Women and Electoral Politics in Canada

Women and Electoral Politics in Canada

Edited by

Manon Tremblay and
Linda Trimble

OXFORD
UNIVERSITY PRESS

OXFORD
UNIVERSITY PRESS

70 Wynford Drive, Don Mills, Ontario M3C 1J9
www.oup.com/ca

Oxford University Press is a department of the University of Oxford.
It furthers the University's objective of excellence in research, scholarship,
and education by publishing worldwide in

Oxford New York

*Auckland Cape Town Dar es Salaam Hong Kong Karachi
Kuala Lumpur Madrid Melbourne Mexico City Nairobi
New Delhi Shanghai Taipei Toronto*

With offices in

*Argentina Austria Brazil Chile Czech Republic France Greece
Guatemala Hungary Italy Japan Poland Portugal Singapore
South Korea Switzerland Thailand Turkey Ukraine Vietnam*

Oxford is a trade mark of Oxford University Press
in the UK and in certain other countries

Published in Canada by Oxford University Press

National Library of Canada Cataloguing in Publication

Women and electoral politics in Canada / edited by Manon
Tremblay and Linda Trimble.

Includes bibliographical references and index.
ISBN-10: 0-19-541744-5   ISBN-13: 978-0-19-541744-9

1. Women in politics—Canada. 2. Women politicians—Canada.
I. Tremblay, Manon, 1964- II. Trimble, Linda, 1959-

HQ1236.5.C2W6254 2003   324'.082'0971   C2002-906138-5

3 4 - 06

Contents

Contributors

Jerome H. Black is an Associate Professor of Political Science at McGill University

André Blais is Professor in the Department of Political Science, Université de Montréal

William Cross is Associate Professor in Political Science and holder of the Edgar and Dorothy Davidson Chair in Canadian Studies at Mount Allison University

Lynda Erickson is Professor in the Department of Political Science, Simon Fraser University

Elisabeth Gidengil is Professor of Political Science, McGill University

Heather MacIvor is Associate Professor in the Department of Political Science, University of Windsor

Richard Nadeau is a Professor in the Department of Political Science, Université de Montréal

Neil Nevitte is a Professor in the Department of Political Science, University of Toronto

Brenda O'Neill is Assistant Professor of Political Studies, University of Manitoba

Sonia Pitre is a Ph.D. candidate, Department of Political Science, Université Laval

Jocelyne Praud is Assistant Professor of Political Science, University of Regina

Shannon Sampert is a Ph.D. candidate, Department of Political Science, University of Alberta

Manon Tremblay is Professor and Directrice du Centre de recherche sur Femmes et Politique, Université d'Ottawa

Linda Trimble is an Associate Professor in the Department of Political Science, University of Alberta

Lisa Young is Associate Professor of Political Science at the University of Calgary

Chapter 1

Women and Electoral Politics in Canada: A Survey of the Literature

MANON TREMBLAY AND LINDA TRIMBLE

INTRODUCTION

The report of the Royal Commission on the Status of Women in Canada (commonly called the Bird Report) was the first major comprehensive study on the living conditions of Canadian women, and a number of its findings remain valid today, 30 years after it was tabled. From their resolutely liberal conception of political representation, the Commissioners observed that Canadian women continued to be denied many of the rights and privileges of citizenship. And yet the Commission's recommendations were scarcely of the kind that could change women's second-rank status, at least in politics. This is particularly true with respect to affirmative-action measures: while the Commission acknowledged that such measures were valid, it did not recommend that they be adopted, suggesting instead that more women be appointed to the Senate, an institution without any real power over federal government decision making. In fact, the Bird Commission's best-known contribution was to foster an awareness among the Canadian public of women's status as second-class citizens. The Commission helped mobilize the feminist movement in Canada and Quebec, and also legitimized the movement's efforts to transform social relations between men and women. For instance, it was following the Report's publication that the National Action Committee on the Status of Women and Fédération des Femmes du Québec were founded.

In the early 1990s, the Royal Commission on Electoral Reform and Party Financing, the Lortie Commission, produced a study on women and Canadian politics in which a number of the Bird Commission's 20-year-old findings reappeared. It seemed that many of the obstacles confronted by women seeking political office had not been cleared away. The Lortie Commission (1991) made a number of recommendations designed to increase the number of women in Canadian politics. For instance, the report suggested that the number of elected female candidates be one of the criteria for reimbursement of political parties' election expenses (273). Unfortunately, that recommendation was not implemented. Thus, not surprisingly, three federal general elections later the proportion of women in the House of Commons (as in the provincial legislatures and most large Canadian municipalities) remains below critical mass (Dahlerup 1988; Kanter 1977). Moreover, the number of women elected in the 2000 federal election remained the same as after the 1997 vote. It seems that women have hit a glass ceiling in Canadian politics—at least in the House of Commons—and that to break through it, special measures will have to be taken to promote the election of women to federal, provincial, and territorial legislatures.

Although the space women occupy on the various political scenes in Canada has increased incrementally, the same cannot be said of research generated on the theme of women and politics, where considerable work has been done in four overlapping areas since the Bird Report was issued. While the 'women and politics' field is flourishing overall, studies conducted in Canada often unfortunately reflect the two solitudes: some claim to examine Canada but in fact focus exclusively on English Canadian realities, while others concern only Quebec (Arscott and Tremblay 1999).

The first area covered by studies on women and politics is women and political thought. Research efforts here essentially focus on the study of women's political relationships, or the lack thereof, as constructed in philosophy and political theory. Examples include Lorenne M.G. Clark and Lynda Lange's *The Sexism of Social and Political Theory* (1979) and Diane Lamoureux and Micheline de Sève's 'Faut-il laisser notre sexe au vestiaire?' (1989). A second area of research in women and politics is public policy. Studies in this field look at how government decisions—in particular public policy decisions—shape the construction of the genders and at how women influence (or fail to influence) public policy. Caroline Andrew's 'Women and the Welfare State' (1984) and Janine Brodie's *Women and Canadian Public Policy* (1996) are leading works in this field. A third orientation in studies on women and politics is social movements. Based on theories of (new) social movements, these studies have focused particularly on the political and identity-based forces shaping the ideas, organization, and strategies of the women's movement. There are many works on this area; we have, in Quebec, Diane Lamoureux's *Fragments et collages* (1986) and Micheline de Sève's *Pour un féminisme libertaire* (1985), and in English Canada, Jill Vickers, Pauline Rankin, and Christine Appelle's *Politics as If Women Mattered* (1993), Catherine L. Cleverdon's *The Woman Suffrage Movement in Canada* (1974), and Alexandra Dobrowolsky's *The Politics of Pragmatism* (2000).

The fourth research orientation on the theme of women and politics concerns the presence of women in electoral politics, that is, women's political involvement as voters, members of political parties, and representatives elected to decision-making bodies, on school boards, and at the municipal, provincial, and federal levels of government. This is the research area with which we are concerned here. In other words, this book focuses on the formal aspects (voting and running for office, for example) rather than the informal aspects (such as being a member of a women's group or taking part in an anti-globalization demonstration) of electoral participation in Canada. This bias in favour of formal politics does not mean that the other forms of involvement are not important to the quality of democratic life but merely reflects a research choice.

In the following pages, we provide a survey of the most recent literature on women and electoral politics in Canada. Our purpose is to show that the relationships women maintain with electoral politics in Canada are both diversified and complex; while some trends identified in the first research studies are still apparent, others have changed and new trends have emerged. But before considering the research on participation by women in electoral politics, it is important to examine the concept underlying that research, the concept of political representation.

ON POLITICAL REPRESENTATION AND WOMEN

In September 2002, Canada ranked 34th in the world for representation of women in its national parliament, reflecting decades of effort by the feminist movement to mobilize more women to enter decision-making bodies. As well, in academe, we have witnessed an increase in the number of women political scientists interested in the theme of women and electoral politics in Canada. Yet the feminist movements in Canada have not developed a theory of representation to guide electoral practices.[1] In fact, the political representation of women is simply not the subject of any public debate in Canada right now.

The absence of an overarching theory of representation does not mean that Canadian women's movements are not committed to activities designed to elect more women in political life. To the contrary, women's groups whose sole purpose is to elect more women emerged in the 1980s and 1990s at the federal and provincial levels, among them Winning Women and the Committee for '94. In fact, these activities essentially have a twofold purpose based on different but related conceptions of political representation: to increase the number of women in politics and to ensure better representation of women's demands, needs, and interests. In the language of political theory, both purposes refer to descriptive and substantive conceptions of political representation (Pitkin 1967).

Descriptive representation is concerned with who the representative is. In other words, it focuses on the representative's socio-demographic characteristics such as sex, race, or ethnic group. According to this view, what the elected person does is less important than who he or she is. At the collective level, the decisions made by an elected assembly are less important than the composition of that assembly. The notion of a mirror is often used to convey the meaning of descriptive representation: the assembly should mirror the socio-demographic characteristics of the population it is empowered to represent. As such, because women constitute roughly one-half of Canada's population, they should be present in approximately the same proportion in decision-making bodies. This descriptive conception of political representation was reflected in the Lortie Commission's observation that 'women are underrepresented by 74.1 per cent relative to their demographic weight. . . . They are only 25.9 per cent of the way to attaining proportional electoral representation' (Royal Commission on Electoral Reform and Party Financing 1991: 94).

Substantive representation refers to the activity of representation, reflecting both opinions and actions. For a person to fully represent a constituency, his or her opinions and actions 'must correspond to or be in accord with the wishes, or needs, or interests, of those for whom he [*sic*] acts . . . [and] he must put himself in their place, take their part, act as they would act' (Pitkin 1967: 114). As a principle, substantive representation implies not only that the elected person shares the opinions and concerns of the persons he or she represents, but also that the elected representative commits to consistent action with a view to representing their interests. That said, a representative still has a degree of independence to interpret the framework of that representation. This flexibility also applies to the political representation of women (Tremblay 1998b). In short, the concept of political representation may be read in two ways: as the politics of presence (or being) and as the politics of ideas (or activity). These notions of representation serve as a basis for the research work done on the participation of English Canadian and Quebec women in electoral politics as voters and party members or as candidates and elected representatives.

CANADIAN WOMEN AS VOTERS AND PARTY MEMBERS

Canadian research on the political participation of women features analyses of the quest for the right to vote and the accompanying suffragist struggles, of the gender gap in the electoral and public policy fields, and of women's involvement in political parties.

Suffragist Struggles
While most white Canadian women obtained the right to vote in federal elections in 1918,[2] major discrepancies exist as to the year in which that right was obtained at the provincial level, the greatest being between Quebec and the other provinces. Quebec women had to wait until 1940 to be able to vote in provincial elections, whereas most women in the other provinces won that right between 1916 and 1925. It is therefore not surprising that a number of studies on the vote and suffragist struggles have sought to explain this difference between Quebec and the rest of Canada; in other words, they have examined the 'specificity' of Quebec (Cohen 1997; D'Augerot-Arend 1991). Another concern in this field of research is the historiography of the suffragist struggles, the arguments for and against female suffrage, and women's movement strategies for achieving formal democratic rights (Bacchi 1983; Cleverdon 1974; Lamoureux 1989; Lamoureux and Michaud 1988).

One idea that characterizes the literature on female suffrage in provincial elections is that the discrepancy between Quebec and the rest of Canada—and, more specifically, Quebec's 'backwardness' in this area—is attributable to cultural and nationalist forces opposed to modernization. Yolande Cohen's argument (1997) is interesting in this respect. In her view, English Canada gave women the vote sooner because English Canadian elites saw this as a way for politicians to legitimize their interference in the private female sphere while securing a reserve labour force. In Quebec, on the contrary, it was the Church, rather than women, that not only became the state's mandatory interlocutor in social matters, but also interpreted the maternal function in terms of the future of the French Canadian nation. Women became the embodiment of the discourse of the French Canadian nation's survival, hence their exclusion from politics and their confinement within the family and by tradition.

Further research on suffrage reveals two opposing conceptions of the role of women. One is a humanistic conception based on grand individual freedoms, including property rights. This, for example, is the basis of the 'no taxation without representation' argument. The other conception refers to the separate spheres for women and men: the private sphere for the former, the public for the latter. Arguments about the incompatibility of woman suffrage and maternity fall within this category. Diane Lamoureux and Jacinthe Michaud (1988) also update other, more unusual findings, notably that in the absence of a countrywide suffrage, provinces that granted women the right to vote had a larger electorate, thus increasing their influence in federal politics.

The debate on parity between women and men in political life is a fertile ground for future research on the right-to-vote and suffragist struggles. Parity is based on the notion that since humanity is dual, or universally divided into genders, the number of elected women should be increased until women hold half of all seats. The equal right to take part in the election of representatives is based on the equal right to sit on decision-making bodies: they are two sides of the same coin of electoral representation. Perhaps because the debate on parity has taken place mainly in France, reflections about its applicability to the Canadian context have occurred almost exclusively in Quebec (Tahon 1998; Tremblay 2000–1, 2002b, 2003). The concept of parity deserves further consideration in the coming years, particularly in the context of reform of representative institutions and the electoral system.

The Gender Gap in the Electoral and Public Policy Fields

A dominant concern in this field of research is the question of whether women and men have identical or different electoral and political conduits, that is, divergent electoral behaviour and electoral and public policy opinions. The idea of a gender gap—a difference between women and men—animates this field of research, although it also forms the basis for other aspects of the study of relations between women and electoral politics in Canada. A number of studies in this field, past and present, highlight the difference between women and men with regard to electoral and political conduits (with the unintended effect of suggesting that women, as well as men, constitute a monolithic group). In most cases, the studies show that women express more conservative opinions, for example, giving less support than men to Quebec sovereignty, which is perhaps merely an effect of their overrepresentation in the older age categories (Tardy 1980). Earlier studies also found that women participate in politics to a lesser degree than men (Black and McGlen 1979; Kay et al. 1987).

Voting research suggests there is a gender gap with regard to candidate choice and partisan preference. In Quebec, a study conducted with French-speaking political science students also revealed that the female students were more likely than the male students to trust women politicians, and that they were more inclined to support various measures to increase the number of women in Parliament (Tremblay 1994). Furthermore, between 1974 and 1988, men were more inclined than women to support a Conservative party led by a man, but that discrepancy disappeared in 1993, when more women supported a Conservative party led by a woman (O'Neill 1998). Similarly, in the 1997 federal election, not only were women voters more inclined than men to vote for the New Democratic Party, they also formed a more positive assessment of the NDP leader (Nevitte et al. 2000). In addition, in analyzing opinion polls conducted in Canada between 1964 and 1990, Joanna Everitt (1998a) found no significant difference between the support offered by women and that by men for a woman in a political leadership position.

A gender gap is also apparent in partisan preferences. In the early 1970s, men were more inclined than women to support the NDP, reflecting at least in part that party's association with the predominantly male unions (Vickers and Brodie 1981). In the 1980s, Wearing and Wearing (1991) showed that more men than women supported the Conservative party, although as mentioned previously that difference changed in 1993, when the party was led by Kim Campbell. More recently, an electoral study conducted following the 2000 federal election revealed that Canadian women are more reserved than Canadian men in their support of Stockwell Day's party, the Canadian Alliance, formerly the Reform party ('Divided by the Gender Thing', *Globe and Mail*, 16 February 2001: A11). This difference may be related to that party's neo-conservative and neo-liberal social and economic positions, which Canadian women are generally less likely to adopt. In Quebec, surveys conducted in 2001 showed that women were less predisposed than men to support the Parti Québécois, led by Bernard Landry, opting more than men for Jean Charest's Liberal party.[3] In reference to an earlier period, Sylvia Bashevkin (1983b) established a link between the preferences of certain Quebec women for the Quebec Liberal party and that party's historic association with woman suffrage. More than the women of other generations, Quebec women born between 1901 and 1915 identified with the Liberal party of Quebec, at least in 1965 and 1979. That generation of Quebec women experienced the suffragist struggles and saw Adélard Godbout's Liberal party grant women the right to vote in provincial elections.

Lynda Erickson's chapter addresses the partisan gender gap issue. How did Canadian men and women perceive the political leaders in the 1997 federal election? Did women and men differ in their assessment of the leaders and, if so, how? While certain differences appeared between women's perceptions of party leaders in the 1997 federal election and those of men, they are not substantial and, in some instance, they are quite intriguing. Ultimately, Canadian men and women view politics differently, although it cannot be said that their views are oppositional or mutually exclusive.

Beyond the strict electoral dimension, a number of studies have recently addressed the gender gap issue in the public policy sphere. Elisabeth Gidengil (1995) revealed a gender gap with respect to the Canada–US Free Trade Agreement: men viewed the issue more from an economic standpoint, women from a social perspective, their greatest resistance to the agreement stemming from their skepticism about workings of market forces and concerns about welfare provision. She also showed that Canadian women were more favourable than Canadian men to measures such as quotas to increase the number of women in Canadian political institutions (Gidengil 1996). Looking at the years from 1971 to 1990, Everitt (1998a) observed a more than 27-percentage-point difference between male and female opinions on issues concerning the use of force (nuclear war and cruise-missile testing) and 6- to 9-point variations on social welfare questions (see also Wearing and Wearing 1991). More recently, the 2000 Canadian Electoral Study (CES)[4] revealed some interesting differences of opinion between women and men on certain social topics, including 'law and order' issues, gay rights, and gender equality.

Elisabeth Gidengil, André Blais, Richard Nadeau, and **Neil Nevitte** have explored these figures from the 2000 CES in their chapter here. They develop six scales (Free Enterprise, the Welfare State, Health Policy, Feminism and Gender-Related Issues, Moral Traditionalism, and Crime and Punishment) on which they reveal numerous differences between women and men. In the 2000 federal election, women were more reserved about free enterprise, more reluctant to trust the market, and more supportive of the welfare state than men. According to the 2000 CES team, the most convincing reasons for the differences observed between women and women are socio-psychological, that is, related to gender-role socialization in childhood. The authors also reveal differences among women themselves that, in some instances, are greater than those between women and men.

Although the gender gap is based on a model of polarization between women and men, it also suggests that women constitute a homogeneous group, although, as **Brenda O'Neill** shows in her chapter here, the reality is more complex than that. One common assertion is that, while they embrace the objectives of the feminist movement, young women are less inclined than their elders to identify themselves as feminists (the 'I'm not a feminist, but . . .' syndrome). In fact, in certain respects, women of various generations have similar attitudes toward feminism and the feminist movement. These cleavages between generations of Canadian women are not unrelated to developments in feminist thinking, in which ideas vary from one generational wave to the next.

Research also attempts to show the extent to which women and men take part in political life. The minimum level of involvement is the exercise of the right to vote: while previously fewer women voted than men, this discrepancy has now all but disappeared (Black and McGlen 1979; Kay et al. 1987; Maillé 1990b; Vickers and Brodie 1981). Studies remain to be conducted in this field to determine whether, for example, women vote in the same proportions as men within those ethnocultural communities in which women's participation in political life is viewed in different terms. This is an important question considering the richly diverse fabric of the Canadian population.

In other aspects of electoral participation, there still appears to be a gender gap, which had already been identified in the early 1960s (Black and McGlen 1979). In their study for the Lortie Commission, Janine Brodie and Celia Chandler (1991) showed that Canadian men were more inclined than Canadian women to discuss politics during the 1980 election campaigns, to help a political party, and to watch the leaders' debate. The same findings remained for the 2000 federal election: fewer women than men paid attention to election news, regardless of whether it was disseminated by radio, television, or a daily newspaper. As well, women were less likely than men to watch the leaders' debate broadcast in English and less inclined as well to be members of a political party or to have previously contacted a parliamentarian (specific analyses drawn from the CES).

However, prudence is called for in analyzing the participation of women and men in the political and electoral processes since these data can be very much influenced by the social roles assigned to each sex and by women's specific experiences (Ollivier and Tremblay 2000; O'Neill 1995). The indicators used to measure participation are based more on men's than women's experiences of everyday life. For example, Statistics Canada data show that women still have greater responsibility for children. It is therefore not surprising that they are less able to discuss politics, watch the leaders' debate, or help a political party. Future research in the area should be sensitive to this type of sexist bias and might focus on developing new, more gender-neutral indicators. Similarly, it is to be hoped that the research will go beyond a mere description of polarized differences between men and women into a study of the very structure of opinion. For example, O'Neill recently revealed the different role that religious values play in the structuring of opinions in Canadian women and men (2001b). O'Neill also outlines a women's culture characterized by a care ethic as a way of understanding the political opinions and behaviours of Canadian women (2002).

Women in Political Parties
Research on women's involvement in political parties has focused mainly on the following question: What relationships do women maintain with the parties? This is an important question since the parties play a key role in electoral politics in Canada, including in the political socialization of the population, the formalization of a vision of political governance, the recruitment and selection of political personnel, and competition within the electoral game. They are also an unavoidable stepping stone for anyone wishing to be elected, except perhaps in some municipalities.

Women's Presence in Political Parties
Previous research revealed dual horizontal and vertical models for women's entry into partisan politics. The notion of *horizontal entry* reflects the fact that women are active in fields of activity traditionally defined as female: education, health, welfare, and the environment, not to mention the former women's branches of certain political parties (Bashevkin 1993; Brodie and Vickers 1982). However, those fields of activity are often considered of lesser importance. Today it is likely useful to reassess the relative importance of various areas of activity. For example, who could argue that health, a jurisdiction traditionally defined as feminine, is of lesser importance considering that portfolio's weight in the overall government budget and its scope in political governance in the coming years? This issue deserves more extensive research.

Women's *vertical entry* into political parties refers to what Robert Putnam (1976) describes as the law of increasing disproportion: the farther up you go in party hierarchies, the fewer women there are, apart from a few who act as symbols (Kanter 1977). In other words, women find themselves in what Bashevkin (1993) characterizes as pink-collar jobs, namely clerical and service positions in parties (see also Brodie and Vickers 1982; Vickers 1978; Vickers and Brodie 1981). However, considerable progress has been made. In 1990, women occupied 38 per cent of seats on the national executive of the federal Liberal party, 43 per cent in the Progressive Conservative party, and, as a result of an affirmative action resolution passed, 58 per cent in the New Democratic Party of Canada (Bashevkin 1993: 79; for Ontario, see also Bashevkin 1982; Bashevkin and Holder 1985). The pinnacle of power, party leadership, remains dominated by men, with minor exceptions, including the Conservative party (for a brief moment and in a context of political disaster) and the NDP, traditionally a leftist party more open to women but also a party far removed from power (Whitehorn and Archer 1995; Young 2000). As of 2002, only 20 women have ever been selected to lead competitive Canadian parties, that is, parties holding seats in the legislature (Trimble and Arscott, forthcoming). One woman, Alexa McDonough, led two parties, the Nova Scotia NDP and later the federal NDP.

Jocelyne Praud has extensively examined the question of women's presence in party structures in English Canada and Quebec (Praud 1995, 1998a, 1998b). As she shows in her chapter here, the presence of women in the decision-making bodies of the two main Quebec political parties, the Liberal party of Quebec and the Parti Québécois, still leaves them in the minority, although near critical mass, with at best one-third of positions (except recently on the PQ national executive). Praud emphasizes that women should mobilize within parties—and target a broad range of female and male members—in order to improve their descriptive representation in the various party offices, even if the structures and strategies they adopt do not always make it possible to achieve those objectives. Given women's continued underrepresentation in political life and the gatekeeper role played by parties, it is appropriate to understand why the parties raise barriers to women and thus determine how to circumvent these barriers.

In this respect, certain political parties in English Canada and Quebec have been a mobilizing ground for women and for the adoption of measures designed to ensure better representation for both sexes in all decision-making bodies and greater influence by women over the decision-making process in the parties. This is the case in the PQ (Praud 1998b), the federal NDP, the Liberal party of Canada (Brodie 1994; Young 2000), and the Ontario NDP (Burt and Lorenzin 1997; Praud 1995, 1998a). These mobilization efforts are driven by the conviction that an increase in the number of women in the parties will have an impact on the substantive representation of women as expressed in the parties' platforms. But this assumed relationship between the descriptive and substantive representation of women has not been proven beyond a reasonable doubt (Gotell and Brodie 1991). New research is needed to gain a better understanding of the link between numbers and impact, as this relationship will inform feminist strategies with regard to the federal and provincial states in the years to come.

Differences Between Female and Male Party Members

In Quebec, this issue has been explored by Évelyne Tardy and others since the early

1980s (Gingras, Maillé, and Tardy 1989; Legault, Desrosiers, and Tardy 1988). In general, the research directed by Tardy on party membership has favoured at least five analytical approaches: political history and path, constraints on the exercise of party membership, conceptions of membership, perceptions of the underrepresentation of women in politics and ways of correcting it, and the socio-demographic characteristics of female and male party members. This research suggests that the idea of systematic differences between female and male party members should be qualified since there are sometimes more similarities between women and men than differences among women themselves.

In English Canada, some studies of the female and male members of political parties have focused on opinions on various social issues. Generally speaking, there appear to be differences between the opinions of female and male members, a phenomenon that has been observed for a number of years now. Bashevkin's study (1985) of female and male delegates to the conventions of the New Democratic, Liberal, and Conservative parties of Ontario in the early 1980s revealed significant gender differences on the appropriateness of affirmative action measures to correct the representation of women in politics. Brodie (1987) found a clear gender gap over the issues of abortion and male–female equality among delegates to the federal Conservative and Liberal conventions in 1983 and 1984. Similar differences were apparent in the NDP when Whitehorn and Archer (1995) observed significant discrepancies between the opinions of female and male party members in 1983 and 1987, particularly on the issue of pornography.

The chapter by **Lisa Young** and **William Cross** makes a major contribution to our knowledge of women's participation in the lives of the parties in Canada. The authors reveal certain differences between female and male members of the five main Canadian political parties in 2000, differences that are more or less pronounced depending on the issue considered, thus recalling Tardy's findings of discontinuous polarizations between women and men. For the future, it would be interesting to examine the impact that women have in the parties: do they manage to make their voices heard, and if so, how and to what effect?

Barriers to the Political Participation of Women in Parties
Notwithstanding the underrepresentation of women in most decision-making bodies in English Canada and Quebec, this issue has received appreciable attention from researchers. Studies show that parties play a strong role in maintaining the descriptive and substantive underrepresentation of women in politics. This finding, moreover, appears across the generations of research on women and electoral politics in Canada. In the early 1970s, the Bird Commission found

> a number of impediments to women seeking candidature: in particular, prejudice in the constituency associations, inadequate financial resources and limited mobility. The constituency association has autonomy in the selection of the candidate and jealously guards this right. It is at the constituency level . . . that disparagement of women candidates and the belief that a woman candidate will lose votes are usually encountered. Women who have been successful at the polls confirm that

winning the nomination is a more formidable hurdle than winning the election. (Royal Commission on the Status of Women 1970: 349)

Of course, the political parties are not the only barrier to the election of women: the socialization process and the social roles of the sexes also play a role (Bashevkin 1983a; Brodie 1985; Gingras, Maillé, and Tardy 1989; Kay et al. 1988; MacInnis 1972), as does the electoral system, to which we will return later.

Current research now supports the notion that, contrary to what certain local political elites fear, women are not 'losing' votes when they run for office (Hunter and Denton 1984; Tremblay 1995a, 2002a). In fact, the most recent studies tend to confirm that where the shoe pinches is in nominations (Erickson 1997a, 1998; Erickson and Carty 1991; Norris et al. 1990). Women find it hard to win nominations for several reasons, including financial constraints, limited networks of contacts within the parties, and a larger number of opponents for the nomination than faced by their male counterparts (Bashevkin 1982, 1991, 1993; Brodie and Chandler 1991; Brodie and Vickers 1981; Erickson 1991b, 1993; Gingras, Maillé, and Tardy 1989; Maillé 1990a; Vickers 1978; Vickers and Brodie 1981).

However, when they do win nominations, women are not confined to uncompetitive ridings (Pelletier and Tremblay 1992; Studlar and Matland 1994, 1996). In fact, a significant proportion of the problems women encounter in winning a nomination are related to the pre-eminence of *homo politicus*; that is, the attributes required to access the spheres of power are more in keeping with the profile of men than women. One of the electoral ground rules in Canada is that a political party selects only one candidate per constituency. Consequently, the parties attempt to present the person who is perceived as most likely to win the election. Norris and Lovenduski (1989) believe that an informal model candidate inspires local executives in their choice of person to defend the party colours on election day and that women thus do not fit the model.

Sonia Pitre explores this issue in this volume for New Brunswick in an effort to understand the process of recruiting, selecting, and nominating candidates in provincial elections. She asks which factor best explains the percentage of women in the New Brunswick Legislative Assembly: the degree of a party's centralization, the institutionalization of its candidate recruitment process, the centralization of its candidate nomination process, its ideology (leftist or rightist), or the adoption of strategies to increase the presence of women in the parliamentary arena. In conclusion, Pitre asserts that the objective of increasing the number of women in politics cannot be treated independently of the will of the parties to have more women in their ranks.

Since parties are the gatekeepers to legislative office and have the potential to address the problem of women's underrepresentation, how do they react to the idea of putting into place measures designed to promote the election of women in politics? This is a relatively recent question in the Canadian studies, probably because it is now clear that in the absence of such measures, the presence of women in politics will continue to be marginal. In their chapter, **Lisa Young** and **William Cross** reveal a certain degree of dissatisfaction among female party members (particularly in the federal Liberal party) with their party's efforts to improve the descriptive representation of women in their organization. This kind of gender gap is also apparent at the elite level. Focusing on male and female candidates to the 1993 federal election, Lynda Erickson showed that women provided stronger support than their male counterparts for measures designed to increase the number of women in politics (1997b). Manon Tremblay and Réjean Pelletier came to substantially the same findings (2000, 2001). Using qualitative methodologies, future research could explore the rationales developed by the political elites to explain the low numbers of women on decision-making bodies. It would also be interesting to see whether those elites believe that the virtual exclusion of women from politics is a thorn in the foot of democracy and, if so, what changes they are prepared to make to correct the situation.

Women's Groups and Political Parties

From a substantive perspective of women's political representation, the relationship between parties and the women's movement is an important issue since it concerns the ability of women and women's groups to make their demands heard by the political parties. The Bird Commission recognized women's significant contribution to various groups in civil society and their impact on political governance. This dynamic in relations between women's groups and the political parties has not been the focus of research in English Canada or Quebec, at least until quite recently, when Young (2000) published her book on this topic (see also Young 1998, 2002a).

Lisa Young develops her ideas here with an examination of the efforts made by the feminist movement between 1970 and 2000 to influence political parties on the Canadian federal scene. She bases her work on a bold question—can feminists change politics?—a question she explores on the basis of two concerns: first, how have women's groups dealt with political parties and what strategies have they used for that purpose, and second, how have the parties responded to feminist efforts? Young observes that the mobilization of feminists in electoral politics has created a certain openness toward women in the parties, but the parties' receptiveness to feminists' demands has not been constant over time. The impact feminists have had on the parties has been modulated by a number of factors, the most powerful of which is the ability of women's groups to provide the parties with the commodity they feed on: votes. Thus, the relations between women's groups and the political parties must be monitored closely. It would also be interesting to understand how women and the feminist movement in English Canada and Quebec view their relations with the polity and, in particular, with the political parties, where right-wing governments hold power.

CANADIAN WOMEN IN THE POLITICAL ELITE

Thus far, we have mainly considered research on mass political participation—the activities engaged in by 'ordinary' women in the population. Other studies have focused on women's elite-level electoral participation, as candidates and elected representatives, including at the pinnacle of power.[5]

Difficulties Faced by Women Candidates

This issue deals mainly with the electoral system itself and its rules: once they have won their party's nomination in a given constituency, what forces can limit the election of women? The main factors are the plurality electoral system and the rate of turnover of political personnel.

The electoral system is a set of rules and practices under which the electorate chooses its representatives. In Canada, it is a single-member plurality system. Following a single ballot in each constituency, the person who receives the largest number of votes is declared the winner, without an absolute majority being necessary. Many studies suggest that this system does not favour the election of women; proportional systems—in particular list systems, which permit a number of representatives to be elected by riding—would be more favourable (Matland 1998a; Rule 1987). Under the majority system in federal and provincial elections, every political party designates a single candidate per constituency, unlike certain proportional arrangements in which each party puts up a number of names per election area. While it is important in a majority system that the party designate 'the right person', it is a disadvantage in a proportional system to present a list consisting solely of persons of a single trait (men, for example). The proportional system would also be more conducive to the election of women than the majority system because of the *contagion effect*, the process by which political parties adopt policies initiated by rival parties, such as gender quotas, in an effort to maintain their electoral competitiveness (Matland and Studlar 1996).

In her chapter, **Heather MacIvor** addresses the question of the effect of the majority electoral system on the descriptive representation of women in the House of Commons. While it is correct to think that the adoption of a proportional system in Canada could increase the number of women in the lower house, it is incorrect to believe that this is the magic solution to the underrepresentation of women in Parliament. MacIvor emphasizes that the proportional system's ability to elect women depends on the will of the parties to achieve that objective, in particular by putting women candidates on lists for eligible positions. In fact, the underrepresentation of women in Canadian politics is an indicator of a greater malaise, a malaise of representative democracy—and not only of an electoral system—which, from a descriptive standpoint, is not representative.

The rate of renewal of political personnel can also limit the election of women candidates. A Canadian parliamentarian can currently seek a new mandate as many times as he or she wants. MPs wishing to continue their careers on Parliament Hill enjoy a definite advantage over their opponents if only because they can rely on a well-oiled electoral machine or on name recognition. This is the phenomenon of *incumbency*, which has been identified as a significant cause of underrepresentation of women in politics (Brodie 1985; Erickson 1997c). However, Young (1991) qualifies the advantage of the outgoing member; she believes the high rate of turnover in the House of Commons represents an asset for, rather than a barrier to, women's re-election. But to get elected, women must be candidates in safe ridings, or at least in inherited ridings, initiatives explored by Pelletier and Tremblay (1992) and Tremblay (2002a, 2002c). Furthermore, there is a growing tendency among the more competitive parties to run woman candidates against each other, at least on the Quebec political scene (Tremblay 2002b). To the extent that the riding is competitive for one of the political parties, this procedure does not foster an increase in the number of female members in the Quebec National Assembly—in fact, it is more likely to generate an image of women losing in politics, something that is definitely not needed in or out of Quebec.

The problems raised by the electoral system and its rules offer a promising field of research for the coming years. Very little research has been done in Canada on the effect the majority electoral system has on the election of women in federal and provincial politics. However, while the electoral system is an important factor, the will of the political parties to have more women elected is equally important, if not more so, and it would be appropriate to ascertain the scope of both factors. It would also be useful to delve more deeply into the effect of incumbency on the ability of women to get elected. The results of the 2000 federal election, in which the turnover rate was very low, appear to confirm the conclusions of Pelletier and Tremblay (1992) and Young (1991) that the increase in the number of women in politics is contingent on the nomination of women candidates in the most competitive ridings (Tremblay 2002a).

The Position of Women in Politics

As is the case with their entry into the universe of parties, women's access to power is modulated by a dual vertical and horizontal division. Studies have shown that elected women have been confined to subordinate positions, that is to say, positions of lesser power (Clarke and Kornberg 1979; Vickers 1978). Women politicians also found themselves addressing issues traditionally defined as suited to female abilities (Brodie and Vickers 1982; Spencer 1985; Vickers and Brodie 1981). Some studies have also shown that women were more likely to be elected in urban and metropolitan ridings, at least in provincial elections (Brodie 1977; Matland and Studlar 1998; Moncrief and Thompson 1991).

While this model of women's vertical and horizontal entry into electoral politics remains relevant, it is no longer entirely accurate. Gary Moncrief and Donley Studlar (1996) evaluated the portfolios held by women in provincial government cabinets from 1976 to 1994; during that period, women gradually occupied increasingly important positions in cabinets, in all provinces, although in an uneven fashion. In fact, women are better represented in the executive than at the legislative level (Studlar and Moncrief 1997; see also Trimble and Arscott, forthcoming). Furthermore, while it is true that women are still concentrated in so-called female portfolios, they now cover an increasingly broader range of portfolios and high-level departments (see Crossley 1997 for Prince Edward Island). The same is true at the federal level. On the one hand, it appears that the few women admitted to the pinnacle of federal power as senior ministers were responsible for a very limited range of portfolios: justice and health, two areas associated with traditional female roles. On the other, it seems difficult to support the idea that the women who acted as junior and intermediate ministers were responsible for primarily human and non-economic departments, as women have been appointed to the head of departments such as foreign trade, consumer and corporate affairs, energy, national revenue, and employment.

Extensive work remains to be done to gain a clear understanding of the ways in which women enter electoral politics. For example, how do male political elites perceive the abilities of women in politics? What processes govern the assignment of ministerial responsibilities? What barriers limit women's access to the very limited and powerful cabinet circle? What are the relationships between women ministers, women members, and women's groups, and how do these influence women's substantive representation?

Identities of Political Women

The question of the identity of political women is an important one since it relies on the descriptive conception of political representation. Generally speaking, research on the socio-demographic characteristics and experience of political women relative to their male colleagues can be reduced to two major historical periods. First, studies conducted up to the first half of 1980 describe women as following in men's footsteps because they did not have the resources available to them to enter political life. At that time, women entered the electoral arena later than men, once their children had reached a certain degree of independence (Bashevkin 1982, 1983a; Brodie 1985; Brodie and Vickers 1981; Kohn 1984). Although political women had more education than women in the population at large, they had less than their male colleagues (Bashevkin 1983b; Brodie 1977; Brodie and Vickers 1981; Kohn 1984; Langevin 1977). They were more likely than women in the general population to be in the labour force (Brodie 1977), but they were in less prestigious and more diverse occupations than men (Bashevkin 1982, 1983a; Brodie 1977; Brodie and Vickers 1981, 1982; Clarke and Kornberg 1979; Kohn 1984; Langevin 1977; Vickers and Brodie 1981). And although political women at that time participated actively in various organizations (Brodie 1985), they were also less likely than their male colleagues to have held high-level political responsibilities prior to their election (Vickers 1978).

Research conducted since the second half of the 1980s shows a change in the socio-demographic characteristics of today's political women relative to their elders. What is more, this new generation of political women enjoys resources comparable to those of men. This can take one of two forms: some women possess the same resources as their male counterparts but in greater quantity, while others exhibit different resources, reflecting women's gender-based experiences in society. For example, today's political women are more likely than those in the past to have never been married; more of them than men are never-married, separated, divorced, or widowed (Arend and Chandler 1996; Black and Erickson 2000; Tardy, Tremblay, and Legault 1997). Furthermore, young children now appear to be less of a barrier to their political involvement than in the past, although the active support of spouses is an essential condition for elite-level political engagement (Tremblay and Pelletier 1995). Focusing on women candidates in the 1993 federal election, Jerome H. Black and Lynda Erickson (2000) showed that 91 per cent of women had attended university, compared to 78 per cent of men. Nearly identical percentages of female (60 per cent) and male (57 per cent) candidates were managers, professionals, or business persons (Black and Erickson 2000). In addition, political women and men had comparable party experience (Tremblay and Pelletier 1995). However, men had been more involved in political and socio-economic groups and women in cultural, educational, and community groups, in which they had held positions of responsibility (Gingras, Maillé, and Tardy 1989; Tardy, Tremblay, and Legault 1997; Tremblay and Pelletier 1995). Black and Erickson found that a greater percentage of female than male candidates in the 1993 Canadian election had been involved in interest groups (2000).

Apart from the study by Black and Erickson (2000), there is very little recent data on the socio-demographic characteristics of political women, especially office-holders. The chapter here by **Linda Trimble** and **Manon Tremblay** fills an obvious void in the descriptive conception of the political representation of women. The authors analyze certain socio-demographic characteristics (in particular, country of birth, marital status, age at election, education, and occupation) of women elected to the House of Commons and provincial and territorial legislatures from 1917 to 2000. The analyses show that political women form an elite more closely representing their male colleagues than Canadian women in general. Furthermore, they in no way constitute a monolithic group. These findings call into question the descriptive conception of the political representation of women. First, political women do not reflect the population of women, a fact that moreover raises questions about the effects on the substantive representation of women. Second, the descriptive conception suggests that the contribution of women to the representative nature of Parliament is limited to gender, whereas the diversity of political women argues in favour of a more substantial contribution.

Jerome Black examines this diversity among women, in particular by linking gender and ethnicity in the 35th, 36th, and 37th Parliaments. From the scant studies on minority women elected to the House, it appears that, generally speaking, they have a higher level of education and occupation than minority men and majority women (see also Black 1997, 2000a). But that is not all that distinguishes these minority women from minority men and majority women. In fact, although they remain largely underrepresented in federal politics, the 1993, 1997, and 2000 elections saw an ever-increasing proportion of minority women elected to the House of Commons. Black suggests in his chapter here that minority women, elected primarily in Ontario under the banner of the Liberal party, offer a 'double value' for parties wishing to project an image of inclusion and diversity.

The question of the identity of women in politics intersects that of the construction of the image of political women by the mass media. This is a relatively new field of research in Canada. Linda Archibald, Leona Christian, Karen Deterding, and Dianne Hendrick published the first study on the question in 1980, underscoring numerous sexist prejudices in the journalistic treatment of women candidates to elections held in 24 major Canadian municipalities between 1950 and 1975. Other studies, conducted in the 1990s, came to substantially the same conclusion: political women do not always enjoy neutral treatment, that is, coverage free of sexist prejudice, by the media (Gidengil and Everitt 1999, 2000a; Gingras 1995; Robinson and St-Jean 1995; Robinson, St-Jean, and Rioux 1991; Tremblay and Bélanger 1997).

The final chapters of this volume add to our knowledge of the way in which the media image of political women is constructed. Focusing on the 1993, 1997, and 2000 federal elections, **Joanna Everitt** and **Elisabeth Gidengil** show that, even when they are no longer a novelty in the upper levels of electoral politics, women are still subject to symbolization, in the sense intended by Kanter (1977). The media analyzes their words and actions against a male standard, thus reinforcing the idea that politics is a male universe. One of those standards is confrontation: politics is a struggle. However, in a society where aggressiveness is viewed as alien to the identity of women, applying this standard to the analysis of female party leaders has paradoxical effects: if they do not conform to it, they are disregarded by the media, but if they play the game, the media overemphasize their aggressive behaviour. This paradoxical treatment attests to the fact that women are still marginalized in politics, a phenomenon that is accentuated by the understated treatment given to Alexa McDonough by television news media in the 2000 federal election. The idea that politics is a male universe is taken up by **Shannon Sampert** and **Linda Trimble**, who also consider the media's treatment of McDonough in the 2000 federal election. The authors suggest that by favouring a media treatment based on the game frame rather than the issue frame, Canada's English-language national newspapers marginalized McDonough and the NDP. Their findings recall that of Tremblay and Bélanger (1997): there is likely no longer clear discrimination in the media treatment of women, but rather a universe of subtle and informal discrimination.

In today's world of modern telecommunications, there are numerous research issues that could be addressed. For example, what are the relations between political women and the Internet? Do their relations differ from those of political men? Can the Internet contribute to the substantive representation of women, and if so, how? Can it enhance the operational link between politicians and women's groups? Although numerous studies have shown that the media are not perfectly objective with regard to political women, we still do not know what effect that treatment had on women's election: does the media treatment of women limit their opportunity to be elected?

Beliefs and Actions of Women in Politics

This last issue leads us to the heart of the substantive conception of political representation: Do political women speak and act in such a way as to defend and promote the needs, demands, and interests of women? Asked another way, the question is this: Do women make changes in politics? This is a recent issue in research on women and electoral politics in Canada, reflecting the very recent entry of women into legislatures in numbers approaching critical mass.

One of the first papers in this area was published by Margrit Eichler in 1979. Her study of MPs and MLAs in the second half of the 1970s showed that men in politics attached less importance than their female counterparts to gender equality; as well, they were less likely to perceive inequalities in female–male relations. Tremblay reached similar findings from her survey of female and male candidates in the 1989 Quebec election (1992, 1995b): women were more inclined than men to support various demands expressed by the feminist movement and to champion the idea of political representation of women. The gender difference is not always systematic, however; it is modulated by variables such as political affiliation, feminist awareness, and the political and parliamentary ground rules (Tremblay 1999). In fact, as Lise Gotell and Janine Brodie write, not all women in Parliament are spokespersons for the feminist cause, and some may simply be anti-feminist (1991; see also Desserud 1997).

More recently, studies have addressed the question of whether women, as women, make a difference in politics. Trimble believes this is the case (1997; see also Trimble 1993; Young 1997). She feels that women can make a difference by speaking on women's behalf in at least five ways: they can bring women's experiences to the political arena, experiences that were previously considered private under the traditional division of gender roles; they can be in contact with the feminist movement and put its demands in the political arena; they can consider the criterion of gender when speaking out on legislation; they can make policies deliberately intended to change and improve the living conditions of the female population; and they can promote a different parliamentary style. In one study conducted on women elected to the House of Commons of Canada in 1993, Tremblay and Pelletier (1993) discovered that political women felt they make a difference in politics, whether by altering the political agenda, exercising influence over public policy orientations, or affecting parliamentary style (see also Brock 1997; Carbert 1997). Erickson also feels that women have the potential to alter Canadian politics: while the cleavage between women and men is not systematic, it appears women have more liberal ideas than men, particularly those in the left-wing parties (1997b). Based on speeches made in the House of Commons during the first session of the 35th Parliament, Tremblay made the following observation: women members were more likely than their male counterparts to speak and act with a view to supporting women's issues, although that representational activity remained marginal (1998a).

The question of whether women make a difference in politics should receive greater attention in the coming years. In the recent past, the Quebec feminist movement has shown a lack of interest in federal power. However, if the election of women could constitute a strategy for achieving substantive representation of women, the feminist movement might be encouraged to review its positions and strategies with regard to government. Furthermore, if it were to appear that women and men manage political power differently, women could play an important role in a reform of political and electoral institutions in Canada at the dawn of the twenty-first century (Tremblay 2000–1).

Finally, we must mention one category of political women who, while not elected, still participate in the political representation of women: senators. For the time being, there is no known study of female members of the Canadian Senate. Who are they? Where do they come from? What do they think? How do they position themselves in regard to women's political representation? These are valuable questions since senators are important role models for women. Because they study and vote on bills just like their colleagues in the House of Commons, senators may occasionally even make a difference to the substantive representation of women. For instance, in the early 1990s, women's mobilization in the Senate led to the defeat of a bill adopted by the House of Commons that would have recriminalized the provision of abortion services in Canada. Reflections in this field are essential in order to better grasp the potential contribution of senators to the descriptive and substantive representation of women.

CONCLUSION

One thing is clear: a lot of work remains to be done. Our purpose here is to present the most recent work on the diversified and complex relations women have with electoral politics in Canada.

The book is divided into four sections. Part I concerns the electoral system and political representation. Heather MacIvor (chapter 2) assesses the electoral system's impact on the election of women to the House of Commons of Canada. Linda Trimble and Manon Tremblay (chapter 3) address the issue of the descriptive representation of Canadian political women in the twentieth century, while Jerome Black (chapter 4) more specifically considers the presence in the 35th, 36th, and 37th Parliaments of minority women.

Part II looks at the participation of women in political parties. Lisa Young (chapter 5) examines the efforts of the feminist movement on the political scene to influence political parties and promote women's interests. Lisa Young and William Cross (chapter 6) investigate women's recent and current involvement in political parties. Sonia Pitre (chapter 7) focuses on a significant barrier to the election of women in politics, the candidate selection process in the political parties of New Brunswick. Lastly, Jocelyne Praud (chapter 8) analyzes the efforts made to feminize the provincial political parties of Quebec.

Part III concerns the values and attitudes of the Canadian population. Elisabeth Gidengil, André Blais, Richard Nadeau, and Neil Nevitte (chapter 9) explore the idea of a gender gap in the electorate during the 2000 federal election. Lynda Erickson (chapter 10) examines the perception that Canadian women and men had of their political leaders in the 1997 federal election. And Brenda O'Neill (chapter 11) looks at support for feminism throughout the generations.

Part IV addresses the relations between women politicians and the media. Joanna Everitt and Elisabeth Gidengil (chapter 12) analyze a very subtle form of sexism exercised against political women, that is, the manner in which they are viewed through a purportedly neutral frame of reference that in fact is defined on the basis of male realities, here focusing on television coverage of the 2000 leaders' debates. Shannon Sampert and Linda Trimble (chapter 13) follow in the same vein, revealing some of the (sexist) parameters underlying the media treatment of the NDP leader in the 2000 federal election in national newspaper headlines.

NOTES

1. We would not like to give the impression here that there is a consensus on electoral issues within the feminist movement in Canada, particularly that all feminists and all self-styled feminist groups agree that women should get involved in government and be

elected to decision-making bodies. In fact, certain feminists and feminist groups reject the electoral and government arena either in the name of co-opting or because they perceive civil society (in particular social movements) as a more appropriate ground for the political representation of women.

2. It was, in fact, mainly white women who obtained the right to vote, since Japanese Canadian, Chinese Canadian, and Indo-Canadian men and women were denied the federal franchise until 1948 and 1949. Furthermore, the Inuit—women and men—were denied the right to vote between 1934 and 1950, and it was not until 1960 that the Parliament of Canada passed legislation granting the vote to all adult Aboriginal persons (Crête and Blais 2000).

3. SOM Recherches et Sondages, 'Vote comparatif des hommes et des femmes', July 2001, available at <www.som-inc.com/SondagesPublics/Vote%20HF/Vote.html>.

4. The data from the 2000 CES may be consulted at <www.fas.umontreal.ca/pol/ces-eec>.

5. In Canada, very little research has been conducted on the few women who have made it to the pinnacle of executive power, as prime minister or premier, with the exception of studies on their electoral support (O'Neill 1998) or media coverage (Gidengil and Everitt 1999, 2000a, and in this volume; Tremblay and Bélanger 1997). However, a new volume by Trimble and Arscott (forthcoming) examines the experiences of female party leaders, including first ministers.

Part I

The Electoral System and Elected Women

Chapter Two

Women and the Canadian Electoral System

Heather MacIvor

Introduction

The influence of electoral systems is a central theme in political science (e.g.,
Duverger 1964; Farrell 1997; Lijphart 1994; Milner 1999; Rae 1971). Since the
mid-1980s, electoral systems have been particularly prominent in analyses of
women's political representation. Generally speaking, female parliamentarians are
most numerous in states with proportional systems, while those with single-
member systems lag behind. The differences between electoral systems are often
identified as the most important reason for the wide variance in women's representation across the spectrum of national parliaments (e.g., Norris 1987, 1997a; Rule
1987, 1994b; see Tables 2.1 and 2.2).

The electoral system is the set of rules and procedures by which the citizens of a
given country choose their national legislators.[1] Those rules and procedures are
both formal and informal. The formal aspects of an electoral system are codified in
legal and constitutional documents, such as the Canada Elections Act and Section 3
of the Canadian Charter of Rights and Freedoms.[2] The informal aspects arise from
the interaction of the formal rules with the unique contextual (cultural, socio-economic, and political) conditions in a particular country. Taken together, the formal
and informal components of the electoral system create incentives for the political
actors who operate within it. Those incentives affect both the number of female
candidates and their chances of electoral success.

Unlike most democracies (see Table 2.1), Canada uses the *single-member plurality (SMP)* system for its national elections. While the proportion of women in the
Canadian House of Commons exceeds the world average, it is well below that in
most Western European countries. But after decades of electoral-system stability
in Canada, electoral reform has become a major issue during the past decade
(Norris 1997a; Norris, ed. 1995). Opinion surveys reveal substantial public discontent with the status quo and a willingness to consider alternatives (Blais and
Gidengil 1991; Howe and Northrup 2000). The movement toward electoral reform
appears to be gaining momentum.[3]

This chapter argues that while electoral systems do not by themselves determine
the level of women's parliamentary representation, disproportional systems impose

Table 2.1

The Representation of Women in National Parliaments, Selected Countries, September 2002

	Women in Lower House of Parliament (%)	Type of Electoral System
Sweden	42.7	list-PR
Denmark	38.0	list-PR
Finland	36.5	list-PR
Norway	36.4	list-PR
Iceland	34.9	list-PR
Netherlands	34.0	list-PR
Germany	31.7	MMP
New Zealand	29.2	MMP
Spain	28.3	list-PR
Austria	26.8	list-PR
Australia	25.3	AV
Belgium	23.3	list-PR
Switzerland	23.0	list-PR
Canada	**20.6**	**SMP**
Portugal	19.1	list-PR
United Kingdom	17.9	SMP
Luxembourg	16.7	list-PR
WORLD AVERAGE	14.8	–
United States	14.0	SMP
Ireland	13.3	STV
Israel	13.3	list-PR
France	12.3	SMM
Italy	9.8	mixed
Greece	8.7	list-PR
Japan	7.3	MMP

SOURCE: Inter-Parliamentary Union, 'Women in National Parliaments' (Available at:<www.ipu.org/wmn-e/classif.htm>, accessed September 2002).

Table 2.2

Average Representation of Women Under Different Types of Electoral System

	Average % of Women in Lower House of Parliament	Comparison to Average % of All Cases in Table 2.1
Plurality/Majority	18.0	-5.5
MMP	20.9	-3.4
List-PR	27.3	+3.8
STV	13.3	-10.2
Total	23.5	–

formidable barriers to the nomination and election of female candidates. The electoral system is an intervening variable in the political equation. In other words, it determines neither the supply of female aspirants nor the demand for female candidates;[4] these are largely determined by forces external to the electoral system. But once a woman decides to enter the political fray, her electoral success will be either fostered or hindered by the particular electoral system in place. Unlike highly proportional systems, which create both incentives and opportunities for parties to nominate women, Canada's SMP system imposes disincentives that militate against female candidates despite the growing willingness of parties to run women in winnable seats.

The electoral system in each country interacts with other unique factors—political culture, attitudes toward gender equality, the socio-economic status of various groups within the electorate, voting patterns, the structure of the party system, and the ways in which individual parties select candidates for parliament—to create a set of incentives for political actors. The actors in question include national and local party officials, aspiring candidates, and voters. Figure 2.1 shows that the representation of women in Parliament varies across democracies. To understand why this is the case, we must take into account the entire structure of incentives in each country. As we will see, SMP is a major reason for women's underrepresentation in the Canadian House of Commons despite the presence of contextual factors that are relatively favourable to female political participation.

Figure 2.1

Factors Determining the Representation of Women

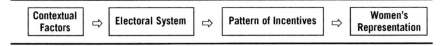

Major Types of Electoral Systems

For the sake of simplicity, we will focus on three major categories of electoral systems: plurality/majority, proportional representation (PR), and mixed (Blais and Massicotte 1996). (See Table 2.3 for a brief synopsis of the basic types.) Five concepts are key to understanding the differences between these systems, and their impact on the election of women:[5]

- *Electoral formula*: the procedure used to count the votes and determine the winning candidate(s)
- *Ballot structure*: the way in which the voter expresses his or her electoral preference(s)
- *District magnitude*: the number of MPs elected from each constituency
- *Threshold of election*: the percentage of valid votes required to elect an MP, determined by the electoral formula and the district magnitude; the lower the threshold, the more proportional the system
- *Proportionality*: the accuracy with which the electoral system translates votes into

Table 2.3

Major Electoral Systems

	Full Name	Description	Examples
SMP	single-member plurality	The country is divided into single-member constituencies. The voter chooses one of the candidates on the ballot. The candidate with more votes than any other wins the seat.	Canada, the United Kingdom, the United States
SMM	single-member majority	The country is divided into single-member constituencies. The voter chooses one of the candidates on the ballot. If no candidate wins a majority of the valid votes, a run-off election between the top two or three candidates is held.	France
AV	alternative vote	The country is divided into single-member constituencies. The voter rank-orders some or all of the candidates on the ballot. The ballots are counted and a majority quota is calculated. If a candidate reaches the quota in the first round of counting, he or she is declared elected. If no candidate receives a majority of the vote, the last-place candidate is eliminated and his or her second preferences are redistributed among the remaining candidates. The counting continues, eliminating the lowest candidates, until one candidate receives at least 50% + 1 of the votes.	Australia (House of Representatives)
STV	single transferable vote	The country is divided into multi-member constituencies. The voter rank-orders some or all of the candidates on the ballot. A quota is calculated on the basis of the valid votes cast, and the first-preference votes are counted. Any candidate with more first preferences than the quota is declared elected, and his or her surplus votes are redistributed among the remaining candidates on the basis of second preferences. The counting continues, eliminating the lowest candidates and redistributing the surplus votes of the winners, until all the seats have been filled.	Ireland
List-PR	list-proportional representation	The country is divided into multi-member constituencies (or is designated as a single multi-member constituency). Each party lists its candidates on the ballot, and the voter chooses one of those lists. The lists can be open (the voter can express a preference among the candidates of his or her favourite party) or closed (a simple vote for a party). The seats are allocated on the basis of either a highest-average or a largest-remainder formula. When the number of seats for each party has been determined, seats are filled by the candidates at the top of the lists.	The Netherlands, Israel, the Scandinavian countries
MMP	mixed-member proportional	Each voter casts two ballots: one for a candidate in an SMP constituency and one for a party list. In corrective MMP, the number of seats for each party is calculated on the basis of the list-PR votes and the number of SMP seats is subtracted to determine the number of list-PR seats to which each party is entitled. In parallel MMP, the two groups of MPs are elected separately, and their combined totals determine each party's seat allocation.	Germany, New Zealand

SOURCE: Heather MacIvor, 'Proportional and Semi-Proportional Electoral Systems: Their Potential Effects on Canadian Politics', presentation to the Elections Canada Advisory Committee, Ottawa, May 1999.

parliamentary representation. If a party wins 25 per cent of the votes and is awarded 25 per cent of the seats in parliament, that is a highly proportional result. In recent years, the concept of proportionality has been expanded beyond party representation to embrace demographic representation within the national parliament. In this sense, a truly proportional electoral system would produce a legislature that mirrored the gender, ethnic, and occupational make-up of the entire electorate.

Plurality/Majority

All of the systems in this category have a district magnitude of 1 (each constituency elects one MP). Therefore, each sets a high electoral threshold and each is highly disproportional.[6] The differences between them arise from variations in electoral formula and ballot structure. Under SMP, the candidate with more valid votes than any other is declared the winner, without needing an absolute majority. In a *majority* system, the winner must receive at least half of the valid votes.

The disproportionality produced by single-member electoral systems was graphically illustrated by the results of the 1997 Canadian general election. The Reform party (now the Canadian Alliance) and the Progressive Conservative party each won roughly 19 per cent of the vote, but Reform took three times as many seats (60 to the PCs' 20; MacIvor 1999: 32). This type of perverse result has often provoked discussion of electoral reform in Canada.

Proportional Representation: List-PR and the Single Transferable Vote

Under *list-PR*, the country is divided into multi-member districts (except in the Netherlands and Israel, where the entire country is a single constituency), and each party nominates as many candidates in each district as there are seats to be filled. The candidates for each party are listed on the ballot in rank order, as determined by national or local selection committees. The candidates at the top are far more likely to be elected than those at the bottom. When the votes are counted, the returning officers calculate the share of the vote received by each party. Then a mathematical formula is used to determine how many of the district seats each party has won. To simplify: If Party A wins 30 per cent of the vote in a 10-member district, it is awarded 3 of those seats. The top 3 candidates on its district list are declared elected. Party B, with 20 per cent of the vote, earns 2 seats, and so on.

A few countries use a *single transferable vote (STV)* system, which employs an ordinal ballot in relatively small multi-member districts. Each party may nominate as many candidates as there are seats in a given district, and the voter rank-orders some or all of the candidates according to preference. Because of the low district magnitude, STV is the least proportional of the PR systems. Some political scientists even place it in a separate, 'semi-proportional' category (e.g., Norris 1997a).

Mixed Systems

Since the early 1990s, various 'mixed' electoral systems have been adopted in both emerging and established democracies. *Mixed-member proportional (MMP)* systems combine a plurality or majority system with list-PR (Massicotte and Blais 1999).

Most mixed systems elect two distinct groups of MPs simultaneously: one group represents single-member constituencies, while the others are elected from national or regional party lists. Under *corrective* mixed systems, the number of seats awarded to each party is determined by the list-PR results (Massicotte and Blais 1999). The list seats are used to 'correct' the disproportional effects of the single-member district seats. The extent of the correction depends on the relative numbers of list-PR and single-district seats. In *parallel* systems, which produce less proportional outcomes, the two groups of MPs are elected separately. Each party's share of seats is the sum total of the successful constituency and list candidates. The latter do not correct the disproportionality of the former.

Most Canadian advocates of electoral reform have proposed corrective systems with relatively small numbers of list-PR seats (Seidle 1996). Therefore, the discussion of electoral reform in this chapter will focus on the possible effects of MMP on women's parliamentary representation.

ELECTORAL SYSTEMS AND THE REPRESENTATION OF WOMEN IN NATIONAL LEGISLATURES

Measuring the Effect of Electoral Systems on Women's Representation

While the electoral system does not solely determine the percentage of women in a national legislature, it is clear that majority/plurality systems reduce female representation (see Tables 2.1 and 2.2, p. 23). On average, as Table 2.2 indicates, countries with list-PR and mixed systems elect significantly more women to their national parliaments than those with single-member systems. When multiple-regression analysis is used to measure the relative influence of different variables on female representation—including the socio-economic status of women, cultural attitudes toward gender equality, and the strength of left-wing parties—the electoral system often emerges as the single most important factor (Matland 1998; Norris 1996, 1997b; Rule 1987).

Further evidence of the effect of electoral systems on women's parliamentary representation comes from Australia, which uses a different system to elect each of its two houses of the federal parliament. As of March 2001, women accounted for 23 per cent of the Lower House—elected by alternative vote (AV), as described in Table 2.3 (p. 25) —and 30.3 per cent of the Upper House, which is elected by a more proportional STV system.[7] The experience of France and New Zealand is also suggestive, although it may be contaminated by a time-lag effect: in both cases, the replacement of a single-member system by a more proportional system (list-PR in the French case and a mixed system in New Zealand) resulted in an immediate and significant increase in women's electoral success. When New Zealand switched from SMP to a mixed system in 1996, the proportion of women in its parliament rose from 21.2 per cent to 29.2 per cent overnight (Matland 1998).[8] One comparative study concluded that 'for industrialized democracies, changing from a majoritarian to a PR system [would] result in a 15.6 per cent jump in the female proportion of the national legislature' (Matland 1998: 115).

Despite the clear association between electoral systems and women's representation, we should not overstate the independent influence of the electoral system. Contextual factors cannot be overlooked (Norris 1997a). In particular,

> the comparative extent of women in parliament is best explained by a combination of early full female political participation, welfare state socialism, party list PR seats, and leftist seats. Of these four factors, early full female participation and welfare state socialism are clearly more important than having party list PR and leftist seats. In other words, party list PR and leftist parties in parliament help a bit, but much less than broader contextual points. (Siaroff 2000: 206)

Table 2.1 (p. 23) shows that Australia and Canada, both of which use single-member systems, elect more women to their parliaments than either Israel or Greece, which use list-PR systems. So list-PR cannot, by itself, explain the electoral success of women in Scandinavia and the Netherlands (Matland 1993). Nevertheless, the comparative evidence suggests that single-member electoral systems reduce the percentage of women in parliament—all other things being equal—and that proportional systems do not.

Explaining the Relationship
Theories about the effects of electoral systems on women's representation may be divided into two categories: those that focus on the characteristics of electoral systems themselves and those that emphasize the incentives produced by the interaction between the electoral system and contextual factors.

Electoral-System Characteristics
Of the five electoral-system characteristics discussed earlier, district magnitude is usually identified as the strongest predictor of women's parliamentary representation.[9] The case for district magnitude is simple: the more seats in a given district, the more candidates each party nominates and the greater the odds that one or more women will be included (Norris 1996). Most countries with large multi-member districts have high percentages of female parliamentarians (recall, however, that Israel has both an extremely proportional list system and low female representation). Conversely, single-member districts tend to reduce the number of female candidates.

The claim that list-PR automatically increases female representation should be taken with a grain of salt. As Pippa Norris puts it, 'arguably a party list system is a necessary but not sufficient condition for high levels of female representation' (1993: 314). The key point is that women candidates will fail unless they are placed near the top of their respective party lists. Elina Haavio-Mannila and colleagues distinguish among three categories of list positions: those at the top are 'mandate' positions, which virtually guarantee election to parliament; those at the bottom are 'ornamental' positions; and those in-between are 'fighting' positions, neither hopeless nor promising (in Matland and Taylor 1997). The rank-ordering of women candidates depends on contextual factors, such as cultural attitudes, internal party rules, and pressure from women's groups, and not on district magnitude as such

(Matland and Taylor 1997). In a few cases, such as elections to the Argentine Senate, parties are required by law to nominate a certain percentage of women and to place them in favourable positions on their lists (Norris 1997a). In most cases, however, the percentage and positioning of female list-PR candidates is determined by the parties themselves. So while a large district magnitude *permits* parties to nominate more women, it does not *require* them to do so.

Context and Incentives

We have seen that the electoral system itself does not entirely explain the variance in women's political representation. We have also seen that contextual factors interact with the electoral system to produce the incentive structure for political representation in each Western democracy. Three contextual factors are particularly noteworthy: candidate-selection practices, cultural attitudes toward gender equality, and the socio-economic status of women. The latter two factors have changed dramatically in most Western states, including Canada, over the past three decades. The percentage of women who work outside the home, particularly in non-traditional and professional jobs, has multiplied, along with the proportion of women who pursue higher education. Egalitarian attitudes and enhanced socio-economic status for women increase both the supply of female aspirants and the demand for female candidates (Rule 1987; Studlar and Matland 1994). These crucial contextual factors operate independently of the electoral system and are not amenable to rapid institutional reform.

The electoral system does have a direct impact on candidate selection, however.[10] The district magnitude, together with the ballot structure and the electoral formula, imposes particular organizational requirements on parties. Of particular importance is the nomination process used by each party, which directly affects the demand for female candidates (and indirectly affects the supply). But the electoral system is only one factor at work. Left-wing parties are considerably more willing to nominate female candidates in mandate positions, largely for ideological reasons (Norris 1993). Where socialist, labour, and Green parties have adopted mandatory gender quotas—as they have in most Western European states—the numbers of female candidates and legislators have risen dramatically (Royal Commission on Electoral Reform and Party Financing 1991). List-PR, combined with centralized candidate selection, allows progressive parties to translate incentives for greater female representation into effective change (Matland 1993). SMP, as the NDP discovered in 1993, does not.

ELECTORAL SYSTEMS AND INCENTIVE STRUCTURES: THE CANADIAN CASE

Federal legislation creates the framework within which our national parties contest elections to the House of Commons. Within that framework, Canadian parties are free to conduct their internal affairs as they see fit. For example, the Canada Elections Act forbids a registered party to nominate more than one candidate in each riding, but it does not require parties to follow any particular selection procedure (apart from section 65, which disqualifies particular classes of prospective candidates). The omission is deliberate. Since before Confederation, local constituency associations have been free to select candidates for Parliament with little interference from their national parties. This tradition of local autonomy contrasts sharply with the centralized control of candidate selection in most Western democracies, where national party committees either compile lists of candidates (usually with some input from local party organizations) or lay down strict rules for their district associations to follow.

Canada's 'local patronage' model of candidate selection (Norris 1996) is at the core of the incentive structure for political aspirants of both sexes. It is the logical outcome of an electoral system that divides the country into separate single-member districts. This institutional structure, combined with a localistic political culture, has produced a strong and fiercely guarded tradition of local party control over candidate selection (Carty, Cross, and Young 2000; Sayers 1998). The *patronage* element of the model refers to the weakness of institutional rules for candidate nomination: 'Gatekeepers have considerable discretion, the steps in the application process are familiar to participants but rarely made explicit, and procedure may vary from one selection to another' (Norris 1996: 203). In recent years, Canada's national parties have taken tentative steps away from the local-patronage process (Erickson 1997b). For example, the federal Liberal party allows its leader to appoint candidates when he or she deems it necessary. On the whole, however, Canadian constituency associations retain virtually complete discretion over the selection of parliamentary candidates. They are also substantially less likely to nominate women than to nominate men (see Table 2.4).

Single-member districts, combined with local-patronage candidate selection, restrict the demand for female candidates in at least three ways. First, single-member districts reduce candidate selection to a zero-sum game (Studlar and Matland 1994). Each party chooses one standard-bearer in each constituency. The decision to nominate a male candidate rules out the nomination of a woman, and vice versa. Whereas candidate selectors in multi-member systems can choose—or be compelled—to 'balance the ticket' by including women on their district lists, no such balance is possible in a single-member system (Matland and Studlar 1996).

Second, the weakness of central party control makes it almost impossible to impose national quotas or guidelines for the selection of particular types of candidates. In 1991, the federal NDP decided that half of its candidates in the next general election would be women (Erickson 1993). The proposal faced stiff resistance from NDP constituency associations, partly because of its 'undemocratic' character (Erickson 1997b: 42). In the end, the requirement to nominate women was watered down into a set of 'guidelines', from which ridings with incumbent MPs were explicitly exempted. In the 1993 election, only 38 per cent of NDP candidates were female (Matland and Studlar 1996: 719)—a respectable figure, but not quite gender parity.

Third, incumbency is particularly strong in single-member systems. A constituency association with a sitting MP is unlikely to oppose his or her wish for renomination, both because an incumbent is a proven winner and because the MP usually dominates the local party organization (Sayers 1998). Because most incumbents are men, their re-nomination reduces the number of seats available to female aspirants (Studlar and Matland 1994).

The Canadian evidence suggests that the most important restriction on demand for female candidates is low district magnitude. There is no evidence that local party associations discriminate against female aspirants because of sexism, or that they regard women as an electoral liability (Erickson 1997b). Even under SMP, the major parties nominated substantially more women in the 1984 election than they had previously (Studlar and Matland 1994), and they continued to do so until 1997.[11] At the same time, the incumbency effect is weaker in Canada than in most other single-member systems; the turnover rate for Canadian MPs is unusually high, partly because the volatility of the electorate is exaggerated by the effects of SMP (Erickson 1997b; Norris 1996; Young 1991). This high turnover provides greater opportunities for aspiring candidates, including women. So does the

Table 2.4

Numbers of and Success Rates (Percentages) for Female Candidates, Canadian General Elections, 1984–2000

	1984	1988	1993	1997	2000
Liberal	44 (15.6%)	53 (18%)	64 (21.7%)	84 (27.9%)	65 (21.6%)
PC	23 (8.2%)	37 (12.5%)	67 (22.7%)	56 (18.6%)	39 (13.0%)
NDP	64 (22.7%)	84 (28.5%)	113 (38.3%)	107 (35.5%)	88 (29.2%)
Reform[a]	–	8 (11.1%)	23 (11.1%)	23 (10.1%)	32 (10.7%)
BQ	–	–	10 (13.3%)	16 (21.3%)	18 (24.0%)
Total major parties	131 (15.5%)	182 (19.0%)	277 (23.7%)	286 (23.7%)	242 (19.0%)
Female major-party candidates elected (% of major parties)	27 (20.6%)	39 (21.4%)	53 (19.1%)	62 (21.7%)	62 (25.6%)
Female candidates for other parties	83	120	199	122	133
Total female candidates (% of all candidates)	214 (14.8%)	302 (19.2%)	476 (22.1%)	408 (24.4%)	375 (20.7%)
Total female candidates elected	27 (12.6%)	39 (12.9%)	53 (11.1%)	62 (15.2%)	62 (16.5%)
Total male candidates	1235	1273	1680	1264	1422
Total male candidates elected	255 (20.6%)	256 (20.1%)	242 (14.4%)	239 (18.9%)	239 (16.8%)
Margin of difference between % of successful male and female candidates	8.0	7.2	3.3	3.7	0.3

SOURCE: Elections Canada, Official Voting Results of the 1988 General Election (Ottawa: Minister of Supply and Services Canada, 1988) (available at <http://www.elections.ca>, accessed April 2001).

[a] Called the Canadian Reform Conservative Alliance in 2000.

unusually open and uncompetitive nomination process in most constituency asso-ciations. We may conclude, therefore, that single-member districts are the most important institutional reason for women's underrepresentation among Canadian parliamentary candidates.

Historically, female candidates have been less successful in Canadian elections than male candidates (although the results of the 2000 federal election are heart-ening). If the survey evidence is correct, this gender gap does not reflect a weak demand for women legislators among the Canadian electorate (Matland and Studlar 1996). Historically, female candidates have been less successful because they were more likely to run in constituencies where their parties were weak, or because they ran for small parties or as independent candidates. In other words, they were ornamental candidates. However, most of the major parties have devoted consider-able effort in recent years to increasing the number of women in mandate and fight-ing constituencies, an effort that is reflected in the growing number of women in the House of Commons.

To summarize, while the demand for female candidates in Canada is reduced by single-member districts, contextual barriers to the nomination and election of women are relatively weak. We must therefore look at the supply side of the equa-tion to fully explain the underrepresentation of women in the Canadian House of Commons. There are at least three contextual factors that limit the pool of poten-tial female candidates (MacIvor 1996). First, the gendered division of labour within Canada's political parties may discourage women from pursuing nominations. The establishment of women's auxiliaries by the Liberal and Conservative parties in the 1920s relegated most female party members to housekeeping chores: providing refreshments at meetings, minding campaign offices, and keeping track of mem-bership lists. Although this division of labour has certainly weakened since the 1970s, particularly for younger and better-educated women, there is still an unspo-ken assumption in some local constituency associations that men should make policy and women should make coffee.

Second, women in Canada still hold fewer of the resources—money, professional contacts, education, leisure time—that nurture political careers. Third, the nature of Canadian politics itself, with its intense partisanship and aggressive posturing, is uncongenial to many women (and men). None of these supply-side factors can be attributed to the electoral system, and none can be cured by electoral reform. Having said that, there is reason to expect that both the supply of and the demand for female candidates would increase under a more proportional electoral system. The replacement of some or all of the existing single-member districts with list-PR seats would lower the barriers to female aspirants and increase the proportion of women in the Canadian House of Commons. It would allow the parties to balance their tickets by including more female and minority candidates, and strengthen the contagion effect from parties that are more committed to the political representa-tion of women.[12]

CONCLUSION: ASSESSING THE EFFECT OF MMP ON WOMEN IN CANADIAN POLITICS

While the adoption of MMP would almost certainly increase the numbers of female candidates and MPs, it would be a mistake to treat electoral reform as a panacea. There are at least two reasons for caution. First, the success of female list-PR candidates would depend on the rank-ordering of the lists. Without strong formal or informal incentives for the parties to place women at the top of their lists, such as the recent French *parité* law, which penalizes parties for nominating fewer than 50 per cent women, most female standard-bearers would be ornamental.

Second, the adoption of formal incentives, such as legally binding quotas for female candidates, is unlikely for at least two reasons. For one, the parties—whose parliamentary caucuses have the right to amend and reject proposed legislation—would almost certainly reject such interference with their candidate-selection procedures. When, in 1991, the Royal Commission on Electoral Reform and Party Financing proposed amendments to the Canada Elections Act that would have given parties financial incentives to increase the number of women in their parliamentary contingents, the major parties rejected the idea outright (Dobrowolsky and Jenson 1993).

Furthermore, public opinion in this country does not appear to favour mandatory gender quotas. In a recent survey of attitudes toward Canada's representative institutions, only one-third of respondents agreed that the underrepresentation of women was a serious or very serious problem. Two-thirds considered the gender imbalance in Parliament to be a minor problem or no problem at all (Howe and Northrup 2000: 72). When asked whether they would favour or oppose requiring the parties to choose equal numbers of male and female candidates, the respondents were evenly divided: 40.9 per cent approved of such a requirement, while 40.5 per cent were opposed (Howe and Northrup 2000: 73). (Not surprisingly, women were significantly more enthusiastic about the idea than men.) At the same time, however, just over half of the respondents (51.2 per cent) approved the idea of 'requiring the parties to choose more female candidates than they do now' (Howe and Northrup 2000: 74). So Canadians might be willing to accept some formal measures to increase the nomination of women, but not an outright quota system.

In this context, the fate of the Nunavut gender-quota proposal is instructive. The Nunavut Implementation Commission proposed in 1997 that the legislature in the new territory be elected from 10 dual-member districts, each of which would send one male and one female MLA to Iqaluit (Nunavut Implementation Commission 1997). A May 1998 plebiscite in the new territory rejected the proposal by 57 per cent to 43 per cent (Dahl, Hicks, and Jull 2000). If we conclude that formal incentives for Canadian parties to nominate women in mandate positions will not be implemented, then the impact of MMP on women's parliamentary representation will depend on informal incentives.

On the surface, these look promising. Since 1993, when New Zealand abandoned SMP in favour of MMP, Canada has had the highest proportion of female legislators among the SMP countries. Under MMP, the barriers arising from single-member districts would be lowered (to a greater or lesser degree, depending on the mix of SMP and list seats). The supply of female candidates would likely continue to increase as women's socio-economic and political status continued to improve. We may assume, therefore, that most of the registered parties would include substantial numbers of women on their lists and place at least some of them in mandate and fighting positions.[13] Given the relatively strong demand for female candidates in Canadian elections and the probability that women's groups would take advantage of the publicity surrounding a new electoral system to pressure the parties for favourable list positions, the introduction of a multi-member element would likely promote the election of women to Canada's House of Commons.

However, the New Zealand experience with MMP provides a reason for caution. It suggests that under mixed systems, most female MPs are elected from party lists. Of the 35 women elected in New Zealand in 1996, 25 (71.4 per cent) were list MPs and only 10 (28.6 per cent) won constituency seats (Arseneau 1999: 139). Three of the major parties failed to elect a single woman in the constituencies and had to rely entirely on the list seats for female representation. In the last election before the adoption of MMP, 21.2 per cent of those elected to the New Zealand parliament were women—the highest proportion among the SMP democracies at that time, just above Canada, with 18 per cent (Norris 1996: 191). In effect, the proportion of female MPs in SMP districts fell from 21.2 per cent to 15.4, even as they captured 55.6 per cent of the list-PR seats introduced in 1996. So women's performance in the SMP seats worsened significantly under electoral reform despite the overall increase in female representation. The balance between SMP and list seats was a little more even in the 1999 election: fewer women were elected from the list seats and more from the electorate seats, while the overall number rose by 2 to 37 (Vowles 2000: 14). Nonetheless, there were still fewer women among the electorate MPs than in the ranks of list MPs.

If we could assume that SMP and list-PR MPs would enjoy equal status, then the overrepresentation of women in the latter category need not worry us. As former New Zealand prime minister Jim Bolger points out, 'how [the] women got into Parliament matters less than the fact that they're there now'.[14] But some Canadian opponents of electoral reform argue that a mixed system would create two classes of MPs: the constituency representatives, who would have personal ties to the voters, and the list MPs, who would represent only their parties (see Katz 1999; Seidle 1996). If the latter were regarded as second-class parliamentarians, and if female MPs were disproportionately concentrated in this second class, the status of women in Canadian politics might not improve quite as much as electoral-reform advocates predict.[15] It is also worth noting that the proportion of women in the New Zealand Cabinet did not keep pace with growing legislative representation. Women accounted for 20 per cent of the MPs in the National Party–New Zealand First coalition government formed after the 1999 election, but only 5 per cent of Cabinet ministers (Arseneau 1999: 139). This illustrates a crucial point, which advocates of electoral reform would do well to remember: getting more women into Parliament will not automatically make things better for those outside Parliament. Until women account for a substantial proportion of party leaders and Cabinet ministers, rising female representation in Parliament will have little effect on public policy.

Despite these caveats, a more proportional electoral system would be a positive development for women in Canadian politics. It would almost certainly increase the numbers of women MPs in most, if not all, party caucuses. Instead of being shut out of 'safe' seats by male incumbents, female aspirants would have a chance to gain favourable positions on party lists. The increased demand arising from ticket-balancing would encourage a growth in supply, as the incentives for women to seek elected office through the party system improved. At the very least, greater representation of women in the Canadian Parliament would be a symbolic move toward gender equality. At most, it could improve both the process and the outcomes of our political system. A representative democracy that denies equal electoral opportunities to identifiable groups among its population is neither representative nor particularly democratic. If we are truly committed to improving the representation of women in Canadian politics, then we should place electoral reform high on our list of priorities.

NOTES

1. While electoral systems at the sub-national level—that is, state or provincial—are also significant, this paper will focus on the election of national parliaments.

2. 'Every citizen of Canada has the right to vote in an election of members of the House of Commons or of a legislative assembly and to be qualified for membership therein.'

3. After the 2000 federal election, a grassroots group called Fair Vote Canada began to organize conferences and media events to raise awareness of electoral reform. In early 2001, the Law Commission of Canada identified the electoral system as a top priority. In May 2001, the Green party filed a lawsuit against the federal government, challenging the constitutionality of the electoral system under the Charter of Rights.

4. The distinction between the supply of and the demand for female candidates is based on Norris (1997b).

5. This discussion is based on MacIvor (1999a).

6. The disproportionality produced by single-member electoral systems was particularly evident in the 1993 Canadian general election. The Conservatives won only 2 seats with 16 per cent of the national vote, while the Bloc Québécois took 54 seats with 13.5 per cent of the national vote.

7. Inter-Parliamentary Union, April 2001, available at <www.ipu.org/wmn-e/world.htm>.

8. Some of the best sources for further information on New Zealand's electoral system are Vowles et al. (1998), Vowles et al. (2002), and most of the research papers and journal articles available from the New Zealand Election Study Web site at <www.nzes.org>.

9. One study found that ballot structure was the key factor, but this is an exception; see Norris (1997b).

10. *Candidate selection* is the informal process that occurs within a particular party organization by which aspirants for office are recruited, evaluated, and eventually narrowed down; *nomination* refers to the formal process determined by law under which the names of candidates are placed on the ballot.

11. The sudden decline in female candidacies in the 2000 election is a disturbing development, but one that cannot be fully addressed here. However, it is likely that the high rate of incumbency in that election provides a partial explanation.

12. The *contagion theory* holds that competitive political parties tend to copy each other's innovations. Where one party in a given jurisdiction decides to appeal to female voters

by nomination more women candidates, its rivals may feel pressured to follow suit. See Matland and Studlar (1996).

13. While it is tempting to make predictions about the numbers of women elected under a hypothetical new electoral system, such predictions are too unreliable to carry much weight. Voting patterns and party systems change with the introduction of new electoral rules, and there are so many undetermined variables, such as the percentage of list seats in an MMP system, that any prediction would almost inevitably rest on incorrect assumptions. Therefore, any speculations about the possible effects of MMP on women in Canada's Parliament should be approached with caution.

14. James Bolger, remarks to the Institute for Research in Public Policy Conference on Electoral Reform, Ottawa, 3 May 2001.

15. On a more positive note, the New Zealand parties deliberately recruited a host of political newcomers to run for list seats in 1996. While the influx of non-professionals caused some unforeseen problems for the party leaders, who found themselves swamped with basic questions about political procedures, the newcomers brought a welcome infusion of energy and enthusiasm into the country's political elite (Jo Kenelly, former assistant to James Bolger, personal interview, Ottawa, 4 May 2001).

Chapter 3

Women Politicians in Canada's Parliament and Legislatures, 1917–2000: A Socio-demographic Profile[1]

LINDA TRIMBLE AND MANON TREMBLAY

INTRODUCTION

> [In 1971, Dave Barrett, then leader of the BC New Democratic Party] said he wanted to encourage me to seek an NDP nomination for the next provincial election. Bill and I had a good chuckle over that at home that evening, because we both knew that no Vancouver riding would choose a person who was Black, female and an immigrant to be its elected representative. (Brown 1989: 94)
>
> —*Rosemary Brown, a Black woman born in Jamaica, was elected to the BC legislature in the riding of Vancouver-Burrard in 1972.*

Between 1917 and 2000, 618 women were elected or appointed to Canada's Parliament and legislatures; many of them served more than one term in office. We know a bit about some aspects of these female parliamentarians' lives and careers, including when and where they were elected (Brodie and Vickers 1982; Vickers 1978; Vickers and Brodie 1981), the political parties they represented (Arscott and Trimble 1997; Studlar and Matland 1996), and the obstacles and opportunities they faced when contemplating and seeking elected office (Brodie and Chandler 1991; Tremblay and Pelletier 1995). But their social and demographic characteristics remain largely a mystery, especially in the case of women senators. There is little information about how old these women politicians were when first elected or appointed, where they were born, whether they were married, divorced, or single, and what kind of education and employment backgrounds they had before seeking office (Arend and Chandler 1996; Brock 1997; Crossley 1997; Spencer and Spencer 1992; Tremblay and Pelletier 1995). As yet, no comparisons over time have been made between elected and appointed women parliamentarians, or between women elected national and provincially.

This chapter is based on a study of selected personal and social characteristics of all women elected and appointed to Canada's Parliament and legislatures from 1917 to 2000. This time period begins with the election of the first women MLAs, Alberta's Louise McKinney and Roberta MacAdams, who won office in 1917, and the first female member of Parliament, Agnes Macphail, who entered the Commons in 1921 (see Trimble 1999). It spans the appointment of the earliest woman senator, Cairine Wilson, in 1930, and the first women to enter legislatures in provinces where suffrage was granted to most women later than in the west. For instance, in PEI, where most women won the vote in 1922, no woman sat in the legislature until 25 years later, in 1967. Similarly, while women acquired the franchise in Quebec in 1940, no female member of the National Assembly was elected until 1961. Women began to win election to Parliament and provincial and territorial legislatures in record numbers in the mid- to late 1980s, constituting more than 10 per cent of the elected representatives in most jurisdictions. And in the year 2000 about 20 per cent of elected legislators and almost 30 per cent of senators were women. In short, the first 83 years of women in politics reflect a dramatic change in the political environment for Canadian women.

The chapter begins by describing the methodology for our study of women elected to Canada's Parliament and legislatures between 1917 and 2000. The second section provides an overview of the literature on social and demographic characteristics of Canada's women politicians, accompanied by a discussion of why these characteristics matter. We identify trends and unanswered questions, and formulate several hypotheses that inform our own investigation. The third section, describing research findings from this study, offers a general profile of elected women in Canada, followed by an examination of differences across time and jurisdiction on five measures: country of birth, marital status, age at first election, education, and occupation. The conclusion speculates about the implications of our findings for the substantive representation of women's diverse experiences and policy needs in Canada's Parliament and legislatures.

Methodology

This study reports some of the research findings from a statistical analysis of information about the political and personal backgrounds of all Canadian women elected to the Parliament and legislatures or appointed to the Senate between 1917 and 2000.[2] The newest women legislators, elected in British Columbia and Alberta in 2001, were not yet been included in the database at the time of writing and were not analyzed in this study. The data were gathered from a variety of publicly available sources, including government Web sites, the *Canadian Parliamentary Guide*, and other published works describing the characteristics and careers of Canada's women politicians. We collected information, where possible, about each woman's country and date of birth; age, marital status, and jurisdiction when first elected or appointed; educational and occupational background; party affiliation; political and volunteer experience; and political career while in office.

Female legislators were not interviewed or surveyed for this study; thus, the data are limited by the availability of published information. For instance, we were unable to determine the ethnicity of most women politicians, so our study cannot address the many very important questions about the ethnic diversity of women politicians in Canada. However, we do know that most visible minority women have been elected very recently, and Jerome Black's chapter in this volume addresses part of this research gap (see chapter 4). As well, because our data set includes information on only women politicians, we cannot make comparisons with male legislators.

We can, and do, compare the occupational, age, marital, and other characteristics of modern women legislators to those of Canadian women by referring to Statistics Canada data.

SOCIAL CHARACTERISTICS OF ELECTED WOMEN

Much of the Canadian literature on women in politics has focused on why such a small number of women have sought and won elected office. Before the late 1980s, very few women contested, won, or were appointed to legislative posts, so Canadian political scientists examined patterns of underrepresentation and outlined the many barriers to women's quest for formal political power (Bashevkin 1993; Brodie 1985; Megyery 1991). This attention to the electoral recruitment and success of women remains important, for even though women are now winning close to 20 per cent of the seats in Canada's legislative assemblies, the goal of equal representation is far from realized and is unlikely to be attained soon (Arscott and Trimble, forthcoming). The number of women elected to the House of Commons plateaued in the 2000 election and dropped in recent elections in British Columbia (2001), Alberta (2001), and Nova Scotia (1999).

With women now constituting between 15 per cent and 30 per cent of the legislators in most Canadian jurisdictions, thus forming a critical mass of elected representatives, scholars have begun to ask whether electing women makes a difference. In other words, researchers are asking if female legislators are willing and able to change the style and content of legislative debate and to influence public policy outcomes in meaningful ways (Tremblay 1992, 1998a, 1999; Trimble 1997). Jane Arscott and Linda Trimble summarized early research on this question, arguing that the ability of women representatives to make a gender-sensitive difference while in public office is shaped, at least in part, by the characteristics and beliefs of the female legislators themselves (1997). The social backgrounds, ideological positions, and personal characteristics of women politicians may help determine what they do while in political office, though party affiliation continues to be a very powerful predictor of the attitudes and behaviour of female politicians (Erickson 1997b; Tremblay 1997, 2002c). Female politicians' political beliefs, including ideas about representation, can influence their willingness to represent women's diverse interests and goals, and evidence suggests that social and demographic characteristics matter too (Ship 1998; Trimble 1998). In other words, Canadian researchers have found that who legislators are may be as important as how many women occupy political office. Yet we do not have a complete sense of who they are, especially at the provincial and territorial level, and we know very little about the social, political, and demographic characteristics of women senators in particular.

But why does it matter who these political women are? After all, the idea that representatives in liberal democracies must mirror the population at large is controversial, with many democratic theorists insisting there is little or no connection between the characteristics of legislators and their ability to represent the interests of their constituents (Vickers 1997). For instance, according to Jennifer Smith, elected officials cannot be accused of being unrepresentative of a given group on the grounds that they do not share the characteristics of members of that group (1991). As Anne Phillips says, 'in the conventional understandings of liberal democracy, difference is regarded as primarily a matter of ideas. . . . The personal characteristics of the representatives barely figure in this' (1995: 1). To put this idea another way, representation should be about ideas, not identities, about what representatives do, not who they are.

Feminist political scientists have disagreed, arguing that what representatives actually say and do is indelibly stamped by who they are. According to Iris Marion Young, it is difficult, if not impossible, for legislators to think through political questions without being influenced by their own background, experiences, and standpoint (1990). Many studies have demonstrated the link between the sex of representatives and their political attitudes, opinions, and behaviours while in office (Bystydziensky 1992; Carroll 1992, 1994; Lovenduski 1986; Skjeie 1991; Tremblay 1992, 1998a; Trimble 1997, 1998). And scholars have shown that the social backgrounds and personal characteristics of women politicians shape their willingness and ability to articulate women's diverse experiences and to advocate policy measures designed to raise the status of women (Trimble 1998). In short, who women are may be an important determinant of what they think and do in legislatures, as well as of how effectively they represent women's varied and various interests. A key element, then, of the electoral project—the goal of representing women and women's ideas, beliefs, and policy interests in elected political bodies—is the representation of women's different identities (Young cited in Vickers 1997). Recognition of women's diversity is therefore central to a feminist understanding of representation, for women are by no means a monolithic group with uniform policy interests (Butler 1990; Spelman 1988; L. Young 1994).

The literature on the recruitment of female politicians to public office shows that gender is a key variable shaping access to electoral office, as women's attributes are, in some important respects, different from those of their male counterparts (Black and Erickson 2000; Tremblay, Pelletier, and Pitre, forthcoming). For example, female candidates and office-holders have higher levels of education and more political experience than male candidates, suggesting that women must compensate for the role conflict inherent in entering a traditionally masculine domain. Women politicians' exceptional qualifications reflect a continued need to overcome gender-, class-, and race-based hurdles to political power. For instance, Black's finding that ethnic minority women members of Parliament have a higher socio-economic profile than non-minority women MPs indicates that race barriers are layered on top of gender-based obstacles to elected office (2000a). And class has always acted as a key determinant of success for all political office-seekers, male and female.

Many analyses of Canada's women politicians to date have explored the social, political, and demographic characteristics of candidates for public office. Janine Brodie's examination of women who stood as candidates for municipal, provincial, territorial, and federal office between 1945 and 1975 produced the general observation that women take distinct pathways to political office and their experiences reflect the gendered nature of social life and political competition. For instance,

Brodie found that 79 per cent of the women candidates who responded to her survey were married and 21 per cent were single, separated, widowed, or divorced when they sought office (1985: 83). Most (79 per cent) had professional occupations, albeit many in female-dominated professions such as teaching, nursing, secretarial and administrative, and social work, while 10 per cent were homemakers (1985: 85). Brodie's findings support the idea that women's qualifications are different and that they reflect a need to compensate for gender-based barriers. But most of the women in Brodie's sample—about 88 per cent—did not win office (1985: 20). They contested elections at a time when most women candidates were selected by competitive parties to run in 'unwinnable' ridings or were chosen to serve as standard-bearers for fringe parties. Therefore it is entirely possible that the characteristics displayed by Brodie's sample will differ from those of more recent, more successful candidates.

Jerome Black and Lynda Erickson's study of male and female candidates in the 1993 Canadian federal election identified the educational attainment, occupational status, party involvement, and volunteer experience of these political aspirants (2000). While their research did not compare women over time, it did contrast women with men. The study confirmed Brodie's notion of gendered pathways to public office, as it discovered important differences in the personal attributes and political experiences of male and female office-seekers. For instance, male candidates were more likely than female candidates to be married, and they also had more children (2000: 11). Women candidates displayed higher levels of education than their male counterparts, and different employment backgrounds, with women more likely than men to be in professional occupations and men more likely than women to be self-employed (2000: 13). Women candidates also displayed a greater tendency than male candidates to hold office within political parties and interest groups (2000: 15–16).

Black and Erickson explored various explanations for these gender-based differences, including the idea that the sexual division of labour and the persistence of sexism in Canadian society affects the recruitment of women politicians (2000). Because women have different social and economic backgrounds, their professional and personal experiences diverge from those of their male counterparts. For instance, given the existence of female-dominated professions and a still largely gender-segregated workforce, it is not surprising that women candidates often have different occupational backgrounds than do male candidates. As well, female candidates tend to compensate for entrenched societal gender biases by attaining exceptional qualifications, such as high levels of education or greater political experience, in an effort to prove that they have 'the right stuff' for public office.

Black and Erickson's findings are very interesting because they suggest that, to be successful in political life, women candidates must in some respects be just like the men who win power, but that in other respects they must surpass them (Tremblay and Pelletier 1995). Do these observations regarding marital status, occupation, education, and political experience apply to elected and appointed women in the early years and at both levels of government? The literature indicates a generational effect, with women elected in the 1960s to the early 1980s exhibiting fewer political

resources than their male colleagues, including lower levels of education, less prestigious occupational backgrounds, and less important political responsibilities
(Bashevkin 1982, 1983a; Brodie 1977; Brodie and Vickers 1982). But by the mid-
to late 1980s, the status of white able-bodied Canadian women had changed quite
dramatically. The second wave of the women's movement and other social forces
brought women into postsecondary education and the labour market, and in particular women began to enter the types of professions considered good recruiting
ground for political parties seeking candidates. Therefore, from the mid-1980s to the
present, a new generation of political women was elected, and these women clearly
reflect the trends highlighted by Black and Erickson (2000). Contemporary female
legislators display similar resources to their male colleagues, sometimes even exhibiting higher levels of qualification, but they also continue to reflect areas of difference
(Tremblay, Pelletier, and Pitre, forthcoming).

Research conducted by Louise Carbert, Kathy Brock, and John Crossley provides
glimpses into the occupational backgrounds of female members of provincial legislatures elected in the 1980s, illustrating the tendency of women to take distinct
occupational paths to political office. Carbert (1997) determined that most of the
13 women who served in the Saskatchewan legislature between 1991 and 1995
were in professional occupations before entering political life. Brock (1997) compared male and female MLAs serving in the Manitoba legislature from 1981 to
1995, noting in particular that male MLAs were much more likely to be farmers or
involved in agricultural businesses while the female MLAs tended to be teachers or
nurses before running for office. Crossley's examination of male and female MLAs
serving in the PEI legislature between 1966 and 1994 (a sample of 88 men and 12
women) discovered that women 'are not recruited from the same occupational
groups as men' (1997: 296). Female MLAs serving during this time period were
drawn from occupational categories traditionally associated with women: teaching,
homemaking, and health care. These findings support the hypothesis that women's
differential labour-force participation is reflected in the personal backgrounds of
women politicians.

Provincial studies also add weight to Black and Erickson's contention that
women politicians may compensate for perceived 'deficiencies' (that is, overcome
the hurdle of not being male) by displaying exceptional qualifications for public
office, especially age and education (2000). Brock (1997), Crossley (1997), and
Samia Spencer and William Spencer (1992) found the female representatives they
studied in Manitoba, PEI, and Quebec to be better educated than their male counterparts, and discovered that MLAs of both sexes have a higher level of educational
attainment than the general population. Crossley's study of PEI legislators points
to a different age profile for men and women, with women tending to begin their
legislative careers later, in their mid-forties or early fifties, and with elected women
concentrated in a narrow age range; in contrast, men elected to the PEI legislature
between 1966 and 1994 sought office earlier, often while in their twenties and thir-
ties, and reflected a wider distribution of ages (1997: 299).

Spencer and Spencer's survey of Quebec politicians who served in the House of
Commons or the Quebec National Assembly between 1961 and 1991 asked

respondents questions about their age, marital status, place of birth, education, and social background (1992). The researchers observed that the vast majority of male and female legislators were born in Quebec and identified themselves as originating from the middle class (1992: 334–35). But the women were slightly older than their male counterparts, were significantly less likely to be married, and had fewer children. Sylvie Arend and Celia Chandler (1996) also pointed to differences in the marital status of male and female office-holders. These scholars conducted surveys of all elected women in Canadian legislatures, and a sample of elected men, in 1983 and again in 1986. Because their focus was on the sex- and gender-role constraints experienced by female political aspirants, Arend and Chandler measured marital status when first elected; they found that women legislators were more likely than male legislators never to have been married or to have been widowed, divorced, or separated (1996: 16). The persistence of patriarchal ideas about a married woman's proper place acted as a barrier to the political aspirations of female aspirants with children; many mothers who sought a political career between 1945 and 1975 deliberately delayed their entry to politics until their children were grown (see Brodie 1985).

Several hypotheses can be drawn from these research findings. First, a general observation can be made that, like male politicians (Dyck 2000), female legislators do not mirror the social characteristics and political experiences of women in Canadian society. They are older, less ethnically diverse, better educated, more politically active, and more likely to hold professional occupations, all because of the selection process itself. Successful candidates for elected public office must be able to represent the party to the electorate, a public role implying a certain level of knowledge, financial and organizational resources, and support from the party and community. But for women, the task of convincing parties to select female candidates requires them to confront sex-based assumptions about these qualifications. Legislative institutions in Canada initially excluded women on the grounds that they were by nature unqualified to vote and run for public office (see Cleverdon 1974). Since winning the right to vote and to contest office, women politicians have found themselves in male-dominated political institutions. To break into a traditionally male occupation, women must overcome the subtle attitudinal barriers to the idea of women's entering a 'man's world'. Parties recruit candidates who mirror the qualifications and characteristics of office-holders.

Second, the literature suggests that women politicians of different generations entered political life with different characteristics and qualifications. The pioneers—women who were elected or appointed shortly after most women won the right to vote and run for office—were likely highly educated and professionally accomplished in many respects, but they had to jump the social, economic, and attitudinal barriers to women's seeking a political role. Before the 1970s and 1980s, most women did not have the social qualifications and economic resources available to male candidates, thus we expect to find differences in the socio-demographic characteristics of early women legislators (1917–1983) compared to those elected since the mid-1980s. The second wave of the Canadian women's movement undoubtedly shaped the life experiences and career paths of women elected in the 1980s, 1990s, and early 2000s. While Canadian women continue to experience a sexual division of labour in the home and workplace, some female political aspirants have been able to achieve the same qualifications as male candidates. As well, there is considerable support for the 'exceptionalism' hypothesis, the notion that women who have won office since the mid-1980s display qualifications, such as high levels of educational attainment, age, and professional status, that set them apart from their male counterparts. Although we do not compare male and female legislators, we do examine the characteristics of women politicians and expect to find that they were, and are, predominantly middle-aged, married, well-educated professionals.

The literature gives little guidance with respect to the impact of jurisdiction and method of selection. Appointed political office represents a different selection mechanism, but it nonetheless reflects similar assumptions about the appropriate qualifications for parliamentary service. Formally, the prime minister appoints senators who meet certain constitutional requirements. Senators must be at least 30 years of age, own $4,000 in real property, and claim a net worth of at least $4,000. But these are less significant qualifications than the unwritten understandings about the nature of the appointment. Senators are chosen on the basis of region, party service, standing in the community, age, and experience. The post is considered the capstone of an individual's political career and is often a reward for faithful party service; as such it comes fairly late in life. Since many senators were once legislators, it is reasonable to expect that their occupational, educational, and social characteristics, other than age, will be similar to those of elected women. However, Lorna Marsden and Joan Busby show that the first 13 women appointed to the Senate had extensive volunteer backgrounds and were all involved in women's organizations (1989: 74). Prime ministers have made appointments that reflect gender-based claims for representation, and thus it is possible that senators display different characteristics than their elected counterparts.

Among elected women politicians, jurisdiction may also be a determinant of qualifications and social characteristics. Studies conducted in the United States suggest that sub-national legislatures tend to be associated with lower levels of professionalism, power, and prestige, and with less competition for office, than national legislatures (Studlar and Matland 1996). For these reasons, coupled with the fact that provincial office may be more appealing to married women with children because it is literally closer to home, more women are elected to sub-national legislatures than to federal parliaments in some countries. However, Donley Studlar and Richard Matland found that in Canada, a slightly larger percentage of women were elected at the national level than to provincial legislatures in the 1980s and early 1990s (1996: 273). Arscott and Trimble (forthcoming) report that this trend continued, though it was less marked, in 2001. Provincial governments have considerable policy-making power in the Canadian political system; this level of government is therefore highly competitive and the role carries considerable prestige, and as a result the expectations for Canadian women politicians may not be lower at the sub-national level than at the federal level of government. However, it is possible that gender barriers associated with public–private role conflict (blending domestic and public roles) are lower at the provincial and territorial level. There may be fewer hurdles for younger women, especially married women with children, in sub-national legislatures.

Because of the dramatic social and political changes inspired by the women's movement, and because provincial legislatures are in many respects as competitive and powerful as Parliament, we expect to find greater variations in the social backgrounds and qualifications of women politicians over time than across jurisdiction. As well, since senators are often chosen because of their long party service or legislative careers, we do not expect to find senators to differ greatly from their elected women counterparts, with the exception of their age.

WOMEN POLITICIANS IN CANADA, 1917–2000

Between 1917 and 2000, 404 women were elected to serve as representatives in Canada's provincial and territorial legislatures, 154 women were elected to the Parliament of Canada, and 60 women were appointed to the Senate (see Table 3.1). Almost half of these female representatives were elected or appointed in the 1990s and 2000. At the provincial and territorial level, 134 (33 per cent of the sample) were elected since 1993, 73 (47 per cent) of female MPs won office in 1993 or later, and 28 (42 per cent) of the senators had been appointed since 1993. Many of these women politicians were very successful, winning re-election at least once, and many served several terms in office. Women who succeeded in winning election clearly

Table 3.1

Elected and Appointed Women Politicians in Canada's Legislatures[a]

	MPS	Senators	MLAS
Year of first election/appointment			
1917–1983	38 (24.7%)	19 (31.7%)	121 (30.1%)
1984–1992	43 (27.9%)	13 (21.6%)	147 (36.6%)
1993–2000	73 (47.4%)	28 (46.7%)	134 (33.3%)
Region when first elected/appointed			
Atlantic	16 (10.4%)	16 (26.7%)	75 (18.5%)
Quebec	43 (27.9%)	15 (25.0%)	57 (14.2%)
Ontario	50 (32.5%)	16 (26.7%)	67 (16.7%)
West/territories	46 (29.7%)	13 (12.7%)	203 (50.5%)
Type of first election			
General	139 (90.3%)	–	360 (89.6%)
By-election	15 (9.7%)	–	41 (10.4%)
In government or opposition when first elected			
Government	88 (57.1%)	–	275 (68.2%)
Opposition	66 (42.9%)	–	128 (31.8%)
Number of times elected			
Once	54 (35.0%)	–	176 (44.1%)
Twice	50 (32.5%)	–	114 (28.6%)
Three or more	50 (32.5%)	–	109 (27.3%)

[a] Percentages may not add up to 100% because of rounding.

benefited from incumbency, that is, the tendency of successful candidates to win re-election (Erickson 1998).

Most of the women MPs were elected in Canada's most populous provinces, Quebec and Ontario, and just over half of female senators were appointed from these provinces. This is not surprising as federal seat distribution and Senate appointments reflect the concentration of population in the central Canadian provinces. Almost half of Canada's senators (48 of 105) are appointed from Ontario and Quebec. In contrast, the size of provincial and territorial legislatures varies greatly with respect to the legislator/constituent ratio. For instance, Alberta now has 83 ridings and a population of close to 3 million, while Ontario's 103 constituencies serve a population almost four times larger. This factor, plus the early and continued electoral success of women in the western provinces,[3] leads to a different pattern at the provincial and territorial level. Between 1917 and 2000, more women MLAs were elected in the four Western Canadian provinces than in Ontario and Quebec combined. The Atlantic provinces account for the fewest elected women[4] (see Arscott 1997; Crossley 1997).

Table 3.1 offers two additional observations about pathways to success for women politicians. It shows that when first elected, more women served in governing parties at the provincial and territorial level than at the federal level. This difference likely reflects the recruitment of women candidates by the NDP and the PQ, as both parties have recruited women candidates in considerable number and both have formed governments at the provincial and territorial level (Arscott and Trimble 2003; Studlar and Matland 1996; Tremblay 2002b). The NDP has won office in five provinces and territories, more than once in Yukon, BC, Manitoba, and Saskatchewan. The success of the PQ in electing women in Quebec has also boosted the number of provincial women politicians elected to serve in governing parties (Arscott and Trimble forthcoming; Tremblay 2002b). Table 3.1 also shows that while the vast majority of elected women in Canada first won office in a general election, the proportion who experienced their first success in by-elections is worth noting. By-elections provide important windows of electoral opportunity for women seeking election at both levels of government.

Three Generations of Women Politicians
Canada's female political pioneers, women elected between 1917 and the early 1980s, often served as the lone woman in any given legislative chamber, and many felt isolated and distinctly out of place in environments designed for and dominated by men (Brock 1997; Copps 1986; LaMarsh 1968; McLaughlin 1992; Sharpe 1994). When Canada's first female MP, Agnes Macphail, reported for duty in the House of Commons in 1921, an employee tried to stop her from entering the Chamber. 'You can't go in there, miss!' he shouted (Sharpe 1994: 36). One of the very few women who contested a nomination in PEI legislature in the 1950s (unsuccessfully) told an interviewer that the male activists in her party 'didn't want women mixed up in it. It was a man's legislature' (Elsie Inman, quoted in Crossley 1997: 282). Early women politicians defied the definition of politics as a 'man's game' and the concomitant assumption that women did not

have the characteristics or qualifications necessary for a life in politics.

At a time when patriarchal norms defined a married woman's place as in the home, women who succeeded in winning office often were political substitutes for male relatives, accepted by party gatekeepers because it was believed they would faithfully represent the ideas and wishes of their departed fathers or husbands. Of 17 women elected to the House of Commons between 1921 and 1964, 7 were political surrogates for their dead husbands (Sharpe 1994: 77). Our analysis found 9 women who served as political substitutes in the House of Commons, one as recently as 1982. At the provincial level at least 6 women were elected to replace deceased fathers or husbands.[5]

Were the pioneers different in other respects as well? It seems reasonable to hypothesize that they were, as winning acceptance within male-dominated polit- ical parties was likely no easy task. To answer this question we divided the sample into three generations reflecting shifts in women's electoral success. The first gen- eration, women who served in office between 1917 (1921 at the federal level) and 1983, were the path-breakers and were elected or appointed in very small numbers indeed (38 MPs, 19 senators, 121 MLAs). This time frame represents the sporadic and gradual entry of women into political office. The second generation, 1984 to 1992, corresponds to the term in federal office of the Mulroney Conservatives and to a series of watershed elections that saw the number of elected women grow from under 10 per cent to over 15 per cent in many juris- dictions. Forty-three women were elected to the House of Commons and 13 female senators were appointed between 1984 and 1992. Provincially, the pattern is similar, with elections during this time period breaking the 10 per cent mark, and in some cases (BC, Saskatchewan, Ontario, and PEI) even surpassing 20 per cent. The plurality of provincial women politicians won their seats in this time period (147, or 36 per cent).

The third generation comprises women first elected between 1993 and 2000, when the number of elected women continued to climb, reaching 20 per cent in the House of Commons and surpassing 25 per cent in several provinces and the Yukon. At the federal level, the third generation corresponds to the Chrétien Liberals' three mandates, the election of 73 women MPs, and the appointment of 28 female sena- tors. Provincially, the picture is more complex, with significantly more women winning office in some provinces and territories (such as the Western Canadian provinces, Yukon, Quebec, and PEI) than in others (Ontario, the Atlantic provinces, NWT, and Nunavut). As Arscott and Trimble (forthcoming) show, the end of this period signals a slowdown in the percentage of women elected, with the most recent elections failing to significantly increase women's representation.

Social Characteristics
Country of Birth
Yasmeen Abu-Laban summarizes the continued underrepresentation of people of non-British, non-French origin in the House of Commons, noting that only a small percentage of visible minority MPs have been women. For instance, 2 visible minor- ity women, of 11 visible minorities MPs in total, were elected in 1993 (2002: 272).

Black's study of the 1993 federal election concludes that the 'Canadian Parliament is more reflective of the country's ethnoracial diversity than ever before but does not yet fully mirror it' (2002: 361; also see chapter 4 of this volume). Judith Ship points out how few visible minority women have been elected at the federal and provincial levels of government, and shows the fairly recent nature of their entry to politics (1998). For instance, Rosemary Brown was the first black woman elected to a Canadian legislature when she won office in BC in 1972. These studies suggest that people with non-British or non-French ancestry, in particular members of visibly minorities, face greater barriers to electoral success.

We could not determine the ethnicity of most Canadian women senators, MPs, and MLAs for this particular study because of the lack of published information. However, we were able to identify the countries in which Canada's women politicians were born. We do not conflate country of birth with ethnicity by assuming that most immigrants are visible minorities; this measure simply indicates the relative success of immigrant and non-immigrant women across time and jurisdiction.

Table 3.2 (p. 50) shows that the vast majority were born in Canada, regardless of jurisdiction, generation, or method of selection. The largest proportion of immigrant women MPs and MLAs were represented in the first generation of women politicians, those elected between 1917 and 1983. The first part of the twentieth century was a time of widespread immigration to Canada, reflecting the settlement of the Canadian West in particular (Brown and Cook 1974; Prentice et al. 1996). In 1901, the foreign-born population of Manitoba, BC, and the North-West Territories (later to become Alberta, Saskatchewan, and the NWT) ranged from 15 per cent to 30 per cent (Prentice et al. 1996: 113). Many of the first wave of newcomers, those entering Canada between the late 1800s and the late 1920s, originated in the United States of the British Isles; thus it is not surprising that many of the first women politicians were born in these countries. For instance, Irene Parlby, born in London, England, and elected to the Alberta Legislature in 1921, and US-born Cornelia Wood, elected in Alberta in 1940, were part of the immigration wave of the early 1900s (Palamerek 1989).

Before the early 1970s, Canadian immigration policy for women favoured those who were white, preferably from England and Scotland, and willing to do domestic labour (Abu-Laban 1998). Since then, immigrants have become more ethnically diverse, though Abu-Laban writes that women immigrants continue to face barriers because of their race, class, and gender (1998). However, the number of immigrant women elected to Canada's Parliament and legislatures declined between the first and subsequent generations of women politicians. The number of women immigrants elected to the House of Commons dropped in the Mulroney years, when only one woman born outside Canada was elected, but rose after 1993 to 10 MPs.

Provincially, the pattern is different in a couple of ways. First, a smaller proportion of immigrant women won office at this level than at the federal level. Second, although the provinces and territories are like the federal Parliament in one respect—proportionally more women immigrants were elected to provincial legislatures in the first generation—the number has dropped steadily since then. The Senate displays yet another pattern, as more women born outside Canada were appointed to the Senate during the Mulroney years than during the first or third generations.

As of 1996, close to one in five Canadian women (18 per cent) were immigrants (Statistics Canada 2000: 10). Women elected to the House of Commons since 1993 best reflect this reality, if not perfectly. Women politicians appointed to the Senate or elected to provincial and territorial legislatures between 1993 and 2000 are not as representative of this characteristic. While our study does not conflate ethnicity with place of birth, we do recognize the relationship between the two measures in present-day Canada. For instance, Black reports that about 45 per cent of visible minority MPs in 1993 were foreign-born (2001a: 12). Therefore, the continued underrepresentation of immigrant women in Canada's legislatures suggests that the distinct experiences and interests of immigrant and visible minority women are not fully represented in legislative discourses and decisions.

Marital Status

Brodie (1985) argued that gender role constraints imposed by marriage and motherhood do not stop women from seeking office but do affect the pace and direction of women's political careers. In particular, her study of female candidates suggested that homemaking duties and motherhood acted as a brake on women's candidacy, delaying their entry into political life. Perhaps this is why Black and Erickson (2000) and Spencer and Spencer (1992) found that women politicians were more likely to be single than their male counterparts. We expected to discover more single women entering political office in the first generation (1917–1984), when the dividing line between public and private roles acted as a barrier to mothers seeking political careers. This hypothesis was born out for MPs, but not for senators or MLAs. Over a quarter of the women MPs elected between 1921 and 1983 were single; this proportion declined steadily in later years. In contrast, the number of single women elected to provincial and territorial legislatures grew slightly. As well, more single women were appointed to the Senate between 1993 and 2000 than in previous generations. Clearly marriage proved less of a barrier to early women contenders in Canada's provinces and territories than to MPs, perhaps because serving at this level involves less travel and time away from home, thus lessening the role strain associated with combining motherhood with political life.

It should be noted that most women politicians were married when they first won office: marriage in and of itself is not a hurdle. In fact, it may be an enduring electoral and personal asset; few women enter the political fray when divorced or separated. Indeed, the number of divorced or separated women politicians has increased only slightly from the first generation to the third. Despite a dramatic increase in marital breakdown and a climbing divorce rate since 1971 (Statistics Canada 2000: 32), it is notable that most contemporary women politicians start their careers when married. Brodie found that 70 per cent of married candidates she surveyed had the support of their husbands (1985: 90). Marriage may indeed be an important political qualification, and a source of resources, especially at the federal level. Arend and Chandler (1996) note that marriage can be a source of advantage for women politicians, especially if the spouse has a high income and is capable of providing financial

Table 3.2

Socio-demographic Characteristics of Women Politicians Across Generations and Jurisdictions (Totals with Percentages)

	1917/21–1983			1984–1992			1993–2000			Total		
	MPs	Senators	MLAs	MPs	Senators	MLAs	MPs	Senators	MLAs	MPs	Senators	MLAs
Country of origin												
Canada	31 (81.6)	17 (89.6)	106 (87.6)	38 (97.4)	10 (76.9)	132 (89.8)	63 (86.3)	26 (92.9)	124 (92.5)	132 (88.0)	53 (88.3)	362 (90.0)
Other	7 (18.4)	2 (10.5)	15 (12.4)	1 (2.6)	3 (23.1)	15 (10.2)	10 (13.5)	2 (7.1)	10 (7.5)	18 (12.0)	7 (11.7)	40 (10.0)
Civil status												
Married/common-law	28 (73.7)	15 (83.3)	97 (80.2)	30 (69.8)	11 (84.6)	102 (69.4)	51 (69.9)	16 (64.0)	87 (64.9)	109 (72.7)	42 (75.0)	285 (71.1)
Single	10 (26.3)	1 (5.6)	13 (10.7)	8 (18.6)	0	23 (15.6)	5 (6.8)	4 (16.0)	24 (17.9)	23 (15.3)	5 (8.9)	60 (14.9)
Divorced/separated	0	0	2 (1.7)	1 (2.3)	0	9 (6.1)	4 (5.5)	2 (8.0)	11 (8.2)	5 (3.3)	2 (3.6)	22 (5.5)
Widowed	0	2 (11.1)	1 (0.8)	1 (2.3)	2 (15.4)	2 (1.4)	6 (8.2)	3 (12.0)	2 (1.5)	7 (4.7)	7 (12.5)	5 (1.2)
Age at first election/appointment												
Under 40	8 (21.6)	0	31 (30.4)	8 (19.0)	0	33 (25.6)	12 (16.9)	0	22 (23.4)	28 (18.7)	0	86 (26.5)
40–49	16 (43.2)	2 (10.5)	35 (34.3)	24 (57.1)	6 (46.2)	67 (51.9)	29 (40.8)	1 (3.6)	45 (47.9)	69 (46.0)	9 (15.0)	147 (45.2)
50–59	10 (27.0)	5 (26.3)	30 (29.4)	8 (19.0)	4 (30.8)	29 (20.9)	28 (39.4)	10 (35.7)	23 (24.5)	46 (30.7)	19 (31.7)	82 (24.6)
60 and over	3 (8.1)	12 (63.2)	6 (5.9)	2 (4.8)	3 (23.1)	2 (1.6)	2 (2.8)	17 (60.7)	4 (4.3)	7 (4.7)	32 (53.3)	12 (3.7)
Over 50 (% only)	(35.1)	(89.5)	(35.3)	(21.8)	(53.9)	(22.5)	(42.2)	(96.4)	(28.8)	(35.4)	(85.0)	(28.3)

Trimble/Tremblay: Women Politicians in Canada's Parliament and Legislatures 51

Table 3.2 (continued)

Socio-demographic Characteristics of Women Politicians Across Generations and Jurisdictions (Totals with Percentages)

	1917/21–1983			1984–1992			1993–2000			Total		
	MPS	Senators	MLAS	MPS	Senators	MLAS	MPS	Senators	MLAS	MPS	Senators	MLAS
Education												
Less than university	23 (62.2)	12 (80.8)	79 (69.9)	10 (27.0)	3 (23.1)	58 (40.8)	29 (40.3)	8 (30.8)	52 (38.9)	62 (42.5)	23 (42.6)	188 (48.7)
University	14 (37.8)	3 (20.0)	34 (30.1)	29 (73.0)	10 (76.9)	84 (59.2)	43 (59.7)	18 (69.2)	80 (61.1)	84 (57.4)	31 (57.4)	198 (51.3)
Occupation												
Professional	26 (68.4)	13 (81.3)	81 (66.9)	40 (93.0)	10 (83.3)	128 (87.1)	67 (91.8)	22 (78.6)	104 (77.6)	133 (86.4)	45 (78.9)	313 (77.9)
Self-employed	3 (7.9)	0	2 (1.7)	1 (2.3)	2 (16.7)	3 (2.0)	0	5 (17.9)	14 (10.4)	4 (2.6)	7 (12.3)	19 (4.7)
Technical/manual	1 (2.6)	1 (6.7)	4 (3.3)	1 (2.3)	0	5 (3.4)	6 (8.2)	1 (3.6)	6 (4.5)	8 (5.2)	2 (3.5)	15 (3.7)
Homemaker	8 (21.1)	1 (6.7)	27 (22.3)	1 (2.3)	0	6 (4.1)	0	0	7 (5.2)	9 (5.8)	3 (5.3)	40 (10.0)

support for the family, including paying for domestic labour.

Marriage may help women achieve political office, but it sets them apart from the women they represent. Between two-thirds and three-quarters of the women who entered politics since 1993 were married or living with a male partner. In contrast, in 1996, only 58 per cent of Canadian women were living with a spouse or common-law partner (Statistics Canada 2000: 29). Fully 19 per cent of women with children are single, divorced, separated, or widowed (Statistics Canada 2000: 29). Family status is a key determinant of women's everyday lives, shaping everything from the division of labour inside and outside the home to income, leisure time, and social standing. Therefore it may indeed be important that the lives of woman legislators do not reflect the family experiences of most Canadian women. The realities and policy demands of single mothers, divorced women seeking custody and maintenance, elderly widows living in poverty, and women in the workplace searching for high-quality child care are far removed from the experiences of most woman politicians when they enter Canada's legislatures.

Age When First Elected or Appointed

Canadian women politicians tend to be older than their male counterparts, perhaps in part because women often delay candidacy until their children are grown (Brodie 1985: 84). As well, age is regarded as a crucial qualification for politicians, particularly women, because age implies both experience and maturity. Political parties may take older women more seriously than younger women. Moreover, because of the time and labour demands associated with child rearing, it can take women longer to establish their educational and occupational qualifications, not to mention to gain the political experience essential for successful candidacy. Certainly older women are more likely to be chosen for the Senate, where the minimum age is 30 and long experience in the political trenches is a key qualification. For all these reasons, we expected the vast majority of women politicians to be middle-aged, but we also anticipated that this trend would diminish slightly over time for elected women because of women's changing social roles. Contemporary women are used to the 'double shift' of paid work and family responsibilities, and now attain professional qualifications, social stature, and political experience at an earlier age. Growing social acceptance of women in the public realm means younger women may face fewer attitudinal barriers when seeking political careers.

As expected, most women elected or appointed to Canada's legislatures were middle-aged when they started their political careers. Overall, more than three-quarters of MPs and MLAs, and all of the senators, were over 40 when first elected or appointed. One would expect senators to be older than the norm, and this is indeed the case. We found key differences across time and jurisdiction on the age measure, but our hypothesis about the impact of the women's movement and women's changing social roles on the age of female politicians was not supported at the federal level. Table 3.2 (pp. 50–51) shows the percentage of women legislators who entered politics at the age of 50 or over, by generation, and illustrates three patterns.

First, the proportion of women over 50 entering politics declined during the second generation (1984–1992), regardless of jurisdiction or method of selection.

This trend is most dramatic for female senators. Second, instead of declining, the percentage of older women has actually increased at the federal level in the most recent generation. Third, it is only at the provincial and territorial level that our hypothesis receives some support. And as Table 3.2 (pp. 50–51) indicates, younger women, those under 40, are more likely to be elected at the provincial level than at the federal level, though the proportion of women MLAs beginning their careers under the age of 40 has dropped over time. If we isolate elected women, we see that MPs tend to be older than their provincial and territorial counterparts, especially those elected since 1993. In sum, there are more dramatic differences across jurisdiction than over time.

In 1999, over 27 per cent of Canadian women were between the ages of 15 and 34, just under 31 per cent were aged 35 to 54, and about 23 per cent were over 55 (Statistics Canada 2000: 17). Women over 55 are the fastest growing segment of the female population in Canada, at 14 per cent of all women in 1999, up from just 5 per cent in 1921 and 11 per cent in 1981 (Statistics Canada 2000: 17). While the growth in the number of older women politicians at the federal level arguably reflects this population trend, it is clear that elected and appointed women in Canada's Parliament are significantly older than the average Canadian woman. Provincial legislators more closely reflect the age distribution of the female population generally, but nonetheless are still older than most of the women they represent.

The age gap between Canadian women and female politicians has a couple of implications. First, growing political alienation and cynicism, reflected in lower levels of political participation, is evident among Canada's youth (Pammett 2001). For young women, it is possible that this phenomenon is exacerbated by the lack of political role models: women like them are rarely seen in political life. With respect to substantive representation of women's diverse interests, the relatively advanced age of Canada's female politicians has both positive and negative implications. Older women politicians may not have any understanding of youth culture or of the increasingly difficult economic realities faced by young women, such as high unemployment rates and the escalating costs of postsecondary education. On the other hand, age may bring the occupational background or policy experience necessary to pose political solutions to the problems confronting Canada's youth.

Education

In the early part of the twentieth century, while women were seeking the right to vote, activists were also demanding entry into universities. By 1920, women constituted almost 14 per cent of college and university students in Canada (Prentice et al. 1996: 175). This number climbed to 20 per cent of undergraduate students in 1940, to 37 per cent in 1970, and crossed the 50 per cent mark in the 1980s (Prentice et al. 1996: 279, 396–97). Although women are now the majority of undergraduate students in colleges and universities, they remain concentrated in certain areas of study, such as arts, health sciences, education, and home economics (Prentice et al. 1996: 476). Few women students pursue the pure sciences or engineering, and more men than women obtain postgraduate degrees. It is also important to note that until the 1970s, few Canadian women *or* men attended university.

The research indicating that the vast majority of women politicians in Canada are very well educated led us to expect that the educational attainment of Canada's female legislators would be very high, much higher than the average for Canadian women, and that it would have increased significantly over time. This is certainly the case; more than half of the women elected or appointed since 1917 had university degrees and over 60 per cent of women elected or appointed after 1993 boasted a university education. As Table 3.2 (pp. 50–51) illustrates, there are interesting trends reflecting the impact of time and jurisdiction. First, the number of women politicians with university degrees has grown over time, as predicted. At all levels there was a dramatic increase from the first generation to the second, though the increase was greater for senators than for MPs and MLAs. But the percentage of female MPs and senators with university degrees dropped in the third generation, perhaps reflecting a degree of willingness among political parties to recruit women that dampened the 'exceptionalism' requirements. In contrast, the percentage of MLAs with degrees increased slightly in the most recent generation, those elected since 1993. Finally, while in the first two generations female MPs were better educated than their provincial and territorial counterparts, this is no longer true for women elected between 1993 and 2000.

During the first generation, when very few Canadian women (or men) attended university, female legislators were truly exceptional, especially MPs, almost half of whom had completed university. The number of Canadian women with university degrees has increased dramatically over the last three decades, from 3 per cent in 1971 to 12 per cent in 1996 (Statistics Canada 2000: 85). Yet, in contrast, over 60 per cent of women politicians entering office in the 1990s had a university education. Education remains a key social attribute for women politicians, one that clearly contributes to their political success. A university education signals intelligence, motivation, and high socio-economic status. Similarly, a professional occupation indicates the type of success noticed by party gatekeepers. Women politicians have levels of education and professional qualifications not shared by the majority of Canadian women.

Occupation

Women's occupations have changed considerably since the entry of the first woman to a Canadian legislature in 1917. First, more women work for pay. In 1921, only 18 per cent of Canadian women over the age of 15 participated in the paid labour force, and it was not until 1981 that over half of women had paid work (Prentice et al. 1996: 474). The expectation that women perform domestic work inside the home, including child care, has waned but continues to affect women's labour-force participation. In 1999, 55 per cent of women over 15 had paid employment, compared with 67 per cent of men (Statistics Canada 2000: 117).

Second, women now enter a wide range of occupations, though the labour force continues to reflect a sexual division of labour. Men are more likely than women to be self-employed; in 1999, 20 per cent of men were self-employed, compared with 13 per cent of women (Statistics Canada 2000: 126). While women continue to be concentrated in clerical and service occupations, the number of women in professional and managerial jobs has climbed significantly since the early 1900s. For instance, women constituted only 3.6 per cent of managerial workers in 1901, but were over 41 per cent of managers in 1993 (Prentice et al. 1996: 474). And 15 per cent of employed women were in professional occupations such as business, teaching, health care, and social-service work in 1901, compared to 28 per cent in 1993 (Prentice et al. 1996: 475). Women now outnumber men in professional occupations (Prentice et al. 1996).

These social trends led us to expect that the percentage of self-employed and professional women politicians will have increased over time, while the proportion of women politicians who were homemakers before entering politics will have declined. Table 3.2 (pp. 50–51) shows that this is indeed the case, though we were surprised by the high numbers of women with professional occupations elected or appointed during the first generation, 1917–1983. The first women senators had professional qualifications to support the merit of their appointments; all but two of the women appointed during this era (81 per cent) were in a professional occupation before entering the Senate. Clearly this status was more important for early appointees than for the first elected women, as fewer MPs and MLAs were in this job category, though the numbers were still large. These numbers climbed for elected women in the second generation, 1984–1992, and continued to climb in the third generation (1993–2000) for MPs and senators, but not for MLAs. Self-employment is a growing trend among provincial and territorial women politicians and senators, but the reverse is true for MPs.

Another interesting trend shown by Table 3.2 (pp. 50–51) is that very few homemakers have been elected or appointed at the federal level. Only nine MPs had careers in the home prior to political life, eight of them elected in the first generation. Not surprisingly, since most senators are appointed after long political or public service, only one senator was a homemaker before her appointment. None of the contemporary (1993–2000) federal women politicians were homemakers before seeking office. But the provincial and territorial level tells a different story. Over one-fifth of the women elected to Canada's legislatures between 1917 and 1983 were homemakers. This declined dramatically after 1984, but unlike federal politicians, provincial and territorial women with this occupational background continue to win elections.

To some extent, the occupational backgrounds of women politicians reflect labour-force trends. However, in many respects elected and appointed women exhibit exceptional occupational qualifications. Few women politicians worked without pay in the home before seeking political careers. Most had professional jobs in areas such as teaching, social work, nursing, law, the civil service, business, and journalism. Like their male counterparts, women MPs, senators, and MLAs 'do not reflect the population very well in terms of education, occupation or class' (Dyck 2000: 547).

CONCLUSIONS

This study has two key findings. First, as predicted, women elected and appointed to Canada's Parliament and legislatures have more in common with their male colleagues than they do with Canadian women. They were, and still are, older, more likely to be married, and less likely to be first-generation Canadians. As well, Canadian women politicians have significantly higher levels of education and higher occupational status than most women. Second, women elected and appointed to Canadian legislatures have been, and still are, different from each other. The social and demographic characteristics of Canada's female politicians reflect differences across time, jurisdiction, and method of selection.

Time and social change have had less effect on some measures than we anticipated. For instance, more immigrant women were elected in the first generation, 1917–1983, when few women sat in legislatures, than have been since women began serving as politicians in record numbers. The women's movement and changing social norms may be reflected to some degree in the family status of many Canadian women, but the tendency of female politicians to be married when seeking office has not varied greatly over time. Similarly, the age profile of elected and appointed women has shifted a bit, but women politicians remain concentrated in the over-40 category. What has changed is education and occupation. Education stands out, and reflects the dramatic metamorphosis of education patterns since the 1970s, as the proportion of women politicians with university degrees doubled from the first generation to the third. As well, female politicians are now more likely to have professional occupational backgrounds than the pioneer women elected and appointed between 1917 and 1983. Better occupational and educational opportunities for women have thus assisted women in their political careers, but expectations about the personal and professional qualifications of politicians have not really been transformed. Public office remains largely inaccessible to many Canadian women.

Jurisdiction accounts for some of the variation as well. Since 1993, immigrant women have been better represented in the House of Commons than in the Senate or provincial and territorial legislatures. The number of single women politicians has declined in the House of Commons but has risen in the Senate and provincial and territorial legislatures. MPs and senators elected since 1993 are getting older, while MLAs elected since 1984 were slightly younger than the pioneers at the provincial and territorial level. In the first two generations, female MPs were more likely than their provincial and territorial counterparts to have university degrees, but this is no longer the case among women elected since 1993. Women elected at the sub-national level are now more likely to be self-employed than female MPs, almost all of whom had professional occupations before running for election. These findings suggest greater barriers for women seeking office at the federal level, thus stronger pressures for women candidates to meet and even exceed the qualifications achieved by male candidates. Candidacy for the House of Commons is often more expensive, and may be more competitive, requiring additional personal, financial, and political resources.

Finally, the method of selection reflects certain patterns too. Senators are more like their elected federal counterparts than like women elected to provincial and territorial legislatures. As with MPs, senators are slightly more likely to be immigrants, married, and university-educated. However, as we anticipated, female senators are significantly older when first appointed than are female legislators when first elected, reflecting the tendency of prime ministers to choose people who are at the end of their political or professional careers.

We have found that given the constraints and barriers posed by the informal rules of political recruitment, most women do not have more access to political power now than they did 83 years ago. More women conform to the gender, class, and race-based prototype of the model legislator (older, married, well-educated, employed in a professional career, and born in Canada), so there are more women for parties to choose from. But they are very similar in socio-demographic terms to the men who are chosen.

The fact that women in legislative office have not mirrored women's social and demographic diversity has a couple of possible consequences for women's substantive representation. First, many Canadian women do not see themselves reflected in the legislative institutions that are supposed to represent them. Young women, women from ethno-racial minority groups, lower-class women, and single, separated, and divorced women are not winning elected or appointed office in numbers proportional to their presence in the Canadian population. The women in office are socially rather homogenous, thus the diversity so vital to the women's movement is absent at the level of 'official' politics.

The second possible consequence reflects the feminist observation that identities and ideas intersect. The inadequate representation of women's diverse identities suggests the partial representation of the ideas, experiences, and policy goals associated with these standpoints. Trimble discovered that in the Alberta legislature between 1972 and 1995, women's diversity was neither mirrored nor voiced; while 'the white, able-bodied, heterosexual woman, in the guise of "generic woman," has at times been represented in the Alberta legislature, most of her real-life sisters have not' (1998: 258). Yet Trimble also found that a white, middle-aged, professional woman legislator, New Democrat Marie Laing, did articulate the diverse realities and policy needs of women of colour, immigrant women, lesbians, and poor and Aboriginal women. The relationship between representation *by* women and representation *for* women—that is, the link between identities and ideas—needs further exploration.

NOTES

1. The authors acknowledge the financial support of the Social Sciences and Humanities Research Council of Canada; funding for this project was provided by Grant Number 816-99-0005. As well, we would like to thank our research assistants: Kathy McNutt (University of Alberta), who compiled the data on provincial and territorial legislators, and Mélanie Maisonneuve (Université d'Ottawa), who gathered information about MPs and senators.

2. This project is the first stage of a larger study that includes a mail-back survey of all sitting female legislators in Canada and a representative sample of male legislators (conducted Spring 2002). The survey asks representatives about their attitudes, ideological positions, and legislative goals, allowing comparisons based on gender, party, political role, and ideology.

3. Brodie found that 'the distribution of female candidacies is partially a reflection of population size and of the number of political offices open to contest, but it also reflects regional differences. In particular, women are more likely to run for office in the west than in the east. . . . The west has provided a more favourable climate for women in politics for years' (1985: 19). See also Erickson (1997c) for explanations of women's relative success in the west.

4. For the purposes of this paper, all are referred to by the most common acronym, MLAs.

5. We do not have an accurate count of the number of political substitutes at the provincial level, but there were at least six: one in BC, two in Quebec, and one in each of NB, PEI, and NS.

Chapter 4

Differences That Matter:
Minority Women MPS, 1993–2000

Jerome H. Black

INTRODUCTION

Research carried out on the 1993 election has revealed that minority women, defined as those with ethno-racial backgrounds outside of the two majority origin categories (British and French) in Canada, were elected as MPs in noticeable numbers for the first time that year (Black 1997).[1] Although this amounted to only 11 women, the outcome represented a fairly significant increase relative to previous elections, considering that only 2 minority women had been elected in 1988 and altogether just 5 had won seats in Parliament over the entire 1965–88 period.[2] Such an unprecedented increase in numbers helped draw attention to minority women as a new social group seeking access to elite-level positions in federal politics. That they nevertheless clearly remained one of the most underrepresented social categories in the 35th Parliament raises the question of whether there have been any further boosts following the 1997 and 2000 elections. Answering this question is one of several tasks taken up in this chapter.

One of the justifications for this task is the importance of understanding the extent to which the federal legislature mirrors the diversity of Canadian society, particularly those population segments that have traditionally been absent from Parliament. This study is equally motivated, however, by the fact that minority women have also been underrepresented in studies of Canadian politics, with the predictable result that little is known, especially of an empirical nature, about them as political actors. Unfortunately, neither the literature about women women in politics nor that concerning minorities in politics set has taken up the opportunity to study minority women in a systematic way. This is not terribly surprising in the case of the minorities literature, which is underdeveloped in nearly all aspects, a neglect explained by a variety of factors (Wilson 1993), including an almost exclusive focus on ethnicity understood in terms of biculturalism (Stasiulis and Abu-Laban 1991). But even in the much larger 'women in politics' literature, only a handful of studies have explored or even referenced the involvement of minority women in formal politics (Abu-Laban 2002; Black 1997, 2000a; Ship 1998; Trimble 1998). The better news is that a consensus has been forming around the need to avoid generic approaches to the study of women in politics and to replace them with investigations that are sensitive to the varied circumstances and interests of differently situated women across multiple social axes (e.g., Agnew 1996; Stasiulis 1999; Vickers 1997; Young 2002b).

The explicit study of the diversity of women is particularly important for those whose lives and experiences are conditioned not only by their gender but also by their subordinate status, stemming from their class position, sexual orientation, physical ability, place of birth, or ancestral origins. While these particular characteristics, and the various combinations they give rise to, have their own individual features and implications, they all reference women who, one way or another, confront a reality of compounded subordination and disadvantage. This fundamental fact of double minority status (at the very least) is what renders monolithic characterizations problematic and what compels the specific investigation of the differences between women.[3]

From this perspective, the broader purpose of this chapter is to validate the claim about the importance of such differentiation and the need to carry out 'intersectional' analysis (Stasiulis 1999) as a general approach, by demonstrating the benefits of focusing on the particular case of ethno-racial diversity. Additionally, the stress on ethnic and racial distinctions in Canada is of particular importance given the tremendous significance these distinctions have as lines of demarcation and the great influence they exercise in shaping the social and political lives of many Canadians. Certainly, minority women are distinctive and are of particular interest because they live at the juncture of two influential forces that contribute toward defining both advantage and disadvantage in this country—forces that together have produced a 'gendered vertical mosaic' (Abu-Laban 2002).[4] The emphasis here on minority women in the formal political process is not meant to deny the value and indeed the importance of examining the arenas of 'unofficial politics' (Vickers 1997), including local political contexts and communal organizations (Abu-Laban 2002; Agnew 1996); that said, the significance of studying the formal process at the national level should not itself be underestimated.

In more specific terms, the contribution here is multiple in nature. The rudimentary state of knowledge about minority women in politics sets a premium on informative descriptive analysis. This includes not only charting the numbers attaining seats in recent Parliaments, but also assembling relevant background information about the parties they are affiliated with, the regions they represent, their educational and occupational levels, and the degree of ethno-racial diversity in their constituencies. As will be seen, moreover, discussing these attributes of minority women, particularly relative to other gender and origin combinations, also provides opportunities for more interpretative inferences and, indeed, generates some hypotheses for future contemplation. This chapter also discusses more generally some of the areas of research where a focus on minority women is likely to be of great interest and value.

The next section deals with a few key methodological elements that characterize the approach used to collect information on ethno-racial backgrounds and the way that the data on ancestral origins are organized for analysis. The core empirical results are presented in the two subsequent sections: the first on the outcomes of the 1997 and 2000 elections, the second profiling minority women MPs. The section after that presents broader characterizations of the recruitment experiences of minority women MPs and offers some hypotheses for future consideration. The conclusion suggests some promising additional areas of research.

Methodology

The key methodological challenge in analyzing the relevance of ethno-racial distinctions is their careful measurement. Both the inherent complexity of ancestry as a construct and the limitations associated with relying on singular measurement procedures point to the value of a multiple-methods strategy.[5] One such eclectic approach, developed by the author, employs three specific procedures. The preferred one is the use of survey methods to query origins in a direct fashion, but where contact is not possible or where there is no response, then the approach relies on a combination of two other methods: searching through biographical records and the application of a surname analysis (aided by surname dictionaries). This multiple measurement strategy has been applied to determine the origins of MPs elected in 1993 (Black and Lakhani 1997) and to code ethno-racial background in an existing survey of 1993 candidates (Black 2000a). Most recently, it has been used to discern the ancestral backgrounds of MPs elected in the 1997 and 2000 elections (Black 2000b, 2002b). These latter efforts provide the basis for reckoning the incidence of minority women in the last two Parliaments.

A second prefatory note about methodology concerns the specificity of the origin distinctions that can be drawn within the category of minority women. While data patterns are always examined for broader groupings, where possible the results for more specific categories of minority women are also displayed. Both historical and contemporary readings of Canadian society and politics unequivocally demonstrate the dramatically divergent experiences of the different individual minority communities and, more to the point, the variability in the degree of their outgroup status. It is easy to single out 'visible minorities,' understood as racial minorities,[6] as the most distinctive category because they are the furthest removed from full acceptance by the majority communities. It is also a straightforward matter to place those descent groups associated with Northern and Western Europe at the opposite pole (indeed, their status as minorities might even be reasonably debated). In between, one could perhaps identify Eastern Europeans, Southern Europeans, and individuals of Jewish origin as separate categories, and likely in this order of increasing distinctiveness.

Because there are few minority women politicians to begin with, this differentiation means, of course, that only a limited number of cases can be drawn upon to support the inferences made. In fact, the prospect of working with reduced numbers inhibits consideration of further breakdowns of the origin categories, in spite of the fact that such a move would be in keeping with the spirit of the current analysis.[7] As it is, the findings shown for each of the five existing categories might be fairly regarded as having only tentative status. All the same, there is the compelling argument that the small numbers merely register the basic reality that few minority women have become MPs. In any event, to remind the reader of the small number of cases, the findings for the five categories are given in absolute numbers rather than in percentage form. Another, more conventional strategy is also adopted here, namely, bolstering the number of cases. It specifically involves pooling the MPs across the three elections, thus yielding a working data base of 446 legislators who were elected in one or more of the three last general elections.[8]

A third point pertaining to methodology concerns the employment of benchmarks to situate the results for minority women. Comparisons of minority women with majority women provide the most pertinent vantage points, since they focus directly on the possible relevance of ethno-racial differences among women. Still, comparisons involving minority women with their male counterparts can also be instructive, not the least by allowing for judgments about the relative effects of gender and origin.[9]

MINORITY WOMEN IN PARLIAMENT, 1993–2000

Eleven minority women were elected to the 35th Parliament that was convened following the 1993 election, an unprecedented increase relative to earlier elections. In retrospect, this jump in numbers may not be so surprising, given that the 1993 contest also witnessed spikes in the total number of both women and minority MPs elected. While 39 women had been elected in the 1988 election, five years later 53 won their constituencies, pushing their share of seats in the House up from 13.2 per cent to 18 per cent. For their part, minorities saw their numbers rise over the same period from 48 to 71, a boost in representation from 16.3 per cent to 24.1 per cent.[10] Given these fairly large increments for women and minorities separately considered, perhaps it stands to reason that minority women, at the intersection of these two categories, would simply be part of such an upward trend.

If this logic of an overlapping effect were to be applied to the two subsequent elections, it would suggest little subsequent growth in the numbers of minority women elected, since women and minorities registered only modest increases in their numbers for the 1997 election and none for the 2000 contest. Altogether, the net increase for women in 1997 was 9, bringing their share of Commons seats to 20.6 per cent, while for minorities it was 4, representing a share of 24.9 per cent (Black 2000b: 107–8). Three years later, the number of women elected remained exactly the same, while minorities saw their category shrink back down to the 1993 level (Black 2002b). However, any anticipated corollary of little subsequent growth in the number of minority women is not borne out. As Table 4.1 documents, they actually increased their presence over the course of the last two elections. Even if these upward movements are of a modest nature, the stagnation of growth in the two broader categories makes this trend stand out.

Table 4.1 also shows that minority women constituted an ever-increasing proportion of women MPs across the three elections. These growing proportions, moreover, contrast with the pattern evident for their male counterparts: minority men did not at all enhance their position relative to male legislators as a whole. Given these two data configurations, it is not surprising that minority women made up an increasing proportion of minority MPs as a group. In particular, minority women constituted 15.5 per cent of all minorities elected in 1993, 22.7 per cent in the 1997 election, and 26.0 per cent in 2000.

Finally, Table 4.1 breaks down the primary figures for minority women according to the five origin categories already identified. Apart from being of descriptive interest, this more detailed examination allows for an assessment of whether the increments over the 1993–2000 time frame occurred for most of the groups or were concentrated in a few. By and large, the former seems to be the case. For women of Northern and Western European background, the increments are the smallest ones possible. For Eastern Europeans and Jewish women, slightly more improvement can be seen. Only for Southern European women are the numbers more or less stable. Visible minority women saw their numbers double in 1997 and then hold steady.

In short, the election of minority women to the 35th, 36th, and 37th Parliaments forms an unexpected pattern of modest growth and, furthermore, exhibits some breadth. At the same time, none of this takes away from the fact that minority women still remain heavily underrepresented in Parliament. This essential reality is readily summed up in the figure of 19 and its translation into a meager 6.3 per cent share of the seats in the 37th Parliament. The underrepresentation of visible minority women, the most distinctive minority category, is especially striking. Considering their demographic weight in the population, visible minority women have not even reached the one-fifth mark on the road to proportional numerical representation.[11] Alternatively put, it would require the election of 21 visible minority women altogether to bring about parity with their share of the general population. There are, then, two stories about minority women MPs and recent elections: a new one about greater relative success in penetrating the ranks of the legislative elite and a much older one about continuing underrepresentation on a fairly large scale.

Table 4.1
Minority Women MPs Elected in 1993, 1997, and 2000

	1993	1997	2000
Minority women MPs			
Total (% of all MPs)	11 (3.7%)	17 (5.6%)	19 (6.3%)
Minority women as % of all women	20.8	27.4	30.6
Minority men as % of all men	24.8	24.3	22.6
Minority women as % of all minorities	15.5	22.7	26.0
Minority women by category (totals)			
Northern/Western European	–	1	2
Eastern European	2	5	5
Southern European	5	4	5
Jewish	1	3	3
Visible minorities	2	4	4
Mixed European	1	–	–

SELECTED CHARACTERISTICS OF MINORITY WOMEN MPS

The parties that minority women run for is the first characteristic examined as part of an attempt to learn more about their backgrounds and experiences. For this segment of the analysis, the pooled data set of 446 MPs is employed. The tendency of the Liberal party to provide candidacy opportunities for minorities, as part of its broader electoral association with many ethno-racial groups (especially Southern Europeans, Jews, and visible minorities), has been long understood even if it has only been recently documented (Black 2000b, 2002b; Black and Lakhani 1997; Pelletier 1991). The ordinary expectation is that this pattern would extend across gender lines and take in minority women as well.

Table 4.2 verifies the general affiliation of minority MPs with the Liberal party. A larger percentage of minority MPs won election as Liberal candidates between 1993 and 2000 than did legislators with majority origins. Indeed, Liberal affiliation is even stronger among minority women than it is among their male counterparts. The fact that party links are pretty much the same for both women and men among those with majority ancestry reinforces the characterization that for minority women both gender and ethno-racial origin appear to matter. Another interesting revelation is how few were elected under the Reform/Alliance banner; this, however, seems to have more to do with gender than with origin effects. As skewed as the association of minority women with the Liberal party is, it remains even more so for those who can be regarded as the more distinctive minorities. Remarkably, 13 of the 14 women MPs with origins associated with the visible minority category or with Jewish or Southern European backgrounds were elected

Table 4.2

Party and Region Distributions for Origin and Gender Categories of MPs, 1993–2000 (pooled data, column percentages)

	Minority			Majority		
	All	**Women**	**Men**	**All**	**Women**	**Men**
Party						
Liberal	62.6	72.7	59.7	50.2	52.9	49.6
Reform/Alliance	25.3	13.6	28.6	14.8	9.8	15.8
BQ	1.0	–	1.3	24.1	23.5	24.2
NDP	9.1	9.1	9.1	4.1	11.8	2.5
PC	2.0	4.5	1.3	6.5	2.0	7.5
Independent	–	–	–	.3	–	.4
Region						
BC	12.1	13.6	11.7	10.0	9.8	10.0
Prairies	29.3	22.7	31.2	12.4	9.8	12.9
Ontario	41.4	40.9	41.6	22.7	25.5	22.1
Quebec	12.1	22.7	9.1	36.4	33.3	37.1
Atlantic	5.1	–	6.5	17.9	19.6	17.5
North	–	–	–	.7	2.0	.4
N	99	22	77	291	51	240

as Liberals. Again, a similar link is evident for their male counterparts but not to the same degree (32 of 41).

The strong tendency of minority women to be elected under the Liberal banner is also partially reflected in patterns of regional representation (also shown in Table 4.2). Their concentration in Ontario ridings, where the party is hegemonic, is particularly noteworthy, but the clustering seems to be more bound up with the general association of minorities with the party. Elsewhere, minority women were less likely to represent Prairie constituencies than were their male counterparts, but noticeably more likely to do so than majority women. Conversely, they were more likely to be associated with Quebec electoral districts than were minority men but less likely than majority women. Finally, none of the minority women sat as legislators for constituencies either in Atlantic Canada or the North.

The contextual characteristics of constituencies provide another vantage point on the geography of representation. A natural question to pose in a study such as this is whether minority women are more likely to be linked to ridings that are ethno-racially heterogeneous. First, extrapolations from the broader literature about recruitment and its emphasis on supply-and-demand explanations may be pertinent (Norris 1996). On the supply side, there is a straightforward demographic argument that reasons that more minority individuals (who have the requisite ambition and resources) will come forward as office-seekers in areas where the overall candidate pool of minority individuals is larger. From a demand perspective, there is the possibility that officials (and perhaps members) in local party associations, which have traditionally dominated the nomination function in Canada, may encourage such candidacies in heterogeneous areas, believing that there are electoral benefits in doing so. To be sure, these gatekeepers are often responsible for the impediments and biases that minority office-seekers confront (Simard et al. 1991; Stasiulis and Abu-Laban 1991), but constituency associations vary so much in their relevant characteristics and practices (Carty, Cross, and Young 2000) that it is certainly plausible that some are inclined to nominate minorities in mixed areas.[12] In other cases, national officials, who are motivated by broader interests and perspectives, including the cultivation or bolstering of an image of inclusiveness for the party, may exert some pressure on local associations to nominate more minority candidates, in the same way that they have tended to do with regard to women (Carty, Cross, and Young 2000).[13]

Second, there is some empirical evidence that minority candidates are indeed associated with more diverse ridings. In his research on candidates in the 1988 federal election, Alain Pelletier (1991) found a clear tendency for ethnic candidates to be selected in constituencies where the ethnic population was larger than average. Also relevant are two studies of MPs elected in Quebec in the 1997 federal election, one focusing on the Montreal area (Simard 1999), the other on the province as a whole (Black 2001b). Using divergent measures of ethno-racial diversity, both found that minority MPs did indeed tend to be elected in more heterogeneous ridings.

A third basis for the relationship might be regarded as a by-product of the already documented and pervasive association of minority parliamentarians with the Liberal party (bearing in mind the party's dominance in the larger urban centres). It might even be hypothesized that minority women stand out most of all in being elected in more heterogeneous ridings in light of their very high levels of affiliation with the party. At the very least, this pattern suggests that the examination of the link between MP origins and constituency diversity should consider party distinctions to determine if the association holds once party is controlled for or, alternatively, if it extends beyond the confines of the Liberal party.

This analysis uses 1996 census data to index constituency heterogeneity; in particular, three overlapping diversity measures are used: the percentages of the population composed of visible minorities, of immigrants, and of individuals with a non-English and non-French mother tongue. Because the 1996 data have been keyed to the 301 constituencies that are common to the 1997 and 2000 election results, only the 354 MPs elected in one or both of these elections are considered here. Table 4.3 displays the mean scores for the three composition indicators for minorities and majorities as a whole and for the breakdowns by gender. The arrangement of mean scores is quite unequivocal: they depict a rather sharp relationship between MP ancestry and constituency mix, with a heightened effect from gender. Simply put, minority MPs, and minority women MPs most of all, are very much distinguished by being elected in markedly diverse constituencies. Among males, there is a parallel gap between minority and majority legislators, while it is somewhat wider among females. The incidence of visible minorities in the constituency is highest for those won by minority women. Similarly, the immigrant composition of ridings held by minority MPs is almost twice that for constituencies where majority MPs were victorious. For minority women, the mean percentage is

Table 4.3

Constituency Diversity for MPs, 1997–2000 (Pooled Data)

	Visible Minorities (%)	Immigrants (%)	Non-English, Non-French (%)	*N*
All minority MPs	15.2	23.3	23.4	83
Women	18.5	27.7	27.7	20
Men	14.2	21.9	22.0	63
All MPs	7.6	12.3	10.7	229
Women	7.9	13.9	11.2	40
Men	7.5	11.9	10.6	189
Liberal MPs	13.3	20.9	18.9	182[a]
Minority women	22.9	34.1	31.5	15
Minority men	18.2	28.0	26.3	39
Majority women	8.2	18.3	14.1	18
Majority men	10.5	15.6	13.5	92
Other party MPs	5.9	9.6	10.2	172[a]
Minority women	5.2	8.4	16.0	5
Minority men	7.8	12.1	15.1	24
Majority women	7.6	10.4	8.8	22
Majority men	4.7	8.4	7.8	97

[a] Includes mixed minority-majority and Aboriginal categories.

higher yet. A similar figure for these women emerges when the diversity indicator is the population with a non-official mother tongue. Consistent with the previous two indicators, the next highest average score occurs in connection with minority men. The data indeed show that minority status fundamentally drives the relationship with constituency diversity and that gender nevertheless makes a secondary contribution.

The results broken down by party (Liberal/non-Liberal) provide for further refinement and indicate that the minority MP–mixed constituency pattern is indeed a circumscribed one, largely bound up with Liberal party politics and recruitment.[14] As expected, the ridings of Liberal and non-Liberal MPs differ significantly in their diversity. For instance, immigrants constituted, on average, 20.9 per cent of the constituencies held by Liberal MPs and only 9.6 per cent of those belonging to the opposition parties. Moreover, for these latter parties, origin and gender do not seem to be linked to the modest differences in constituency diversity that do occur; indeed, in a couple of instances, majority MPs are (slightly) more likely to have been elected in more heterogeneous ridings. Among Liberal MPs, however, minority origins are unquestionably associated with more diverse constituencies. For minority women, the mean scores are stunningly high whether constituency composition is gauged by the presence of visible minorities, of immigrants, or of those with a mother tongue other than English or French. Finally, it can be noted that the figures are even higher for the four visible minority women MPs, all of whom won as Liberals (specific data not shown).

Information available on the education and occupation experiences of MPs can also be used to profile minority women. However, in addition to being of descriptive interest, their examination also provides an opportunity to investigate the kinds of backgrounds that office-seekers from socially disadvantaged groups seem to need in order to be effective challengers. This can be done through a consideration of two career-path models introduced elsewhere (Black 2000a; Black and Erickson 2000). One, dubbed the *similarity model*, anticipates that newcomers need to have the same resources and experiences, including high levels of education and high-status occupations, that well-established groups have, since these are the qualifications that the system 'requires' for elite-level involvement. This perspective holds that new groups will have a greater presence in the legislature as more individuals from these groups develop the appropriate requisites. A second model, labeled the *compensation model*, has a more critical take on the underlying recruitment process and emphasizes how its biases operate to privilege more established groups at the expense of new ones. The discouragement and discrimination that new challengers face means that they must do more than simply match the credentials of entrenched groups; rather, they must outdo them.

The compensation model has, in two studies so far, drawn more support than the similarity model. One study examined the profile of female and male candidates who ran for the five main parties in 1993 and found that female office-seekers not only had stronger educational and occupational credentials but also had more experience as party-office holders and as participants in non-political organizations (Black and Erickson 2000). A second study actually gauged minority women relative to majority women (and, indirectly, relative to males); along with the 1993 candidate survey, the analysis also used a data set that had a number of background variables pertaining to MPs elected that year (Black 2000a). The model's expectation that minority women, because of the additional impact of their ethno-racial origins, would surpass the credentials and experiences of majority women was largely substantiated, and generally along the same lines as in the gender-only study.

The educational and occupational accomplishments of minority women MPs elected over the last three contests provide another opportunity to assess the similarity and compensation models. Table 4.4 suggests that there is evidence for both models but that overall there are more significant aspects of support for the compensation perspective. The compensation model finds the least general support in the case of education, where there is more similarity than difference in the numbers. The educational training of minority women as a whole is, to be sure, quite high, but these levels are only slightly higher than those achieved by majority women and minority men. Furthermore, while all of these groups are more likely to have a first degree than majority men, this is not the case with regard to a second degree. These figures may very well mean that some positive changes have occurred and that new groups, minority women included, are no longer required to exceed existing standards.

As for occupation, Table 4.4 presents evidence that minority women still 'need' to be better. They were considerably more likely to have had professional occupations than their majority counterparts, and the gap is slightly wider when the comparison is drawn with minority men. These latter two results are not too far off the one for majority males, suggesting that the situation might have improved for the two groups with a singular subordinate status. At the same time, this pattern of similarity brings the situation for minority women into sharper relief and implies the operation of double disadvantage. Moreover, Table 4.4 indicates that the occupation result has breadth: most of the women in all groups had professional occupations. Note as well that these breakdowns show an important exception to the education results: each of the four visible minority women had at least a first university degree and three had a

Table 4.4

Education and Professional Occupations of MPs, 1993–2000 (pooled data)

	Completed University	Second Degree	Professional Occupation	*N*
MPs by origin/gender				
Minority women	76.2%	42.9%	72.7%	21–22
Minority men	74.7%	42.7%	58.4%	75–77
Majority women	73.3%	40.0%	61.2%	45–49
Majority men	67.5%	44.7%	59.4%	228–39
Minority women MPs by category				
Northern/Western European	1	–	–	
Eastern European	3	3	4	
Southern European	4	1	5	
Jewish	3	1	3	
Visible minorities	4	3	4	

second degree. The fact that the education and occupation patterns reflect the assumed workings of the compensation model for the most distinctive category of minority women suggests that racial differences (and the attendant biases) continue to matter a great deal.

Toward Understanding the Recruitment of Minority Women

The indications of at least partial support for the compensation approach (bearing in the mind the broader 1993 results for minority women as candidates) provide an appropriate transition as the analysis turns to speculate on, and offer some hypotheses about, the circumstances surrounding the recruitment of minority women in federal politics. It may very well be the case that these higher qualifications that many minority women have help to explain how—in comparison to other groups—they alone have (modestly) increased their numbers in the last two elections. Even if they are required to surmount higher hurdles, their strong backgrounds may provide them with the necessary confidence to come forward as office-seekers and ultimately be selected.

Another hypothesis bearing upon the exceptionalism of the increased numbers of minority women can also be offered: the parties that believe it important to promote an image of inclusiveness have a strong incentive to recruit them. This is simply because each individual minority woman on the candidate team or in the legislative caucus enhances the party's profile of diversity simultaneously along gender and origin lines, in effect providing double value toward an impression of the party's openness. By favouring minority women, a party is able to do more with less, as it were, than if it were to privilege the selection of both majority women and minority men. In other words, the recruitment of minority women involves less of a deviation from existing practices by requiring that fewer candidacies and seats be taken away from more established forces within the party. This allows the commitment to diversity to be both 'efficient' and limited.

While the explicit adoption of such a double-value strategy might be varyingly contemplated by the federal parties (and presumably not at all by Reform/Alliance, given the results reported here), it likely has the most practical relevance for the Liberals, as the dominant party and as well as as a party that has taken some modest steps to increase the number of women and minority candidates (Carty, Cross, and Young 2000). The point is that there are constraints on the party's ability to do more and, in large measure, this is bound up with its very electoral success. In particular, the Liberal party's ascendancy means that at the same time as it attracts potential office-seekers from both traditional and non-traditional groups, the party has fewer openings available to meet their aspirations. The result of consistently winning in so many constituencies means that the norm of protecting incumbents from renomination challenges ends up sharply limiting the number of seats that might be available to newcomers.[15] Openings are particularly at a premium in Ontario, where the party has reached saturation strength, especially in many of the major urban centres where minorities might be particularly expected to run. Under such circumstances, the party, mindful of the need to make ongoing gestures about increasing diversity but perhaps unwilling to go beyond a certain point in imposing a large number of candidates on local associations, may find it more effective to act in more limited fashion by favouring the recruitment of a few minority women.

No doubt, this double-value hypothesis is best explored while taking into account the larger array of forces and pressures that work both for and against the selection of minority women. Such a broader perspective would help set this particular proposition in context and, more generally, capture what is in reality a far more complex and fluid recruitment process, one influenced by party and riding-association variability. At the very least, a more encompassing portrayal is needed to nuance a characterization that otherwise may appear contradictory, as it stresses that minority women may endure double bias on the one hand, but may also possibly provide double value to parties on the other. A more fine-tuned analysis would presumably proceed with an explicit analysis of the commitment to diversity that the parties and their local organizations have made, taking into account what antecedent factors (e.g., urban location, heterogeneous populations) might have influenced their outlook as they weighed the advantages of running certain 'kinds' of candidates. By itself, there is no reason to assume that the national or regional officials will have the same outlook as constituency-based personnel.

Certainly, the little that is known suggests that multiple factors are at play in accounting for the recruitment experiences and success of minority women and that within-party response may be important. For instance, the 1993 study of minority women candidates found that these women (especially Southern European and visible minority women) were most likely to have reported that they had been encouraged to contest the nomination by party officials, and at all levels. These women also revealed that they were more likely to have been acclaimed as candidates. However, what sharply qualifies these experiences as being indicative of favourable sentiments toward their candidacies is their placement in ridings where their party was normally expected to lose (Black 2000a). Since the 1993 election was anything but normal, some minority women ended up winning in spite of their placement, not because of it; these were, of course, Liberal candidates who benefited from the unexpected fragmentation of the vote on the right (Black 1997).

One straightforward interpretation of the selection of minority women in weaker constituencies in 1993 is, of course, that they were indeed encouraged to run as part of a token effort to create the *appearance* of diversity, at least in the Liberal party team. While party symbolism is a more important preoccupation of more centrally placed officials, local party people may have, in the circumstances, acquiesced in meeting the broader objective of building an appropriate team-wide image, since the candidates were not expected to win in any event; that is, less was thought to be at stake. Indeed, in some instances they might have welcomed the candidacies of these women, especially if they were having difficulty finding candidates in ridings with limited electoral prospects.[16] Furthermore, these women did have, for the most part, impressive qualifications. Matters might have been different had there been a recognition that the prospects of victory were greater.

Since the 1993 election, partisan patterns have stabilized to the Liberals' advantage, and this may have given more impetus to the double-value strategy. As a matter of speculation, it may be that more local associations have since placed greater emphasis on the recruitment of minority women to enhance their chances of electoral success. What gives this hypothesis first-blush plausibility is the empirical association of minority women MPs with ethno-racially diverse constituencies: perhaps this relationship reflects the views of some local parties that minority women candidates are electoral assets. By selecting women rather than men, they meet the objective of running minority individuals and also help out the broader party objective to increase the number of women candidates.[17]

CONCLUSION

In the final analysis, any argument about the value of explicitly incorporating ethno-racial distinctions (or other divisions) into the study of women in politics in Canada requires a demonstration that more can be learned by doing so. Indeed, if variations in origin were of little or no empirical consequence, then they might very well be dismissed in the name of parsimony or generalization. This is clearly not the case here. The present investigation has shown that there are significant empirical (and conceptual) enhancements to understanding involved in extending the analysis beyond a generic approach. First, profiling the composition of recent Parliaments by gender and origin reveals that the growth in the number of minority women was exceptional relative to broader categories. (To be sure, the increases were of a modest nature and minority women, especially visible minority women, remain dramatically underrepresented.) The variables employed to describe the background of minority women also clustered in a somewhat patterned way: minority women, and particularly those with more distinctive origins, were strongly connected to the Liberal party and had a marked propensity to run in the country's most ethno-racially diverse constituencies. Second, many of these descriptive characterizations provided the basis for various forms of explanatory analysis, such as the compensation model and the notion of double value.

These are by no means the only research questions about the recruitment process that are implicated in the study of minority women. Others that come to mind reflect the intricacies and complexities of gender and origin as both independent and interdependent forces that varyingly shape the political context within which minority women find themselves as political actors. In some instances, their origins may be most important, for example, with respect to their ability to draw upon their communities as a resource base, including the mobilization of co-members for nomination contests. As such, community ties may be as important to them as they are for their male counterparts. In other situations, the context for minority women may be more heavily defined by their gender as they may contend with discrimination from the men in their communities (a source that they uniquely face, in addition to what they confront in terms of the wider population). Even so, such prejudice might be motivated less by any traditional disregard for women and their abilities than by a concern to restrict competition for the limited number of political positions available.[18] Other aspects of recruitment politics affecting minority women may be understood more in terms of an interaction between gender and origin. For instance, there is evidence that minority women rely more heavily than minority men on gaining experience and raising their profile by working as activists and office-holders within community organizations and agencies that serve minorities and immigrants (Agnew 1996; Black 2000a).[19] Origin differences can also be said to condition the way gender matters in those situations where traditional segments in some communities voice concerns about women from the community assuming dominant political roles.[20]

The interconnections between gender and origin can also be studied at the level of individual identity and consciousness. Sentiments about group connections might be expressed in a variety of ways (Wilcox 1997). Some minority women might identify equally with both women and minorities as broader categories, while others might have a relatively more developed consciousness with regard to one of the two dimensions. For instance, some visible minority women might regard white women as part of an oppressing class or fear that a focus on gender will divide their communities. Others, however, might see their disadvantaged condition more as a product of their gender. And, of course, it is plausible that some minority women, again probably visible minority women most of all, might have a consciousness that is uniquely focused on their status as double minorities, what one author has called a 'womanist' view (Alice Walker, cited in Wilcox 1997: 76). It would be important to investigate why these different combinations emerge as well as their consequences for political attitudes and action. Finally, contagion effects might also be investigated, such as whether racial consciousness sensitizes gender consciousness and vice versa. This cluster of research questions, moreover, could be investigated in connection with (minority) women not only as office-seekers and legislators but also as voters and community activists.

The contributions to knowledge that explorations such as these promise to make provide additional reasons for the more extensive study of minority women.[21] Such efforts would, of course, do much to remedy current underrepresentation of the subject in the scholarship on women in Canadian politics. Presumably, some of that analysis would also contribute to a greater understanding of a number of the more basic patterns observed in this study. This includes not only the exceptionalism that characterizes the modest increase in the number of minority women elected to Parliament over the last few elections, but also, it is important to remember, their continuing underrepresentation within the four walls of that institution.

NOTES

1. Aboriginal women, another important category of minority women, are not considered here; Aboriginal peoples are, in any event, more properly thought of 'national majorities' (Kymlicka 1998).

2. Two other women with 'mixed majority-minority' origins were also elected over the 1968–88 period (Black 1997). The present analysis focuses on those with only minority origins.

3. Of course, a similar and perfectly valid starting point could be the investigation of gender effects within these different social groups, including among minority individuals.

4. Many minority women could, of course, be easily regarded as 'triple minorities' because of their lower-class positions. The focus here, however, on elite politics, with its near-universal requirement of at least middle-class status, means that class as a status consideration has less direct relevance. At the same time, many of the minority women MPs elected in 1993 were immigrants (Black 2000a), a characteristic that does magnify their outsider status and imply triple-minority status. However, country-of-birth distinctions are not examined in the analysis here.

5. See Black and Lakhani (1997) and Black (2002a) for some commentary in this regard, as well as for a discussion justifying a focus on the 'objective' dimension of ancestry.

6. In the Canadian context, racial minorities are frequently referred to as 'visible minorities', who for the purposes of the Employment Equity Act are defined as 'persons other than Aboriginal Peoples, who are non-Caucasian in race or non-white in colour.' (See also note 7.) For a disclaimer about the employment of the term 'race' and its like, see Black (2000a).

7. Very much illustrative of this is the way that visible minorities, who comprise an incredibly diverse collection of specific origin groups, are collected together here as a single category. In doing so, the analysis follows Statistics Canada's classification, which brackets as visible minorities individuals who are Chinese, South Asian, Black, Arab, West Asian, Filipino, Southeast Asian, Latin American (except Chilean and Argentinian), Japanese, Korean, and Pacific Islander.

8. By-election winners are included in this total if they were subsequently re-elected in a general election.

9. Another point about methodology can also be mentioned, if only briefly. As should be evident, this study relies mostly on background information about MPs taken from published sources and existing statistics. However, as will be seen, several footnotes in the concluding section make reference to interview data. In 1996 (largely in the spring and summer of that year) face-to-face interviews were carried out with 53 MPs as part of a larger research project on minority MPs. Included were 9 of the 11 minority women elected in 1993. The interview material not only serves to provide brief illustrations of a few points raised in the conclusion, but also helps to inform the current analysis more generally.

10. A further 27 MPs (9.2 per cent) were identified as having a combination of both majority and minority origins; see Black and Lakhani (1997).

11. More precisely, the ratio is .19. The numerator is simply the proportion of visible minority women in the 37th Parliament, .013, which, in turn, is divided by a population proportion estimate of .07. This denominator comes from a projection-oriented study produced for Statistics Canada (1995) that estimated that racial minorities would constitute between 14.0 per cent and 14.2 per cent of the population by 2001. The former figure was taken and divided in half. By comparison, the ratio between seat and population shares for visible minority men is .71, and for women as a whole it is .41.

12. Presumably, this is more likely to happen where some of the riding officials are minorities or where minorities make up a significant portion of the standing membership.

13. The Reform party has exceptionally not pushed for more women candidates; see Young (2000).

14. An analysis omitting the BQ from consideration, to take into account the fact that the party had no minority individuals elected in either 1997 or 2000, did not alter the main inferences drawn from Table 4.3.

15. Indeed, this probably helps explain the virtual stagnation in the growth of the number of women and minorities elected in the last election; see Young (2000) for the case of women.

16. One indication of this is the relatively high number of uncontested nomination events that occur; see Carty, Cross, and Young (2000); Carty and Erickson (1991); and Erickson (1997a).

17. Another hypothesis pertaining to the preference for minority women may be tied to the perception by the parties that majority voters find them less 'threatening' as outsiders than minority men.

18. One minority woman MP interviewed summarized how her past unsuccessful attempts at gaining her party's nomination were due to overt and active discrimination: 'The boys in my community worked very much with the boys in the mainstream community in the party'. She was also clear that it was to a large extent about power-sharing, saying at one point simply, 'Males who have the power in the political arena don't want to give it up'.

19. The importance of such experiences for minority women also emerged during several interviews.

20. Several Liberal women MPs (of both minority and majority background) provided unprompted comments in interviews about how their colleague Eleni Bakapanos, a Montreal-area MP, had to deal with considerable hostility from some in the Greek community who did not feel it was appropriate for her to devote time to politics and be away from her young children.

21. Other important areas are suggested by Ship (1998) and Stasiulis (1999).

Part II

Political Parties

Chapter Five

Can Feminists Transform Party Politics?
The Canadian Experience[1]

LISA YOUNG

INTRODUCTION

This chapter focuses on a fundamental strategic question facing feminist activists:
can they reasonably expect to fundamentally alter party politics? Are political parties
merely male-dominated and thus transformable by women with feminist sympa-
thies, or are they inherently patriarchal? Does feminist participation in the formal
political arena hold the potential for changing that arena and its symbolic and
policy outputs? To answer these questions, we briefly examine the strategies of
Canadian feminist activists with regard to the federal party system between 1970
and 2000 (including the 2000 federal election) and then consider in greater detail
the responses of the major Canadian political parties.

Feminist theorists, researchers, and activists are divided on the question of
whether feminists can transform party politics. The liberal feminist view holds that
women can reform political institutions and that integration of women into these
institutions is an essential component of a campaign for political and social change.
This view has spawned an extensive literature cataloguing barriers to women's entry
into formal political institutions (see Bashevkin 1993; Biersack and Herrnson 1994;
Brodie and Chandler 1991; Carroll 1987; Erickson 1991b, 1993; Lovenduski and
Norris, eds 1993; Studlar and Matland 1994; Young 1991). More recently, scholars
working in this tradition have focused on evidence that women's participation in
formal political arenas is different from men's in both style and substance and thus
holds a transformative potential (see Brodie 1988; Bystydzienski 1995; Carroll
1992; Jennings and Farah 1981; Norris and Lovenduski 1989; Skjeie 1988, 1991;
Thomas 1994; van Assendelft and O'Connor 1994; Welch 1985).

The liberal feminist view rests on two key underpinnings. First, it conceives of
the state as a potential ally for feminists. Retaining the liberal focus on the individual and understanding political power in conventional terms, the liberal feminist
project has zeroed in on ending gender-based discrimination and putting women
on an equal footing with men in all realms of social, economic, and political life. In
this view, the state is not inherently patriarchal, but rather a neutral arbiter or
potentially principled agency that could be deployed on behalf of women (Allen
1990). Seeing the state and other political institutions as male-dominated rather

than inherently patriarchal, liberal feminism can conceive of the potential for women's participation to transform them.

This notion illuminates the second assumption underlying the liberal feminist view: that the categories 'woman' and 'feminist' are substantially overlapping. Much of the research examining the extent to which women in the public or in political elites hold feminist views has been conducted in the hope of finding women to be feminists. To a certain extent, this has proven to be the case. Ultimately, however, efforts to equate women and feminism have foundered on the presence of anti-feminist and non-feminist women and on the problem of the irreducibility of women's interests into a single gender-based interest.

The alternative school of thought is grounded primarily in radical and postmodern feminism and has proponents within socialist feminism. This approach characterizes formal political institutions not as male-dominated but as inherently patriarchal. The richest body of literature in this regard deals with the nature of the modern state. For instance, in her radical feminist theory of the state, Catherine MacKinnon (1989) argues that the rule of law and the rule of men are one thing, indivisible. The liberal state coercively and authoritatively constitutes the interest of men as a gender through its legitimating norms and policies. The state is therefore crucial to the maintenance of the patriarchal system and, consequently, inherently and inevitably patriarchal itself.

Radical feminist theorizing has not addressed the character of political parties in as much detail as it has that of the state, but certainly the logic that rejects the modern state as inherently patriarchal can be applied equally to political parties. Just as the state serves the interests of men, political parties allow different factions of men to exercise partial control over some state functions. A coherent radical feminist critique of mainstream political parties is offered by Lise Gotell and Janine Brodie (1991), who argue that these parties have avoided hard programmatic commitments to the women's movement by recruiting highly visible and like-minded women. The recruitment of these women cannot translate into changes in public policy because political parties, particularly those pursuing policy agendas inspired by neo-conservatism, are unwilling to address the structural sources of women's oppression.[2]

These two perspectives are represented within the Canadian women's movement, as some feminists have sought to engage with political parties and others have eschewed such engagement in favour of pursuing autonomous political action such as engaging in political protests and allying themselves with other social movements. When we examine the orientation of organized feminism in Canada toward political parties, we find that autonomous political action has gradually supplanted efforts to engage with political parties. As this has taken place, Canadian political parties have become less responsive to the policy concerns of the women's movement and have focused less attention on including women in political elites.

THE CANADIAN WOMEN'S MOVEMENT AND PARTY POLITICS

Canadian feminism has always had an ambivalent relationship with political parties (see Bashevkin 1993). On the one hand, feminists have called for the opening of partisan political elites to include women and to respond to women's political concerns, such as child care, reproductive freedom, and employment equity. On the other hand, feminists have distrusted political parties as elitist organizations and even as organizations antithetical to women's concerns. This ambivalence was present in first-wave, or suffragist, feminism early in the twentieth century and has been a source of conflict within the contemporary Canadian women's movement.

From the time it mobilized until 1984, the Canadian women's movement exhibited two discrete approaches to electoral and partisan politics. The more visible was the liberal feminist stream's moderate involvement in electoral and partisan politics. This took the form of encouraging political parties to nominate women candidates, monitoring party policies on status-of-women issues, and maintaining informal interpersonal ties between the movement organizations and the three major political parties. This liberal reformist stream can best be described as 'multipartisan' in orientation, which is to say that it maintained ties to all three of the major parties. The closest connection was to the NDP, but there were also significant ties to the governing federal Liberal party. During this period, the National Action Committee on the Status of Women (NAC), the umbrella organization of feminist groups, fell largely into this liberal feminist tradition.

Less visible but equally important was the radical feminist critique of this approach as an endorsement of a patriarchal political system. Radical feminists eschewed engagement with established political parties, and in some cases (such as the Front de Libération des Femmes du Québec) even rejected the idea of a feminist political party on the grounds that it would mean being co-opted by the patriarchal political establishment. Other radical feminists, however, formed the Feminist Party of Canada (FPC) in 1979 (see Zaborszky 1988). The FPC rejected traditional forms of party organization, opting for non-hierarchical structures and voluntary committees instead of a leader. The party never ran candidates in any federal or provincial election.

Conditions at the time were, however, favourable to the engagement of the women's movement organizations in the partisan electoral arena. The governing Liberal party was committed to fostering pan-Canadian citizen groups in an effort to bolster national unity, and the emerging women's movement was able to benefit from this in a number of ways, not least of which was significant financial support. Moreover, the pan-Canadian emphasis of national politics at the time favoured national social programs and relatively interventionist approaches to governing that were in tune with the statism of the women's movement at the time. This statism, or belief in the ability of government to solve problems, contributed to feminist organizations' emphasis on engaging with established political parties because parties are a key route into state decision making.

Through the 1970s and early 1980s, the liberal feminist commitment to the established political process remained the dominant, albeit contested, tendency within the institutionalized women's movement (Vickers, Rankin, and Appelle 1993). NAC's primary focus was on lobbying, not electoral politics, but its leaders remained supportive of women in the parties, and many movement leaders saw taking feminist politics inside the political parties as a crucial element of movement strategy.

In 1980 and 1981, the federal government's initiative to patriate the Constitution from Britain and introduce an entrenched Charter of Rights and Freedoms prompted an extensive and ultimately successful mobilization of Canadian feminists. Although Canadian feminists had never devoted a great deal of attention to the question of constitutional guarantees of equality, once the federal government placed the idea of an entrenched Charter on the constitutional agenda, many feminists (particularly in English Canada) were determined that gender equality would be guaranteed in the document. The battle to ensure that women's rights were protected in the Charter involved an extensive mobilization of feminist activists throughout English Canada and demonstrated the potential political strength of the women's movement.[3] As one woman involved in the fight observed, political parties—and the governing Liberals in particular—were in awe of the political muscle of the women's movement after the Charter episode.

Throughout this period, the Canadian women's movement was essentially multipartisan in orientation, which is to say that it maintained ties with all three of the major political parties, through informal interpersonal ties. The closest ties were to the NDP, followed by the Liberals. Although their numbers were small, there were also a few moderate PC activists involved in feminist organizations. Moreover, almost all of the women who led NAC in its first decade had ties to one of the three major parties.[4]

After the 1984 federal election, the orientation of the women's movement toward electoral politics began to change subtly. The tension between liberal feminists favouring engagement with party politics and radical feminists preferring more oppositional forms of political action became somewhat more pronounced. In part, the existing tension was more noticeable because radical and socialist feminists became a more powerful force within NAC, so the radical feminist critique of engaging with established political parties became a more prominent voice within the national organization. As NAC became more oppositional in stance, it also grew ever more critical of political parties. The new NAC leaders were skeptical of the potential impact and political importance of the integration of women into electoral and partisan politics. After the election of Kim Campbell as leader of the PCs in 1993, for example, NAC president Judy Rebick stated that 'women like that are going to become our most bitter opponents' (cited in Huang and Jaffer 1993: 10). On another occasion, Rebick told a journalist that 'the political system is so patriarchal and so hierarchical—it is such a male culture. What happens to women politicians is they either get sidelined within it or they get co-opted into it' (cited in Sharpe 1994: 213). As NAC grew critical of electoral politics and political parties, its ties to the three major parties eroded. The group's earlier multipartisanship was replaced with an apartisan orientation, which is to say that it emphasized competing with political parties as an intermediary between society and the state. NAC leaders claimed that the failure of political parties to provide adequate representation for the public forced the organization to transform itself into the 'extra-parliamentary opposition' (Gottlieb 1993: 380–81). NAC's changing stance toward parties was a function of its changing internal composition and growing disillusionment among activists with the strategy of working inside established political parties because the results were so much less than had originally been expected.

In the same period, women engaged with political parties and with the project of electing women became alienated from NAC and threw their energies into electoral work. These diverging tendencies in the women's movement did not result in overt conflict between the proponents of the two points of view, but rather created a breakdown in communications whereby advocates of each strategy simply pursued their own courses with little regard for the other approach. Groups focused on the electoral route, such as the Committee for '94, played a prominent role in pushing the parties to include more women in their legislative caucuses through the 1980s and early 1990s. In the latter half of the 1990s, however, these groups became less prominent and in several cases defunct. As a consequence, pressure on the parties to increase the representation of women came from within, if at all.

THE PARTIES RESPOND[5]

In the 1950s and much of the 1960s, women's participation in Canadian party politics tended to take the form of political housekeeping. The roles the parties assigned to women explicitly mirrored the roles society assigned to women within the family. As the PC Women's Association president explained to women involved in the party in 1964, 'every woman knows how to create a home. . . . [The election] is your opportunity to create a "home" for your local campaign' (Harrison Smith 1964). During this period, women's involvement in the Liberal and Conservative parties was channeled into ladies' auxiliaries, which provided important support to party organizations but had little influence. The NDP (formed in 1961 by the CCF and the trade union movement) had no separate women's organization but tended to relegate women to supporting roles. Given these ideas about the appropriate place for women, it is not surprising that there were very few women in the House of Commons and that the parties adopted no policies explicitly related to women.[6]

The secondary role assigned to women began to be challenged in the late 1960s, at roughly the same time that the contemporary women's movement was beginning to mobilize. The women's organizations affiliated with the parties all became founding members of the Ad Hoc Committee on the Status of Women, which later became NAC. Of the three parties, the NDP was the most immediately and directly affected by the emerging feminist movement as it was host to a feminist mobilization closely related to other struggles inside the party at the time. The Liberal party experienced an influx of liberal feminist activists intent on working though the party to achieve social change, and was also motivated to respond to the emerging movement for electoral reasons. The PCs were the least affected but nonetheless experienced some reverberations from the changing times.

The NDP feminist mobilization was integrally linked to the Waffle movement.[7] Many of the young women involved in the Waffle were committed to its socialist ideals but became disillusioned by the treatment of women within the faction. This sexism notwithstanding, the Waffle responded positively to its internal feminist mobilization, 'providing an arena for the development of an analysis and policy proposals that integrated socialism and feminism in a new way' (Vickers, Rankin, and Appelle 1993: 50–51). But feminist mobilization within the party was not restricted to the Waffle. Women involved in the party began to mobilize to challenge the party's leadership on issues of importance to women. This mobilization led to calls for changes in party rules and party policy, including more women as candidates, support for the movement's policy agenda, and representational guarantees for women within the party (Eady 1970; Laxer 1970; NDP 1970a, 1970b).

After a tumultuous national convention in 1971, in which motions calling for gender parity on the party's federal council and for a national convention of NDP women were voted down, relations between feminist women and the party establishment gradually became less conflictual. In 1974, the party sponsored a national conference for NDP women. Delegates to this conference endorsed a document that offered a blistering critique of the treatment of women in Canadian society and that stated that feminism and socialism were inextricably linked (NDP BC POW Committee 1974). Although the party tempered the rhetoric of this document, it nonetheless adopted a Statement on Women's Rights in 1975. This statement committed the Federal Council to full support of the movement for the liberation of women and to a range of policies of particular interest to women, including free 24-hour child care, maternity leave, changes in labour and pension laws, and decriminalization of abortion (NDP POW Committee 1975).

Unlike the NDP, the Liberal party did not experience a spontaneous feminist mobilization among its membership in the early 1970s. Rather, younger women already active in the party continued to challenge the roles assigned to women within the party. They were joined by feminist activists with a pragmatic bent who decided to take their struggles for women's equality inside the governing party. The party's leadership perceived the mobilization of women as significant, and tried, sometimes clumsily, to woo this new electoral constituency. In advance of the 1972 and 1974 federal elections, senior strategists tried with some success to recruit female candidates, and the party targeted female voters for special appeals. In 1973, the party's women's auxiliary was disbanded and replaced by the National Women's Liberal Commission (NWLC), which had a mandate to push for legislation on issues directly affecting women and to encourage women to run as candidates (Myers 1989; Sharpe 1994).

The Conservatives were slower than the other two parties to respond to the emerging women's movement. The PC women's association was resistant to pressure for change, which came from inside and outside the party. Some women within the party wanted to play a more substantive role and to have the party take stands on status-of-women questions, but the women's association responded unenthusiastically (Holt 1973). Despite this lack of enthusiasm, PC policy statements on women suggested a fair degree of responsiveness to feminism, particularly in the aftermath of the Report of the Royal Commission on the Status of Women. During the 1972 election, the party promised legislation protecting women from dismissal during pregnancy and providing maternity leave, making day care facili-

Table 5.1

Female Candidates and MPs, by Party (Percentages)

	Liberal		PC	
	Candidates	**MPs**	**Candidates**	**MPs**
1974	7.6	5.2	4.3	2.1
1979	7.5	5.3	5.0	1.5
1980	8.2	6.8	5.0	1.9
1984	13.6	12.5	8.2	9.0
1988	18.0	15.7	12.5	12.4
1993	22.0	20.0	23.0	50.0[a]
1997	27.9	23.9	18.6	10.0

[a] Only two Conservative MPs were elected in 1993.

ties available to all female federal employees on a contributory basis, and encouraging industry to follow suit (PC party 1972).

After the initial flurry of response to feminism, the three major parties settled into a fairly stable pattern of moderate endorsement of feminist policy issues and gradual inclusion of women into partisan elites. Throughout the period, the NDP remained the most responsive to feminism, while the two mainstream parties lagged behind. In numeric terms, all three parties were slow to integrate women into partisan elites. After the initial burst of enthusiasm for women candidates, progress was slow. As Table 5.1 shows, fewer than 10 per cent of PC and Liberal candidates were women. The NDP nominated considerably more female candidates than the other parties, but many of these women were nominated in unwinnable ridings, so the proportion of women in the NDP caucus was no greater than in the other two parties.

Women won some modest representational gains inside the extra-parliamentary wings of the parties during the 1970s and early 1980s. The NDP reconstituted its Participation of Women (POW) committee in 1977, giving it increased power and legitimacy within the organization (Bashevkin 1991). In 1980, the Liberal party established an ad hoc committee on affirmative action that created an action plan to recruit women as party members and to elected executive positions in the party in the hope of improving the representation of women on such committees from the 25 per cent the committee found in its initial survey (NWLC 1981, 1982).

In their substantive responsiveness to feminism, the three parties varied from left to right. The NDP endorsed key items on the feminist agenda, while the Conservatives were slow to respond. By 1975, the NDP had endorsed almost every policy stance espoused by major Canadian feminist organizations. The party adopted a resolution advocating a pro-choice stance on abortion in 1967, and its 1975 statement on women's rights pronounced its support for public child care, maternity leave, and changes to labour law. To a greater degree than the other two parties, the NDP raised issues of importance to women in Parliament (Steed 1988).

The Conservatives, in contrast to this, had little in the way of policy on issues of importance to women. After Joe Clark became party leader in 1976, the party grad-

Table 5.1 (continued)

Female Candidates and MPs, by Party (Percentages)

	NDP		Reform/CA		BQ	
	Candidates	MPs	Candidates	MPs	Candidates	MPs
1974	15.5	0.0	–	–	–	–
1979	16.7	7.7	–	–	–	–
1980	11.7	6.3	–	–	–	–
1984	22.7	10.0	–	–	–	–
1988	28.5	11.6	–	–	–	–
1993	38.0	11.0	11.1	13.5	13.3	14.8
1997	35.8	38.0	10.1	6.7	21.3	25.0

ually began to adopt more fully developed positions on these issues. During the 1979 and 1980 election campaigns, under pressure from NAC, the party developed policy positions on a range of issues including pay equity, treatment of women under the Indian Act, and removal of the spousal exemption from the sexual assault law. The party did not, however, adopt policy advocated by feminist groups on the issues of child care, maternity leave, or reproductive choice (PC party 1980). It was not until 1981, humbled by losing office after only nine months, that the Conservatives made an all-out effort to respond to organized feminism. This initiative is best understood as part of a broader effort to update the party's image, hoping to appeal to younger urban voters and to women in particular. As a consequence, the party's platform on women's issues became more consistent with the positions of liberal feminists.

The governing Liberals were more difficult to categorize, as the party's relatively weak extra-parliamentary wing appeared open to a feminist policy agenda but the more powerful parliamentary party was bounded by its role in government and by party leader Pierre Trudeau's ambivalence toward feminism. The extra-parliamentary wing of the party adopted numerous resolutions addressing issues raised by the women's movement. The NWLC found that the Trudeau government enacted legislation establishing the principle of pay equity within the federal government, allowing Canada and Quebec Pension Plan contributions to be split upon divorce, prohibiting layoff and dismissal on the grounds of pregnancy, and introducing the child tax credit. The government did not, however, adopt measures guaranteeing equal treatment for Status Indian women or initiating family law reform (NWLC 1978). Overall, this mixed record of policy responsiveness suggests that the Liberal government was more willing to adopt feminist policy stances on issues relating to employment and income security than to thornier cultural issues such as abortion or equal rights for Indian women. Employment issues were less controversial and did not expose the government to opposition as cultural issues did.

From the mid-1980s until 1993, there were substantial representational gains for women numerically, and moderate gains substantively. What is noteworthy about this period is, first, the increased rate of improvement of women's representation, and second, the convergence of all three major parties in support of moderate, liberal feminism.

The NDP again led the way on representational gains. In 1983, the party adopted a resolution guaranteeing gender parity on both the federal executive and the federal council, and the party's executive is balanced by gender so that women hold roughly half the vice-presidential positions. In 1986, the Liberals adopted a rule requiring that half their vice-presidential positions be held by women, but they dropped the measure in 1990. The Conservatives implemented no analogous measures. Both the Liberals and Conservatives did, however, put in place measures guaranteeing women places at conventions. The Liberals passed a constitutional amendment in 1990 requiring that 50 per cent of all convention delegates be women, and the PCs required that at least 33 per cent of constituency delegates be women as of 1991.

The same pattern holds for nomination of candidates. As Table 5.1 (pp. 82–83) shows, the NDP led the way in terms of nomination of candidates, but the Conservatives posted the largest gains in numbers of women elected. For all three parties, the rate of change between 1980 and 1988 was substantial. The NDP is the only Canadian party that tried to implement an affirmative action plan for women and other underrepresented groups as candidates. The first iteration of this plan, set in motion after the 1988 election, clustered federal ridings together and applied a quota to the group of ridings. This ultimately did not prove workable, so a policy approved by the 1991 convention empowered the federal council to oversee greater female involvement in each region. The most significant power given to the federal council under this plan was to freeze nominations for a cluster until a more inclusive nomination process had been achieved (Whitehorn and Archer 1995).

Although it did not adopt an analogous plan, the Liberal party increased its efforts to recruit female candidates in the late 1980s and early 1990s. This involved informal efforts to recruit female candidates, a mentorship program linking new candidates with experienced ones, financial contributions for all female candidates, campaign colleges for women candidates and their staffs, and a campaign manual directed at female candidates. The party amended its constitution in 1990 to give the leader the power to appoint candidates; Jean Chrétien used this power prior to the 1993 election to appoint nine women candidates. The Conservatives undertook similar measures, many of them originating with the Conservative women's caucuses in several major cities.

The late 1980s and early 1990s also saw the election of the first two female leaders of national political parties: Audrey McLaughlin of the NDP and Kim Campbell of the Conservatives. Both experienced substantial difficulties during their tenures as party leader, and both were blamed by many for their parties' electoral defeats.

During this period, all three parties' emphasis on representational gains outstripped their efforts to respond to feminist issues. Nonetheless, all three remained moderately responsive to feminism throughout this period, and none came to define itself in opposition to feminism.[8] Although tensions emerged between the NDP and the women's movement during the debate over the Charlottetown Accord, the NDP remained the party most closely in harmony with the movement's policy agenda.

The NDP was also the only party to share NAC's ongoing opposition to economic restructuring in general, and to the North American Free Trade Agreement (NAFTA) in particular (Leger and Rebick 1993).

The Liberal and Conservative parties were moderately supportive of traditional status-of-women issues but considerably less responsive on the broader economic issues that became the primary focus of the women's movement at the time. Many Canadian feminists took issue with the Mulroney government's neo-liberal economic agenda, which involved privatization of government-owned corporations, entry into continental free trade agreements, elimination of restrictions on foreign investment, and reduction of government spending on a variety of programs, including social programs. One issue that caused particular controversy was child care, as the Conservatives had promised to introduce a national child care program but failed to do so in their nine years in government. On questions unrelated to the role of the state in regulating the market and not requiring significant government transfers, the Mulroney government's record was considerably more positive, although not uniformly so. Brian Mulroney found himself trying to mediate between competing factions in the Conservative party on these issues while trying not to alienate a perceived community of women voters. On the controversial questions of abortion and sexual assault legislation, the government endeavoured to broker compromise legislation. In the case of abortion, this compromise pleased neither side and was defeated in the Senate. In her comparative study of women's movements under Margaret Thatcher, Ronald Reagan, and Mulroney, Sylvia Bashevkin concludes that the Canadian Conservatives were 'far less ideologically driven' neo-conservatives than their British or American counterparts (Bashevkin 1998: 236).

In general terms, the pattern that prevailed from the feminist mobilization of the 1970s until 1993 was one of accommodation. The three parties varied somewhat in their commitment to the numeric and substantive representation of women, but all three actively tried to accommodate women (as mobilized by feminism) within their party. This is in keeping with several defining characteristics of the party system in place from 1957 to 1993.[9] First, the women's movement was a pan-Canadian, non-territorially based movement which looked to the national government for policy change; as such, it shared the pan-Canadian political focus of the three parties. Second, the kinds of policies the Canadian women's movement was calling for during this period essentially involved removal of discrimination and extension of social benefits. This was in harmony with the Keynesian consensus embodied in the party system of the time. Third, the party system was characterized by a politics of accommodation. All three parties tried to bridge cleavages rather than exacerbate them.[10] No party sought to become the party of feminism (or of women), but none sought to become the antithesis of this.[11] Instead, all three parties converged on a moderate endorsement of liberal feminist policy stances. Finally, this party system was characterized by considerable similarity in organizational form among the three parties. The three parties all sought to represent pan-Canadian constituencies and all adopted various representational mechanisms intended to encourage inclusion. This meant that all three parties adopted similar, although not identical, measures designed to ensure the inclusion of women within party affairs. None of the parties rejected the group-based conception of representation underlying this model. This allowed for, among other things, a demonstration, or contagion, effect whereby the NDP forced the two larger parties to adopt mechanisms furthering women's representation within their party organizations and in Parliament. But with the breakdown of this party system, all of the characteristics that favoured some representational gains for women came into question.

Both the Canadian party system and the parties' responsiveness to organized feminism changed in the aftermath of the 1993 election, which reduced the governing Conservatives to only two seats in the House of Commons, decimated the NDP, and catapulted the Reform party and the Bloc Québécois onto the national stage. This change in the party system coincided with and contributed to the Canadian women's movement's shift away from engagement in electoral politics. As a consequence of these two developments, partisan responsiveness to the women's movement has declined substantially.

Although the BQ has proven to be an ally for feminists, its narrow basis in Quebec and its separatist ideology have prevented it from taking strong stands on national issues. In both its representational practices and its substantive policy stances, the Reform party and its successor, the Canadian Alliance, have proven hostile to the representation of women. The Reform party resolutely avoided taking a position of any kind on women's issues on the grounds that there are no problems specific to women, but simply social or family issues. It is telling that this stance was recommended by a party task force led by Preston Manning's wife, Sandra Manning (Flanagan 1995). Because the party did not recognize women as a political group, questions of gender and, more specifically, of gender equity disappeared from political discussion. As Tracey Raney (1998) has demonstrated in her work on Reform, the party's conceptualization of citizenship and equality relied on equal treatment for undifferentiated citizens; in this view, public policy should not take into account difference of any sort. Raney notes that Reform's rejection of difference extended to the argument that social groups that claim to be different undermine the stability of the community. The party's ideological commitment to a highly formalized notion of equality means that it would not endorse policies (such as child care) intended to address systemic, rather than direct, discrimination. As a result, the party's policy platform was on most issues antithetical to organized feminism. Reform opposed state-funded child care, affirmative action, abortion on demand, and public financing for feminist organizations; on at least one occasion, Manning mused out loud about eliminating maternity benefits provided under the national unemployment insurance system (Sigurdson 1994). In March 1999, the party's parliamentary caucus championed the cause of Beverly Smith, a homemaker who was taking her claim that Canadian tax law discriminated against single-income two-parent families to the United Nations (Reform Party 1989).

Although the Reform party did not adopt policies relating explicitly to women, its platform included initiatives directed toward strengthening the family. At the core of these policy proposals were changes to the Income Tax Act designed to facilitate, and perhaps even encourage, one parent to stay at home with children.[12]

Although these policy stances are gender-neutral on the surface, they do suggest an assumption of traditional family forms. The suspicion that Reform's intent was to reduce the role of the state in providing caring services and return such services to the family (mainly women) is supported by Manning's public statements to the effect that 'family is the most important primary caregiver in our judgement' (Manning cited in Raney 1998: 127).

The Reform party appeared to have ties of some sort to anti-feminist and pro-family groups. For instance, the Web page of the Canada Family Action Coalition, a Christian group opposed to abortion, extension of rights to homosexuals, and tax discrimination against single-income families, featured a guest column by Reform MP Rob Anders entitled 'How to Get Involved in Canadian Politics,' which provided a step-by-step guide to capturing a constituency association (FAC Web site: <www.familyaction.org>). Although there were no formal ties between the Reform party and the leading anti-feminist group REAL Women, the latter organization apparently had some proprietary sense toward the party. In the group's November/December 1998 newsletter, REAL Women endorsed Reform's United Alternative (UA) initiative to merge with the Conservatives, arguing that 'a realignment of our political parties is desperately needed to end our one-sided political system. There *must* be a strong, national alternative to the Liberal party, for the sake of democracy, if nothing else' (REAL Women 1998, emphasis in original). Giving members registration information for the UA conference, REAL Women told its members 'we *must* attend this convention so that there will be a large critical mass of social conservatives who will not be overruled by those who [are] merely fiscal conservatives. The future stability of Canada is dependent on our presence there. Please consider attending this Convention with as many friends, neighbours and relatives as you can muster together, in order to change the course of Canadian politics' (REAL Women 1998, emphasis in original).

In numeric terms, the inclusion of women in the Reform party followed roughly the same pattern as that of the other parties: the higher the position, the fewer women. Although no comprehensive statistics are available regarding the participation of women in the Reform party, a study based on 58 constituency association executive lists available on the Internet revealed that 24 per cent of riding presidents listed were women, as were 12 per cent of vice-presidents, 30 per cent of treasurers, and 58 per cent of secretaries.[13] More striking, and arguably more significant, is the pattern of women's representation among Reform candidates and MPs. As Table 5.1 (pp. 82–83) shows, the party had fewer candidates than any of its competitors in the 1993 election; in 1997, the number of women running under the party's banner actually declined, as did the proportion of women in its caucus. After the 1997 election, Reform achieved the lowest rate of representation of women of any major Canadian party at the federal level in 15 years.

The Canadian Alliance, formed as a successor to the Reform party in 2000, differs little from Reform in its policy stances. Like Reform, the Alliance does not mention women specifically in its core policy document (Canadian Alliance 2002), emphasizes the role of family over the state in caretaking, and promises to refer contentious issues like abortion to national referendums.

While the Reform party was emerging as a significant party in English Canada, the NDP was decimated. In the aftermath of the 1993 election, the party lost official party status, and it barely regained this status after the 1997 election. This meant that organized feminism all but lost its closest ally in the partisan arena. The decline of the NDP put a stop to the dynamic toward greater representation of women that the party had created. In its place emerged the Reform party, with its refusal to recognize women as a political group or to encourage women's candidacies. It is not surprising, then, that the election of women has dropped from the political agenda since the 1993 election and that the rate of growth has slowed somewhat. This trend can be seen more clearly in women's candidacies than in the numbers of women elected. Table 5.1 (pp. 82–83) shows that the proportion of female candidates declined between 1993 and 1997 for the New Democratic, Conservative, and Reform parties. The Liberal party continued to nominate an increasing number of women, as did the Bloc.[14]

In substantive terms, issues of importance to women have all but disappeared from the policy agenda of government. As Janine Brodie notes, in the 1993 election 'the federal parties were virtually silent about so-called women's issues. Indeed the two major parties obviously felt gender was so irrelevant that they could refuse to debate women's issues as they had in the two previous federal campaigns without paying any electoral penalties' (1998: 21). As discussed earlier, this can be attributed in part to the fiscal climate in which the new party system is emerging. But it also has to do with the new dynamics of party competition. With the Liberals and Conservatives both competing primarily against the Alliance in English Canada, women's issues have become peripheral to the contest for votes.

In the 2000 general election, the Liberal party returned to its earlier practice of appealing to 'women voters'; such an approach appeared politically expedient. At the outset of the campaign, the Canadian Alliance was the Liberals' primary competitor outside Quebec, and the Alliance enjoyed considerable momentum because of the popularity of its new leader, Stockwell Day. The Liberals sought to halt this momentum by highlighting what they perceived as a disjuncture between the values held by the majority of Canadians and those espoused by Day. Party pollster Michael Marzolini recalls that one of the 'key events of the election campaign' was a 'carefully placed reference to the abortion issue in a speech delivered by the Prime Minister to one thousand women the weekend before the debate', a speech in which the prime minister 'outlined his pro-choice position on abortion and quietly dropped the issue on the table' (Marzolini 2001: 269). Marzolini reveals that Liberal polling prior to the election 'indicated that the abortion issue was a "magic bullet" to use against the Alliance' (Marzolini 2001: 269). The strategy of using abortion as a wedge issue representing a range of other social issues, such as gay rights, was apparently successful. Marzolini reports that 'women voters abandoned the Alliance en masse. Indeed, women made up some two-thirds of all those who deserted the Alliance during the campaign' (Marzolini 2001: 269).[15]

CONCLUSION

Have Canadian feminists transformed party politics? When we examine Canadian parties' responses to the mobilization of feminism, it is clear that this mobilization has opened the doors of Canadian political parties to women's participation. Since Canadian feminists began to pressure the parties for changes to their internal practices in the early 1970s, the number of women holding party office and running for office has increased substantially. That said, the status quo falls far short of the gender parity envisioned by feminist activists.

In substantive terms, Canadian parties have been somewhat responsive to the feminist policy agenda—at least they were from 1970 to 1993. For the Liberal and Conservative parties, however, this responsiveness was driven primarily by a desire to appeal to a poorly defined group of 'women voters'. The Liberal party first responded to the feminist policy agenda in the early 1970s because it saw the mobilization of the women's movement as a potential threat to the party's ability to win votes from women. The Conservatives followed suit in the early 1980s in an effort to shed their backward image and appeal to younger, urban voters, particularly women. It is noteworthy that the only election in which there was a nationally televised leaders' debate on women's issues was the 1984 election, which took place in the aftermath of the successful feminist mobilization around the Charter of Rights and Freedoms. This mobilization impressed the parties with the potential strength of the women's vote, thereby prompting them to respond. The pattern of highlighting feminist issues only when they have the potential to yield electoral benefit continues to the present day, as became clear with the Liberal party's sudden championing of the pro-choice stance on abortion in the 2000 election, not out of concern for principle but as a wedge issue to discredit the leader of the Canadian Alliance. Given this pattern, it is clear that feminist mobilization has not had a lasting effect on the policy stances of Canadian parties.

As organized feminism in Canada has turned its attention away from electoral politics, it has become easier for the parties to downplay or even ignore feminist issues. There is little pressure on the parties to respond to issues that are of primary concern to feminist activists. But even if the Canadian women's movement were focused on electoral politics, the potential for transformation of the policies and internal practices of Canadian parties is decidedly limited. Political parties exist to contest elections, and electoral gain is their primary motivation. We can expect parties to respond to the feminist policy agenda only when that agenda is espoused by a significant electoral constituency. The route to transformation of parties' policy agendas lies in creating demand for such transformation in the electorate at large, thereby creating pressure on the parties. In the absence of such pressure, feminist concerns will remain peripheral to the electoral politics of the day. At the level of strategy, the implication of this for organized feminism is clear: if feminists want to transform party politics, they must start by mobilizing support for their claims in the electorate, and then engage with the parties to point out this support and the potential electoral benefit it might bring them. Neither strategy alone will be sufficient to change the ways in which parties deal with the issues raised by feminists.

NOTES

1. This chapter is drawn in part from Young (2000). Thanks to UBC Press for allowing portions of the text from that book to be used here.

2. Gotell and Brodie use the term *neo-conservatism* in their work (1991). The term generally refers to ideologies that advocate for a limited government role in regulating the economy but for a more extensive government role in regulating social affairs, such as by banning abortion. Arguably, Gotell and Brodie's claim could be applied equally to neo-liberalism.

3. For a detailed description of this mobilization, see Hosek (1983). It should be noted that there was a significant split between English Canadian and Québécois feminists over the Charter issue.

4. For instance, NAC's first president, Laura Sabia, ran as a candidate for the Conservative party after her tenure as NAC president, and her successor Grace Hartman ran as an NDP candidate. NAC's third president, Lorna Marsden, was active in the Liberal party during her NAC presidency and was subsequently appointed to the Senate. Among later NAC presidents, Kay Macpherson and Lynn McDonald both ran for the NDP after their presidencies, and Doris Anderson and Chaviva Hosek both ran for the Liberals.

5. This account is based on interviews with activists and extensive archival research (see Young 2000).

6. During the 1950s and 1960s, the number of women in the House of Commons ranged from a low of one (after the 1968 election) to a high of five (after the 1962 election).

7. The Waffle movement comprised radical activists, many of whom were students or academics, who wanted the party to 'waffle to the left'; see Morton (1986).

8. This is a contrast to the American experience: from 1980 on, the Republican party defined itself in opposition to feminism.

9. For a discussion of the evolving Canadian party system, see Carty, Cross, and Young (2000).

10. The exception to this is the NDP's effort to represent the interests of working-class voters.

11. This stands in contrast to the American case in the 1980s and 1990s, as the Democrats became the party of feminism and the Republicans the party of anti-feminism (see Young 2000).

12. This policy stance is not necessarily antithetical to feminism. In fact, feminist organizations have made positive comments about tax policies designed to increase the choice available to women with young children.

13. This research was undertaken by Amy Nugent. This study is not a scientific sample, but it does give a basic indication of the representation of women in governing Reform constituency associations.

14. The Bloc's increase might be attributed to the decline in the party's fortunes. Having lost its charismatic founding leader and the 1995 Quebec referendum on sovereignty, the Bloc had clearly become the 'B Team' for Quebec sovereigntists. As a result, Bloc candidacies presumably became less competitive. The party did not take any formal measures to encourage women candidates prior to the 1997 election.

15. One might question whether it was abortion or the health care issue, on which the Liberals also questioned Day's credibility, that resulted in women voters abandoning the Alliance.

Chapter Six

Women's Involvement in Canadian Political Parties[1]

Lisa Young and William Cross

Introduction

The liberal democratic promise of equal participation for all citizens in political life has only very slowly been fulfilled for women and members of various minority groups in Canada. No women could vote in federal elections until 1918, and Asian and Aboriginal women were not enfranchised until much later. Even once women won this basic democratic right, they were largely excluded from the political life of the country. Electoral democracy in Canada is structured by political parties, and participation of women in these organizations is a necessary condition if the liberal democratic promise is to be fulfilled. The involvement of women in political parties is also important for other reasons: there is evidence suggesting that women's participation in the extra-parliamentary wings of political parties is related to greater numbers of women elected (Caul 1999) and that women's involvement may make political parties more responsive to women's concerns (Young 2000; but see also Gotell and Brodie 1991).

Feminist research over the past 25 years has gained considerable insight into the barriers to women's participation in political parties (Bashevkin 1993), feminist activism inside parties (Praud 1998a; Young 2000), the role of parties in encouraging and discouraging women's political candidacy (Brodie and Chandler 1991; Erickson 1991, 1993, 1998), and attitudinal differences between women and men in party elites (Brodie 1988; Tremblay and Pelletier 2001). However, despite this extensive research, we know relatively little about why women join political parties, how active they are in the parties, and how party members of either gender view the status of women within the parties.[2] In this chapter, we analyze the findings of a survey conducted in 2000 of members of political parties in order to address these issues. More specifically, we set out to determine how women were recruited into party membership and to what extent they participate in party activities. We also examine their views regarding women's influence in the parties and the appropriateness of guarantees of representation for women.

As the previous chapter discussed, women were involved in Canadian political parties throughout most of the twentieth century, but until the 1970s their participation tended to be channelled into supportive roles. Despite the activism of women within all three of the parties, women remained underrepresented in most facets of party life through the 1980s. Indeed, the closer one came to political power, the fewer women were to be found. A 1991 survey of constituency associations found that this pattern persisted, with women making up 20 per cent of riding presidents, 32 per cent of treasurers, and 69 per cent of riding secretaries (Carty 1991: 55). Women did, however, win some modest representational gains inside each of the three major parties during this period, including guarantees of women's representation on national party executives and positions as convention delegates (see chapter 5).

The Canadian party system was shattered in the 1993 election by the entry of two new parties, Reform and the Bloc Québécois, and by the virtual decimation of the Conservative and New Democratic parties. Chapter 5 described the advent of this new party system and the profound consequences it had for the participation of women in Canadian political parties, such that in the 2000 election, the percentage of women in the House declined for the first time in over 30 years.

In light of this trend, we are left with the question of the current state of women's participation in Canadian political parties. Have the efforts of the past 30 years to make women equal players both in society generally and within parties in particular yielded results that make these representational guarantees obsolete? To provide at least a partial answer to this question, we turn to an examination of the participation of women as members of the five major Canadian political parties.

Methodology
This study of Canadian political party members is based on a mail-back survey of randomly selected members of the five major Canadian political parties conducted between March and May 2000. The survey was mailed to a regionally stratified random sample drawn from the membership lists of each political party.[3] A total of 10,928 surveys were mailed to partisans; 3,872 completed surveys were returned, yielding an overall response rate of 36 per cent.[4] Membership in Canadian political parties fluctuates significantly over the course of an election cycle (Carty, Cross, and Young 2000), so the timing of the survey is significant. Because the study was undertaken during a period when there was no election anticipated and no leadership contests underway,[5] we expect that the members sampled are longer-term, more active members than would have been captured had the survey been conducted when leadership or nomination contests were underway.

WOMEN AS PARTY MEMBERS

Because no figures are available from the five major parties with respect to the gender breakdown of their membership, it is impossible to determine whether there was gender bias in the rate of response to the survey. It is, of course, possible that female party members were more or less likely than their male counterparts to return the survey. Given this, we cannot verify the representativeness of the sample with respect to gender. Women constituted 38 per cent of the respondents to the survey. This breakdown is roughly consistent with data available from public opinion surveys. Paul Howe and David Northrup report that when members of the

Canadian public were asked whether they had ever been a member of a political party, 19 per cent of male respondents and 13 per cent of female respondents answered in the affirmative (2000: 89); in their research, 43 per cent of individuals who had belonged to a political party were women. Broken down by party, the proportion of female respondents to the Study of Canadian Political Party Members was as follows: Liberal, 47 per cent; NDP, 46 per cent; BQ, 37 per cent; PC, 33 per cent; CA, 32 per cent. This pattern corresponds with what one would expect given that both the Liberal and the New Democratic parties have maintained policies designed to involve women in their parties in recent years, while the BQ, Conservatives, and Alliance have eschewed such policies. It also corresponds generally with the patterns of gender difference in electoral support for the parties (Nevitte et al. 2000).

It is noteworthy that the apparent underrepresentation of women within Canadian political parties is not a phenomenon that we can expect to leave behind as younger women join the parties in larger numbers. On the contrary, an age breakdown of respondents to the survey demonstrates that young women make up an even smaller proportion of female party members than young men do of male party members (see Table 6.1). Individuals under the age of 30 constitute a stunningly small proportion of party members overall, and this is even more the case for women. Gender differences in age breakdown were relatively small, except in the Conservative party

The greying of Canadian political parties reflects declining confidence in parties among younger Canadians, accompanied by an increasing faith in the efficacy and appropriateness of unconventional protest tactics and interest group involvement (Howe and Northrup 2000; Nevitte 1996). That the increasing age of Canadian party members is all the more pronounced among women reflects a tendency for women to express greater confidence in interest groups than in political parties[6] and to channel their political and community activism accordingly (Rankin and Vickers 1998).

Even though the parties are apparently not particularly successful in recruiting young women, there is evidence that women have been joining parties in greater numbers in recent years. When we examine the gender breakdown by length of membership, we find that for all the parties except the Conservatives a larger proportion of women than men have been recruited to the party in the five years leading up to the time of the survey (see Table 6.1). This may represent a gradual trend toward equalization in the willingness of women and men to join political parties as perceptions of politics as a male preserve gradually decline.

There are a number of other socio-demographic differences between male and female party members that warrant mention. Female party members are less likely than their male counterparts to have graduate or professional degrees, a finding that is not particularly suprising given the age of most members. Female members are also more likely to report a lower family income than their male counterparts, again a predictable finding in light of the generally lower incomes of older women in Canada. As is also the case in the Canadian population as a whole, women who belong to the parties are less likely than their male counterparts to be employed full-time outside the home; 26 per cent of women surveyed reported full-time employment, as compared to 43 per cent of men. For the most part, this difference is a result of the 12 per cent of female party members who are homemakers and the 12 per cent (as compared to 6 per cent of men) who work part-time. Of the party members who work full-time, we found that women are far less likely to be business owners (28 per cent compared to 43 per cent of men) and more likely to be employed in the public sector (43 per cent versus 25 per cent of men).

RECRUITMENT

Involvement in Canadian party politics is usually characterized as a cyclical phenomenon. In his study of Canadian parties' constituency associations, R. Kenneth Carty found clear evidence that the Liberal and Conservative parties' membership numbers fluctuated vastly between election and non-election years, leading him to conclude that 'when party elections are to be held—to nominate a candidate in an election, or select delegates for a leadership contest—membership takes on its meaning and worth, and individuals are mobilized for these contests with little concern for longer-term involvement or participation' (1991: 38). These findings reflect the traditional understanding of patterns of recruitment into Canadian parties: individuals are mobilized through social networks to join parties during contested nomination and leadership contests, and the parties' local associations are run by a relatively small number of committed partisans during the interim periods. Beyond this, relatively little is known regarding individuals' reasons for joining political parties in Canada.

Is there reason to expect gender differences in patterns of recruitment into party affairs? The answer to this is not clear, but we can speculate that there may be some gender differences. Because party activism has traditionally been a largely male preserve, we might anticipate that women, particularly those who joined a party some time ago, may be more likely to have been recruited by family members or friends, as opposed to having joined the party at the urging of a party official or on their

Table 6.1
Age and Length of Party Membership (Percentages)

	PC		Liberal		NDP		BQ		CA	
	Women	Men	Women	Men	Women	Men	Women	Men	Women	Men
Age										
<30	2*	8*	14	14	3*	4*	4	7	3**	2**
31–45	9*	11*	12	17	14*	23*	17	16	6**	11**
46–60	22*	25*	31	33	34*	34*	36	35	25**	23**
>60	67*	56*	43	37	50*	39*	43	42	67**	64**
Years of membership										
<5	29**	29**	39	32	28	26	48	40	42	40
6–10	8**	13**	16	18	13	10	48	56	43	49
11–20	18**	22**	16	22	21	24	4	3	14	11
>20	46**	36**	30	28	38	40	–	–	–	–

*Chi-square significant at p=.01; **p=.05

own initiative. Moreover, research regarding women's candidacies has found that women are more likely to contest a party nomination if they are invited to do so, as opposed to initiating their candidacy unsolicited (Erickson 1998). By analogy, we might find women more likely to wait to be asked to join a political party, reflecting gender-differentiated patterns of socialization.

As Table 6.2 shows, this pattern does, in fact, hold for all five major Canadian parties. It is important to note that for both women and men, the most common response to the question 'Who asked you to join the ___ Party?' was that they joined on their own initiative. That said, men were considerably more likely to report having joined on their own initiative and women to having been recruited by family members, friends, and relatives.[7] This difference is most marked in the Alliance, with women five times as likely as men to report recruitment by a family member. Women in the Conservative party were three times as likely to report this, and in the NDP and the Bloc women were more than twice as likely to report recruitment by a family member. Although it is impossible to ascertain exactly why women, especially in the two right-of-centre parties, are so much more likely to be recruited by a family member, we can speculate that this reflects different patterns of political socialization whereby some women continue to see political parties as something of a male domain and thus wait to be invited to join, particularly by a male relative already involved in the party.

This pattern is not simply an artefact of a bygone era in which women joined the political parties of which their fathers or husbands were members. Rather, we found that 26 per cent of women, but only 11 per cent of men, under the age of 30 were asked by a relative to join the party. Similarly, only 32 per cent of women under 30, as compared with 55 per cent of men in the same age group, reported joining the party on their own initiative. In both instances, these differences are greater than the gender difference for any other age group. In addition, gender differences among individuals who first joined their party during the five years leading up to the time of the survey are of a similar magnitude as gender differences among longer-term partisans. It is clear that differential patterns of recruitment into party politics endure to some extent to the present day and are particularly pronounced among young women. Although we lack the data that would be necessary to draw definitive conclusions linking these differential patterns to ongoing gender differences in political socialization, these findings strongly suggest their existence.

Table 6.2
Patterns of Recruitment

	Asked by Relative			Joined on Own Initiative		
	Women	Men	Difference	Women	Men	Difference
PC*	25%	7%	+18	50%	63%	-13
Liberal	17%	12%	+5	43%	49%	-6
NDP**	16%	6%	+10	49%	54%	-5
BQ***	11%	5%	+6	62%	71%	-9
CA*	16%	3%	+13	63%	74%	-11

*Chi-square significance for relationship between gender and method of recruitment into the party is significant at *p*=.001; **p*=.01; ***p*=.05

While the patterns of recruitment in party politics vary somewhat by gender, this does not tell us whether women and men have different reasons for joining parties. We can categorize the reasons for joining political parties into material, relational, transitory, and purposive incentives. *Material incentives* relate to financial or other benefits that might stem from party membership, while *relational incentives* refers to inducements based in relationships to family members, colleagues, or friends. *Transitory incentives* refers to temporary or short-lived reasons for joining a party, such as supporting the candidacy of a friend or fellow member of a group; in the Canadian experience, there is a well-established tradition of mobilizing party members in this way (Carty 1991). *Purposive incentives* relate to the motivation to work with others to achieve shared ideological or policy-related objectives. Although there is little research regarding incentives to membership in Canadian political parties, one recent study concluded that, at least for the Reform party, activists were motivated predominantly by purposive incentives (Clarke et al. 2000).

Given that women are more likely than men to report being recruited to party membership by family members or friends, it would follow that they might have been recruited in support of a nomination or leadership contestant, in which case they would be more likely to report relational and transitory incentives to membership. To determine which factors were important to Canadian party members' decision to join their party, we asked survey respondents to rank a series of possible reasons for joining their party as 'not at all important', 'somewhat important', or 'very important'. Table 6.3 summarizes their responses, broken down by gender and party.

As Table 6.3 shows, material and relational incentives were the least important reasons for joining Canadian parties, and transitory and purposive incentives the most. Women were slightly less inclined than men to rate material incentives as important. This pattern was particularly clear within the Liberal party, in which 11 per cent of men but only 5 per cent of women indicated that helping their career was a very important reason for joining the party.[8] This may reflect ongoing gender

Table 6.3

Incentives to Membership by Gender, 'Very Important' as Percentage

	Women	Men
Material		
Thought it would help me get a government job	1% (11)	2% (32)
Thought it would help my career*	2% (28)	5% (88)
Relational		
Friend asked me to	5% (57)	6% (121)
Family member asked me to**	8% (88)	6% (113)
Transitory		
To support a candidate for the local nomination**	56% (713)	38% (781)
To support a candidate for the party's leadership**	45% (546)	30% (597)
Purposive		
Believe in the party's policies	85% (1135)	83% (1823)
Wanted to influence party policy on an issue*	18% (212)	19% (378)

*Chi-square significant at $p=.01$; **$p=.001$.

imbalances in certain professions such as law, but may also indicate a lesser propensity among women to seek personal gain from partisan activism. Even though women were more likely to report that friends or family members recruited them into a party, only a small minority reported a request from a friend or family member as important or very important. Women were nonetheless more likely than men to report that a request from a family member was very important (8 per cent of women versus 6 per cent of men) or somewhat important (18 per cent versus 8 per cent). This pattern did not vary substantially by party.

Where women and men differed substantially was with respect to transitory incentives to membership. As Table 6.3 shows, women were far more likely to report that supporting a candidate for the local nomination or the party's leadership was a very important reason for joining the party. Table 6.4 shows that this pattern is consistent across all five parties but is most pronounced in the NDP and the CA. Given women's greater emphasis on transitory incentives and the absence of substantial gender differences with respect to purposive incentives, we conclude that women conform more closely to traditional expectations with respect to recruitment into Canadian parties: they are more likely to be recruited through social networks for leadership and nomination contests. It is noteworthy that leadership and nomination contests are the moments when partisans are most actively recruiting new party members, and other findings suggest that women are more likely than men to wait to be invited into the party. In this respect, vibrant contested nomination and leadership battles may have the unanticipated consequence of increasing women's participation in party life.

PATTERNS OF PARTICIPATION

To what extent, and in what ways, does women's participation in political parties differ from men's participation? We already know, assuming the responses to this

Table 6.4

Transitory Incentives by Party and Gender, 'Very Important'

	Women (%)	Men (%)	Difference
Support candidate for nomination			
PC*	62	46	+16
Liberal*	64	50	+14
NDP*	50	27	+23
BQ	49	36	+13
CA*	49	30	+19
Support candidate for leadership			
PC*	56	39	+17
Liberal*	42	32	+10
NDP*	33	11	+22
BQ	42	29	+13
CA	50	31	+19

*Chi-square significant at $p=.001$; the chi-square measure is sensitive to sample size, so it is likely that the gender difference for the BQ is not statistically significant because of the relatively small number (410) of BQ respondents.

survey are reasonably representative, that women are numerically underrepresented among political party members. In part, this may be because women wait to be recruited into partisan activism rather than join on their own initiative. It may also reflect a continuing skepticism among many women about the efficacy of activism within political parties, as well as time constraints because of family responsibilities.

Most accounts of women's involvement in political parties in Canada and elsewhere have echoed Robert Putnam's law of increasing disproportion: the higher one goes in party elites, the fewer women there are (1976). Sylvia Bashevkin's research in the early 1990s demonstrated that Putnam's law applied to Canadian parties, with women constituting as many as 70 per cent of riding association secretaries but only 46 per cent of convention delegates, 35 per cent of party executive members, 20 per cent of campaign managers, and an even lower proportion of candidates, legislators, or party leaders (1993: 67). Carty (1991) reported similar findings, which also confirmed the conclusion that Harold Clarke and Allan Kornberg had drawn based on a study of urban constituency associations in the 1970s. They found that women tended to work harder than their male counterparts inside parties while expecting fewer tangible rewards for their commitment (in Bashevkin 1993: 68). A study of members of the British Labour party, however, found that 'more women than men were passive members [of the party], spending no time on party work (55–46 percent respectively)' (Lovenduski and Norris 1993: 43).

Figure 6.1 illustrates the rate of involvement for women and men in a range of partisan activities. There are few gender differences with respect to basic activities such as attending a riding association meetings or contributing funds to the party. This latter finding is somewhat surprising given that Canadian women, on the whole, earn less than men and that women who responded to the survey also reported lower family incomes than their male counterparts. Of course, the survey item tells us only that women are as likely as men to contribute, not the amounts

Figure 6.1

Party Activities by Gender

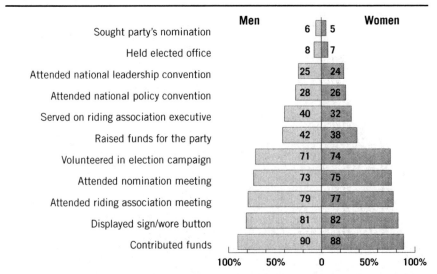

involved. Women were slightly more likely than their male counterparts to attend a riding association meeting or volunteer in an election campaign, echoing Clarke and Kornberg's findings. They were, however, slightly less likely to report having raised funds for the party or having served on a riding association executive.[9] Women were also slightly less likely to have attended a national convention or sought or held elected office.

Gender differences are relatively small, and they certainly do not support the idea that there are large patterns of gender difference in either extent or form of partisan activism. When this is broken down by party, essentially the same pattern remains. Intriguingly, on the items where there are statistically significant gender differences within parties, these differences tend to appear within the NDP and the Liberals.[10] Women in all the parties except the Conservatives are significantly less likely than men to have served on a riding association executive.

It should be noted that these findings do not imply that women are equally represented in political parties, their campaign offices, or their national conventions. Rather, once women have joined a party, they are as likely or almost as likely as their male counterparts to participate in party activities. But as long as women constitute less than half the members of political parties, they will not be proportionally represented within party bodies.

It is noteworthy that the gender differences with respect to seeking party nominations are relatively small: 6 per cent of male party members and 5 per cent of female party members report having sought a federal nomination. Given research that suggests that women's unwillingness to seek nominations is a major factor contributing to the relatively small number of women in Canadian legislatures, this finding is significant (Erickson 1991b, 1993). It suggests that once they are members of political parties, women are almost as likely to seek a nomination as men. The crucial difference is that men are more numerous among party members. In short, one part of the solution to the persistent numeric underrepresentation of women in Canadian legislatures may lie in the recruitment of more women into party membership.

Is there any evidence that women are more likely to be passive party members, as Lovenduski and Norris report in the British case (1993)? As Table 6.5 shows, women are more likely than men to report spending no time at all on party activities in an average month. When we control for party, however, we find that the difference is statistically significant only among Liberals and New Democrats. Given differences noted above with respect to patterns of recruitment into party membership, we also controlled for recruitment and found that women were significantly more likely to spend no time on party affairs only if they had been recruited by a friend, relative, or co-worker, or if they had joined on their own initiative. The largest gender difference was among women recruited into the party by relatives or friends. This indicates the existence of a subset of party members, predominantly but not exclusively female, who have been recruited into party membership by a family member, friend, or co-worker and whose activism is limited to occasionally attending nomination meetings or voting in leadership contests. This may be attributed to a lower level of interest in party affairs among these women, but it may also reflect a failure on the part of the parties to find ways to involve members recruited into the party in this way.

WOMEN'S INFLUENCE AND REPRESENTATIONAL GUARANTEES

Having found that, for the most part, women are almost as active within Canadian political parties as men, we are left with the question of how influential women believe themselves to be within their parties and whether they think that representational guarantees for women are warranted. *Influence*, particularly in a gendered context, can take on different meanings. Traditional conceptions of women's political influence held that women could affect political outcomes through their womanly influence over male family members. These men, once influenced, acted upon these opinions in the public sphere. This conception of women's influence underlay arguments against granting women the vote, on the grounds that men could cast a family vote reflecting the consensus view of family members. Feminist conceptions of women's influence differ markedly from this. Women, in the feminist view, are entitled to directly and independently exercise influence over events, people, and outcomes. The notion of influence is particularly crucial to liberal feminism, which has celebrated 'women of influence' in all walks of life. Because this latter conception of influence is the one more commonly accepted in contemporary Canadian society, our assumption was that party members would interpret the idea of influence in this way. As the results show, however, this is not uniformly the case.

The findings summarized in Table 6.6 tell us a great deal about the perceptions of party members with respect to the influence women have and should have within their party, which in turn illuminate the extent of gender-based conflicts in each of the parties. In the survey, party members were given a list of groups within their party (including women, visible minorities, ordinary members, riding associations,

Table 6.5
Party Members Reporting No Hours Spent on Federal Party Work in an Average Month, by Gender

	Women (%)	Men (%)	Difference
Party			
PC	35	31	+4
Liberal,** V=0.152[a]	27	17	+10
NDP,* V=0.264	68	44	+24
BA	61	53	+8
CA	47	43	+4
Recruited by			
Friend/relative/co-worker,* V=0.165	48	35	+13
Party or MP	35	34	+1
Candidate for nomination or leadership	36	31	+5
Own initiative or group,* V=0.122	46	38	+8
Overall,* V=0.103	45	36	+9

[a] Cramer's V is a measure of association that shows how strong a relationship between two variables is. It ranges from 0 to 1, with 1 representing perfect association. In other words, the higher the statistic, the stronger the relationship.

*Chi-square significant at $p=0.001$; **$p=0.01$

business, unions, the party leader, and pollsters) and were asked to rank how influential each group was on a scale from 1 (not at all influential) to 7 (very influential). As Table 6.6 shows, respondents in all five of the parties ranked women as relatively influential. In all the parties except the Canadian Alliance, however, male party members perceived women to be more influential than did the women themselves. This gender difference was of negligible size in the NDP and the BQ, and was the largest (and statistically significant) among Liberal party members.

There is almost no variation among parties in male party members' average ranking of women's influence in their party. In contrast to this, female party members' average rankings vary considerably by party. Women in the Liberal party give themselves the lowest influence ranking, women in the CA the highest. It is intriguing that women in the CA perceive themselves to be so influential given the absence of representational guarantees for women and of substantial numbers of women in senior party positions or the party's caucus. It is possible that the kind of influence they perceive themselves to exercise is a more traditional, behind-the-scenes influence of women over men rather than a feminist notion of influence as women's ability to affect outcomes directly. Certainly, a feminist conception of women's influence would see the relative absence of women from senior positions in the party as indicative of a lack of influence.

Party members were also asked what influence women *should have* in the party, measured on a 7-point scale. As the Table 6.6 demonstrates, the mean score on this item for women in each party is higher than the mean score for men, and women in every party believe that they should exert considerable influence over party affairs. To put this in perspective, women think women should exercise *more* influence than

Table 6.6

Perceptions of the Influence of Women Within Respondent's Party

	Gender	Influence Women Have (mean)	Influence Women Should Have (mean)	Influence Differential (mean)[a]
PC	Women	4.20	4.88	−0.79
	Men	4.32	4.61	−0.32
	Difference	−0.12	0.27**	−0.47*
Liberal	Women	4.07	5.25	−1.23
	Men	4.37	4.64	−0.29
	Difference	−0.30**	0.61*	−0.94*
NDP	Women	4.33	5.23	−0.92
	Men	4.36	4.95	−0.58
	Difference	−0.03	0.28***	−0.34**
BQ	Women	4.26	5.33	−1.11
	Men	4.32	4.91	−0.60
	Difference	−0.06	0.42**	−0.51**
CA	Women	4.51	4.73	−0.35
	Men	4.30	4.42	−0.14
	Difference	0.21***	0.31**	−0.21***

[a] The influence differential for each respondent is calculated by subtracting the score for 'influence women should have' from the score for the 'influence women have'. The figures reported the third column of Table 6.6 are means of the influence differentials for respondents in each category.

*ANOVA significant at p=.001; **p=.01; ***p=.05

pollsters, unions, business, visible minorities, and youth, but *less* influence than riding associations, ordinary members, and the party leader. For each of the five parties, we find statistically significant gender differences on this item, indicating that women's expectations of the influence they should have exceed those of men. This gap is largest in the Liberal party and smallest in the Alliance and Conservative parties. In fact, more men in the two left-leaning parties believe that women should be more influential in their parties than CA *women* believe they should be within the Alliance. This reflects the vast differences between parties in their acceptance of feminism. Feminist principles are well-entrenched in the NDP and BQ as a result of years of women's activism,[11] but are explicitly rejected by the Alliance (Young 2000).

To calculate the differential scores in Table 6.6, we subtracted the 'influence women should have' from the 'influence women have' for each respondent. The resulting figures in are averages for this variable, which essentially measures a belief that women are insufficiently influential within the party. It is noteworthy that party members of either gender believe, on average, that women should have more influence in their party. Women in the Liberal party are the most inclined to believe that they are not accorded the influence they should be. Women in the BQ and NDP trail not far behind Liberal women in this belief, and women in the Conservative party behind them. In contrast to women in the other parties, women in the Alliance appear relatively content with the extent of their influence Although men in all five parties believe, on average, that women are not as influential as they should be, the smaller magnitudes of their mean differential scores suggest that they do not consider women's lack of influence to be as substantial as do their female counterparts. In all five parties, the mean influence differential among women is greater than among men. The magnitude of this gender gap is the greatest in the Liberal party, where there is apparently a substantial gender divide on the question of women's influence. Consistent with earlier findings, the gender difference is smallest in the Alliance.

Figure 6.2 shows that female party members' attitudes toward the women's movement are important determinants of their views of women's influence within their party. In each of the five parties, women who indicate a belief that 'the feminist movement encourages women to be independent and stand up for themselves' are far more likely to perceive women as inadequately influential within their party than are women who believe that 'the feminist movement encourages women to be selfish and think only of themselves'. In other words, those who have a favourable opinion of the women's movement are more inclined to perceive a deficit in women's influence than are those who view the movement unfavourably. In this respect, feminist orientations apparently make female party members more demanding of their party as well as more inclined to perceive lack of influence.

Given the strong relationship between feminist attitudes and perceptions of women's influence within the parties, differences among parties in terms of influence differentials become easier to explain. Only 37 per cent of women in the CA indicated a positive orientation toward feminism, as opposed to 87 per cent of women in the four other parties. This suggests that the majority of members of the CA hold traditional views of gender relations and are consequently more content with the limited role women play in their party.

One of the issues that has formed a focus for women's activism within Canadian political parties since the 1970s is the increasing of the relatively small number of women nominated as candidates for and elected to the House of Commons. Research focusing on gender differences among partisan elites on these issues have found consistent gender differences but have also found that feminism is a stronger predictor of support for such measures than is gender (Tremblay and Pelletier 2000).

To determine party members' evaluations of their party's efforts (or lack thereof) to nominate female candidates, we asked them whether they thought that their party had done enough, about the right amount, or too much to nominate women. As Table 6.7 clearly demonstrates, the majority of party members in every party and of either gender believe that their party has done about the right amount in this area. Satisfaction is the greatest among CA members. The Alliance has taken no formal or informal measures to increase the number of women running under its banner and has the smallest proportion of women in its parliamentary caucus; this is contested by very few party members of either gender, suggesting that the party's approach to this issue is in no way a source of conflict within the party.

The only groups that are noticeably dissatisfied with their party's efforts to nominate women are Liberal women and, to a lesser extent, women in the BQ. The gap between Liberal men and women is particularly noteworthy. Women in the party are twice as likely as men to believe that the party is not doing enough to nominate women. Women in the Liberal party have been particularly active over

Figure 6.2
Influence Differential (Women Only) by Attitudes Toward the Feminist Movement

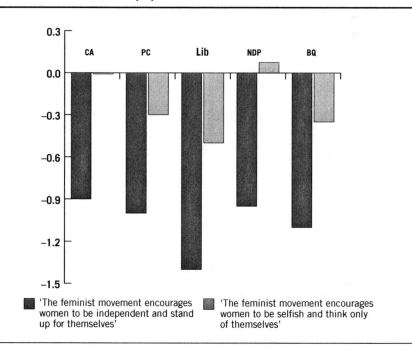

■ 'The feminist movement encourages women to be independent and stand up for themselves'

▨ 'The feminist movement encourages women to be selfish and think only of themselves'

Table 6.7
Evaluation of Parties' Efforts to Nominate Women Candidates, and Circumstances for Agreement with Leader Appointment of Candidates (*N* in parentheses)

	PC		Liberal		NDP***		BQ**		CA	
	Women	**Men**	**Women**	**Men**	**Women**	**Men**	**Women**	**Men**	**Women**	**Men**
Efforts to nominate women										
Not enough	28%***	25%***	43%*	20%*	23%***	18%***	33%**	18%**	9%	8%
	(73)	(130)	(166)	(86)	(61)	(56)	(46)	(44)	(29)	(55)
About right	72%***	72%***	54%	70%*	75%***	77%***	66%**	79%**	90%	90%
	(190)	(378)	(210)	(310)	(199)	(244)	(93)	(188)	(276)	(597)
Gone too far	1%***	4%***	3%*	11%*	2%***	5%***	1%**	3%**	1%	2%
	(2)	(21)	(13)	(49)	(4)	(16)	(1)	(7)	(2)	(16)
Agreement with appointment										
High-profile	55%***	62%***	47%***	54%***	42%	45%	45%***	58%***	44%	45%
	(139)	(330)	(172)	(234)	(104)	(136)	(49)	(128)	(131)	(299)
Interest group	69%	69%	57%**	67%**	49%	54%	52%	52%	65%	62%
	(168)	(360)	(201)	(284)	(118)	(162)	(59)	(109)	(193)	(402)
More women	43%	39%	52%**	41%**	62%*	36%*	57%	47%	24%	21%
	(106)	(201)	(184)	(172)	(155)	(105)	(65)	(98)	(68)	(134)
More visible minorities	34%	29%	42%	39%	57%*	34%*	52%	43%	19%**	12%**
	(81)	(150)	(144)	(162)	(142)	(100)	(57)	(88)	(54)	(75)

*Chi-square significant at *p*=.001; **p*=.01; ***p*=.05

the past decade in their efforts to improve the number of women nominated and elected in the party (see Young 2000). The party's response has apparently been insufficient in the eyes of many female party members, but excessive in the eyes of a substantial minority of male party members, considerably more than in any other party. Moreover, the Liberal party is the only party that has given its leader the power to appoint candidates, and the leader has used this power in the past ostensibly to appoint female candidates. Controversy over this issue relates in part to a perception that the leader claimed to be appointing female candidates in order to increase the number of women in the party's caucus when his real intent was to stop other candidacies, notably those of members of the anti-abortion group Liberals for Life (Young 2000).

On this issue, party members were asked whether they approved of their party leader appointing a candidate under certain circumstances. The circumstances identified were to nominate a high-profile candidate, to prevent an interest group from capturing the nomination, to increase the number of women candidates, and to increase the number of visible minority candidates. As Table 6.7 demonstrates, the first two reasons are considered more acceptable by most party members than are the second two.

Women in all five of the parties are, with minor exceptions, less inclined than their male counterparts to agree with the leader's appointing candidates in order to ensure that high-profile candidates run for the party or to prevent interest-group takeover. The only exceptions to this are in the Conservative party, where men and women are equally inclined to agree with leader appointment to prevent interest-group takeover, and in the CA, where women are slightly more inclined to agree with leader appointment under these same circumstances. This pattern reversed when respondents were asked whether they agreed with leader appointment in order to nominate more women and visible minorities. In all five of the parties, women were more inclined to agree with appointment to increase the demographic representativeness of candidates. The gender differences on this issue were the greatest within the NDP, though there remains substantial, but not overwhelming, support for affirmative action measures for women within the Conservatives, Liberals, and BQ. As anticipated, Alliance members of either gender were not favourably inclined toward this kind of affirmative action measure directed either toward women or visible minorities.

Taken as a whole, these findings suggest that there is considerable ongoing support, particularly among female party members, for representational guarantees for women. In all parties except the CA, female party members see themselves as lacking influence, and a substantial proportion of them support measures such as appointing female candidates. Intriguingly, the female party members who are the most content with the status quo are NDP and CA women. These two parties represent opposite ends of the spectrum in their approaches to women's participation in party affairs, with the NDP activist in its efforts to include women in party elites and the CA explicitly rejecting such efforts. These disparate approaches are apparently in tune with the very different ideological predispositions of women in each party. Where discontent appears to be greatest is in the Liberal party, which has adopted some measures to accommodate women's participation but has apparently not gone far enough to satisfy its female members—but too far for many of its male members.

Beyond these differences between parties, we also find differences between men and women. Male party members perceive women to be more influential than the women themselves do, and they are apparently not as concerned about this perceived lack of influence. Following from this, men are less inclined to support representational guarantees for women. The magnitude of all these gender differences varies by party, and the pattern of variation is consistent across items. As we might expect, gender roles are least contested in the Alliance, and tend not to be hotly contested in the NDP (although NDP women and men differ substantially on the question of appointing women candidates). Where gender roles appear to be most hotly contested is in the Liberal party.

These findings regarding women's influence in the parties and attitudes toward representational guarantees present a portrait of very different levels of gender-based conflict within the parties. In the CA, consensus reigns, as women and men apparently share similar beliefs with respect to the role of women. These party members do not, for the most part, contest their party's ideological stance that gender and other ascriptive characteristics should not be acknowledged by party or public policy. In the NDP, conflicts over women's participation in the party have apparently subsided as most party members of either gender have come to accept feminist arguments regarding the role of women in party affairs (see also Archer and Whitehorn 1997). This relative consensus is the legacy of years of women's activism on these issues, and also reflects the left's acceptance of feminist tenets. In the Liberal party, and to a much lesser extent the Conservatives and the Bloc, there remains gender-based conflict as the issues that have been resolved within the NDP continue to cause conflict. It is not coincidental that these conflicts remain greatest in the parties with the least coherent ideological stances. Because the Liberal party is ideologically flexible, there is space within the party to accommodate both feminist and their critics, and this is reflected in the ongoing gender differences found in this research.

CONCLUSION

The data presented in this chapter suggest that women have made significant progress with respect to their involvement in party politics over the past 30 years. Although they remain somewhat less inclined than men to join political parties, women are apparently almost as active as men in all levels of party activity. That said, we cannot overlook the apparent reluctance of women to join political parties and their greater inclination to wait to be asked to join rather than joining on their own initiative. These patterns raise the possibility that political parties committed to women's equal involvement should be recruiting female members more actively.

Despite the pattern of general equality with respect to women's involvement in all levels of party activity, female party members still see themselves as insufficiently influential and, with the exception of women in the CA, are generally supportive of measures to increase their influence and the number of women holding elected office. That the women directly involved in party affairs perceive this influence deficit and support measures to remedy it suggests that the parties should not rush to reverse representational guarantees for women. Apparently, these measures have not outlived their utility in the eyes of women active in the parties.

The findings of this study illustrate the considerable diversity of opinion among Canadian women involved in electoral politics. These women range from CA members satisfied with traditional indirect influence to members of other parties who continue to demand direct influence and representation. Arguably, democracy is well served when both points of view can be accommodated within the party system.

Finally, we return to the question of whether the participation of women in Canadian political parties has achieved the promise of liberal democracy. Certainly, evidence that barriers to women's participation are declining and that women's participation is as extensive as men's leads us to conclude that we are moving in the direction of fulfilling that promise. However, there remain some reasons for caution. That young women are not joining political parties in large numbers and that there are ongoing expressions of discontent with the influence of women in party politics remind us that the gains women have won are reversible, and that equal participation requires considerable vigilance.

NOTES

1. This research was made possible by a standard research grant from the Social Sciences and Humanities Research Council of Canada. Research and other assistance was provided by Patrick Fournier, Diane Roussel, Anamitra Deb, Pam Mitchell, Kevin Snedker, Tracey Raney, Elizabeth Moore, Charlie Gray, and James Miller. We thank the staff of the national offices of the five political parties and the members of the parties who took the time to complete the survey for their invaluable assistance. The authors wish to thank Manon Tremblay and Lynda Erickson for helpful comments on earlier versions of this chapter.

2. The exception to this is studies of convention delegates; see Brodie (1988) and Archer and Whitehorn (1997).

3. The regional sampling process varied by party. For details regarding this, please contact the authors. For all the parties except the Liberals and the BQ, a regional weighting variable was created to correct for sampling procedures. Accurate regional membership breakdown was not available for the Liberal party, and regional weighting was not relevant for the BQ as its membership is restricted to Quebec.

4. A total of 241 surveys were returned as undeliverable. This number was subtracted from the number of surveys sent when calculating the response rate. The response rate by party was PC, 44 per cent; CA, 43 per cent; BQ, 34 per cent; Liberal, 32 per cent; NDP, 29 per cent. To increase the response rate, each survey mailed was followed approximately one week later by a reminder card with contact information for the researchers.

5. The Canadian Alliance did have a leadership contest beginning in May 2000, but the list from which the sample was drawn was closed prior to the beginning of that leadership contest. This ensured that none of the members recruited by leadership candidates were included in the survey.

6. Howe and Northrup found that, when asked which is a more effective way to work for change, joining a political party or an interest group, 56 per cent of men, as compared to 63 per cent of women, chose an interest group (2000: 95).

7. There were gender differences on other patterns of recruitment, but they were smaller and inconsistent across party.

8. Chi-square significant at $p=.01$.

9. Riding association secretary was not separated out from this, so it is impossible to compare directly with Bashevkin or Carty.

10. Women in the Liberal party are less likely than men to have contributed funds to or raised funds for the party. Women in the NDP are less likely to have attended a national policy convention, raised funds for the party, displayed an election sign or worn a button, or attended a riding association meeting; chi-square significant at $p=.05$ or less.

11. There is little evidence of such activism in the Bloc, but an extensive history of women's activism in the Parti Québécois, which is closely affiliated with the Bloc.

Chapter Seven

Political Parties and Female Candidates: Is There Resistance in New Brunswick?

SONIA PITRE

INTRODUCTION

Whether we embrace a descriptive approach to representation, calling for more women in the different political institutions, or a substantive approach, demanding that women's issues, interests, and needs receive equal attention on the political agenda, important obstacles continue to prevent our goals from being achieved. In Canada in the November 2000 federal election, women won 62 of the 301 seats in the House of Commons (20.6 per cent), the same proportion as in 1997: at only one-fifth of all elected MPs, female representation already faces stagnation. In New Brunswick, following the 1999 election, women held 18.2 per cent (10/55) of Legislative Assembly seats, which must nonetheless be considered progress since the proportion of female MLAs had dropped slightly from 17.6 per cent to 16.4 per cent between 1991 and 1995.[1] These numbers serve as evidence that there are still important barriers limiting half of the population's access to electoral politics.

Informal discrimination from the political system as an obstacle to women's representation has been the focus of many recent studies (see Caul 1999; Erickson 1997b; Norris, ed. 1997; Rule 1994a, 1994b; Tremblay 1999; Tremblay and Pelletier 2001). This 'systemic discrimination', argue Manon Tremblay and Réjean Pelletier (1995), can arise from the rules of the electoral game as well as from within political parties. In the same vein, Pippa Norris and Joni Lovenduski (1995) maintain that parties can create important obstacles to women's political integration. However, the role of political parties in women's underrepresentation is a subject that has yet to be analyzed in New Brunswick. This paper assesses whether formal party characteristics may serve as indicators of a party's efforts to recruit and select female candidates in the context of New Brunswick provincial politics.

The first part of the recruitment process is the distinguishing of political aspirants from the large pool of those eligible for candidacy (Norris and Lovenduski 1995). This process consists of identifying people in the greater population or among party activists who may be interested in running or could be convinced to run for office. The second part, the selection process, is the recruitment of the candidates from the smaller pool of aspirants. It 'determines which citizens from the pool of those recruited into political activity are deemed to be qualified for a political position and put up as candidates' (United Nations, Centre for Social Development and Humanitarian Affairs 1992: 40).[2] In fact, this screening process not only determines which names will get on the ballot, but also who will have legislative power and who will form the government.

Parties play a crucial role in the recruitment process because the elites in charge must not only motivate aspirants to run, but also provide those who become candidates with the necessary resources. Furthermore, without the support of the party organization and the selectorate it is difficult—if not impossible—to make it to the political scene (L. Young 1994, 2000). Some studies have suggested that parties simply do not encourage women to run (Nelson and Chowdhury 1994; Norris 1997b). What, then, motivates political parties to seek female candidates?

While the nature of the electoral system may influence parties' propensity to retain female candidates or not (Matland 1995; Rule 2001; Rule and Norris 1992; for Canada, see Matland and Studlar 1996; L. Young 1994), Caul (1999) believes that party characteristics—that is, party structure, party ideology, female party militancy,[3] and party rules—are better indicators of their efforts to recruit and select women as candidates.

FORMAL PARTY CHARACTERISTICS

Party Organization

According to Miki Caul's model (1999), three variables of party organization can influence women's representation: party centralization, institutionalization of the recruitment process, and the nature of candidate selection. She argues that the centralization of power within a party can influence the proportion of female candidates. In a highly centralized party, the leader can create opportunities for women and respond to requests for greater representation (Matland and Studlar 1996)—it is all just a matter of having the will to do so. It is also easier to hold centralized parties accountable for women's political integration (Caul 1999). This variable will be analyzed according to the position of the party leader and the frequency of party congresses.[4]

As for the recruitment mechanisms, the more rule-oriented the party is, the more institutionalized, or regulated, the recruitment process will be (Norris and Lovenduski 1995). Institutionalization actually prevents arbitrary dismissal of candidates in favour of others. This said, people who seek nomination in weakly institutionalized parties may rely more heavily on personal political capital to be recruited, which may disadvantage women and other categories of people traditionally excluded from the political sphere (Guadagnini 1993; see also Darcy, Welch, and Clark 1994). This leads to the following hypothesis: the more institutionalized the recruitment process, the higher the proportion of female candidates. In order to test this hypothesis, the questions presented by Gideon Rahat and Reuven Hazan (2001) have been modified and applied to the recruitment of candidates. They now read as follows: Who can be recruited (eligibility)? Who recruits candidates (the recruiters)? How are candidates nominated (mechanisms and criteria used)?

Caul (1999) also looks at the level of the nomination process, which Rahat and Hazan (2001) approach by asking who can be selected, where the candidates are selected, and how candidates are nominated.[5] Although some may be inclined to believe that localized nominations are more favourable to female candidates because of women's greater community involvement, Richard Matland and Donley Studlar (1996) argue that a more centralized process may increase the number of female candidates and offer more structured opportunities for women to climb the internal party hierarchy (see also Czudnowski 1975). However, in Canada federally and in New Brunswick, nomination practices are very decentralized (Matland and Studlar 1996; Sayers 1998). This leads to the following hypothesis: the more centralized the nomination process, the higher the proportion of female candidates.

Party Ideology

Caul (1999) identifies party ideology as an indicator of openness to women. Although right-wing parties may include female candidates because they view women as 'an important societal group—as mothers, as workers, as religious adherents', left-wing parties, with a more egalitarian standpoint, can be expected to have better gender representation (Beckwith 1992: 10; see also Beckwith 1986; Young 2000). Matland (1995) found that left-of-centre parties in Norway had a greater proportion of female candidates than parties with a right-wing inclination, although one could also argue that this may be the result of Norway's proportional representation system. Still, Caul (1999) argues that a mere look at the coming to power of left-wing parties shows how they coincide with the increase of elected women. In Canada, the Ontario experience lends credence to this assertion. The election of the Ontario NDP to power in 1990 significantly increased the proportion of women in the provincial Parliament from 15 per cent to 22 per cent, a proportion that was brought back to 15 per cent with the Conservative victory of 1995 (Burt and Lorenzin 1997). Given this, a second hypothesis could be formulated: left-wing parties recruit more female candidates than right-wing parties.

Party Rules

Caul (1999) suggests that by adopting specific rules or measures, parties could significantly increase the number of female party nominations (see also Rule 2001; L. Young 1994). These initiatives, such as quotas or target numbers, are also important indicators of parties' eagerness to solve the problem of women's underrepresentation. According to Matland (1995), gender quotas established by the Norwegian Labour party in 1983 increased the proportion of female party nominations from 33 per cent in 1981 to 51 per cent by 1989. In Canada, the same could be said about the NDP, which is not only the most obvious defender of gender representation but also had the highest proportion of female candidates in the 2000 federal election (Young 2000).

Caul (1999) also maintains that the implementation of formal rules to increase women's representation may be the result of party organization and party ideology (see also Erickson 1997b; Tremblay and Pelletier 2000, 2001): while party organization can influence a party's ability to enforce rules for gender or minority representation, whether it chooses to do so or not is a product of its ideology. Lovenduski and Norris (1993) also believe that a left-wing party is more likely to see the need to intervene in order to help underrepresented groups than is a right-wing party, which might see special measures as a form of discrimination (see also Tremblay, Pelletier, and Pitre, forthcoming; Young 2000). In the same vein, I found that while NDP constituency elites in New Brunswick believed that their party should implement special measures for marginalized groups, Conservatives were diametrically opposed (Pitre, forthcoming). This suggests a third hypothesis: parties that have adopted rules to increase female representation have a higher proportion of female candidates.

METHODOLOGY

This study focuses on the three official parties in New Brunswick: the Progressive Conservative party, the Liberal party, and the New Democratic Party. Inspired by Caul's causal model, the main purpose of the analysis was to look at how formal party characteristics determine parties' openness to women's political representation, if at all. However, Caul's analytical framework refers to an aggregate of quantitative data that was not available in the context of New Brunswick. On the other hand, Rahat and Hazan's (2001) framework, with its qualitative approach, allowed an in-depth analysis of the candidate recruitment and selection process using the available data. The goal was to assess how formal party characteristics influence women's representation. Data has been collected using document analysis and interviews: the analysis of party documents focused on party rules and procedures in preparation for the 1999 New Brunswick election, and 42 semi-directed interviews were conducted with top party officers, provincial party organizers, and provincial and constituency party elites.

FEMALE REPRESENTATION IN NEW BRUNSWICK

Women's entry to New Brunswick's political institutions has been a long time coming, and women's political representation there remains among the lowest in Canada (Desserud 1997). While the proportion of elected women went up 6.1 percentage points between 1987 and 1999, this increase has not been constant. In 1987, a Liberal avalanche swept all of the province's 58 seats and led to the election of all of the party's 7 female candidates, allowing the proportion of women at the legislature to double to past the 10 per cent threshold—from 6.9 per cent in 1982 to 12.1 per cent. Substantial party differences emerge regarding the percentage of female candidates and elected representatives (see Table 7.1, pp. 114–15).

Although the first woman elected in New Brunswick (in 1967) was a Conservative, PC women were absent from the Legislative Assembly between 1987 and 1995. In 1999, however, 8 of the 10 female MLAs elected to the legislature ran and won under the PC banner; 4 of them managed a feat of strength by dethroning Liberal incumbents. Liberal women, on the other hand, have had better success getting elected; in 1999, however, only 1 of 10 Liberal women was elected. In contrast, while the NDP has always had the highest percentage of female candidates, the party has had a harder time getting women elected (or any candidate, for that matter). Only 1 NDP candidate has been elected since 1991: Elizabeth Weir, the party leader.

THE ROLE OF PARTY CHARACTERISTICS

Party Organization
The first aim was to establish whether the centralization of power within the party or control over decision making could influence the number of women running for office. To do so, the position of the party leader and the frequency of party congresses have been analyzed.

The New Brunswick Conservative party had the most frequent change in leadership: six leaders since 1987. In contrast, the NDP had only two leaders during the same period. The Liberals, for their part, had four leaders between 1987 and 2001. Second, the Conservatives met on an annual basis, while the NDP and the Liberals held one party convention every other year.

Following Jan-Erik Lane and Svante Ersson's assumption concerning party leadership and party conventions (1991), these indicators when combined allow us to place the three parties on a continuum from the most centralized, the NDP—with its leadership concentration and biennial conventions—to the least centralized, the Conservative party—with its frequent leadership changes and annual meetings. The Liberals appear somewhere in the middle with a moderately frequent change in leadership and biennial conventions. The fact that the Conservatives ranked as the most decentralized is most likely not a coincidence. Jonathan Hopkin argues that parties that have experienced electoral decline or defeat may try to reform their organization by decentralizing the decision-making process as a way of attracting new or fleeing members (2001; see also Katz 2001).

Finally, supporting Caul's argument (1999), the most centralized party, the NDP, had the most female candidates, followed by the Liberals, then the Conservatives— the least centralized party, with the smallest slate of women running for office. This said, the findings do not support Caul's assumptions regarding party centralization and the proportion of elected women: the most centralized party, the NDP, did not have the most elected female MLAs—the Liberals did. As was previously noted, the latter enjoyed a strong majority from 1987 until 1999. Then again, most Liberal candidates, male or female, have experienced electoral success, lending credence to Pelletier and Tremblay's (1992) assertion that the advent of women to power may be a question of party competitiveness, rather than women's serving as token candidates, as argued by Alfred Hunter and Margaret Denton (1984). However, the Liberal party's high level of competitiveness, combined with its weak proportion of female candidates and its high incumbency rate, gives strength to Jorgens Rasmussen's (1983) and Elizabeth Vallance's (1984) arguments that parties are less likely to risk selecting women in highly competitive ridings when the number of seats up for grabs is limited.

Table 7.1

Representation of Women Among Candidates and Elected MLAs, New Brunswick

	Liberal		PC	
	Candidates	**Elected**	**Candidates**	**Elected**
1987	7/58	7/58	6/58	–
1991	10/58	9/46	7/58	0/3
1995	8/55	8/48	5/55	0/6
1999	8/55	1/10	10/55	8/44

SOURCE: Report of the Chief Electoral Officer, available at <www.gnb.ca/elections/publications-e.asp#prov>.

[a] The number of female candidates does not include independent female candidates or candidates from the Natural Law party, which is not an official party in New Brunswick; [b] Pierrette Ringuette-Maltais left the provincial scene shortly after her election to run federally.

Institutionalization of the Recruitment Process

Using Rahat and Hazan's (2001) analytical framework, the aim was to test the level of institutionalization of the recruitment process in relation to the proportion of female candidates, that is, to see how rule-oriented the recruitment of candidates is.

Eligibility

The results show that, in theory at least, the New Brunswick Elections Act, not political parties, regulates eligibility to run: any person who has the right to vote can become a candidate. New Brunswick thus has a very inclusive recruitment process.[6] This suggests that, in theory, there are no limitations that could affect the 'size and nature of the potential candidate pool' (Rahat and Hazan 2001: 298).[7] However, because the rules of eligibility stem from electoral law and not from the political parties, eligibility was not retained as an indicator of the level of institutionalization of the recruitment process. Nonetheless, as will be addressed further, political parties insist that aspiring candidates become party members before their nomination meetings.

The Recruiters[8]

The Conservative party has made some attempts to institutionalize the process of candidate recruitment. PC recruitment efforts were led at two levels: provincially, by the appointed Provincial Search Committee (PSC), and at the constituency level, by Local Search Committees (LSCs) made up of appointed constituency party executives or other party activists.[9] With provincial and local recruiters, the PC candidate recruitment may be considered a multi-layered process. The LSCs seem to qualify as exclusive selected party agencies, while the PSC qualifies as a relatively exclusive non-selected party agency.[10]

Beyond certain similarities, the Liberal recruitment process seems much more informal and less rule-oriented. This may be due to the party's overwhelming success between 1987 and 1995, with people manifesting their interest in running ahead of time and making candidate recruitment that much easier. Yet a very informal Campaign Readiness Committee had been put together. This committee, appointed by the party leader or his entourage, was mandated to coordinate the provincial campaign and help LSCs identify prospective candidates. However,

Table 7.1 (continued)

Representation of Women Among Candidates and Elected MLAS, New Brunswick

	NDP		Confederation of Regions		Total	
	Candidates	Elected	Candidates	Elected	Candidates[a]	Elected
1987	17/58	–	–	–	30/174	7/58
1991	26/58	1/1	9/48	1/8	52/222	11/58[b]
1995	20/55	1/1	5/36	–	38/201	9/55
1999	28/55	1/1	1/18	–	47/183	10/55

it must be added that during the 1999 provincial campaign, the Liberal party did very little recruitment. Out of 55 ridings, 35 had returning Liberal MLAs and 1 had a returning candidate, leaving only 19 (34.5 per cent) candidacies open. This supports authors who argue that the incumbency effect has an impact on the recruitment of candidates (e.g., Carty and Erickson 1991; Krashinsky and Milne 1985, 1986; Sayers 1998). In all, LSCs were established in very few ridings. Liberal recruiters are also members of a multi-layered process: LSCs should also be ranked as exclusive selected party agencies and the PSC as a relatively exclusive non-selected party agency.

The NDP functions somewhat differently. A document entitled *Guidelines for the Candidate Search Committees* (New Brunswick NDP 1998) explained how to recruit candidates, and who and what was involved in the process. First, a PSC was established. In terms of participation restrictions, the guidelines were slightly more rule-oriented than those of the other two parties, ordering that this committee be co-chaired by members of both linguistic communities and both genders. The committee's role was to coordinate recruitment efforts at the provincial level and to help local and regional recruiters with their searches. Interestingly, representation guidelines for the traditionally excluded groups were also established for the party's Local and Regional Search Committees: the committees—provincial, local, or regional— were to have an equal number of representatives from both genders, from the labour movement, and from youths, as well as representatives who would reflect both regional and linguistic differences. The NDP made a conscious effort to include traditionally marginalized groups, including women, which could in fact influence women's political integration.

According to Tremblay and Pelletier (2001), depending on the party at hand, more women constituency party presidents of federal parties can influence the proportion of women who get recruited. This also follows Caul's (1999) argument concerning the influence of female party elites on women's political representation. On Rahat and Hazan's continuum, these representation guidelines seem to give the NDP a slightly more inclusive—or less exclusive—tendency at both the local and provincial levels. Essentially, when compared to the other two parties, the NDP also has a multi-layered process and should be ranked, locally, as a less exclusive selected party agency and, provincially, as a less exclusive non-selected party agency. In spite of their efforts to include traditionally excluded people, the relative size of these committees still makes them exclusive.

Mechanisms for Candidate Selection

Although all eligible voters are also eligible candidates in theory, in practice not all citizens are approached. The next question touched on how candidates are recruited. That is, what are the mechanisms used and the criteria according to which candidates have been recruited?

According to the PC interviewees, many aspiring PC candidates came forward by themselves for the 1999 provincial election, which was a welcome change from the 1991 and 1995 elections, when the party's general performance was at its lowest. This lends credence to Sayers's (1999) argument that recruitment is much easier when parties have a reasonable chance of being elected. In the remaining ridings, a very informal process was used. Provincial and local elites both favoured a word-of-mouth approach to recruitment: either they were informed by party members of possible candidates or they approached people they wanted on their campaign team. As for the party's criteria, to borrow from Rahat and Hazan (2001), the process seemed very inclusive: there were no specific rules or guidelines concerning who the potential candidates could be. The PC watchword was to look for the 'winning candidate' and not to overlook anybody—card-holding member or not. As was to be expected, the party had no goals or requirements in terms of gender or minority representation, nor any way of ensuring that an actual and effective candidate search had been conducted. In large, the Conservatives' actual candidate recruitment is inclusive but very informal and not at all institutionalized.

The Liberal recruitment mechanisms were very similar. Word of mouth was also the most common strategy. However, as mentioned previously, little recruitment was done during the 1999 campaign. As some provincial interviewees have pointed out, not only were there only 19 open seats, but a handful of prominent community figures (7, to be precise) had manifested their intentions to run under the Liberal banner, thus leaving just 12 seats (21.8 per cent) open for aspiring Liberal candidates. As with the Conservative party, there were no set guidelines or criteria for the prospective candidates. While almost anyone could be seen as a potential candidate, party member or not, the best candidate was the so-called star candidate: a well-known, well-respected leader in the community, 'a name' that people could easily recognize. The Liberals' mechanisms and criteria, then, were also inclusive and not at all institutionalized.

The NDP adopted a more institutionalized approach, seeking consistency throughout the province. The party's campaign document even ordered that the recruitment process remain 'opened, democratic, fair and done diligently' (NDP 1998: 3). Although some candidates came forward by themselves, the party relied heavily on recruitment of prospective candidates. This supports Sayers's (1999) argument concerning the role of party competitiveness in the recruitment of candidates. Besides word of mouth, the party used a more structured approach of going through lists of local public figures—social, community, and labour activists, local politicians, and so on. The party also had somewhat different criteria: while the NDP preferred to look among card-holding members and long-time party activists, as is usually the case with mass parties (Sayers 1999), it also counted on non-members who embraced the party's philosophy. Like the other two parties, the

NDP's approach is not to overlook anybody, although belief in the party's principles remains essential. If local NDP candidates could not be found, the PSC tried to find someone from another part of the province, as did the Liberal and Conservative parties. In sum, the NDP's mechanisms and criteria make the recruitment process much more institutionalized than the PCs' or the Liberals'. Furthermore, the fact that NDP candidates are expected to embrace party principles may also make the party's criteria seem slightly less inclusive.

While recruitment for the NB parties is mostly led at the grassroots level, then, the parties have made some efforts to centralize the process. Nonetheless, the recruitment of candidates remains largely informal and not very rule-oriented, although interesting party variations arise.

So, how does this translate in terms of female representation? The findings seem to lend credence to Caul's (1999) argument that the more institutionalized the recruitment process, the higher the level of female representation, at least as far as the number of candidates is concerned. In fact, a clear continuum seems to emerge: in 1999, the most institutionalized party, the NDP, also had the most women running for office (see Table 7.1, pp. 114–15). However, one could argue that this may be due to the party's ideological inclination or its lack of electoral success rather than the level of institutionalization of the party's recruitment process—although these may not be mutually exclusive. In contrast, the least institutionalized, the Liberal party, also had the fewest female candidates, of whom only three were not incumbents. The Conservatives appeared between the two. Interestingly, the Conservatives also got the most women elected in 1999, which may be attributed to general turnover (Krashinsky and Milne 1985, 1986; Young 1994).

The Selection Process
Who Can Be Selected

While almost all adults living in New Brunswick could be approached to run, becoming a candidate through a nomination meeting is slightly more restrictive.[11] The results suggest that the three New Brunswick party constitutions have the same participation restrictions in regards to candidacy: in order to run for nomination, individuals must be members in good standing of the party. Although this would qualify according to Rahat and Hazan (2001) as an inclusive condition, some party variations do emerge in terms of the membership requirements, that is, the membership dues and the minimum party membership period before the nomination convention.

The Conservative party had the shortest waiting period, of at least 72 hours; the Liberals' minimum waiting period was anywhere between 72 hours and 30 days, depending on the local party constitution; and the NDP's minimum membership period was set at 30 days before the nomination convention, which made the integration of new members and the search for candidates much more difficult. However, it must be noted that at the 2001 NDP biennial convention, the party made an effort to recruit new blood by reducing the minimum membership period to 14 days before the nomination meeting. According to Lane and Ersson (1991), short membership periods facilitate the integration of new members. As for membership dues, the Conservatives and the NDP ask for a five-dollar donation, while the Liberals prefers free membership cards; all can be considered very inclusive.

The Selectorate

As a general rule, to run for nomination a person must be able to vote for his or her own nomination. In other words, membership requirements established for the selectorate are exactly those for candidacy: a minimum membership period and membership fees, which vary according to the party. The classification on the inclusive–exclusive continuum thus remains the same: although all three are at the inclusive end of the axis, the Conservative party comes out as the most inclusive, followed by the Liberals, and then the NDP, which appears slightly less inclusive.[12]

Nature of the Nomination Process

The data for the three parties show similarities in where and how candidates are selected and how this influences women's representation. First, the selection process is led at the constituency level. Grassroots members are called upon to nominate the candidate they believe is the best person for the job (one member, one vote). Nominations are made at nomination meetings using a multi-round majoritarian voting system.[13] However, if there is only one person running, she or he will be nominated by acclamation. Although this may seem like a locally based procedure, some efforts have been made to centralize the process, and party variations have been observed.

While nomination meetings are held locally and organized by the constituency party executives, the time, date, and location of these meetings are to be determined in consultation with the Provincial Council, apparently for strategic reasons. This may, nonetheless, be perceived as an attempt for greater central control over the process. In fact, the process appears much more structured than that for the recruitment of candidates. In the Conservative party, additional attempts to centralize the nomination have been made: the party has detailed provincial guidelines concerning the roles and responsibilities of the riding associations, the campaign readiness chairs, and the provincial headquarters in the nomination process. The Liberals, on the other hand, barely mention the selection process in their constitution and, as previously outlined, do not have a document to assist local executives, thus suggesting a more informal and decentralized process. This may also be due to the party's high incumbency rate. The NDP has made efforts to centralize the nomination process. The party's constitution states that nomination meetings are to be held and organized locally by the constituency party executives, except where circumstances prevent it, in which case the provincial executive will organize the meeting. Furthermore, as in the Conservative party but less explicitly, the NDP's campaign document also seeks provincial consistency by giving important guidelines to riding executives who have been mandated to organize the conventions.

Stages in the Nomination Process

Beyond these few attempts to centralize the process by implementing some provincial party guidelines, there is another level to the nomination process: the party leader. All three party constitutions state that if constituency party executives are unable to find a candidate, the leader will appoint one. The leader is also involved in the signing of the candidate's papers, one of two requirements of the New Brunswick Elections Act. First, the law requires that every candidate obtain at least 25 signatures from eligible voters to secure their nomination. Second, as at the federal level, the party leader's signature is needed to run as a member of the team. In other words, the leader has a right of veto over who may run for the party. This is a way of ensuring some central control over the process. However, in reality, the option of not signing a selected candidate's papers is very seldom exercised. First, alternatives such as 'political bullying' or talking people out of running have been used to escape the negative media attention that could come out of the refusal to certify someone's papers. Second, in the case of an unwanted aspiring candidate, the leader, with the help of the local party organization, may rally behind another candidate for the nomination. As some interviewees have explained, although the leader would not publicly support one candidate over another, whom the leader is endorsing is usually quite obvious.

The fact that there are two selectorate levels (the grassroots and the party leader) makes the selection of candidates a multi-stage process. Rahat and Hazan argue that even if the veto is 'activated only on rare occasions, one must still consider the impact of this agency' over the outcome (2001: 303). It could be argued that since no provincial party leader in New Brunswick has ever officially refused to certify a candidate's papers, the veto has no impact on candidate selection. However, the point must be made that the other informal strategies employed to avoid the application of the veto right may have a dissuasive effect and may very well affect women's representation in the province. One line of reasoning would suggest that the mere possibility of the veto's use is evidence enough of a very centralized multi-stage process.

While the Conservative party seemed to have a slightly more centralized and regulated nomination process than the two other parties, it did not have the highest proportion of female candidates. This contradicts Caul's argument concerning the concentration of nomination process as an indicator of higher female representation (1999); other elements must be at work. It also implies that the third hypothesis—that the more centralized the nomination process, the higher the proportion of female candidates—could not be verified. On the other hand, the Conservatives did manage to get the most women elected in 1999. This can be attributed to two factors: first, as Pelletier and Tremblay (1992) argue, women's election to office is less about women in lost-cause ridings than about the party's level of competitiveness; second, as mentioned by Don Desserud (1997), some advancements concerning women's representation can be attributed to a party's unexpected success in what were thought to be uncompetitive ridings where female candidates happen to be running. This supports Studlar and Matland's (1996) argument that electoral volatility is favourable to female representation.[14]

Party Ideology

Do left-wing parties recruit more female candidates than right-wing parties? Table 7.1 (pp. 114–15) shows that between 1987 and 1999, the NDP had the highest proportion of women running for office, followed by the Liberals and then the Conservatives. In 1999, the Conservatives, who always had the smallest slate of female candidates, bumped the Liberals out of second place. One could only suggest, on the one hand, that this may be due to a reluctance on the part of the local Liberal elites to recruit and select female candidates where there were no incumbents running or, on the other, that Conservative elites were less reluctant to do so, possibly because they did not expect they could win. The NDP had the highest proportion of female candidacies. The data also show a clear difference between parties in the change in the proportion of female candidates: the NDP had the greatest increase, the Conservatives were second, and the Liberals were last.

From an ideological standpoint, the NDP is a left-of-centre party, the Conservative party the farthest right, and the Liberal party somewhere between the two, near the centre of the continuum. Party ideology was also assessed for this study by provincial party elites' self-placement on a left–right scale. The resulting data seem to lend credence to Caul's (1999) argument that left-wing parties have better female representation, at least as far as the proportion of women candidates is concerned (see also Beckwith 1992; Matland and Studlar 1996). The NDP, which ranked farthest left on the ideological spectrum, also had the most women running for office in 1999—and since 1987, for that matter. In contrast, the party farthest right, the Conservative party, has always had the smallest slate of female candidates—except in 1999—and the Liberals could be found somewhere between the two. However, in 1999, only two female candidates separated these last two. Apart from the incumbency effect and the level of competitiveness, one could suggest that this minimal variation may be due to the very little ideological difference between the province's two traditional parties (Arscott 1997; Desserud 1997; Forbes 1978; Kenny 1999; Pitre, forthcoming; Thorburn 1961).

Table 7.1 (pp. 114–15) also shows, however, that while the NDP has had the highest proportion of female candidates, it has had more difficulty getting women elected. Notwithstanding the fact that the number of women involved make statistically significant observations impossible, one can at least make the observation that the results do not support Caul's idea that the more left-wing parties elect more women to office (1999), at least not in New Brunswick. The results suggest that women's electoral success is more a question of the party's competitiveness than of party ideology as such. However, one thing is certain, if women are not being nominated they certainly cannot be elected, and that goes for all parties.

Party Rules

There is very little to be said about the influence of party rules on the proportion of female candidates because only one party has adopted such guidelines: the NDP. Their campaign document orders that the process be conducted in such a way to make 'potential candidates from all sectors of society, including women, aboriginal, visible minorities, handicapped people, and youths, stand out' (NDP 1998: 3). As for the other parties, even though Conservative and Liberal provincial elites asserted their parties' goals in terms of female representation, in reality no such goals can be read in any of their party documents. Essentially, gender representation is neither an institutionalized party guideline nor an official goal for either the Conservatives or the Liberals.[15]

The fact that the NDP is the only party to have these rules and that it also has the greatest proportion of female candidates gives credence to Caul's argument (1999) and thus allows the verification of the hypothesis (see also Rule 2001). The same observation applies on the federal scene, where the NDP has similar rules and the largest slate of female candidates (see Young 1994, 2000). Furthermore, this also supports the idea that left-wing parties are more likely to feel the need to help marginalized groups than right-wing parties (Lovenduski and Norris 1993; Tremblay, Pelletier, and Pitre, forthcoming; Young 2000), which might see special measures as a form of discrimination.

CONCLUSION

In Richard Katz's words, 'a party's candidates in large measure define and constitute its public face in elections. Collectively, they manifest the democratic, geographic, and ideological dimensions of the party. They articulate and interpret the party's record from the past and its program and promises for the future' (2001: 278). If Katz's conception of political parties is accurate, then, the public face of New Brunswick parties could be described as mostly, if not exclusively, male. As for the parties' programs and promises for the future, women are also conspicuous by their absence, particularly from the Liberal and the Conservative parties.

Inspired by Caul's causal model (1999) and using most of Rahat and Hazan's analytical framework (2001), this study focused on formal party characteristics. It examined party structure, rules, procedures, and ideology as possible indicators of parties' efforts to recruit female candidates. Five hypotheses have been tested and all were confirmed, except one. Contrary to Caul's assumption, the most centralized nomination process did not have the highest proportion of female candidates: while the Conservative party appeared to have the most centralized nomination process, it did not have the highest proportion of female candidates. However, the party did manage to get the most women elected following the 1999 provincial election, supporting Matland and Studlar's argument that legislative turnover is a significant factor in women's political integration (1996). As for the rest of the hypotheses, the NDP—the most centralized party, the party with the most institutionalized recruitment process, the most left-wing ideology, and the only one to have special rules to increase female representation—was also the party with the highest proportion of female candidates. However, the results did not seem to apply to the number of women elected, which also supports Pelletier and Tremblay's claim that women are not necessarily candidates in 'lost cause' ridings, but that their election depends on the party's level of competitiveness (1992; Tremblay and Pelletier 2001). Furthermore, the Liberals' high incumbency rate and weak proportion of female candidates may also support Rasmussen's (1981, 1983) and Vallance's (1984) arguments that when the number of open seats is limited, parties are less likely to select women to run for office.

In light of these results, could it be argued that there is resistance in New Brunswick parties as far as the recruitment of female candidates is concerned? The answer must be qualified. In the case of the NDP, the answer is no. The answer is not so clear for the Conservatives and the Liberals. To borrow from Caul (1999), the implementation of formal rules to increase women's representation is the result of the party organization and party ideology. While the party's organization may influence its ability to enforce such guidelines, the actual will to do so is a result of party ideology. The problem of the weak proportion of female candidates in the Conservative and Liberal parties may be a question less of resistance to female candidates as such than of the willingness to do something about it. It may lie with the party elites' false perception that the recruitment and selection of candidates is an entirely neutral process, which is not the case. As Susan Carroll argues, the candidate recruitment process is more unfavourable toward women not for sexist reasons, but because of the rules of the game: 'Barriers in the existing political opportunity structure work to keep outsiders out, regardless of gender, and to perpetuate the power of those who hold political positions. Since those who are in power are disproportionately men, the present structure of political opportunity helps to maintain the power of those men' (1994: 158–9). This said, could the recruiters, who are mostly men, even unconsciously recruit male candidates because traditional 'male' characteristics (those of *homo politicus*) are what they know best? Are women more likely to be recruited in ridings where there are more female constituency party executives? Are female constituency party executives more opened to special measures to increase female representation? As suggested in Caul's model (1999), it would be interesting to see what the effect of female party activists is on the recruitment of female candidates. These are a few of the questions that need to be addressed in future research.

In conclusion, if these parties have turned to more decentralized practices in the name of greater party democracy, how in the name of democracy can they justify having so few women as candidates? Based on the results presented here, it would seem that a combination of party centralization and institutionalization of the recruitment process might facilitate the implementation of the special measures to increase female representation. However, it is clear that without the willingness to implement such measures, changes in formal party characteristics will not increase the number of women running for office.

NOTES

1. This translates into 10 women out of 58 MLAs in 1991 and 9 out of 55 in 1995. While these differences may seem irrelevant, they suggest that women's gradual political integration cannot be taken for granted.
2. It must be added that *recruitment process* is sometimes used to refer to the greater operation that includes both the recruitment and selection of candidates (for more explanation, see United Nations, Centre for Social Development and Humanitarian Affairs 1992: 30).

3. The variable of female militancy will not be analyzed here because of the lack of sufficient data. For more information on the role of female party activists, see Caul 1999; Sainsbury 1993; Tremblay and Pelletier 2001; Young 2000.

4. Lane and Ersson (1991) have found that the more frequent the change in party leadership, the less centralized the party; such change implies greater grassroots involvement. As for party congresses, it seems that the longer the period between party conventions, the more centralized the party, suggesting that decisions are centralized at the top of the hierarchy. As with leadership conventions, frequent party conventions allow for greater grassroots involvement.

5. According to Rahat and Hazan (2001), candidates can be nominated at the national, regional, or local level, and the selection process can be placed on an inclusiveness–exclusiveness axis. The most inclusive form of selection would be opened to the entire electorate (e.g., American or non-partisan primaries); at the exclusive end, the leader would singlehandedly appoint all candidates (e.g., the Degel Ha Torah, an ultraorthodox party in Israel in which one rabbi decides all nominations on the party list). Other selection methods would fall anywhere between these two extremes.

6. According to Rahat and Hazan, criteria for candidacy can be all-inclusive, that is, opened to all citizens; very exclusive, meaning that candidacy is only opened to a few select people; or somewhere between the two, when it is restricted to party members, in which case the level of inclusiveness would depend of the restrictions imposed on party membership (2001).

7. Yet, as relates to women, the literature has repeatedly shown that, in practice, the sexual division of labour, sexual identity, and socio-demographic characteristics still keep most women from entering the legislature (Andrew 1991; Bashevkin, 1993; Erickson 1991a; Maillé 1994; Tremblay and Pelletier 1995; for New Brunswick, see Gaudet and Lafleur 1988–89; Pitre 1998).

8. For lack of a better word, those who seek the potential candidates in the general population will be referred to as *recruiters* to distinguish them from the selectorate. Rahat and Hazan (2001) place the latter on an inclusive–exclusive continuum, going from the electorate (the most inclusive), to party members, selected party agency, non-selected party agency, and finally the party leader (the most exclusive). The authors argue that 'In the "selected party agency" zone we find various party agencies that may be distinguished by different parameters. Inside each party, the relative size of each agency is a sign of its inclusiveness. . . . In addition, the more inclusive party agencies contain delegates selected by party members, while the more exclusive ones include representatives who were selected by such delegates.' The 'non-selected party agencies' zone, on the other hand, has 'special selection committees whose composition is ratified *en bloc* by a selected party agency. The more exclusive selectorates in this zone are represented by a gathering of party founders, in new parties, or an informal gathering of faction leaders in older ones' (2001: 302–3). This inclusive–exclusive axis has also been applied to the recruiters.

9. PSCs were especially active in ridings where local committees had asked for help. In fact, the recruitment process is something constituency party executives hold dearly; outside intervention may be perceived as intrusion, especially if the assistance is not requested (Carty and Erickson 1991).

10. Using Rahat and Hazan's (2001) classification, the PC LSCs are qualified as exclusive selected party agencies because they are very small groups of local party elites—'representatives' who have previously been selected by grassroots party members to become constituency party executives, and then appointed to 'delegates' (that is, constituency party presidents, also previously selected by local party members) to join the LSC. As for the PSC, it qualified as a relatively exclusive non-selected party agency: access is very limited and its members have neither been previously appointed by the party leader or his entourage nor elected by grassroots members.

11. According to Rahat and Hazan (2001), the most inclusive selection process would allow any member of the electorate to run, while the most exclusive would only allow a small number of party members who respected some additional requirements to run.

12. Although the five-dollar fee imposed on PC members may appear more restrictive than the Liberals' free membership, interviews reveal that candidates running for nomination may offer to pay the membership fees for new members in exchange for their support at the convention. This cost is actually considered an integral part of nomination expenses. The fact that it is only five dollars and that it can easily be sidestepped makes it minimally restrictive. There was no mention of such practices in the NDP.

13. That is, the first person to get an absolute majority of the votes (50 per cent plus one) wins the nomination. When there are three or more contenders, the person with the fewest votes is eliminated at each round.

14. No one had expected such a landslide victory in the 1999 election for Bernard Lord's Conservatives, who won 44 of the 55 seats and elected 8 of their 10 female candidates; this as also the case for Frank McKenna's Liberals in 1987, when they won all 58 seats and elected all of their 7 women candidates. As argued by Erickson and Carty (1991), one could only hypothesize that women might have faced more contested nominations if these seats had been considered winnable ridings.

15. One could argue that the Liberal party has the Tony Barry Fund in place in order to help women with the financial costs of winning an election. However, while this fund is an interesting initiative, it is not a rule or guideline. Furthermore, this initiative emanates from the Liberal Women's Association and not from the party's mainstream and does not appear in the party documents.

Chapter Eight

The Parti Québécois, Its Women's Committee, and the Feminization of the Quebec Electoral Arena[1]

Jocelyne Praud

INTRODUCTION

During the feminist agitation of the 1970s, North American and Western European centre-left/social democratic parties began to give more recognition to women and issues of concern to them. They incorporated feminist claims into their programs, sanctioned the replacement of women's auxiliaries with feminist women's committees, and provided support services (such as information and training workshops, financial assistance, and child care arrangements) to women aspiring to become party officials and candidates. Resorting to more formal, mandatory means to enhance women's involvement in party affairs and electoral politics, some left-leaning parties even passed statutory rules requiring that certain party positions and riding nominations be reserved for women. For instance, in the 1970s, the Parti Socialiste Français and the Norwegian Labour party set aside, respectively, 10 per cent and 40 per cent of party positions and extended these provisions to candidacies shortly thereafter (Praud 1993).

In Canada, the first parties to use such formal measures to 'feminize'[2] their internal organization and the electoral arena were the federal and Ontario NDP. In the early 1980s, following several years of lobbying by their women's committees, they inserted into their statutes the requirement that their governing bodies (councils and executives) and committees comprise at least 50 per cent women. Later on, they extended this rule to candidacies (Bashevkin 1993; Praud 1995). By contrast, the Liberal and Conservative parties have relied primarily on informal (voluntary) measures, such as support services, to enhance women's participation in party life and electoral politics.

Although Canadian parties have endeavoured to address issues of concern to women in their platforms and to recruit more women party officials and candidates since at least the 1970s, their informal and formal pro-feminization initiatives have not aroused much interest among students of women in politics.[3] A general survey of the studies published in the past two decades on Canadian women in politics highlights two main trends.[4] First, this literature has tended to deal with women occupying visible elite positions (candidates, mayors, legislators, and Cabinet ministers) rather than with women occupying less visible party positions. Specifically, the link between the low proportion of female party officials and women's under-representation in electoral politics and democratic institutions has not really been explored.[5] Second, researchers have thoroughly documented the obstacles facing aspiring women politicians but not the initiatives launched within political parties to help women overcome obstacles and increase their share of party positions, candidacies, and legislative seats. In Canada, for instance, the few existing studies of such initiatives have dealt mainly with the formal gender-balance rules and quotas that political parties have used to boost the number of women party officials.[6] Consequently, a study focusing on a major party that has resorted to extensive informal means to boost women's involvement in its internal organization and the electoral arena would contribute to the literature on Canadian women in politics.

The Parti Québécois (PQ) could serve as the object of such a study. Since its first electoral victory in 1976, the PQ and its main rival, the Quebec Liberal party (PLQ), have dominated Quebec politics. This means that women have had a greater chance of being elected to the Assemblée Nationale by running for one of these two parties; that is, the feminization of the Quebec electoral arena depends on the PQ and PLQ and on their willingness to facilitate women's access to it. Thus far, the PQ appears to have been somewhat more willing to do so than its rival. In 1977, it established a special women's committee, the Comité National de la Condition Féminine,[7] responsible for increasing women's involvement within the party hierarchy and as candidates and for bringing issues of concern to women to the attention of the party. (The PLQ lacks such a committee.)[8] Lastly, in part because of PQ activists' resistance to formal gender requirements, which they tend to view as infringing on the principle of equality of opportunity, the Committee's many initiatives to feminize the internal organization and the Quebec electoral arena have remained largely informal (Gingras, Maillé, and Tardy 1989; Legault, Desrosiers, and Tardy 1988; Praud 1998b).

This study assesses the impact that the Committee's initiatives have had on the participation of PQ women in party affairs and electoral politics. It is divided into two main sections. First, the activities organized by the Committee to boost women's involvement are presented. Second, longitudinal statistics on the proportion of Péquiste women as riding and regional presidents, national executive officials, candidates, MNAs, and Cabinet members are analyzed and compared to similar statistics from the PLQ. This study is based on original research materials, including interviews with past and present PQ and Committee activists,[9] documents (such as reports, minutes, and correspondence), and statistics made available to the author by the Committee. This chapter argues that while the Committee has worked assiduously to feminize the PQ, these initiatives have thus far generated only moderate gains for women in the party organization and the Quebec electoral arena.

FROM THE COMITÉ RÉGIONAL DE LA CONDITION FÉMININE TO THE COMITÉ NATIONAL D'ACTION POLITIQUE DES FEMMES

The women's committee of the PQ was started early in 1976 by a group of Péquiste women from the Montréal-Centre region who felt that the sections of the party program addressing women's condition needed to be substantially revised. As soon as the Montréal-Centre executive approved the establishment of the Comité Régional de la Condition Féminine (CRCF), these women moved into action. First, they invited PQ and non-partisan women activists as well as PQ leaders to a symposium on women's condition entitled 'Solitaires ou Solidaires'. In workshops on the family, education, justice, politics, health, and employment, participants discussed the particular problems faced by women and the means to remedy them (Région Montréal-Centre du PQ 1976; Rowan 1976a, 1976b).

Inspired by these discussions, the women from the CRCF put forward a lengthy resolution calling for maternity leave, public child care services, and free abortion at the May 1977 PQ convention. Despite the strong opposition of René Lévesque and other executive members to the section on free abortion, the resolution carried. Anticipating the resistance of the executive toward their resolution, CRCF members had spent the months prior to the convention building support for their proposal at the local level. They went to numerous riding and regional meetings and educated party activists, many of whom were going to be delegates at the 1977 convention, about the resolution. Their efforts to reach out to the rank and file eventually paid off: the resolution passed, and four women, including two young feminists—Louise Thiboutot, one of the founders of the Committee, and Denise LeBlanc—were elected to the executive in spite of the objections of party elites.[10] At the provincial council meeting that followed the 1977 convention, the new executive presented a resolution providing for the creation of a Comité National de la Condition Féminine (CNCF) that was to defend the interests of women throughout Quebec. The resolution did not encounter any opposition. Thus, as of September 1977, the PQ had a women's committee that was to promote and coordinate all the riding- and regional-level efforts related to women, suggest policy stands to the party, and reach out to women outside the party:

> [Le] Comité national de la condition féminine . . . verrait . . . à:
> a) promouvoir et coordonner l'action décentralisée des régions et des comtés tant au niveau de l'actualité que du programme et de l'action politique.
> b) faire connaître et améliorer le programme en ce qui concerne la situation de la femme.
> c) suggérer au Parti, après l'établissement des priorités, des prises de position: i) concernant les problèmes de la femme; ii) concernant les actions et/ou les projets de loi du gouvernement.
> d) sensibiliser les femmes du Québec à la question du référendum et sur l'indépendance. (PQ, Conseil National de Sherbrooke 1977)

Although this resolution did not mention the role of the CNCF in enhancing women's participation in party affairs, this was one of its main objectives. Some of the first initiatives of CNCF activists confirm this. Through the late 1970s, they travelled tirelessly to meet with PQ women all across Quebec and to encourage them to become more active in party bodies. During these visits, they held workshops on the structures, policy making, and offices of the PQ. They also emphasized the need to gather PQ women interested in women's condition in riding or regional women's committees and provided advice on how to establish such committees (CNCF 1977, 1978). In the view of two founding members, the experience women were to gain from their committee involvement was intended to prompt them into contesting riding or regional executive positions. With regard to the establishment of women's committees, the efforts of CNCF activists were particularly fruitful; by 1979, 106 PQ ridings (out of 110) and 11 regions (out of 13) had one (Rowan 1979).

Shortly after the 1980 referendum campaign, the CNCF decided to alter its official mandate and name. In order to rally Quebec women to the yes side, it set up the Comité des Québécoises pour le Oui and organized two large demonstrations, one whose message was 'La politique c'est l'affaire de toutes les femmes' and the other to commemorate the 40th anniversary of Quebec female enfranchisement (CAPF 1980b). These events, however, were overshadowed by the Yvettes rallies of the PLQ, which received extensive press coverage.[11] As journalist Françoise Guénette wrote, the Yvettes episode forced the members of the women's committee to re-examine their goals (1981). Realizing that the chronic absence of women in the decision-making positions of the party hampered their actions, they decided to change the official mandate and name of the committee. In August 1980, the coordinator of the recently renamed Comité d'Action Politique des Femmes (CAPF) sent a letter to regional presidents to inform them that from now on the official mandate of the committee would include getting more women involved at all levels of the party: 'Le mandat . . . se li[ra] comme suit: Associer les femmes du Parti Québécois à l'élaboration et la promotion des actions du Parti et plus spécifiquement sur les conditions de vie des femmes et *leur représentation au sein du Parti*' (1980a, my emphasis). Many of the Committee's subsequent initiatives were aimed at fulfilling this new mandate. For instance, to sensitize party activists to the poor level of women's participation in party affairs and the need to remedy this situation, the CAPF organized several colloquia. The Committee also offered training workshops on the functions of PQ bodies, the party policy-making process, and how to contest party positions and prepare a speech (CAPF 1982a, 1982b; Legault, Desrosiers, and Tardy 1988).

Given the CAPF's concern for women's low level of involvement within the party organization, its behaviour during the 1985 leadership campaign was surprising. For the first time in the history of the PQ, two women, Pauline Marois and Francine Lalonde, came forward to contest the party leadership. Although the Committee saluted Marois's and Lalonde's candidacies, it chose not to support any candidate. The president of the CAPF justified the Committee's decision by saying that 'on ne peut pas dire "votez pour une femme parce que c'est une femme"; ce serait une insulte pour les autres' (Chantal Mallen, cited in Beaulieu and Rowan 1985). Instead, it asked candidates to provide written comments on three issues: female employment, the role of the state, and women and power (Mallen 1985). Of six leadership candidates, four (Luc Gagnon, Pierre-Marc Johnson, Pauline Marois, and Francine Lalonde) complied with the Committee's request. According to journalists Carole Beaulieu and Renée Rowan (1985), the most concrete and innovative responses came from Marois and Johnson. Yet, with respect to women and power, Marois's comments appeared to be more substantive than Johnson's. While the latter emphasized the need to encourage women, the former pledged to prevent ridings without a PQ incumbent from holding their nominating convention until they found at least one woman to contest the nomination (Beaulieu 1985; Beaulieu and Rowan 1985). It is somewhat peculiar that the Committee, the goal of which since its inception had was to stimulate party women's participation, did not come out in support of Marois or Lalonde, instead limiting its involvement to asking candidates to present positions.

After the defeat of the PQ in the 1985 election, the CAPF undertook to promote the issue of party women's involvement more forcefully. The small number of female PQ candidates (20, or only 4 more than in 1981) and the cancellation of the leaders' debate on the status of women appear to account for this more vigorous approach. The debate was cancelled because of Liberal leader Robert Bourassa's refusal to participate in it. But what angered the Committee was not so much Bourassa's refusal as the PQ's lack of reaction to the cancellation. In the CAPF's view, this would not have happened had more women been in top party positions:

> Le manque de femmes aux hauts niveaux de décision du parti s'est fait sentir à plusieurs reprises. Un seul exemple parmi d'autres: si le PQ n'a pas 'utilisé' le refus de Bourassa de rencontrer les groupes de femmes, c'est, en bonne partie, parce qu'on ne 'sentait' pas l'importance de ce dossier, et ceci depuis le début de l'organisation du débat. Les seules personnes qui en voyaient l'importance ont été des femmes même non impliquées dans le 'féminisme', mais elles étaient trop rares au niveau décisionnel. (CAPF 1986f)

In the post-election period, the CAPF was determined to increase women's share of party positions. Many of its 1986 documents list as the priorities of the Committee, first, increasing the presence of women at all levels of the party; second, collaborating with other, non-party women's groups to keep abreast of different ways to improve women's living conditions; and third, preparing for the 1987 party convention. Furthermore, in May 1986, the Committee invited PQ women (including former party officials, CAPF members, and candidates) to discuss strategies to improve women's participation within the party hierarchy (CAPF 1986b, 1986c, 1986g, 1986h).

The initiatives that the CAPF launched in the second half of the 1980s were directed at two groups within the PQ: elites and female activists. For instance, the Committee lobbied riding and regional presidents to recruit women to serve in their executive and as convention delegates (CAPF 1986a, 1986e, 1986h, 1987). The following is an extract from a letter sent to party elites by the CAPF to remind them about the need to promote women:

> Dans vos comtés, dans vos régions et au niveau national, on procède à une réorganisation et en particulier on comble plusieurs postes vacants. Parmi les critères qui vous guident dans ces choix, nous voudrions vous en rappeler un: *la nécessaire et normale présence des femmes.* . . .

> Par conséquent, nous faisons appel *aux femmes et aux hommes* qui militent au
> Parti québécois: il est non seulement juste mais également rentable que les femmes
> soient plus présentes *à tous les niveaux du parti*. (CAPF 1986a)

The party leadership was not spared the CAPF's lobbying—hence its pledge to present at least 50 per cent women candidates in the 1989 election (CAPF 1988a; Normand 1989). During this period, CAPF members also undertook to provide party women with the tools necessary to become more actively involved. For instance, they held training workshops called 'À Moi la Parole' in different ridings and regions. The workshops, modelled on the public-speaking sessions of the newly created organization Femmes Regroupées pour l'Accès au Pouvoir Politique et Économique (FRAPPE), dealt with public speaking, the functions of party bodies, and the PQ program (CAPF 1986d, 1986g). Also, just before the 1989 election, the CAPF reached out to aspiring female candidates by organizing information and training sessions and meetings with former PQ candidates and with PQ leader Jacques Parizeau (CAPF 1988a, 1988b; Lessard 1989).

In the following year, the Committee continued to lobby party elites and offer support mechanisms to women interested in ascending the party ladder or contesting a nomination. Beginning in 1990, the Committee also undertook to find a woman in each riding and region willing to act as its local representative. These representatives were expected to remind their local executives about the need for a greater female presence at all levels of the party, compile data on the number and position of women in riding and regional executives, and establish links with women's groups potentially interested in the PQ program and propose additions and changes to it (CNAPF 1993, 1993–94, 1994). In April 1991, 65 ridings (out of 125) had a representative, and by the spring of 1993, this number had increased to 82 (CNAPF 1993–94). This informal network was partly formalized at the August 1993 convention when delegates passed a resolution calling on the 14 regional executives to also include a CNAPF representative. Elected at regional conventions, CNAPF representatives sit on the regional executive and have speaking and voting rights at party council meetings (see PQ 1994).

Under the presidency of Diane Bourgeois (1995–2000), the CNAPF continued to promote women and their concerns within the party organization and the electoral arena. Specifically, the Committee applied its energies to ensuring that all riding and regional executives included a CNAPF representative. Despite the resistance of certain executives and the hesitation of some women to take on such a responsibility, the Committee eventually succeeded in having a representative in place in all 125 ridings and all 17 regions. At the time of writing (summer 2002), the total number of CNAPF members was 156: 14 CNAPF executive members, 17 regional representatives, and 125 riding representatives. In the second half of the 1990s, the Committee was also very active in seeking out and supporting (financially and otherwise) women candidates. Lastly, it is worth noting that during this same period, the CNAPF devoted considerable time to communicating with women's groups, taking part in the 1995 Women's March Against Poverty and the 2000 World March of Women, and making policy recommendations to the PQ party and government.

THE IMPACT OF THE COMMITTEE'S INITIATIVES

The following assessment focuses on the numerical gains that PQ women have made since the inception of the Committee. Numerical representation (as opposed to substantive representation) was selected as a measure because the first goal of the Committee was to increase the number of women in positions of power. To be able to assess the substantive gains made by PQ women, one would have to closely examine the party's programs, policy statements, and resolutions from the past 25 years. Although this would be a worthwhile endeavour, it is beyond the scope of the present study.

More specifically, this assessment relies on longitudinal data from the 1970s onwards related to the proportion of women among PQ riding and regional presidents, national executive officials, candidates, MNAs, and Cabinet ministers as well as on statistics related to PLQ women.[12] Overall, these data suggest that the Committee is in large part responsible for the moderate gains that Péquiste women have made within the party organization and in electoral politics. For one thing, the involvement of PQ women in party bodies and electoral politics increased significantly right after the establishment of the Committee. Furthermore, on the whole, PQ women have played a more extensive role in party affairs and elections than Quebec Liberal women, who do not have an established women's committee to promote their interests.

It is true that the percentage of female riding presidents increased almost tenfold between 1978 and 1981, from 3 per cent (3/100) to 29 per cent.[13] Nevertheless, through the mid-1980s, it remained at 23–5 per cent (see Table 8.1). Finally, by 2001, close to a third of riding presidents were women.

Before comparing PQ and PLQ women's participation in riding executives, it should be noted that since 1971, Liberal riding executives must reserve one vice-presidential position (out of two) and one youth position (out of two) for women (Legault et al. 1988). Despite these requirements, PLQ men have held the reins of riding executives. The PLQ had no female riding presidents in 1978 (compared with 3 per cent, or 3/100, in the PQ). Twelve years later, 17 per cent of Liberal riding presidents were women (compared with 23 per cent in the PQ; CSF 1978: 316; Richer 1991: 19).[14] As of 2001, Liberal women held 20.3 per cent (24/118) of riding presidencies (compared with 28.8 per cent, or 36/125, in the PQ; PLQ statistics).[15] In short, the PLQ's two designated female positions in riding executives[16] do not seem to have given Liberal women a significant edge over PQ women.

Table 8.1

Female Local Riding Presidents in the PQ, 1978–2001

1978	1981	1985	1987	1990	1992	1993	2001
3.0%	29.0%[a]	24.0%[a]	23.3%	23.0%[a]	25.6%	23.2%	28.8%
(3/100)			(27/116)		(32/125)	(29/125)	(36/125)

SOURCES: Comité d'Action Politique des Femmes, 'Rapport d'activités au Conseil national', June 1986; Comité National d'Action Politique des Femmes statistics; Ginette Legault, Guy Desrosiers, and Évelyne Tardy, *Militer dans un parti provincial: Les différences entre les femmes et les hommes au P.L.Q. et au P.Q.* (Montreal: Centre de Recherche Féministe, 1988): 114; PQ statistics; Jocelyne Richer, 'Femmes de pouvoir: On revient de loin', *La Gazette des femmes* 12 (1991): 19; thanks also to Évelyne Tardy, Guy Bedard, and Rébecca Beauvais.

[a] Only percentages were available.

PQ women appear to have had difficulties imposing themselves as regional presidents. Through the 1980s, their share of regional presidencies actually decreased, from 23 per cent (3/13) in 1981 to 15.3 per cent (2/13) in 1985 and none in 1987. Women did not fare much better in the following decade, holding only 7.1 per cent (1/14) of regional presidencies in 1991 and none in 1993. As of 2001, 3 regional presidents out of 17 (17.6 per cent) were women (CAPF 1986a, 1986e; CNAPF statistics; Legault et al. 1988: 114; PQ 2001).

Overall, the proportion of women on the PQ national executive appears to have progressed fairly regularly (see Table 8.2). In 1973, the election of two women to the previously male national executive brought their representation to 18.2 per cent. As mentioned earlier, the 1977 convention not only passed the Committee's first lengthy resolution, it also elected four women to the national executive. By 2001, almost two-thirds of the national executive were women.

One interviewee suggested that most PQ national executives since 1979 have been made up of one-third or more women because PQ elites wanted to ensure that women's share of these visible positions would not drop to an embarrassing level. For instance, in order that CAPF members would support the 1987 changes to the party's internal structures (namely, the transfer of national committee presidents from the national executive to the less powerful national bureau), party leader Jacques Parizeau pledged to seek female candidacies for the national executive. According to the interviewee, Parizeau kept his promise. The steady proportion of women on the national executive through the second half of the 1990s and, more recently, the appointment of Marie Malavoy as first vice-president of the PQ indicate that Lucien Bouchard and Bernard Landry decided to follow Parizeau's lead.

Comparable PLQ data suggest that PLQ elites may not be as concerned with the promotion of women to top party positions. Between 1978 and 1992, the percentage of women on the PLQ executive committee was always about 10 per cent lower. Women held 14.3 per cent (1/7) of the PLQ executive committee positions in 1978, about 14 per cent in the late 1980s, and 27.1 per cent (13/48) in 1992 (CSF 1978: 316; Desrochers 1993: 64; Legault et al. 1988: 65). By August 2001, only 15 per cent (6/40) of the PLQ executive committee were women (PLQ statistics).[17] In other words, the two positions the PLQ reserves for women in its executive committee (one vice-presidential position and one youth representative position) did not significantly increase the number of women holding top party positions (see PLQ 2000).

PQ women have fared less well in their proportion of candidacies (see Table 8.3).

Table 8.2
Women in the National Executive of the PQ, 1973–2001

1973	1974	1977	1979	1981	1984	1986	1990	1992	1994	2001
18.2%	6.7%	26.7%	33.3%	33.3%	33.3%	33.3%	27.5%	36.4%	33.3%	58.3%
(2/11)	(1/15)	(4/15)	(5/15)	(5/15)	(5/15)	(5/15)	(3/11)	(4/11)	(4/12)	(7/12)

SOURCES: Comité National d'Action Politique des Femmes statistics; Lucie Desrochers, *Femmes et pouvoir: La révolution tranquille* (Quebec City: Publications du Québec, 1993): 64; Ginette Legault, Guy Desrosiers, and Évelyne Tardy, *Militer dans un parti provincial: Les différences entre les femmes et les hommes au P.L.Q. et au P.Q.* (Montreal: Centre de Recherche Féministe, 1988): 114; Marcel Léger, *Le Parti québécois: Ce n'était qu'un début* (Montreal: Québec/Amérique, 1986): 343–45; Parti Québecois, *Régions et circonscriptions: Régions* (Available at: <http://partiquebecois.org/regions_regions.phtml>, accessed 15 May 2001); Jocelyne Richer, 'Femmes de pouvoir: On revient de loin', *La Gazette des femmes* 12 (1991): 19.

After improving steadily through the 1980s, their share appeared to stagnate in the 1990s. A record 25.6 per cent (32/125) in 1989 may have resulted from the CAPF's active lobbying of the party leadership. PLQ women's share of candidacies was somewhat behind that of PQ women, at least up until 1989 (see Table 8.3). On the whole, however, it appears to have evolved in a similar manner. Interestingly, in the 1994 and 1998 elections, the PLQ presented the same number of women candidates as the PQ, thus indicating that Liberal women have also reached a ceiling. And although the 1998 election saw the two parties vying for women's vote by address-ing issues of concern to them or showcasing their women candidates, neither appeared willing to really outdo the other in terms of female candidacies (Binder 1998; Hébert 1998).[18]

The data contained in Table 8.3 also suggest that the proportion of women in the PQ and PLQ caucuses and, thus, the total proportion of women MNAs have pro-gressed, albeit slowly, since 1976. Both caucuses had less than 10 per cent women MNAs in 1976 and 1981. The total percentage of female MNAs more than doubled between 1981 and 1985. This upward trend, however, was temporarily halted by the 1994 election. At the time of writing, almost one-quarter of MNAs are women.

Since the lonely days of PLQ ministers Claire Kirkland-Casgrain (1962–73) and Lise Bacon (1973–76), women's share of Cabinet positions has increased steadily. For instance, it went from less than 10 per cent (1–2/24–27) through the 1970s and the early 1980s to about 15 per cent (4/28) in the mid- and late 1980s, then to 20 per cent (6/28) in the early 1990s (Drouilly and Dorion 1988: 82; Richer 1991: 18). From 1994 to 2001, PQ premiers appointed women to one-quarter to one-third of Cabinet positions. In 1994, 30 per cent (6/20) of Parizeau's Cabinet were women. Most notably, 3 of these women were in his 7-member inner Cabinet (D'Amours 1995: 16). When Bouchard became premier in early 1996, he appointed one fewer woman to his Cabinet, which slightly reduced women's share

Table 8.3

Quebec Women Candidates and MNAS, 1976–98

	1976	1981	1985	1989	1994	1998
Candidates						
PLQ	2.7%	10.7%	13.5%	16.8%	22.4%	22.4%
	(3/110)	(13/122)	(17/122)	(21/125)	(28/125)	(28/125)
PQ	6.4%	13.1%	16.4%	25.6%	22.4%	22.4%
	(7/110)	(16/122)	(20/122)	(32/125)	(28/125)	(28/125)
MNAS						
PLQ	3.8%	7.1%	14.1%	16.5%	17.0%	20.8%
	(1/26)	(3/42)	(14/99)	(15/91)	(8/47)	(10/48)
PQ	5.6%	6.3%	17.4%	27.6%	19.5%	26.3%
	(4/71)	(5/80)	(4/23)	(8/29)	(15/77)	(20/76)
Total	4.5%	6.5%	14.7%	18.4%	18.4%	24.2%
	(5/97)	(8/122)	(18/122)	(23/120)	(23/124)	(30/124)

SOURCES: Lucie Desrochers, *Femmes et démocratie de représentation: Quelques réflexions* (Quebec City: Bibliothèque de l'Assemblée nationale, 1994): 74; Pierre Drouilly and Jocelyne Dorion, *Candidates, députées et ministres: Les femmes et les élections* (Quebec City: Bibliothèque de l'Assemblée Nationale, 1988): 60–61; 'Quebec Election '98' (1998), Cnews, <http://www.canoe.ca>, accessed 15 May 2001.

of Cabinet positions to 25 per cent (5/20; Séguin 1996). However, after the 1998 election, he assembled a larger and more feminized Cabinet, one-third of them women (9/26, or 34.7 per cent; Clark 1998). On 8 March 2001, Landry, Bouchard's successor, made it clear that his Cabinet would accord an important place to women. Stating that 'l'homme fort du Québec est une femme', Landry announced in July 2001 that Pauline Marois, his main leadership rival, would be deputy premier as well as finance and economy minister. Landry also appointed eight other women to his cabinet, to seven ministries and two secretaries of state, thus bringing women's Cabinet representation to 33.3 per cent (9/27; Joly 2001).

What do these statistics tell us about the impact of the Committee and its initiatives on the enhancement of women's political involvement? To begin with, the Committee's establishment helped to boost the participation of PQ women in party affairs and electoral politics. The proportion of women riding presidents and national executive officials improved significantly in the late 1970s and early 1980s. Between 1977 and 1981, the proportion of women convention delegates also increased considerably, from 25 per cent to 38 per cent (Beaud 1982: 247; '38 per cent des Délégués Étaient des Femmes', *Le Devoir* 7 December 1981: 2). It is more difficult to detect such a pattern with regard to regional presidencies, since the earliest data available are from 1981. Nevertheless, the fact that women's share of regional presidencies has never exceeded this level could suggest that the establishment of the Committee also facilitated women's access to these positions. Lastly, it is worth reiterating that the proportion of women PQ candidates more than doubled between 1976 and 1981 and in 1989, when the CAPF lobbied actively for more women candidates.

Since this initial increase, however, the Committee's pro-feminization initiatives appear to have mainly maintained, rather than markedly enhanced, women's involvement in party and electoral politics. Women's share of regional presidencies actually declined through the 1980s to the point that one woman at most presided over a regional executive between 1987 and 1993. The presently higher percentage of women regional presidents should be viewed with caution as it may be attributed in part to the increase in the number of regional presidencies, from 13 to 17. Given the moderate gains achieved by PQ women over the past two decades, it seems appropriate to conclude that the initiatives that the Committee launched after its inception have generally plateaued at a status quo.

CONCLUSION

This study highlights the need for students of women's participation in electoral politics to devote more attention to women who hold less visible positions within party organizations: the degree of feminization of the electoral arena may depend in part on that of major party organizations. In the case of Quebec, it appears that the more women activists and officials a party has, the more likely it is to present women candidates and ensure that they are elected; conversely, the fewer women activists and officials a party has, the less likely it is to present women candidates. Thus, among the different factors that affect women's involvement in electoral politics, researchers need to focus not only on the ones external to party organizations (such as political culture and women's organizations), but also on those internal to them. More precisely, their analyses should also tackle the situation of women in major party organizations as well as the role of their committees and assess the extent to which these factors have affected the feminization of the electoral arena.

As indicated in this study, since its establishment in 1977, the Women's Committee of the PQ has worked hard to increase the proportion of women in the party's internal bodies and in the Quebec electoral arena. Overall, however, these efforts have resulted in moderate numerical gains for women, maintaining, rather than markedly increasing, the gains made right after the Committee's establishment. Nonetheless, it would be erroneous to infer from this that the Committee has been largely ineffective. If it had not been for the Committee and its constant promotion of women and their concerns, PQ women may not have made even the moderate gains they did make. Moreover, it is worth noting that PLQ women, who do not have an established women's committee, have tended to trail behind PQ women. One could even suggest that the moderate gains that PQ women made thanks to the Committee might have prompted the PLQ to promote women within the party hierarchy and, more recently, as candidates. Alternatively put, this moderate feminization of the PQ may have had a contagion effect on the PLQ.[19] In any event, it is important to appreciate the fact that the Committee is largely responsible for the feminization of the PQ organization and caucus and that such a task is quite difficult to carry out since the party lacks formal gender representation rules for internal positions and candidacies.

It should be stressed that the study does not argue that the Women's Committee of the PQ is solely responsible for the greater presence of women in Quebec political institutions (namely, party organizations, the Assemblée Nationale, and the Cabinet). Clearly, factors external to political parties, including women's organizations such as the Fédération des Femmes du Québec, the Association Féminine d'Éducation et d'Action Sociale, and Femmes Regroupées pour l'Accès au Pouvoir Politique et Économique (see Maillé 1990a), have played a very important role in the feminization of Quebec political institutions. Rather, the study simply highlights the need for researchers studying the involvement of women in electoral politics to pay closer attention to factors internal to political parties and, in particular, the women's committees of political parties.

In the absence of such rules, one of the main challenges currently facing the Committee appears to be the different attitudes of PQ activists and elites toward the feminization of the party organization and the electoral arena.[20] As the longitudinal data from the 1990s show, PQ women's share of riding and regional presidencies and candidacies has tended to be lower than their share of provincial executive and Cabinet positions.[21] The extent to which party activists and elites are involved in selecting the individuals who are to fill these positions help to explain this gap. While local party activists have a considerable influence on the selection of riding and regional presidents and candidates, provincial elites have an important influence on the selection of provincial executive officials (see Praud 1997). Needless to say, the party leader as premier also determines the composition of the Cabinet.

Although PQ activists are aware of the low proportion of women in party positions and electoral politics, they are somewhat reluctant to address this problem themselves. In their view, the Committee is responsible for stimulating women's involvement; they are not (Praud 1998b). In contrast, Parizeau, Bourassa, and Landry have made a point of including women in the national executive and Cabinet and of assigning important responsibilities to them.

Clearly, to understand the nature and extent of this lack of interest, more research needs to be conducted on PQ activists' and elites' views on the question of women in politics. As for the Committee, it needs to consider innovative ways of involving local party activists and elites in its pro-feminization activities when designing strategies to increase the presence of women in party bodies and electoral politics. For the Committee to be able to bring about a gender-balanced party organization and electoral arena, it needs to have not only the active support of provincial PQ elites, but also that of local party activists and elites.

NOTES

1. The author thanks Diane Bourgeois, Chantal Mallen, and Christiane Monarque for providing information on the history of the Women's Committee of the Parti Québécois; Évelyne Tardy, Guy Bédard, and Rébecca Beauvais for very generously sharing the findings of their forthcoming research on gender differences among the activists of the Parti Québécois (PQ) and the Quebec Liberal party (PLQ); Karl A. Henriques, Christiane Monarque, Manon Tremblay, and Sylvia Bashevkin for commenting on previous drafts of this paper; and the Social Sciences and Humanities Research Council of Canada and the Faculty of Arts at the University of Regina for funding this research. Since this study examines how women's involvement in Quebec electoral politics has evolved since the 1970s, consideration will be given not only to the PQ, but also to the PLQ. The majority of the party documents used in this study were made available privately to the author by individuals involved in the Women's Committee.

2. Throughout this paper, the term *feminization* simply refers to the increase in the number of women as party officials, candidates, elected representatives, and Cabinet members.

3. On the specific initiatives launched by federal and provincial Canadian parties, see Bashevkin's seminal study (1993).

4. See, for example, Arscott and Trimble, eds (1997); Brodie (1985); Maillé (1990a); Megyery, ed. (1991b); Spencer and Spencer (1992); Tardy et al. (1982); Tardy and Legault (1996); Tremblay and Pelletier (1995); Young (2000).

5. One exception is Bashevkin's 1993 study, the first results of which were published in 1985. Legault, Desrosiers, and Tardy's fascinating study of the women and men involved in the PQ and the PLQ (1988) does not really address party activists' involvement in electoral politics.

6. The perception that formal measures may be more effective probably explains this focus. For Canada, see Bashevkin (1993); Praud (1995, 1998a). For other countries, see, for example, Appleton and Mazur (1992); Caul (1998); Kolinsky (1991); Short (1996).

7. This committee changed its name twice: first, in 1981 to the Comité d'Action Politique des Femmes (CAPF) and then, in 1993, to the Comité National d'Action Politique des Femmes (CNAPF). Here it will be referred to as the Committee, the CAPF, or the CNAPF, depending on the period.

8. Liberal women from Quebec used to have their own federation. However, in 1971 they decided to merge with the main Liberal Federation in Quebec (see Lévesque 1993). PLQ

statutes require that the executive committee of the party and riding executives reserve one vice-presidential position and one youth position for women.

9. These interviews were conducted in July 1994 in Montreal.

10. This version of the events surrounding the passage of the CRCF's resolution is based on interviews conducted with CRCF members. On the 1977 convention, see Fraser (1984).

11. For more information on the Yvettes, see Black (1993b); Dandurand and Tardy (1981); Hamilton (1993); Payette (1982); Tardy (1993).

12. It should be noted that the limited availability of such PLQ statistics somewhat restricted the assessment.

13. When percentages are not followed by nominal figures in brackets, parties were not able to provide this information, which was then found in secondary sources.

14. In 1992, 37 per cent (815/2201) of Liberal riding positions and 32.5 per cent (415/1277) of PQ riding positions were occupied by women (CNAPF statistics; Desrochers 1993: 64).

15. At that time, seven riding associations did not have a president.

16. For the composition of PLQ riding executives, see PLQ (2000).

17. At that time, two of the executive committee positions were vacant.

18. For more information on women candidates in Quebec, see Pelletier and Tremblay (1992); Tremblay (1997, 2002c).

19. But see Matland and Studlar (1996), whose study questions the importance of contagion with regard to Canadian women candidates.

20. Clearly, another equally important challenge remains to find women willing to contest party positions and nominations.

21. This phenomenon is not specific to the PQ or to Quebec. In France, it has been referred to as 'le fait du prince' (or, as translated by Appleton and Mazur, 'having a patron' [1993: 110]). French women have had tremendous difficulties obtaining party positions and candidacies and getting elected to the Assemblée Nationale. However, since the 1980s, the presidents of the Republic and prime ministers have made sure to appoint a respectable number of women to Cabinet positions (see Jenson and Sineau 1995; Sineau 2001). In other words, women in France and Quebec have been able to gain Cabinet positions in part because of their connection to a powerful political leader/prince. This has led Fraisse to point out that in France women govern, but they do not represent (1994).

Part III

Values and Attitudes of the Canadian Electorate

Chapter Nine

Women to the Left?
Gender Differences in Political Beliefs and Policy Preferences[1]

ELISABETH GIDENGIL, ANDRÉ BLAIS, RICHARD NADEAU, AND NEIL NEVITTE

INTRODUCTION

The 1993 federal election witnessed the emergence of a significant gender gap in support of the new party of the right: women were much less likely than men to vote Reform, a trend that continued in the 1997 federal election.[2] Although the Reform party subsequently reconstituted itself as the Canadian Alliance party and sought to reshape its image, the gender gap in support persisted in the 2000 federal election.[3] Meanwhile, in the 1997 election, a gender gap also opened up on the left, and it too appeared again in the 2000 election. In both 1997 and 2000, women were more likely than men to opt for the NDP, the traditional party of the left.[4] In this chapter, we examine whether these gender gaps in vote choice are paralleled by differences between women and men in their basic political beliefs and policy preferences.

The gender gap literature suggests that there should be significant differences between women's and men's opinions on questions relating to social welfare policy, free enterprise, and questions relating to the use of force. There is a growing body of evidence that Canadian women are more skeptical about the workings of the free enterprise system and more supportive of the welfare state than Canadian men (Everitt 1998a; Kopinak 1987; Terry 1984; Wearing and Wearing 1991), and women attach a higher priority to social welfare issues than do men (Everitt 2002; Gidengil 1995). There is also compelling evidence that women are more reluctant than men to resort to the use of force (Everitt 1998a; Terry 1984). By contrast, gender gaps on other issues have typically been weak or inconsistent. This is true of feminist beliefs and women's issues more generally (Everitt 1998a, 1998b; O'Neill 1995; Terry 1984)[5] as well as issues relating to questions of morality and social mores in general.

As Pippa Norris (forthcoming) has recently reminded us, though, context matters to both the size and the direction of gender gaps. The 2000 federal election provides a novel context for examining gender gaps in a variety of domains. With a federal budget surplus, the question was no longer where cuts should be made to social programs but where new monies should be allocated. And with the unemployment rate clearly on the decline, jobs were no longer the central issue that they had been in the two preceding elections (Nadeau et al. 2000; Nevitte et al. 2000).

Meanwhile, with the Liberals campaigning to portray the Alliance as a party of social conservatives out of step with mainstream Canadian society, and with the religious beliefs of Stockwell Day, the Alliance leader, a matter of media scrutiny, issues relating to traditional moral standards and lifestyle choices assumed new electoral importance.

We used data from the 2000 Canadian Election Study (CES) to examine gender differences in this changed electoral context.[6] We begin with a review of the reasons that have been advanced for the existence of gender gaps in political beliefs and policy preferences. Then we see how much difference gender makes to opinions in each of the relevant attitudinal domains. For each domain, we had created a scale in order to have a summary indication of the overall gender gap in that domain.[7] In order to get a better sense of the importance (or lack thereof) of these gaps, we compare the male–female differences with the differences across Canada's most consequential electoral cleavage, region. These composite measures also provide us with a parsimonious way of evaluating the various explanations that have been advanced for the gender gap phenomenon.

EXPLAINING THE GENDER GAP PHENOMENON

Structural and Situational Explanations

A recent study of the gender gap phenomenon in the United States was aptly titled 'The Complexities of the Gender Gap' (Howell and Day 2000). As the authors observe, 'no single explanation has been generally accepted, possibly because they all contribute a piece of the puzzle' (859). The various explanations fall into two broad types: the first focuses on structural and situational factors that differentiate the life experiences of women and men, the second on socio-psychological differences that reflect gender-role socialization in childhood.

One of the most prominent structural arguments links the gender gap to women's greater reliance on the state. According to the welfare state dismantlement hypothesis (Erie and Rein 1988; see also Deitch 1988; Piven 1984), women should be more supportive than men of the government's role in providing a social safety net and more opposed to policies that threaten it. The feminization of poverty means that women are more likely than men to need the social safety net provided by the welfare state. At the same time, women are more likely than men to rely on the public sector for their employment. Whether as recipients of social welfare or as service providers, it was women who bore a disproportionate share of the costs of retrenchment in the 1990s (Bashevkin 2000). The implication of this argument is that sex differences in support of the welfare state would disappear if the material circumstances and employment patterns of women and men were more similar.

While the welfare state dismantlement thesis emphasizes women's distinctive experiences, the welfare backlash thesis switches the conceptual focus to men (Greenberg 2000). This argument points to changes in the nature of welfare provision, in particular to the fact that men have ceased to be the primary beneficiaries of social welfare programs (Mettler 1998). The result, it concludes, is an erosion of support for the welfare state among men.

A second structural argument looks beyond women's role as state workers to the effects of gendered patterns of employment more generally (De Vaus and McAllister 1989; Manza and Brooks 1998; Togeby 1994). Entry into the paid workforce is assumed to have a radicalizing effect on women as they find themselves disproportionately concentrated in low-paying jobs or confined to 'pink-collar ghettos'. These distinctive experiences in the workplace may foster a feminist consciousness and a questioning of traditional roles on the part of working women (Klein 1984; Manza and Brooks 1998).[8] Participation in the paid workforce may also enhance support for collective provision, since working women have more need of state services to assist them with child care and other parental responsibilities (Manza and Brooks 1998).

Where these arguments emphasize differences in women's and men's material interests, other accounts of the gender gap focus on interests that are explicitly linked to gender as such. These accounts revolve around the mobilizing effects of feminism. One variant focuses on the impact on women of feminist issues such as abortion, discrimination in the workplace, the lack of female representation in politics, and patriarchal structures in society at large. A second variant switches the conceptual focus to men, pointing to a possible anti-feminist backlash on the part of those men who resent the transformations in gender roles wrought by second-wave feminism (Kitschelt 1995). There are also suggestions that this anti-feminist backlash may be part of a larger resentment of changes in cultural values and practices, changes that have challenged the status of the white male. This resentment is seen as manifesting itself in a renewed emphasis on traditional social values and respect for authority (Ignazi 1992).

These structural explanations all revolve in some way around the notion of gender differences in self-interest, whether material or not. The gender roles interpretation, by contrast, focuses on women's traditional role as caregivers. As Jeff Manza and Clem Brooks (1998) observe, this type of explanation emphasizes the effects of adult socialization as women experience motherhood and parenting. Sara Ruddick (1989) has been the leading exponent of the argument that these experiences foster a form of 'maternal thinking' that promotes a more compassionate view of those in need. While maternal thinking is generally seen as encouraging a liberal stance on issues relating to the use of force and to social welfare, the argument has also been made that having children can be a conservative influence in women's lives, especially on questions of morality (De Vaus and McAllister 1989).[9]

Socio-Psychological Explanations

All of the explanations discussed so far point to objective differences between women and men. A second type of explanation centres instead on socio-psychological differences that transcend these differences in objective circumstances. Socio-psychological explanations focus on differences in women's and men's values and priorities that have their origin in childhood socialization. Their theoretical underpinnings derive from Carol Gilligan's work on gender differences in moral reasoning (1982). Her counterposing of female and male 'voices' suggests that women will be less individualistic than men (see also Phelan 1990). In her study, men's moral reasoning tended to emphasize competing rights and give primacy to the individual, while women's moral reasoning put the emphasis on conflicting responsibilities and treated relationships as primary. And where the moral imperative for men took the form of an 'injunction to respect the rights of others and thus to protect from interference the rights to life and self-fulfilment', the moral imperative for women appeared as an 'injunction to care, a responsibility to discern and alleviate the "real and recognizable trouble" of this world' (Gilligan 1982: 100). Applied to the realm of politics, this contrast in moral reasoning suggests that women will be more skeptical of market solutions than men and more willing to endorse government intervention on behalf of the needy. The implication is that these sex differences will persist regardless of material circumstances, sector of employment, or adult role.

Gilligan's work also provides a possible explanation for sex differences in opinions on issues relating to law and order and the use of force. While the men in her study tended to favour a hierarchical conception of society and to value separation, the women were more likely to conceive of society as a web of connections and to value inclusiveness. These contrasting conceptions translated into differing views about human aggression and how it should be dealt with. As Gilligan argues,

> if aggression is tied, as women perceive, to the fracture of human connection, then the activities of care . . . are the activities that make the social world safe, by avoiding isolation and preventing aggression. . . . In this light, aggression appears no longer as an unruly impulse that must be contained but rather as a signal of a fracture of connection, the sign of a failure of relationship. (1982: 43)

The masculine model of hierarchy and subordination, by contrast, finds its counterpart in a greater readiness to resort to the use of coercion and control, or what Felicia Pratto, Lisa Stallworth, and Jim Sidanius have termed a 'social dominance orientation' (1997).

The gender gap in support for the Canada–US Free Trade Agreement in the 1988 federal election provides some support for Gilligan's model. Not only were women less receptive than men to market-based arguments, but these arguments had less effect on their opinions about the agreement (Gidengil 1995). For women, the agreement's implications for Canada's social programs were the more important concern. Tellingly, these differences in women's values and priorities could not be explained in terms of their material disadvantage. Brenda O'Neill has recently taken Gilligan's model a step further to argue that there is a women's political culture, albeit one that overlaps with men's (2002). As she readily acknowledges, it is difficult to provide direct evidence of the existence of gendered subcultures; but to the extent that gender differences in opinion cannot be explained by differences in other social background characteristics, the idea gains plausibility. Indeed, socio-psychological interpretations of the gender gap imply that the differences between women and men will cut across other social divisions (see Elshtain 1984; Sears and Huddy 1990).

This should not be taken to mean, of course, that women constitute some sort of monolithic opinion bloc. On the contrary, we need to take account of the many differences among women—and men. To this end, we examine a number of possible sources of heterogeneity of opinion among women, including education, marital status, age cohort, and religiosity.

OPINIONS OF WOMEN AND OF MEN

Free Enterprise, the Welfare State, and Health Policy

Previous studies of the gender gap phenomenon have consistently found that women are less sanguine than men about the virtues of free enterprise, more supportive of social welfare programs, and less open to market solutions. It turns out these differences are not just a function of hard economic times and cutbacks in the welfare state.

Even in the changed context of the 2000 federal election, women remained consistently more skeptical than men about the workings of the free enterprise system, though the degree of skepticism depended very much on which aspect of those workings was under discussion (see Table 9.1). Women were especially skeptical of the notion that 'when businesses make a lot of money, everyone benefits, including the poor'. On the other hand, they were clearly less persuaded than men that individual effort will be rewarded. Similarly, women were more reluctant than men to rely on market solutions. For instance, only a minority of women believed that 'the government should leave it entirely to the private sector to create jobs'. Still, a majority of women did seem to prefer the market solution. When these items are combined, we can clearly see that women are more ambivalent than men about the free enterprise system. The difference is fairly modest, but it is statistically significant ($p<.01$) and it exceeds the differences among income groups and across Canada's regional divides.[10]

Similar sex differences appear when we look at views about the welfare system (see Table 9.1). First, improving social welfare programs was clearly a much more important election issue for women than for men. Of the eight issues that respondents were asked to rate, improving social welfare programs (along with health care) revealed the largest difference in the priorities of women and men. Second, women were more likely than men to believe that more should be done to reduce the gap between the rich and the poor in Canada, and they were also more likely to think that governments have a legitimate role in ensuring a decent standard of living. And finally, women were more likely than men to reject the notion that the welfare state undercuts the work ethic by promoting dependency on the state.

However, the fact that a majority of women did *not* reject this argument should temper any characterization of women's support for the welfare state. Only a minority of women rated improving social welfare programs as being very important. And despite both their concern with income disparities and their endorsement of the government's role in providing a social safety net, women, like men, were reluctant to support an increase in welfare spending. By the same token, views about welfare spending provide little support for the notion that resentment of the welfare state is a distinctively masculine orientation.[11]

Table 9.1

Women's and Men's Opinions on Issues (Percentages)

	Women	Men
Free enterprise		
Everyone benefits when businesses make a lot of money***	28	37
People who do not get ahead have only themselves to blame***	66	71
People can find a job if they really want***	75	82
The government should leave job creation to the private sector***	40	49
Jobless should move to regions where there are jobs***	59	67
Welfare system		
Social welfare is a very important issue***	44	31
Should do more to reduce gap between rich and poor***	78	71
The government should see that everyone has a decent standard of living***	68	61
The welfare state makes people less willing to look after themselves (disagree)***	38	30
Increase welfare spending	29	26
Health care		
Health care is a very important issue***	90	78
Health care has gotten worse***	66	6
Increase spending on health care***	89	85
Oppose allowing private hospitals***	56	50
Oppose allowing doctors to charge a fee***	70	60
Feminism and gender-related issues		
Sympathetic to feminism***	60	65
The feminist movement encourages women to be independent***	80	71
The feminist movement just tries to get equal treatment for women***	63	53
Discrimination makes it extremely difficult for women***	57	46
Do not lay off women with employed husbands first	86	86
Society would not be better if more women stayed home***	50	54
Should do more for women***	66	55
Having more women MPs is best way to protect women's interests***	56	36
Lack of women MPs is a serious problem***	41	30
Favour requiring parties to nominate 50% women**	37	31
Moral traditionalism		
Should not allow gay marriage***	35	48
Only married women should be having children	26	30
Should not be more tolerant of different lifestyles*	25	30
Newer lifestyles contributing to societal breakdown***	45	51
Fewer problems if more emphasis on traditional family values*	69	74
Should not adapt our view of moral behaviour**	53	48
Should be difficult to get an abortion*	35	33
Crime and punishment		
Crime is a very important issue***	76	68
Crime has gone up***	55	43
Crack down on crime***	76	72
Tougher sentences for young offenders***	43	53
Favour death penalty***	36	49
Support gun control***	65	49

*Significant at $p<.10$; **$p<.05$; ***$p<.01$

The difference between women and men on social welfare questions should certainly not be overstated. When we combined the items to form a 0 to 1 scale (with 1 representing the highest level of support for the welfare system), the difference between women (.64) and men (.58) is statistically significant ($p<.01$), but it is clearly much smaller than the gap that separated the lowest (.68) and highest (.55) income groups. And with mean scores ranging from a low of .54 in the West to a high of .70 in Quebec, regional differences also outstrip sex differences.[12] The fact remains, though, that the advent of an era of federal budget surpluses had not eliminated the differences between women and men in their views on social welfare.

Opinions about health care provide further evidence that women are more inclined than men to favour state provision. Improving health care was the single most important issue in the 2000 federal election for women and men alike. But the issue was more salient for women than for men (see Table 9.1, p. 145). It is easy to understand why such importance was attached to the issue and also why it was even more important for women: two-thirds of men and fully three-quarters of women believed that the quality of health care had deteriorated over the previous five years. Not surprisingly, women and men largely agreed that this was an area where spending by the federal government should be increased. Interestingly, though, a substantial proportion of both women and men who perceived the quality of health care to have worsened blamed the deterioration on poor management rather than lack of money.

Even though women were more likely to think that the quality of health care had deteriorated, they were more opposed than men to market solutions, such as allowing private hospitals in Canada or allowing doctors to charge a fee for office visits. When we combined these two items into a simple additive scale that ran from 0 (favour both private hospitals and user fees) to 1 (oppose both private hospitals and user fees), women received an average score of .67, compared with .57 for men ($p<.01$). Again, the difference between women and men was hardly huge, but it rivalled the difference between the lowest (.67) and highest (.56) income groups and it exceeded regional differences, at least outside Quebec.[13]

Whether we look at views on free enterprise, the welfare state, or health policy, a similar pattern of gender differences appears. Women were more ambivalent about the free enterprise system, more sympathetic to the welfare state, and more reluctant to turn to the market for solutions. But a key question remains unanswered: Is this because women tend to be more reliant on the state, or is it because women in general tend to be less individualistic than men, as Gilligan's (1982) work suggests?

The welfare state dismantlement thesis implies that women will be less persuaded of the virtues of free enterprise than men because they are less likely to be among its beneficiaries. While the gap was narrower among women (.52) and men (.56) in the lowest income group ($p<.10$), women in the highest income group proved to be only slightly more pro–free enterprise (.54) than less affluent women.[14] A similar pattern held for views about the welfare state. If the welfare state dismantlement thesis explained the gender gap in support of the welfare state, we would expect the gap to disappear once we control for income differences. The gap between women (.69) and men (.67) did narrow in the lowest income group, but affluent women remained significantly more supportive of the welfare system (.61) than similarly affluent men (.52; $p<.01$), and income clearly made less of a difference to women's opinions than it does to men's. Differences in the material circumstances of women and men made even less difference to their views about health care. True, the gap between women (.70) and men (.64) was smaller in the lowest income category, but it still met conventional levels of statistical significance ($p<.05$), and the gap actually widened among the most affluent women (.63) and men (.51; $p<.01$). In fact, high-income women were almost as committed to universal provision as low-income men. Clearly, something other than differences in material self-interest must be driving these gender gaps.

This conclusion is reinforced when we look at the effects of sector of employment. According to the welfare state dismantlement thesis, part of the explanation for these gender gaps in views about the role of the state versus the market lies in the fact that women are more likely than men to be employed in the public sector. It turns out, though, that the gender gaps persist. Whether they were employed in the public sector or in the private sector made little difference to women's and men's opinions about the free enterprise system. A similar pattern held for views about welfare. Men employed in the public sector were no more supportive of the welfare system than their counterparts in the private sector, and women employed in the public sector (.64) did not score significantly higher than women employed in the private sector (.61). Furthermore, far from eliminating the gender gap in support of universal health care, the gap was actually wider among women (.72) and men (.60) within the public sector ($p<.01$).

Similarly, gendered patterns of employment more generally cannot explain these differences in the views of women and men. According to this argument, entry into the paid workforce has a radicalizing effect on women by exposing them to gender inequalities and discrimination. However, labour-force participation had little or no effect on women's (or men's) perceptions of the economic system, and women remained more supportive of universal health care whether they were in the paid workforce or not. As for views about welfare, support for the welfare system was, if anything, a little lower among women who were in paid employment, though they remained significantly more supportive (.62) than men who are employed (.55; $p<.01$).

Having children is also said to have a radicalizing effect on women by pushing them in a more liberal direction, at least on questions having to do with collective provision and the role of the state. Lise Togeby suggests that this effect will be most evident when there is only one child (1994). This gender-roles argument did not fare well, though. If anything, women with a single child were slightly more persuaded (.55) of the virtues of free enterprise. And far from having a radicalizing effect, women who had one child tended to be a little *less* positive in their views about welfare. Surprisingly, having children had no effect on women's views on health policy. The effect was confined to men; consistent with Togeby's argument, having one child has a radicalizing effect whereas having more than one child has the opposite effect.

The fact that none of these structural and situational explanations can account for the gender gaps in views about the role of the state versus the market lends plausibility to socio-psychological interpretations that emphasize gender differences in fundamental values. The extent to which women are less individualistic than men cannot be explained in terms of differences in material interests or experiences in the workforce or the home.

As we noted above, though, there are a variety of differences among women themselves that need to be taken into account. First, the 'women's autonomy' argument suggests that women require economic and psychological independence from men in order to express their distinctive values and priorities (Carroll 1988). To achieve psychological independence, women have to transcend traditional sex-role socialization. One of the most potent factors in encouraging such independence is higher education. Economic independence, meanwhile, is more likely to be achieved by women who are in paid employment and who are not married. As Susan Carroll notes, 'economic independence from men is highly, although not perfectly, correlated with marital status' (1988: 256).

This argument implies that skepticism about the free enterprise system should be most apparent among women who are in paid employment, who are more highly educated, and who have either never married or are separated or divorced. The same should be true of support for the welfare system and public provision of health care. However, these expectations received only mixed and weak support from our study. We have already seen that labour-force participation did not have the expected effect. The same held for marital status: the gender gaps were not confined to those who had never married but appeared regardless of marital status. Women who had never married (.46) were a little more skeptical of the virtues of free enterprise, but married women remained significantly more skeptical (.54) than married men (.61; $p<.01$). A similar pattern held for views on welfare and health care. With one notable exception, education had little effect on women's views on all of these questions. The exception was health care: as the level of education increased, the gender gap widened. The mean score for university-educated women was .70, compared with only .54 for their male counterparts ($p<.01$). Aside from this, though, there is little to suggest that the gender gaps are more likely to occur among women who enjoy sufficient autonomy to express their difference from men.

Pippa Norris, meanwhile, has pointed to the existence of a gender–generation gap that she attributes to the impact of the second-wave women's movement on the cohorts of women who reached maturity in its wake (1999). The effect of this feminist mobilization is to make younger women more liberal in their views than both men and older women.[15] In order to pursue this possibility, we compared opinions across four age cohorts that corresponded to distinct phases in the evolution of the women's movement: the pre–second wave cohort, born before 1942; the second-wave cohort, born between 1942 and 1957; the post-movement cohort, born between 1958 and 1972; and the third-wave cohort, born after 1972 (see Everitt 2001).

However, this feminist catalyst argument fared little better than the women's autonomy argument. Women who came of age during the rise of third-wave feminism were a little more skeptical of the virtues of free enterprise (.48) than women whose formative experiences predated the rise of the second-wave feminism (.56), but a parallel effect appears for men. On the other hand, there was no association between age and support for the welfare system: the gender gap cut across age cohorts. And if exposure to the feminist movement had a radicalizing effect on women's views about health care, that effect was modest and confined to women who came of age during the rise of third-wave feminism (.74). The gender gap persisted, regardless of age cohort; even in the pre–second wave cohort, women (.67) were significantly more opposed to market solutions than men (.58; $p<.01$).

Feminism and Gender

So far, we have been treating feminist mobilization as a possible catalyst for the expression of women's difference, but we also need to compare women's and men's orientations toward the feminist movement, and indeed toward gender issues more generally. One possible explanation for the rightward tilt on the part of some men is a reaction against changes in gender roles over the past three decades, changes that have challenged their traditional position of dominance within both the public and private spheres. Given the central role of the feminist movement in instigating this challenge, we should expect to find much more negative views about feminism among men.

If we focus simply on how much sympathy respondents expressed with feminism, we can immediately discount the notion of an anti-feminist backlash on the part of men. If anything, it is women, not men, who were less likely to be sympathetic (see Table 9.1, p. 145). However, men did tend to have less positive perceptions of the feminist movement. They were less likely than women to think that the feminist movement 'just tries to get equal treatment for women' and encourages women 'to be independent and speak up for themselves'. Significantly, though, only a minority of men opted for the view that the feminist movement 'puts men down' (27 per cent) and encourages women 'to be selfish and think only of themselves' (18 per cent).[16] And these views had less effect on men's sympathy with feminism than on women's: only 42 per cent of men who said the movement puts men down and 50 per cent of those who said it encourages women to be selfish were unsympathetic, compared with 63 per cent and 68 per cent, respectively, of women.

When the three items are combined into a pro-feminism scale, there is a statistically significant, albeit modest, difference in the mean scores of women (.72) and men (.67; $p<.01$) on a 0 to 1 scale.[17] With average scores ranging from a low of .67 in both Ontario and the West to a high of .77 in Quebec ($p<.01$), where a person lives clearly had more of an effect on their views about feminism than whether they were a man or a woman. As the gender–generation gap thesis would lead us to expect, there was even less difference between women (.68) and men (.65) who came of age before the advent of the second-wave women's movement. That said, the differences across age cohorts in support of feminism were surprisingly modest, even among women. It is only among women who were socialized during the rise of third-wave feminism that there was much of an increase in support for feminism (.78).

O'Neill argues that religiosity acts as a countervailing force to feminism in many women's lives (2001b), and this may well be one reason why the gender gap in support for feminism is so modest. Religion is typically a more salient factor for women than for men: Canadian women are more likely to state a religious affiliation than Canadian men, and they are also more likely to say that religion is personally important to them. Religiosity does indeed help to explain why the gender gap in support for feminism is so modest in our study. The gap disappeared altogether between women (.64) and men (.64) for whom religion was very important, and significantly more women (36 per cent) than men (26 per cent) said that religion was important in their lives. Tellingly, secularism was associated with a sizeable increase in support for feminism among women (.80) but not among men (.68).[18]

The women's autonomy argument would predict that support for feminism would also be higher among women who enjoy economic and psychological independence from men. However, labour-force participation had virtually no effect on women's (or men's) support for feminism, and full-time homemakers in particular were no less supportive than women in general. Education, meanwhile, had only very modest effects, with support ranging from .69 among women who did not complete high school to .77 among university graduates ($p<.05$). The one dimension of the women's autonomy argument that did make a difference was marital status, with support ranging from a low of .69 among women in traditional (that is, non–common law) marriages to .81 among those who had never married ($p<.01$). There are no indications that having children has a radicalizing effect on women.[19]

The lack of effect of labour-force participation may seem surprising given that women were more likely than men to believe that 'discrimination makes it extremely difficult for women to get jobs equal to their abilities' (see Table 9.1, p. 145). It turns out, though, that this belief was *less* prevalent among women (and men) who were in paid employment (53 per cent) than among those who were not (63 per cent). This poses something of a challenge to the notion that participation in the labour force radicalizes women by exposing them to gender inequalities.

As with views about feminism, opinions about gender-related issues do not lend much support to the notion of a backlash on the part of men. Women and men alike generally rejected the suggestion that 'if a company has to lay off some of its employees, the first workers to be laid off should be women whose husbands have jobs'. Only a small minority would countenance such blatant discrimination, and they were as likely to be women (11 per cent) as men (12 per cent). And when it comes to conceptions of gender roles, women were actually a little less likely than men to reject the traditional notion that 'society would be better off if more women stayed home with their children'.

On the other hand, women were more likely than men to say that more should be done for women, and they were much more likely to agree that having more female MPs is the best way to protect women's interests. That said, they did not necessarily see the lack of women in the House of Commons as a serious problem, and they were only a little less reluctant than men to endorse the idea of requiring parties to nominate as many female as male candidates.

The questions on discrimination, doing more for women, and having more women MPs were combined into a scale, which revealed a significant gap between women (.62) and men (.54; $p<.01$) on attitudes toward gender-related issues. The gap may be modest, but it rivals the differences to be observed across Canada's regions (ranging from a low of .55 in the West to a high of .64 in Quebec).[20] There is little evidence, though, of any gender–generation gap. Attitudes on gender-related questions were even less affected by age cohort than was support for feminism. Whether socialized before the advent of second-wave feminism or during the rise of third-wave feminism, women on average held very similar views on these questions. And if the gender gap narrowed in the oldest cohort, it was because older men actually scored a little higher than younger men.

There was even less support for the women's autonomy argument. Labour-force participation had little discernible impact on women's views, and marital status, too, made only a small difference (and it was women who were divorced or separated who had the highest mean score at .69). The impact of education was actually stronger among men, with scores ranging from a high of .61 for men who did not complete high school to a low of .50 for university graduates. Education had very little impact on women, and it was women who did not complete high school who scored highest (.67). Finally, far from radicalizing women, if anything having children was associated with a slightly less pro-woman stance on these questions (.60, versus .64 for women who had no children).

Moral Traditionalism

Whether we look at support for feminism or at views about gender-related issues more generally, the differences between women and men were too modest to support a charge of a significant anti-feminist backlash on the part of men. However, this does not preclude the possibility of a more generalized cultural backlash against changes in values and lifestyles.

There are certainly indications that men tend to be a little more conservative than women when it comes to issues of moral traditionalism, but the differences are nowhere near large enough to justify referring to a cultural backlash on the part of Canadian men (see Table 9.1, p. 145). The one issue on which women and men really differed was gay marriage. Only one-third of the women interviewed were opposed to allowing gays and lesbians to get married, compared with almost half of the men. Among women, a clear majority (58 per cent) came out in favour of allowing gay marriages. The other sex differences were much more modest. Women were even less likely than men to agree with the statement that 'only people who are married should be having children' or to reject the notion that 'we should be more tolerant of people who choose to live according to their own standards, even if they are very different from our own'. They were also a little less likely to agree that 'newer lifestyles are contributing to the breakdown of our society' and that 'this country would have many fewer problems if there were more emphasis on traditional family values'. It should be noted, though, that over two-thirds of women did agree with the latter proposition. And when it came to the notion that 'the world is always changing and we should adapt our view of moral behaviour to these changes', women were actually more likely to disagree than were men. Finally, to the extent that there was any difference at all on abortion, it was women who thought it should be more difficult for a woman to get an abortion.

Not surprisingly, then, when these items are combined into an additive scale, women (.47) score only marginally lower than men (.49) on moral traditionalism, a difference that barely reaches conventional levels of statistical significance ($p<.05$).[21] The impact of gender on moral traditionalism pales beside that of other social characteristics. Differences between regions, for example, ranged from a high of .52 in Atlantic Canada to a low of .41 in Quebec ($p<.01$).

Age had an even stronger effect than region, with average scores ranging from a low of .35 for the youngest cohort to .58 for the oldest cohort ($p<.01$). However, the pattern of age effects does not conform to the notion of a gender–generation gap. On the contrary, the effect of age was nearly the same for women and men.

O'Neill (2001) shows that religion has a conservative influence in many women's lives (see also De Vaus and McAllister 1989; Mayer and Smith 1995) and serves to limit the size of the gender gaps on questions relating to civil liberties (such as pornography, capital punishment, and the rights of gays and lesbians). If this argument applies to issues of traditional morality more generally, we would expect the gender gap to be wider between women and men who are more secular. Religiosity was indeed one of the most important correlates of moral traditionalism for both women and men. Average scores on the moral traditionalism scale ranged from a low of .34 among respondents to whom religion was not important at all to a high of .60 among those to whom it was very important ($p<.01$). However, women's greater religiosity does not explain the modest size of the gender gap on these questions as a whole. The gender gap was only slightly wider among women (.30) and men (.36) to whom religion was unimportant ($p<.05$).

A similar pattern holds for marital status. Women who were living in common-law relationships clearly took more liberal positions on these questions (.37) than those who were living in traditional marriages (.50), but the same was true of their male counterparts (.38).[22] Surprisingly, perhaps, having children made no difference to women (or men), despite the assumption of some gender-role theorists that parenthood increases concern on women's part for moral standards in society.

There is some support, though, for the women's autonomy argument. Education had more impact on women than on men. The more education women had, the less likely they were to be moral traditionalists. Average scores ranged from .57 among women who did not complete high school to only .40 among university graduates, compared with a range of .55 to .44 for men. And to the extent that labour-force participation makes a difference, women (but not men) who were in paid employment did tend to take less traditional positions on questions of morality (.44) than women who were not part of the labour force (.51).[23]

Crime and Punishment

As we noted above, Gilligan's work (1982) suggests that women will be less likely than men to favour a punitive approach in dealing with crime. This turned out to be the case. The fact that women were even more concerned about crime than men makes the differences in views about crime and punishment all the more interesting. Among women and men alike, crime ranked second only to health care in the number of times it was described as being a very important issue to the respondent. However, it was even more important to women than to men (see Table 9.1, p. 145).

One reason may be that women were more likely to think that crime had increased over the previous five years. Even among those who thought that crime had gone down, though, women (66 per cent) were more likely than men (56 per cent) to describe it as a very important issue. Three-quarters of women and almost as many men concurred that 'we must crack down on crime even if that means people lose their rights'. Where women and men parted company was on the treatment of those who commit crimes. Women were less likely than men to advocate a punitive approach in dealing with young offenders. Men clearly opted for tougher sentences (53 per cent) over rehabilitation (33 per cent), but women were divided, with almost as many choosing rehabilitation (41 per cent) as the get-tough approach (43 per cent). Similarly, women were much less likely than men to favour the death penalty. Indeed, more women opposed (43 per cent) the death penalty than favoured it. Moreover, there seemed to be a good deal of ambivalence about the question: 20 per cent of women responded that they did not know, compared with 14 per cent of men.

The division was even sharper when it came to gun control. Two-thirds of the women agreed that 'only the military and police offices should be allowed to have guns', compared with only half of the men. This finding is very much in line with prior research in Canada and elsewhere that has consistently found sizeable gender gaps on issues relating to the use of force (Everitt 1998a; Smith 1984; Terry 1984). Surprisingly, perhaps, this reluctance to resort to force even extended to peace-keeping. Women (53 per cent) were much less ready than men (67 per cent) to agree that 'Canada should participate in peacekeeping operations abroad even if it means putting the lives of Canadian soldiers at risk'. As with the other issue of life and death, many women (13 per cent) were unsure how to respond (compared with only 4 per cent of men).

When we combined the two items dealing with offenders into a simple additive scale, running from 0 (rehabilitate young offenders and oppose the death penalty) to 1 (tougher sentences for young offenders and favour the death penalty), men (.58) clearly emerged on the get-tough side, while women (.49) were close to the midpoint (p<.01).[24] Moreover, women's views on dealing with offenders were little affected by the region of Canada in which they lived. The same cannot be said of men, with mean scores ranging from a low of .50 in Quebec to a high of .64 in the West (p<.01).

According to the gender–generation gap argument, younger women should be more liberal than both men and older women. This is very much the pattern that appeared for views about crime and punishment. The gender gap was widest between women (.41) and men (.56) in the youngest age cohort (p<.01). And while young women were clearly more opposed than older women to treating offenders harshly, young men were little different from their elders.

There is also some support for the women's autonomy argument. The key idea here is that women require psychological and economic independence from men in order to express their 'difference'. Two key indicators are education and marital status. As the argument would predict, the more formal schooling women had, the less likely they were to favour a get-tough approach to crime: mean scores ranged from a high of .54 for those who did not complete high school to a low of .37 for university graduates (p<.01) . Meanwhile, education had little effect on men's views, though men with a university education were less likely to embrace the get-tough approach (.49).[25] It is worth emphasizing that the difference across educational levels among women easily exceeded the overall difference between women and men. Marital status also had the predicted effect: women in traditional marriages tended to take a tougher line on crime than did women who had never married; this said, the gender gap persisted. The other factor that is assumed to limit women's autonomy is confinement to the domestic sphere, but participation in the paid workforce had little effect on women's (or men's) opinions. Women who had children at home (.54) were a little less liberal than those who did not (.46) when it came to matters of crime and punishment, but the effect was not consistent enough to claim much support for the gender-roles argument. [26] A similar conclusion holds for the effect of religiosity.[27]

DISCUSSION

Despite the change in the economic context and the advent of budget surpluses, women clearly remained more skeptical of the virtues of free enterprise, more supportive of the welfare system, and more reluctant to endorse market solutions than men in the 2000 federal election. The fact that these gender gaps could not be explained in terms of differences in women's and men's material interests lends weight to the socio-psychological argument that women tend to be less individualistic than men. The gender gap in views about crime and punishment also provides support for a socio-psychological interpretation of the gender gap phenomenon.

    In contrast to a number of earlier studies, we also find consistent evidence of gender gaps in opinions on both feminism and gender-related questions more generally. However, these gaps did not extend to the broader domain of traditional social values, despite the fact that the 2000 election brought questions of traditional morality to the fore. There are signs that men tend to take slightly more conservative stances on these questions than women do, but with the notable exception of gay marriage, the gender gaps were small or inconsistent. And even on the issues that are explicitly gendered, the differences among women themselves exceeded the differences between women and men, as did the regional differences. Religiosity, in particular, clearly served as a conservative influence when it came to views about feminism and questions of traditional morality.

    Other sources of difference among women proved to be less important. Of the factors that might enhance women's autonomy, education and marital status were the most consequential, but their effects were not uniform. There is little indication that participation in the paid workforce makes a significant difference to women's views. Meanwhile, having children either had no effect or had contradictory effects.

    While the socio-psychological approach generally fared better than the structural and situational explanations, the gaps we observed would seem too modest to support the notion of a distinctive women's political culture (O'Neill 2002).[28] That does not mean, though, that they are inconsequential. The gender gaps on free enterprise, health policy, and crime and punishment all exceeded the differences across Canada's regional divides. And because gender is the 'fault line of maximum potential cleavage' (Jennings 1988: 9), even small differences between women and men can have important implications for party fortunes. Finally, to the extent that younger women, but not younger men, are more left-wing than their elders in domains like health care, feminism, and crime and punishment, we can expect these gender gaps to increase through generational turnover. Gender, in short, is a source of cleavage that must be taken seriously in any analysis of Canadian politics.

APPENDIX: QUESTION WORDING

Text in square brackets indicates in which wave of the survey the question was asked: 'cps' indicates the campaign telephone survey, 'pes' indicates the post-election telephone survey, and 'mbs' indicates the self-administered mail-back survey.

Free Enterprise
1. For each statement below, please indicate if you strongly agree, agree, disagree, or strongly disagree:

   - When businesses make a lot of money, everyone benefits, including the poor. [pesg16]
   - People who don't get ahead should blame themselves, not the system. [pesg15]
   - If people really want work, they can find a job. [mbsa11]
   - The government should leave it entirely to the private sector to create jobs. [cpsf6]
   - If people can't find work in the region where they live, they should move to where there are jobs. [cpsf20]

The Welfare State
1. To you personally, in this federal election, is improving social welfare programs very important, somewhat important, or not very important? [cpsa2f]
2. How much should be done to reduce the gap between the rich and the poor in Canada: much more, somewhat more, about the same as now, somewhat less, or much less? [cpsc13]
3. Please circle the number that best reflects your opinion. The government should [mbsb1]:

   i. see to it that everyone has a decent standard of living
   ii. leave people to get ahead on their own

4. For each statement below, please indicate if you strongly agree, agree, disagree, or strongly disagree:

   - The welfare state makes people less willing to look after themselves. [mbsa4]

5. Should the federal government spend more, less, or about the same as now on welfare? [pesd1b]

Health Policy

1. To you personally, in this federal election, is improving health care very important, somewhat important, or not very important? [cpsa2e]
2. Has the quality of health care in Canada over the past five years got worse, got better, or stayed about the same? [cpsc6]
3. Should the federal government spend more, less, or about the same as now on health care? [pesd1d]
4. Would you favour or oppose having some private hospitals in Canada? [pesd7]
5. And would you favour or oppose letting doctors charge patients a [$10][$20] fee for each office visit? [pesd8a/b] [Note: the amount of the fee was randomly varied.]

Feminism and Gender-Related Issues

1. Are you very sympathetic toward feminism, quite sympathetic, not very sympathetic, or not sympathetic at all? [pesg20]
2. Please circle the number that best reflects your opinion.

   a. The feminist movement encourages women [mbsb7]:

      i. to be independent and speak up for themselves
      ii. to be selfish and think only of themselves

   b. The feminist movement [mbsb2]:

      i. just tries to get equal treatment for women
      ii. puts men down

3. For each statement below, please indicate if you strongly agree, agree, disagree, or strongly disagree:

   • Discrimination makes it extremely difficult for women to get jobs equal to their abilities. [mbsa5]
   • If a company has to lay off some of its employees, the first workers to be laid off should be women whose husbands have jobs. [mbsa3]
   • The best way to protect women's interests is to have more women in Parliament. [mbsa15]
   • Society would be better off if more women stayed home with their children. [cpsf3]

4. How much should be done for women: much more, somewhat more, about the same as now, somewhat less, much less, or haven't you thought much about it? [cpsc10]

5. As you may know, there are many more men than women in the House of Commons. In your view, is this a very serious problem, quite a serious problem, not a very serious problem, or not a serious problem at all? [pesg7a]
6. Would you favour or oppose requiring the parties to have an equal number of male and female candidates? [pesg7b]

Moral Traditionalism

1. For each statement below, please indicate if you strongly agree, agree, disagree, or strongly disagree:

   - Gays and lesbians should be allowed to get married. [cpsf18]
   - Only people who are legally married should be having children. [mbse4]
   - We should be more tolerant of people who choose to live according to their own standards, even if they are very different from our own. [mbsa2]
   - Newer lifestyles are contributing to the breakdown of our society. [mbsa7]
   - This country would have many fewer problems if there were more emphasis on traditional family values. [mbsa9]
   - The world is always changing and we should adapt our view of moral behaviour to these changes. [mbsa8]

2. And now a question on abortion: do you think it should be very easy for women to get an abortion, quite easy, quite difficult, or very difficult? [pesg8]

Crime and Punishment

1. To you personally, in this federal election, is fighting crime very important, somewhat important, or not very important? [cpsa2b]
2. Do you think that crime in Canada has gone up, gone down, or stayed about the same in the last few years? [cpsj50]
3. Which is the best way to deal with young offenders who commit violent crime: one, give them tougher sentences, or, two, spend more on rehabilitating them? [cpsj51]
4. Do you favour or oppose the death penalty for persons convicted of murder? [cpsc15]
5. For each statement below, please indicate if you strongly agree, agree, disagree, or strongly disagree:

   - We must crack down on crime, even if that means that criminals lose their rights. [mbse5]
   - Only the police and the military should be allowed to have guns. [cpsf19]

Notes

1. The authors are grateful to the Social Sciences and Humanities Research Council of Canada for funding under its Major Collaborative Research Initiatives Programme. The authors would also like to thank Cameron Anderson for his research assistance.

2. In 1993, 15 per cent of women voted Reform, compared with 23 per cent of men. In 1997, 18 per cent of women voted Reform, compared with 26 per cent of men.

3. The Alliance attracted the votes of 32 per cent of men, but only 22 per cent of women.

4. In 1997, 13 per cent of women voted NDP, compared with 8 per cent of men. In 2000, 12 per cent of women opted for the NDP, compared with 9 per cent of men.

5. Focusing on feminist consciousness, rather than feminist issues, O'Neill (2001b) has recently found evidence of larger gender differences.

6. Funding for the 2000 Canadian Election Study was provided by the Social Sciences and Humanities Research Council of Canada, Elections Canada, and the Institute for Research in Public Policy. The field work was conducted by the Institute for Social Research at York University (outside Quebec) and by Jolicoeur (in Quebec). The study consisted of a 30-minute campaign interview, a 30-minute post-election interview, and a self-administered mail-back questionnaire. The response rate for the campaign survey was 59 per cent. Of the 3,647 respondents interviewed during the campaign, 2,918 completed the post-election survey and 1,539 returned the mail-back questionnaire. This chapter uses items from all three waves of the study. The demographic composition of the three waves is similar, except for the fact that the mail-back questionnaire had fewer respondents in the youngest age group. For any gender gap that is wider among young people, the overall size of the gap may be underestimated.

7. Each scale is a simple additive scale. The individual items were all re-scaled to run from 0 to 1 and then summed to form the scale. Dividing the total scores by the number of items yielded a scale that runs from 0 to 1. Wording for all questions used in this chapter can be found in the Appendix. Scalability was assessed using Cronbach's Alpha. The coefficients ranged from .47 to .74. On the basis of his meta-analysis of the magnitude of alpha coefficients obtained in behavioural research, Peterson reports that the average alpha coefficient for scales measuring values and beliefs is .70 (1994). The average coefficient for the scales used in this chapter is .60. Scales with a small number of items typically yield lower coefficients.

8. As Manza and Brooks (1998) readily acknowledge, it is possible that the arrow runs both ways. In other words, it may also be the case that a growing feminist consciousness encourages women to enter the paid workforce.

9. Togeby (1994) found that the effects of parenthood on women vary depending on the number of children. In her study, having a single child was associated with more left-wing views, while having more than one child appeared to make women more conservative.

10. The pro–free enterprise scale has a reliability coefficient of Alpha = .51. Average scores range from .55 in both Atlantic Canada and Ontario to .58 in the West ($p<.05$), and from .54 in the lowest income tercile to .59 in the highest income tercile ($p<.01$).

11. Twenty-two per cent of men favoured spending less on welfare, compared with 20 per cent of women.

12. The pro-welfare scale has a coefficient of reliability of Alpha = .69. Both the income differences and the regional differences are significant at the $p<.01$ level.

13. The universal health care scale has a coefficient of reliability of Alpha = .47. The income differences are significant at the $p<.01$ level. Regional scores ranged from .60 in the West to .68 in Ontario ($p<.01$). Quebec was the outlier, with an average score of only .55.

14. The gap between women and men in the highest income tercile remains significant at the $p=.01$ level.

15. However, Everitt found that feminist mobilization appears to have affected young men and young women alike, at least on questions relating to feminism and equality (1998b).

16. The figures for women were 15 per cent and 11 per cent, respectively.

17. The pro-feminism scale has a coefficient of reliability of Alpha = .66.

18. The gap is statistically significant at the $p<.01$ level.

19. If anything, women with one child were less supportive of feminism (.65).

20. The gender scale has a coefficient of reliability of Alpha = .58. The questions on the lack of women MPs and on requiring parties to nominate equal numbers of women and men could not be included because they were asked only of a random half-sample. The inclusion of the stay-home item would result in a much lower coefficient of reliability (Alpha = .45). The regional differences are significant at the $p<.01$ level.

21. The moral traditionalism scale has a coefficient of reliability of Alpha = .74.

22. The impact of marital status is significant at the $p<.01$ level for women and men alike.

23. The differences within and among these groups are all significant at the $p<.01$ level.

24. The crime-and-punishment scale has a coefficient of reliability of Alpha = .53.

25. Mean scores ranged from .60 for men who had not completed high school to .62 for those with some postsecondary education.

26. While the overall difference is statistically significant at the $p<.01$ level, the effect of child rearing declined with the number of children. The average score for women with one child at home was .56, compared with .49 for those with three or more children.

27. Mean scores ranged from .45 for women to whom religion was not at all important to .51 for those to whom it was very important.

28. It should be noted that O'Neill looks beyond survey-based studies of public opinion and cites evidence from in-depth interviews that women and men differ in their conceptions of politics and democratic citizenship (2002).

Chapter 10

In the Eyes of the Beholders:
Gender and Leader Popularity in a Canadian Context

LYNDA ERICKSON

INTRODUCTION

The importance of party leaders in vote choice has been a venerable theme in studies of Canadian electoral politics (Clarke et al. 1982, 1991; Gidengil et al. 2000a). As central characters in national campaigns, leaders are a constant focus of media attention and comment (Mendelsohn 1993, 1996; Taras 1990). For many voters, leaders personify what an election is all about. It is not surprising, then, that voters' opinions of leaders become salient when they enter the polling booth. Since leaders and the public's perceptions of them are so important in elections and election outcomes, the question of whether women and men react differently to particular political leaders is of special interest to those interested in the gender dimensions of political life. Yet research on Canadian politics has just begun to address the issue of gender differences in voters' responses to party leaders. Studies have looked at whether leader effects on vote decisions are stronger for women than for men (Banducci and Karp 2000; Gidengil et al. 2000a) and at what kind of effect of women party leaders have on the voting behaviour of women and men (Banducci and Karp 2000; O'Neill 1998). But more general questions of how, and indeed whether, women routinely assess leaders differently than men have attracted less direct attention.

There are a number of reasons to think that women may assess some leaders more favourably or other leaders less favourably than do men. First, some popular notions and research suggest that how women and men perceive public figures may not always be the same (Hyde 1991; Lips 1993; Sapiro and Conover 1997). If women and men characterize leaders differently they may feel differently about them. Second, there is evidence that opinions of women and men differ on a number of social and political values and issues (see chapter 9; see also Erickson and O'Neill, forthcoming; Everitt 1998a; Gidengil 1995; Gidengil et al. 2000c; O'Neill 2001). These differences might also lead to different leader assessments, with women tending to assess more favourably leaders whose political views reflect the 'women's side' on issues. Third, 'resemblance criteria', by which voters give higher ratings to leaders who mirror their demographic characteristics (O'Neill 1998), suggest that women voters will rate women party leaders more highly than will men voters. Certainly, evidence from research on gender and the evaluation of leaders in other organizational contexts has found that men devalue female leaders more than women do (Eagly, Makhijani, and Klonsky 1992).

Not only may women assess particular leaders more or less favourably than men, there may also be gender differences in what factors determine how favourably particular leaders are evaluated. Certain traits attributed to leaders may be more important for women than for men. For example, whether or not a leader is perceived as compassionate may matter more to women and thus have a greater effect on women's approval of that leader. Or certain socio-demographic characteristics among voters may be more (or less) relevant in determining women's assessments of leaders. For example, religious convictions may structure women's ratings of leaders more than they do men's ratings. There is evidence that the factors that affect other political attitudes and that structure voting behaviour differ to some degree between women and men (Erickson and O'Neill, forthcoming; Gidengil et al. 2000c; O'Neill 2001; Sapiro and Conover 1997). We might reasonably hypothesize that this differential salience, or relevance, of factors extends to how leaders are evaluated. Using data from the 1997 Canadian Election Study (CES), this chapter explores the issue of gender differences in Canadians' assessments of party leaders.[1] It determines whether or not there are differences in men's and women's overall familiarity with leaders as well as in their evaluations of leaders' personal traits. The analysis also examines the role various socio-political factors play in the relationship between gender and leader assessments.

GENDER AND LEADERSHIP ASSESSMENTS: PREVIOUS FINDINGS

In the comparative literature, evidence on whether men and women differ in their assessments of party leaders has been mixed. Looking at how women and men in Australia, Britain, and the United States viewed the personal qualities of party leaders in the early 1990s, Bernadette Hayes and Ian McAllister found some gender differences in the assessments of the leaders in each country, but differences were limited to assessments of challengers and did not extend to incumbents (1997). Moreover, they concluded that except for evaluations of Neil Kinnock, the Labour Opposition leader in Britain, gender had no significant net effect on leader evaluations once other factors were taken into account. In other words, when statistical methods were used to control for relevant socio-demographic and political variables, including partisanship and attitudes to the economy, the impact of gender disappeared. They concluded it was these other variables, not gender as such, that produced the gender differences they found. Hayes and McAllister did not, however, examine whether the factors affecting leadership assessments differed for women and men, or whether some factors affected women more than men.

Virginia Sapiro and Pamela Johnston Conover also explored the issue of leader perceptions in their analysis of the relevance of gender in the 1992 American elections (1997). They looked at two aspects of leader assessments: respondents' emotional reactions to the two leading candidates, George H. Bush and Bill Clinton, and the character traits attributed to these candidates. They found gender differences in both emotional responses to and character assessments of both the incumbent (Bush) and the challenger (Clinton). For both the emotional responses and respondents' perceptions of the two leaders' character traits, the effect of gender mostly disappeared once Sapiro and Conover controlled for socio-demographic factors, core values, partisanship, and respondents' positions on a number of key political issues. They concluded that gender as such did not determine the emotional responses to candidates: it was the socio-demographic and attitudinal differences between women and men that produced the gender differences.

However, Sapiro and Conover also looked at whether the factors affecting voters' emotional responses and their perceptions of character traits worked differently for women than men. While they found many similarities between the sexes—there were many parallels in how various factors affected the judgments of women and men— there was evidence of differences as well. As they observed, women and men 'did not assess character traits in precisely the same way' (Sapiro and Conover 1997: 515).

Research on Canada that has looked at gender and leadership has tended to focus on gender differences in how leaders affect the way people vote. The 1993 election attracted attention in this respect because two of the five competitive parties, the Conservatives and the NDP, were headed by women (Kim Campbell and Audrey McLaughlin, respectively): the issue of whether there were gender differences in support for parties headed by women was therefore of particular interest. In her analysis of gender voting, Brenda O'Neill (1998) found that women were more likely than men to be recruited to vote PC and NDP in 1993. In other words, among those voters who changed their party vote from the previous election, or had not voted in that election, proportionally more women than men were attracted to the two parties that had female leaders. O'Neill attributed this difference to the more positive ratings that women gave to the leaders of these two parties.

In a comparative analysis of the impact of women leaders on voting in New Zealand, Australia, Britain, and Canada, Susan Banducci and Jeffrey Karp (2000) also looked at the 1993 Canadian election. They too recorded gender differences in voters' assessments of the female leaders, with women more favourable to the women leaders. But they also noted a significant gender difference in assessments of the Reform party leader, Preston Manning, who was more popular among men. With further analysis, they found that leadership assessments were more important for women than for men in voting Conservative, NDP, and Liberal.

In their analysis of the effects of leadership on voting from 1968 to 1997, Elisabeth Gidengil and colleagues (2000a) also found that leader effects were greater for women than for men in 1993, and, like Banducci and Karp, they found that this difference extended beyond parties headed by women. They found no evidence that having female party leaders involved in an election particularly sensitized women to the leadership issue thus producing a gender gap in leader effects. Gender differences in leader effects over time did not necessarily coincide with elections in which female leaders were present. For example, Gidengil and colleagues found no gender differences in leader effects for the 1997 election, when the NDP again had a female leader (2002a). While such evidence speaks to the question of whether leader popularity is more important in determining the votes of women than of men, it does not directly address the question of how gender affects popularity itself.

Data and Methods

The 1997 CES questioned respondents both during the election campaign and after the vote. The data on leadership evaluations available from this survey include ratings of each party leader in both the pre- and post-election waves of the survey. In each wave, respondents were first asked how much they knew about each leader; names were presented in randomized order. Then they were asked to indicate how they 'feel' about the leaders using a scale from 0 to 100; with 0 indicating that respondents strongly disliked a leader and 100 indicating respondents strongly liked a leader, a score of 50 can be considered the neutral point.

In the pre-election wave, those who said they knew nothing at all about a particular leader were not asked to rate that leader. In the post-election re-interviews, all respondents, regardless of whether they said they knew anything at all about a leader, were asked to rate each leader. The pre-election survey also included questions about various traits of the leaders. Respondents were asked how well each of the following words and phrases fit each leader: 'trustworthy', 'strong leader', 'arrogant', 'compassionate', and 'in touch with the times'. For each trait, interviewees were asked whether it fit a particular leader 'very well', 'fairly well', 'not very well', or 'not at all'. Responses were scored from 0 for 'not at all' to 3 for 'very well'. Again those respondents who said they knew nothing about a leader were not questioned about the personal characteristics of that leader.

Both pre- and post-election questions about the party leaders are used in the analyses below. The items concerning the various traits of leaders are used to explore whether women and men see the same traits in their politicians. In combination with these questions about traits, the pre-election ratings of how respondents felt about each leader allow us to explore whether personal characteristics of leaders, and which particular ones, matter more (or less) to women than to men when they rate political leaders.

Post-election ratings provide the most complete measure of voters' views for looking at the role of socio-political variables in the nexus of gender and leader evaluations. They were collected after voters had been primed by the election campaign to think about to the various leaders,[2] and the questions were asked of all respondents, whether or not they said they knew nothing about a leader. Earlier studies indicate that many of those who say they know nothing about a leader still have views about that leader (Blais et al. 2000; Gidengil et al. 2000a). Accordingly, the post-election ratings are used to explore the implications of gender in the context of various other social and political variables.[3]

In choosing which socio-political variables to use for examining gender differences in this context, two primary criteria were used. First, socio-demographic variables that have been found to be especially relevant in other studies of Canadian electoral politics were selected. These consist of religious variables, including whether respondents were Catholic and whether they considered religion very important in their lives; education variables, including whether respondents had a university degree or did not finish high school; income; union membership; age; ethnicity; and regional variables.[4]

Value dimensions that might be considered a plausible source of gender difference were also identified. These include traditional moralism (Inglehart 1990), feminism (Conover 1988; Erickson and O'Neill, forthcoming; Gidengil et al. 2000c; Inglehart and Norris 2000), the role of government (Erickson and O'Neill, forthcoming; Gidengil 1995; Gidengil et al. 2000c; Gilens 1988; Klein 1984; Seltzer, Newman, and Leighton 1997), attitudes to capitalism (Erickson and O'Neill, forthcoming; Nevitte et al. 2000), and continentalism (Gidengil 1995). Accordingly, scales were developed from the CES data to tap each of these value dimensions,[5] and correlations between scale scores and gender were calculated. The results are displayed in Table 10.1. As the significance tests displayed in the table indicate, all but the traditionalism scale are related to gender. Thus women scored as less continentalist, more skeptical of capitalism, more supportive of governmental playing a role in the economy, and more feminist than men. Because it was thought traditionalism might play a different role for women than for men when they are evaluating leaders, that scale was kept for subsequent analyses.[6]

LEADER FAMILIARITY IN THE 1997 ELECTION

In the 1997 election, voters faced a collection of both new and more familiar leaders vying for their party votes. The prime minister and Liberal leader, Jean Chrétien, and the Reform party leader, Preston Manning, were both running in their second elections as leader. Chrétien's position as prime minister had, since 1993, guaranteed him attention in the media, and hence political visibility. Manning, on the other hand, was leader of the third-largest party in the House. Still, after the 1993 election he tended to attract media attention by virtue of his party's position as the largest opposition party outside Quebec.

Of the newer leaders, Jean Charest had assumed interim leadership of the PCs shortly after the party's disastrous showing in the 1993 election. As head of Canada's oldest political party, Charest attracted media attention, although having a caucus of just two members did limit the media coverage he received.[7] McDonough, the only female leader in the election, had won a hotly contested leadership race in her party in 1995, but even more than Charest she suffered in terms of political visibility as a result of the small contingent she led in the House.[8] The newest leader, Gilles Duceppe of the Bloc Québécois, was not elected to the

Table 10.1

Ideological Orientation by Gender[a]

Traditionalism	−.019
Feminism	.103*
Role of government	.124*
Capitalism	−.156*
Continentalism	−.087*

[a] Pearson correlation coefficients between gender and ideology scales. Gender is scored with women=1, men=0.
*$p=.01$.

leadership of his party until March 1997. However, his party's visibility in the House as the official opposition and its prominence in Quebec as a result of its role as one of the standard bearers of the separatist message guaranteed him attention within the one jurisdiction important to his party: the province of Quebec.[9]

Voters' familiarity with the leaders, both during and after the election campaign, reflected the previous electoral experience the leaders had as heads of their parties and their political visibility going into the election. Table 10.2 presents respondents' average scores on knowledge about leaders, based on whether respondents said they knew 'a lot', 'a little', or 'nothing at all' about each leader.

In both pre- and post-election surveys, Chrétien was clearly the most well known of the leaders, with Manning second.[10] McDonough was by far the least well known. In the pre-election survey, fully 63 per cent of respondents said they knew nothing at all about her, and in the post-election survey 50 per cent still said they knew nothing at all about her. By comparison, just 30 per cent and 23 per cent of respondents said the same about Jean Charest in the pre- and post-election surveys, respectively.

Table 10.2 also records the extent of gender differences in the amount of knowledge respondents said they had about the leaders. Women had significantly lower knowledge scores for three of the five leaders. McDonough, however, is not included in this group. Thus, although she was the least well known of the leaders, she did, apparently, attract the attention of as many women as men. For Duceppe, whose scores are available for Quebec respondents only, the gender differences were also small but not statistically significant.

GENDER AND LEADER EVALUATIONS

Pre-election evaluations

Before the election, as shown in Table 10.3, gender differences in leaders' rankings

Table 10.2

Leader Familiarity[a]

	Pre-election				Post-election			
	All	Women	Men	Difference	All	Women	Men	Difference
Charest	.88	.82	.94	-.12*	.97	.92	1.03	-.11*
		(2056)	(1859)			(1616)	(1523)	
Chrétien	1.22	1.16	1.29	-.13*	1.28	1.21	1.35	-.14*
		(2054)	(1861)			(1615)	(1524)	
Duceppe[b]	1.03	1.00	1.07	-.07	1.25	1.23	1.28	-.05
		(518)	(472)			(387)	(393)	
Manning[c]	1.04	.98	1.11	-.13*	1.10	1.02	1.18	-.16*
		(1526)	(1384)			(1224)	(1133)	
McDonough	.42	.41	.42	-.01	.56	.56	.57	-.01
		(2033)	(1855)			(1612)	(1526)	

[a] Mean scores, with *N* in parentheses; scale ranges from 0 to 2, with low scores indicating that respondents knew little about the leader; [b] Quebecers only; [c] non-Quebecers only.

*$p=.001$

among those who said they knew something about the leaders were evident for just two of the leaders. The largest difference was found with respect to McDonough. Although she was not the most well liked leader among women—she fell behind both Charest and Chrétien—women were clearly more positive about her than were men. This is consistent with evidence from other organizational contexts that men assess women leaders lower than do women (Eagly, Makhijani, and Klonsky 1992). In contrast to McDonough's ratings, women rated Manning lower than did men. He was the lowest-scoring leader among women, third among men.

In order to check if the gender differences in leader evaluations were simply the result of gender differences in traditional support for the parties, leader scores were calculated for those who did *not* identify with the party of the leader being evaluated (called 'Non-identifiers' in Table 10.3).[11] The gender differences described above were essentially unchanged with the introduction of this party control.

This study also looked for any evidence that women appreciate and judge leaders' personal characteristics differently. As with the leader evaluations, only respondents who said they knew something about the leaders were asked about leaders' characteristics. For each trait assessed, average scores for each leader were calculated. Some suggestive findings emerged. First, on all but one of the characteristics, gender differences with respect to assessments of McDonough were the most substantial and significant (see Table 10.4). Indeed, women judged her more positively than did men on every characteristic, but particularly as a 'strong leader' and 'in touch with the times'. The findings on 'strong leader' are consistent with findings from the psychological literature that suggest women are more willing than men to attribute non-traditional but role-positive attributes to women leaders (Kite 2001).

Gender differences were not, however, limited to assessments of McDonough's personal qualities. Scores for Manning also showed a number of gender differences. Women were less likely than men to see Manning as a strong leader, as trustwor-

Table 10.3

Pre-election Candidate Evaluation by Gender[a]

	All			Non-identifiers[b]		
	Women	Men	Difference	Women	Men	Difference
Charest	54.4	54.6	-.20	52.9	52.0	.90
	(1254)	(1318)		(930)	(1000)	
Chrétien	52.7	53.7	-1.0	45.0	46.8	-1.8
	(1745)	(1663)		(1008)	(1035)	
Duceppe[c]	43.4	40.8	2.6	33.7	32.6	1.1
	(313)	(319)		(173)	(208)	
Manning[d]	41.3	46.1	-4.8*	37.6	41.7	-4.1*
	(1108)	(1129)		(909)	(896)	
McDonough	49.6	42.1	7.5*	46.6	39.3	7.3*
	(629)	(635)		(464)	(552)	

[a] Leaders ranked on scale from 0 to 100, with *N* in parentheses; respondents who said they knew nothing at all about a leader are not included; [b] respondents who did not identify with the leader's party; [c] Quebecers only; [d] non-Quebecers only.

*Significant to *p*=.001

Table 10.4

Views on Leaders' Personal Qualities by Gender

		Women	Men	Difference
Strong leader	Charest	2.05 (1156)	2.04 (1227)	.01
	Chrétien	1.91 (1687)	1.91 (1634)	.00
	Duceppe[a]	1.19 (287)	1.03 (303)	.16*
	Manning[b]	1.57 (1035)	1.67 (1094)	-.10*
	McDonough	1.82 (522)	1.50 (539)	.32***
Trustworthy	Charest	1.84 (1040)	1.89 (1165)	-.05
	Chrétien	1.57 (1640)	1.53 (1603)	.04
	Duceppe[a]	1.41 (269)	1.41 (292)	.00
	Manning[b]	1.58 (960)	1.71 (1032)	-.13***
	McDonough	2.09 (476)	1.88 (493)	.21*
Arrogant	Charest	1.07 (1101)	1.11 (1178)	-.04
	Chrétien	1.49 (1628)	1.62 (1581)	-.13***
	Duceppe[a]	1.39 (267)	1.37 (294)	.02
	Manning[b]	1.61 (993)	1.59 (1041)	.02
	McDonough	.83 (489)	.95 (503)	-.12*
Compassionate	Charest	1.88 (1012)	1.95 (1139)	-.07
	Chrétien	1.62 (1577)	1.70 (1561)	-.08***
	Duceppe[a]	1.46 (250)	1.43 (273)	.03
	Manning[b]	1.45 (954)	1.51 (1014)	-.06
	McDonough	2.25 (479)	2.09 (486)	.16***
In touch with the times	Charest	2.00 (1082)	2.04 (1183)	-.04
	Chrétien	1.64 (1610)	1.57 (1591)	.07*
	Duceppe[a]	1.38 (255)	1.16 (288)	.22**
	Manning[b]	1.65 (971)	1.85 (1034)	-.20***
	McDonough	2.05 (475)	1.69 (490)	.36***

[a] Quebecers only; [b] non-Quebecers only.

*p=.05; **p=.01; ***p=.001

Table 10.5

Candidate Evaluations by Personal Qualities by Gender[a]

	Charest			Chrétien		
	All	**Women**	**Men**	**All**	**Women**	**Men**
Woman	–	–	–	–	–	–
Strong leader	7.52	6.61	8.27	7.22	6.61	7.47
Trustworthy	8.09	7.54	8.44	9.61	7.54	9.56
Arrogant	-2.80	2.96	-2.70	-2.80	-2.96	-3.32
Compassionate	3.50	3.57	3.41	3.62	3.57	3.90
In touch with the times	1.82	**3.30**	–	2.82	3.30	2.70
Constant[b]	18.20	19.76	17.83	21.03	21.27	19.77
N	1990	935	1055	2975	1485	1490
r^2 [c]	.38	.37	.39	.48	.50	.47

[a] Unstandardized regression coefficients; only those significant at $p < .05$ are shown. Figures in bold indicate significant gender differences significant to $p=.10$; [b] 'Constant' is the intercept, the value the dependent variable would take if the value of each independent variable was zero; [c] 'r^2' measures the proportion of variance in the dependent variable that is accounted for by the independent variables.

thy, or as in touch with the times. Duceppe, on the other hand, was more likely to be seen as a strong leader and in touch with the times by women than by men. For Chrétien, gender differences emerged only on the question of arrogance; women judged him to be less arrogant than did men. There were no gender differences in the assessments of Charest's personal qualities.[12] Overall, these findings suggest that there are some, albeit limited, differences in how women and men see the personal characteristics of political leaders, with the greatest differences occurring with respect to how a woman leader is perceived.

We also looked for any evidence that the personal characteristics related to voters' feelings about political leaders differed by gender. For example, were some characteristics, such strength, more important to men, or, following Carol Gilligan's argument that women's moral considerations are more motivated by caring and compassion (1982), were women's feelings about leaders more affected by their assessments of whether or not the leaders are compassionate? And was there any evidence for gender differences in leader ratings that were independent of how women and men assessed the traits of the different leaders? In other words, did women and men who assessed the traits of a leader similarly still differ on how much they liked or disliked that leader?

Table 10.5 presents the results of a multiple regression analysis that tested the effects of the trait assessments on respondents' like/dislike scores. It looks at how respondents scores on each trait affected how much they liked or disliked a leader when their scores on the other traits were taken into account. In other words, it shows whether the scores on each of these traits independently contribute to how leaders were rated.

The combined results for men and women include a gender variable ('Woman') to see if gender had a direct impact on leaders' ratings over and above the effects that might have come because women assessed some of the leaders' traits differently from men. The second and third columns present the results of analyses of women's

Table 10.5 (continued)

Candidate Evaluations by Personal Qualities by Gender[a]

| | Duceppe | | | Manning | | | McDonough | |
All	Women	Men	All	Women	Men	All	Women	Men
–	–	–	-1.76	–	–	–	–	–
5.57	–	7.67	4.83	4.99	4.62	7.14	5.88	8.44
12.15	14.23	10.77	8.98	9.01	8.95	7.46	7.96	6.86
-4.09	-2.86	-4.80	-3.61	-4.06	-3.22	-2.89	**-4.16**	–
–	–	–	3.61	**2.70**	**4.44**	–	–	–
–	–	–	5.93	**5.31**	**6.57**	5.90	6.21	5.15
19.52	16.31	22.87	12.67	13.67	10.00	9.39	13.28	7.20
488	228	260	1833	879	954	881	437	443
.49	.51	.49	.50	.50	.50	.38	.36	.39

and men's scores separately in order to assess whether the salience of particular traits was greater for women or men. Only the relationships that were significant, and thus empirically reliable, are included in the table.

The data show that assessments on every trait were relevant to the overall ratings of almost all the leaders. In other words, all the traits appear to matter for leaders' popularity. Of note, however, is that the direct effect of gender on evaluations remains significant, although reduced, for Manning. Even taking into account the differences in how women and men perceived Manning's personal traits, women still scored Manning almost two points lower than did men.

Women and men appeared to be largely influenced by similar personal qualities. (Note that only where figures are in bold can the differences recorded be considered significant.) The biggest effects are for trustworthiness. Indeed, trustworthiness was the most important characteristic for leaders' evaluations for both women and men—with just one exception. For men's assessments of McDonough, being a strong leader seemed to be more important than her trustworthiness.

In other respects there were no real gender differences in how important being a strong leader was in leaders' overall ratings. It seems to have weighed as heavily for women in their judgments of leaders as it did for men.[13] Nor were there gender differences with respect to the importance of compassion for leaders' rating, except for Manning: perhaps contrary to expectations, Manning's scores on compassion were more important to men than to women. For McDonough, who of all the leaders drew the highest scores for compassion among both women and men, rankings on this personality feature were not a significant factor in whether or not respondents liked her. As compassion is a characteristic more stereotypically associated with women then men (Kite 2000) and one that is socially valued (Eagly and Makhijani 1994), it is perhaps ironic that her scores on this quality did little to help her public image.

It is also of note that being in touch with the times showed one pattern of difference for Charest, for whom it had more impact on women's evaluations, and another pattern for Manning, for whom it had more impact on men's evaluations. When combined with the fact that gender differences in the leaders' scores on this trait were among the largest, these findings suggest that understandings of 'being in touch with the times' may differ for women and men.

The last trait for which there was a significant gender difference, arrogance, was important for women's assessments of McDonough but not for those of men. Again, this was a trait on which McDonough scored well among both women and men: she received the lowest scores on this (negative) trait of the five leaders. Nonetheless, for men this had little apparent effect on their feelings about her.

Post-election Evaluations

Like the pre-election evaluations, the post-election assessments show differences in how women and men responded to the leaders (see Table 10.6). McDonough elicited the largest difference, with women scoring her 7.6 points higher than men (a difference that largely held among non-identifiers). For the other leaders, women again rated Manning lower than did the men, but the difference was less than half that for McDonough. Again, however, as a group women placed Manning last among the leaders while men rated McDonough below him.[14] For Chrétien and Charest, there were quite small, albeit positive, gender differences, this time with women assessing both leaders more positively than men.

We next considered whether gender differences remained once we took into account the socio-political factors that affected the ratings of different leaders and if there was any evidence that the factors that affected the popularity of leaders differed between women and men. We found that after controlling for socio-political variables through multivariate analysis, the gender differences in ratings for Chrétien and Manning disappeared but they remained in evaluations of Charest and McDonough (see Table 10.7). In other words, there were gender differences, albeit modest, in how voters assessed these two leaders that were not accounted for by the usual factors that explain political differences.

The evidence also suggests that some of the factors that influence how people

Table 10.6
Post-election Candidate Evaluation by Gender[a]

	All			Non-identifiers[b]		
	Women	Men	Difference	Women	Men	Difference
Charest	51.1	48.8	2.3*	49.4	47.0	2.4*
	(1442)	(1429)		(1243)	(1196)	
Chrétien	55.1	52.3	2.8*	49.2	47.0	2.2
	(1543)	(1487)		(1039)	(1049)	
Duceppe[c]	42.5	38.9	3.6	37.2	35.4	1.8
	(363)	(377)		(273)	(28.3)	
Manning[d]	42.3	45.5	-3.2**	38.5	41.1	-2.6*
	(1113)	(1088)		(967)	(895)	
McDonough	46.3	38.8	7.6***	44.4	37.6	6.8***
	(1229)	(1308)		(1079)	(1188)	

[a] Leaders ranked on scale from 0 to 100, with *N* in parentheses; [b] respondents do not identify with the party of the leader being evaluated; [c] Quebecers only; [d] non-Quebecers only.
*p=.05; **p=01; *** p=.001

Table 10.7

Evaluations of Leaders by Gender[a]

	Charest			Chrétien			Manning[b]			McDonough		
	All	Women	Men	All	Women	Men	All	Women	Men	All	Women	Men
Gender	2.44*	–	–	–	–	–	–	–	–	3.68***	–	–
Catholic	–	4.90***	–	–	–	–	-5.69***	-4.53*	-7.46***	–	–	–
Religiosity	4.06***	–	2.47	–	3.48*	–	-.25***	-.26***	-.23***	–	–	–
Age	–	–	–	–	–	–	–	–	–	–	–	–
Degree	6.77***	–	10.16***	-5.68***	4.89***	-4.98*	–	–	–	8.33***	8.55***	8.20***
Not secondary	-5.49***	-5.37**	-5.43**	-4.17***	-6.67***	-3.49*	–	–	–	-2.87*	–	-4.25*
Union	-2.77**	-2.79*	–	–	-5.09**	4.59**	–	–	–	–	–	–
Public-sector	3.28**	–	–	3.27*	–	–	–	–	–	3.12**	–	3.41*
High-income	–	5.91***	–	2.91*	–	4.29*	–	–	–	–	–	–
Non-European	–	–	–	7.56***	8.19*	7.82**	–	–	–	–	–	–
Northern European	–	–	–	–	–	–	3.84*	6.56**	–	–	–	–
Atlantic	4.73***	–	7.45**	-9.63***	-11.89***	-7.23*	–	–	–	10.88***	9.96***	11.83***
Quebec	5.18***	4.14*	6.44***	-10.56***	-14.19***	-7.83***	–	–	–	–	–	–
Prairies	-5.66***	-7.12***	–	-6.94***	-8.44***	-5.71**	9.05***	5.96**	12.10***	–	–	–
BC	-5.13**	-9.12***	–	–	–	–	5.24**	–	7.52**	–	–	–
Traditionalism	–	–	–	4.70***	–	–	16.58***	12.37***	20.61***	–	–	–
Capitalism	15.07***	12.64***	17.55***	12.92***	16.02***	11.17**	16.40***	20.91***	12.42***	-9.37***	–	-10.63***
Feminism	13.78***	–	21.51***	22.95***	19.96***	26.36***	–	–	–	27.11***	25.31***	28.65***
Role of government	–	–	–	6.33**	–	6.27*	–	–	–	5.03*	7.59*	–
Continentalism	–	–	–	–	–	–	14.20***	14.25***	13.70**	-7.41*	–	-8.41*
Constant	31.10***	40.63***	24.06***	32.69***	37.62***	30.30***	32.05***	30.18***	32.63***	26.70***	28.18***	28.00***
Adjusted r^2	.09	.07	.11	.11	.13	.09	.10	.09	.11	.15	.11	.14
N	2218	1073	1145	1991	956	1035	1745	878	868	1922	898	1024

[a] Unstandardized regression coefficients. Figures in bold indicate gender differences significant to $p \leq .10$; [b] non-Quebecers only.

*Significant to $p \leq .05$; **$p \leq .01$; *** $p \leq .001$

evaluate leaders affect women and men differently. Among the socio-demographic variables, two in particular show significant gender differences (see Table 10.7).[15] Having a university degree was positively related to men's but not women's assessments of Charest, whereas a degree was positively related to women's but not men's assessments of Chrétien. Region also had a differential effect. For Chrétien, being a Quebecer had almost twice the negative effect on women as on men, whereas for Manning, living on the Prairies had twice the positive effect on men as on women.

On the ideological variables, the only gender difference in the findings that met any standard of statistical significance is the relationship of feminism to evaluations of Charest. For men, scores on feminism—that is, the extent to which they scored highly on measures tapping pro-feminist sentiments—were related to how much they said they liked Charest, whereas for women they were not. In other words, the more feminist men were, the more they liked Charest. This pattern—that feminism is more relevant for men than for women—is also hinted at in the numbers for Chrétien. Although the difference is not statistically significant, the apparent positive effect of feminism was higher for Chrétien among men than among women. It is interesting that for McDonough, on the other hand, for whom feminism was also relevant, the apparent effect was not appreciably greater for either gender.

Conclusion

Evidence for a gender dimension in voters' responses to party leaders in the 1997 election is perceptible but not substantial, suggesting a particular but not exclusive relevance for women party leaders. In general, women indicated that they were less knowledgeable than men about each party leader, except with respect to McDonough. Moreover, although women ranked McDonough third in both pre- and post-election surveys, the gender differences on leader scores were largest for her.

In terms of perceptions of leaders' traits, there is again evidence of gender differences. Women and men appear to have seen some aspects of leaders differently, but that also happened most consistently for McDonough. There were also many similarities between women and men for the salience of personal qualities in assessments of leaders. Some gender differences did emerge, but these differences were not generalized to all leaders. Thus, being a strong leader was not generally more important for men than for women, nor was compassion generally more important for women than for men. Instead, the differential effects were related to particular politicians.

With respect to the links between socio-demographic and ideological variables on one hand and leader evaluations on the other, again just a few differences emerged. Perhaps most surprising is that in evaluations of leaders, feminism appears to be more relevant for men, especially in their evaluations of male leaders. Gender, both of voters and of leaders, does seem to matter in how leaders are assessed but it in ways that are usually subtle and sometimes unexpected.

APPENDIX

Socio-demographic Variables

1. Dummy variables[16]

- Catholic: Self-identification as Catholic
- Religiosity: Religion very important
- Degree: University degree
- Not secondary: Did not finish high school
- Union: Respondent or household member belongs to union
- Public-sector: Employed in the public sector
- High-income: Household income—top 25 per cent
- Northern European: Ethnicity Northern European (excluding British or French)
- Non-European: Ethnicity non-European
- Atlantic
- Quebec
- Prairies
- British Columbia

2. Age (in years)

Ideology/Value Scales

Scales range from 0 to 1. To create each scale, component variables were re-coded from 0 to 1, then variable scores were summed and divided by the number of items in the scale.

Traditionalism

A. Only people who are married should be having children.

1. Strongly disagree
2. Somewhat disagree
3. Somewhat agree
4. Strongly agree

B. Views on abortion. Of the following three positions, which is closest to your own opinion:

1. Abortion should be a matter of the woman's personal choice.
2. Abortion should be permitted only after need has been established by a doctor.
3. Abortion should never be permitted.

C. Society would be better off if more women stayed home with their children.

1. Strongly disagree

2. Somewhat disagree
3. Somewhat agree
4. Strongly agree

Capitalism
A. People who don't get ahead should blame themselves, not the system.

1. Strongly disagree
2. Somewhat disagree
3. Somewhat agree
4. Strongly agree

B. When businesses make a lot of money, everyone benefits, including the poor.

1. Strongly disagree
2. Somewhat disagree
3. Somewhat agree
4. Strongly agree

C. Now a few questions about groups using the 0 to 100 scale. 0 means you really dislike the group and 100 means you really like the group. You can use any number from 0 to 100. How do you feel about big business?

Feminism
A. How much do you think should be done for women?

1. Much less
2. Less
3. About the same as now
4. Somewhat more
5. Much More

B. Now a few questions about groups using the 0 to 100 scale. How do you feel about feminists?

Role of Government
A. There's not much any government can do these days to solve the unemployment problem.

1. Strongly disagree
2. Somewhat disagree
3. Somewhat agree
4. Strongly agree

B. The government should leave it entirely to the private sector to create jobs.

1. Strongly disagree
2. Somewhat disagree
3. Somewhat agree
4. Strongly agree

Continentalism
A. It would be a good thing if Canada and the United States became one country.

1. Strongly disagree
2. Somewhat disagree
3. Somewhat agree
4. Strongly agree

B. Do you think Canada's ties with the United States should be much closer, somewhat closer, about the same as now, more distant, much more distant?

1. Much more distant
2. More distant
3. About the same as now
4. Somewhat closer
5. Much closer

C. Now a few questions about groups using the 0 to 100 scale. How do you feel about the United States?

NOTES

1. Data for the 1997 CES were provided by the Institute for Social Research (ISR) at York University, Toronto. The survey was funded by the Social Sciences and Humanities Research Council and was completed for the 1997 Canadian Election Team of André Blais, Elisabeth Gidengil, Richard Nadeau, and Neil Nevitte. Neither the ISR nor the National Election Team are responsible for the analyses and interpretations presented here.

2. Although the evidence suggests that leadership considerations are primed more during some elections than others (Gindengil et al. 2000b), overall, the party leaders as a group and their combined activities are clearly more a focus of media attention during election campaigns than at other times.

3. It should be noted that the questions about some of the leaders were not posed to the sample as a whole. Questions about Gilles Duceppe were asked only of Quebec respondents. Pre-election survey questions about Manning were only asked of respondents from outside Quebec. The post-election rating question about Manning was asked of the full sample. In order to be consistent in the treatment of pre- and post-election data, and because Reform ran only 11 candidates in the province of Quebec during the 1997 election, Quebec respondents are excluded in analyses of responses to Manning. Because of the comparatively small number of respondents who were asked about Duceppe, the regression analyses looking at effects of socio-political variables do not look at the effect on him.

4. For a description of these variables, see the Appendix.

5. Factor analysis was used to develop the scales for traditionalism, the role of government, feminism, and attitudes to capitalism. For details, see Erickson and O'Neill (forthcoming). For the continentalism scale, see Gidengil et al. (2000c).

6. In testing the effects of gender and the difference hypothesis for the post-election leader evaluations, the two kinds of variables, socio-demographic and ideological, were introduced as separate blocks, with the socio-demographic variables tested first and the ideological variables added second. Only those variables that were related to each leaders' evaluations in the first stage were included in the second stage with the ideological variables. (Table 10.7 presents only the results of the second stage of these analyses.)

7. Charest and Elsie Wayne (from New Brunswick) were the only two PC MPs. As a result, the party did not have official party status in the House of Commons.

8. The NDP caucus had only nine members after the 1993 election. It too lacked official party status.

9. Evidence from television coverage suggests that this pattern of political visibility did not change much during the election campaign, with the exception perhaps of the visibility of the Conservative leader. Content analysis of news stories on CBC, CTV, and Radio-Canada stations indicated that in terms of the number of stories each party received outside Quebec, the Liberals had the most coverage, followed by the Conservatives and then Reform. The NDP were last. In Quebec the order was Liberals, BQ, PCs, Reform, NDP (Nevitte et al. 2000). Given that much of the coverage of parties in election campaigns is focused on leaders, it is probably safe to assume the coverage of the leaders follows the pattern for party coverage.

10. If the scores for Chrétien, Charest, and McDonough are based only on respondents from outside Quebec, the same pattern holds.

11. The only significant gender differences in partisanship were the proportions of NDP and Reform loyalists: the percentage of women indicating that in federal politics they usually think of themselves as NDP was 2 points higher than that of men, whereas the percentage of men (outside Quebec) who said they usually think of themselves as Reform was 5 points higher than that of women.

12. The scores were also calculated for those who did not identify with the party of the leader being assessed. The pattern of findings was the same with the exception of assessments of arrogance. Significant (negative) gender differences were found for Charest but not Chrétien, and the difference in scores for McDonough, although in the same direction, were only significant at the $p=.10$ level.

13. It should, perhaps be noted that for Duceppe, the scores on strong leadership were significant only for men, but the number of respondents on which the results are based is small.

14. This finding still holds when only non-Quebec respondents are compared on assessments of the four leaders.

15. Statistical significance was determined by the significance of an interaction variable in the main equation.

16. A *dummy variable* is one that assigns '1' to members of a particular subgroup and '0' to those who are not members of that subgroup. For example, for the dummy variable 'Catholic', those who identified their religion as Catholic were assigned '1' while those who did not were assigned '0'.

Chapter 11

On the Same Wavelength?
Feminist Attitudes Across Generations of Canadian Women[1]

BRENDA O'NEILL

INTRODUCTION

Feminist thought has changed over time, and so has feminist activism. Most researchers and historians now accept a certain set of labels to differentiate periods in feminist thought and activism. The *first wave* of the feminist movement refers to activist women in the early twentieth century who fought for basic rights for women, such as the right to own property, to vote, to run for political office, and to sit in the Senate. The *second wave* refers to a later generation of feminists that emerged in the 1960s and 1970s, and that was dominated by the quest for women's substantive equality with men, a fight often predicated on minimizing gender differences; this was in direct contrast to feminists in the previous wave who more often extolled women's virtues as a means of justifying their inclusion in male-dominated political processes. The *third wave* refers to the youngest feminist activists who came into their consciousness in the 1980s and 1990s, and whose beliefs, values, and activism distinguish them from earlier feminist activists and earlier feminist thought. This most recent wave is identified in part by its unwillingness to limit women to a defined set of gender roles, by its acceptance of gender as only one of women's many identities, and by its use of technology for disseminating feminist material.

This chapter explores generational differences in Canadian women's attitudes toward feminism in Canada and the importance of these differences for electoral politics. The commonly held view is that younger women are less willing to adopt the feminist label than women who came of age in the second wave, in spite of their general support for women's equality. This has been identified as the 'but I'm not a feminist' phenomenon, as in 'I believe in equality for women and in the right of access to abortion services, but I'm not a feminist'.[2] This unwillingness stems in part from the backlash against feminists in mainstream culture and media that creates a number of myths and falsehoods surrounding the feminist movement and its goals (Baumgardner and Richards 2000; Faludi 1991).

Feminism has been particularly successful in selling its message to young Canadian women; the feminist movement has been less successful, however, in getting younger women to identify with the movement itself. The 'but I'm not a feminist' phenomenon appears to be alive and well in Canada. While women do not reveal particularly positive attitudes toward feminist spokespersons, they are nevertheless supportive of the movement's goals and of particular policy positions associated with feminist thought.

The level of public support for feminism, feminists, and feminist policy prescriptions shapes electoral politics in Canada. The literature on the gender gap makes clear that the feminist opinion is associated with more liberal attitudes overall (Conover 1984; Gidengil 1995; O'Neill 2001). Thus the level of support for feminism among the general public determines the likelihood of electing parties into office that will be sympathetic to, if not also supportive of, feminist objectives and feminist policy goals. Moreover, such support is directly relevant to the likelihood of Canadian parties' endorsing alliances with feminist organizations and adopting more feminist policy stances (Young 2000). And perhaps on a somewhat more ambitious note, support for feminists and feminism would seem to be a necessary condition for the electoral success of a decidedly feminist party.

THE WAVES OF FEMINISM

The idea that there are distinct waves of feminism provides the foundation for this study. The existence of distinct waves should not be taken to mean that Canadian feminists within each wave have spoken in a unified voice (Adamson, Briskin, and McPhail 1988). Moreover, there are varying interpretations of the transition points in and focuses of each wave. Barbara Arneil's *Politics and Feminism* (1999) provides an account of the transitions feminism has undergone that is comprehensive in its inclusion of an academic treatment of the most recent third wave.

Feminists of the first wave included among their goals the acquisition of liberal rights for women within a public/private framework that presumed the existence of gender difference. In contrast, second-wave feminism, despite its many manifestations,[3] adopted an acceptance of universality, that is, of the duality of gender with its emphasis on the differences between women as a group and men as a group. This claim rested uneasily with the often-employed argument of the 'sameness' of the genders, adopted in part to allow for a basis on which to demand equal treatment and the challenging of the public/private and culture/nature dichotomies. The difficulty, as identified by Naomi Black, was that 'women wanted to stay different without being disadvantaged' (1993: 153). In the 1960s, women were very much socialized to assume domestic responsibilities, but this socialization came in direct contrast with the fact that many of these same women entered the workforce, in part to escape the 'feminine mystique', as it was identified by Betty Friedan (Baumgardner and Richards 2000).

Canadian feminists of this period fought to remove the many formal and informal barriers that existed, such as 'glass ceilings' in employment (Baumgardner and Richards 2000). The Royal Commission on the Status of Women served as a lightning rod for Canadian feminists in the late 1960s and 1970s, documenting many of these barriers and generating public awareness of such issues as access to abortion, equal pay, pension discrimination, and violence against women (Baumgardner and Richards 2000). Finally, the second wave accorded a higher value to the public than to the private sphere, in part to counter the dominant culture, which assigned women to the domestic sphere; this, however, provided a target for criticisms launched by a subsequent generation of feminists.

Third-wave feminism is distinct from the previous waves of feminist thought in both thought and action (see Arneil 1999). The focus on the 'universal' woman by a previous generation of feminists provided a jumping-off point for the third wave. Many women, particularly lesbians and women of colour, failed to see themselves reflected in the second wave's discourses. Third-wave feminists differ as well in that they 'grew up with feminism as their birthright', and many are 'reaping the benefits . . . of the second wave women's movement's labour' (Steenbergen 2001: 9). These benefits have provided young feminists with the freedom to question second-wave feminist theory and prescriptions. The result is that they are 'pushing the boundaries of who and what constitutes feminist community and defines feminist theorizing' (Pinterics 2001: 15).

As a result, third-wave feminism can be differentiated from its predecessor in several respects. First, the newest feminist wave uses personal narratives as a basis of knowledge development to a greater extent than in the past, in part because such accounts are considered more political (as in 'the personal is political'), accessible to a wider audience, and more respectful of women's diversity than are the more traditional or academic feminist treatments. Second, third-wave feminism adopts a belief in the multiplicity of identity, reflecting the difficulty many women feel in categorizing themselves with unique and singular identities based on gender, race, sexuality, or ability. Women, it is argued, are more than simply women; they also possess a sexual identity, a racial identity, and many others. Third-wavers are less likely to see gender as transcending any of these multiple identities, a belief that very often sets them at odds with the previous generation of feminists. Third, this wave of feminism expresses a desire to openly address the contradictions within feminism while simultaneously challenging the 'perceived rigidities in the ideals of second-wave feminist politics' (Arneil 1999: 153), resulting in a re-embracing of femininity, motherhood, and women's sexuality in an attempt to straddle the contradictory desires of embracing women's similarities (and hence difference from men) and their differences from one another.[4] According to Candis Steenbergen,

> the desire to analyze body image, self-esteem, desire, sexuality and sexual pleasure has been strong in third-wave writings to date. To many, those pursuits have revolved around continual self-analysis and personal negotiation, an attempt to reconcile the desire to create their own version of 'femininity' and the fear of betraying their allegiance to feminism and the struggle for female empowerment. (2001: 11)

Finally, the third wave has adopted a new strategy for the accumulation and dissemination of knowledge, characterized by the grassroots distribution of zines (photocopied and stapled articles distributed through feminist networks) and through the medium of cyberspace, especially e-mail, Web pages, and chat groups.[5]

Feminist thought among feminist activists is, however, distinct from feminist thinking in the broader public, although the two are related. Given feminists' commitment to the cause, their opinions on a number of issues are likely to be more strongly held, more consistent with feminism's core values, and more stable over time. Yet Joanna Everitt's research (1998b) reveals that the movement's efforts have coincided with an increased liberalization of Canadian attitudes on a small set of issues, including the election of women as political leaders and women in the workplace. Moreover, Everitt shows that younger Canadians, both women and men, have been especially open to the feminist movement's arguments, and as such have attitudes that are more in line with those of the feminist movement than do older Canadians. As Everitt notes, 'young adults, who have weaker attachments to traditional ideas, may adopt the policy positions of a movement without adopting a movement identification' (1998b: 749). The movement has had a particularly powerful impact on young, well-educated, employed women, given their greater ability to identify personally with the movement's goals and exposure to the movement's messages during their formative years (Everitt 1998b).

DATA AND METHODS

The data employed in this investigation come from the 1997 Canadian Election Study (CES),[6] which provides a recent survey of Canadian political attitudes that is comprehensive both in the types of questions asked and in the number of Canadians sampled. For the purposes of this investigation, only women respondents were selected for examination (N=2008)[7] and these respondents were grouped into four cohorts:

- Pre–Second Wave: born before 1943
- Second Wave: born between 1943 and 1957
- Third Wave I: born between 1958 and 1968
- Third Wave II: born between 1969 and 1979[8]

The Pre–Second Wave cohort identifies women who entered their young adult years prior to the advent of second-wave feminism. As such, they likely exhibit attitudes that are rather traditional with respect to women's roles. The Second Wave cohort identifies women who came into adult consciousness at the height of the second wave of the feminist movement during the 1960s and 1970s. Their attitudes regarding women's roles are likely to most resemble those of second-wave feminists and activists. The next two cohorts identify women who came of age in the 1980s and 1990s, a period normally identified with third-wave activism and feminist thought. Women in these two groups were anticipated to hold attitudes that more closely resemble the attitudes exhibited by this most recent generation of feminists.

This breakdown provides a significant sample of respondents in each group. The Pre–Second Wave group constitutes 24 per cent of the sample (N=477), the Second Wave group 32 per cent (N=641), the Third Wave I group 24 per cent (N=488), and the Third Wave II group 20 per cent (N=402).[9]

The objective of the analysis was to examine differences in feminist attitudes and beliefs across these four groups in an effort to assess whether attitudes in the general population reflect differences across the waves of feminism as discussed in academic literature and by feminist activists themselves. The first consideration was Canadian women's attitudes toward feminists and the feminist movement; that is, do Canadian women generally identify with feminists? The second was to assess Canadian women's attitudes toward the various policy positions associated with feminist thought; that is, are Canadian women feminist, given the values and opinions they hold? In each case these investigations break down the sample of women down by cohort in order to compare results across women coming of age during each of the three feminist waves. In most instances the examination employs contingency tables to evaluate attitudes across these feminist cohorts.[10]

RESULTS

Attitudes to Feminists and the Feminist Movement

The survey question in the 1997 CES that comes closest to assessing subjective identification with feminists is a thermometer scale asking respondents to rank how they feel about feminists, using a scale from 0 (really dislike them) to 100 (really like them). This is not, it must be pointed out, a measure of subjective identification as a feminist but rather a measure of affect for feminists. The measure can nevertheless be argued to be highly correlated with such a subjective measure; women who identify themselves as feminist would, it is argued, respond positively toward feminists as a group. The measure provides a valid and reliable correlate of subjective feminist identification rather than a measure of that concept itself.[11] Respondents were also asked to rank several additional groups (big business, unions, people on welfare, Aboriginal peoples, the police, racial minorities, the baby-boom generation, and gays and lesbians). Table 11.1 provides the results of several of these questions as well as the average score accorded all groups by cohort.

The results reveal significant differences across the cohorts in the rankings that women assigned to various groups. Every cohort ranked feminists below the midpoint on the 0–100 thermometer scale; there was, however, significant variation in this absolute ranking, with younger women appearing to have ranked feminists

Table 11.1

Thermometer Ratings for Groups by Feminist Cohort

	Third Wave II	Third Wave I	Second Wave	Pre–Second Wave
Feminists*	48.4	45.5	44.1	42.2
Gays and lesbians*	61.2	55.3	51.9	40.6
Racial minorities*	66.1	61.7	59.7	58.9
Aboriginal peoples	58.8	58.8	59.5	59.6
Big business*	60.5	56.8	56.2	56.1
Average *	57.9	55.6	55.7	53.8
N^a	317	363	463	313

[a] Minimum sample size recorded across all variables.

*$p<.01$

more highly than did older Canadian women. But when compared to the average ranking accorded to all groups, women in each cohort ranked feminists roughly 10 percentage points below the average ranking that they assigned to all groups. The difference in the ranking of feminists across the cohorts comes, then, from the differences in the average score each cohort assigns to groups; since younger Canadians provided higher rankings to all groups, feminists only appear to have come out ahead.

The fact that feminists were ranked significantly below average for all groups by all cohorts underscores the effect of the backlash and the negative baggage that accompanies the label. As shown below, despite support for many of the key planks in the feminist movement's platform, feminists as a group were not ranked very highly by women in any cohort. Indeed they ranked well below several of the other groups asked about in the survey and, in particular, significantly below big business, which was ranked above the overall average by each cohort.

When the question turned to gays and lesbians, a significantly different result emerged(see Table 11.1). An acceptance of diversity, particularly with regard to gays and lesbians, is one of the key defining characteristics of third-wave feminism. The results suggest that the ranking provided to gays and lesbians by Canadian women varies significantly by cohort: 20 percentage points separated the youngest and oldest cohorts on this question. And the difference is not simply because of the higher overall average ranking that younger women assigned to groups. While the two cohorts of third-wave women ranked the group 3 points above and roughly at the average, respectively, the two oldest cohorts ranked gays and lesbians at 4 and 13 points below average, respectively. In terms of affect, the difference between old and young women is unquestionable.

A similar, but far less striking, result appears in feelings toward racial minorities. The youngest cohort gave the group a positive evaluation of 66, but this fell somewhat across the cohorts and reached a low of 59 among the oldest cohort. An examination of the relative ranking accorded the group suggests that this difference is not simply because of the higher overall ranking that young women accorded to groups in society. Women in the Third Wave II cohort ranked racial minorities 8 points above the average for the listed groups; among the two oldest cohorts, this ranking is closer to the average, at 4 and 5 points above it. Thus an acceptance of diversity, at least as it extends to feelings toward racial minorities, exists across women of all ages but is somewhat higher among third-wave women.

A slightly different pattern emerges when the group in question is Aboriginal peoples. There is no apparent difference in the rank accorded the group across the cohorts. But given the overall difference in the average rank each cohort assigns to all the groups, a difference emerges in the relative ranking assigned to Aboriginal peoples across the cohorts: older women provide a higher relative rank to the group than do younger women. Thus, if younger women are more open to diversity, this diversity is limited to particular groups, especially gays and lesbians; and most interestingly, this openness to diversity appears to exclude feminists themselves.

Respondents were asked to assess the influence that they believed various groups possessed as well as the influence they believed these same groups should possess.

Positive affect for feminists and the movement can be argued to include a desire to see the group accorded greater political influence. Several of these groups are the same ones that appeared in the closeness thermometer question (see Table 11.1, p. 182). Respondents were asked to judge possessed influence and desired influence on a scale of 1 (very little influence) to 7 (very influential). A measure of desired influence change was created by subtracting the influence believed to be possessed by each group from the influence desired for each group. The results for this 'desired influence change' measure for each cohort appear in Table 11.2.

The results appear, on first glance, to suggest relatively little difference between the cohorts in their attitudes to feminist influence. Respondents seem to agree on the desired change in the level of influence possessed by feminists: each cohort believes that feminists should have *less* influence than they currently possess. The feminist movement has not, then, been very successful in justifying its continued importance to Canadian women.

The cohorts do not, however, agree on the level of desired influence change for gays and lesbians: while the Third Wave II cohort believes the group should possess more influence than is currently the case, the other cohorts, particularly the Pre–Second Wave cohort, believe the group should have less. And the differences are significantly different across the cohorts on this question. On this second measure, then, the youngest cohort of Canadian women is significantly different from other Canadian women in their attitudes to the influence desired for gays and lesbians.

A similar but somewhat weaker result appears in the set of questions tapping the desired influence change for racial minorities. The youngest cohort is willing to accord a slightly higher level of influence to the group overall, but the other cohorts believe the group's level of influence should decrease. Women in the youngest cohort not only 'feel' more positive toward racial minorities and gays and lesbians, they also believe that each group deserves a greater measure of influence in Canadian society. The final rows in Table 11.2 suggest that when the group in question is Aboriginal, it is the Pre–Second Wave cohort that is most willing to accord greater influence to the group. And interestingly, this group is the only one among the four whose influence the oldest cohort is willing to see increased.

Although differences appear in this set of questions across the cohorts, they

Table 11.2

Desired Change in Influence for Various Groups by Feminist Cohort[a]

	Third Wave II	Third Wave I	Second Wave	Pre–Second Wave
For feminists	-.19	-.17	-.30	-.30
For gays and lesbians*	.25	-.13	-.50	-.91
For racial minorities**	.06	-.15	-.47	-.52
For Aboriginal peoples	.05	-.12	-.08	.42
N[b]	168	206	284	184

[a] Average difference between how much influence a group should possess and how much influence they currently possess, ranging from -6 to 6. Negative values suggest the group has too much influence; positive values suggest the group should have more. The midpoint (0) identifies respondents who desire no change in the group's influence level; [b] minimum sample size for each cohort across the questions.

*$p<.01$; **$p<.05$

should not be inflated in importance. A slightly greater acceptance of diversity does appear among the youngest of the Third Wave groups: this cohort would accord a greater level of influence to gays and lesbians and, to a lesser degree, racial minorities and Aboriginal peoples than each group currently possesses, but all would still fall below below the overall average level of influence desired for all of the groups included in the set of questions.[12] And it is clear that this desire is not extended to feminists as a group.

Respondents were also asked to render an opinion on the goals of the feminist movement; these two survey questions are an attempt to assess popular perceptions and support of the movement's objectives rather than affect toward the group's members. Results by cohort for these questions appear in Table 11.3. The breakdown of responses, however, reveals little in the way of differentiation across the cohorts: a majority in each cohort believes that the feminist movement tries to get equal treatment for women and that the movement encourages women to be independent and to speak up for themselves.

Interestingly, however, there is a significant degree of uncertainty regarding the feminist movement's objectives, an uncertainty that occasionally varies by cohort. For instance, on the first question, between 18 per cent and 19 per cent of respondents in each of the cohorts responded that they were not certain whether the feminist movement just tries to get equal treatment for women or whether it puts men down. On the second question, a smaller but equally large share of women gave the same response to the choice of whether 'the feminist movement encourages women to be independent and speak up for themselves or to be selfish and think only of themselves'. On this second question, however, variation is evident across the cohorts: while 15 per cent of respondents in the youngest cohort answered 'not sure', only between 9 per cent and 12 per cent of the other cohorts answered similarly. One could conclude, then, that there exists a significant degree of uncertainty among women in the general public over the goals and objectives of the feminist movement and that, in some cases, this uncertainty is greater for younger rather than older women.

Attitudes to Feminist Positions and Beliefs

Women in the 1997 CES were asked for their beliefs regarding access to abortion. Abortion has been, and continues to be, one of the key political lighting rods for the feminist movement: equal rights for women, it is maintained, must at the very least ensure that women have the right to determine their reproductive choices. The 1997 CES included a question wording experiment to assess the importance of answer order to responses.[13] For our purposes, responses to these three questions have been merged; results, broken down by cohort, appear in Table 11.3.

Table 11.3 confirms that younger women, particularly in the Third Wave cohorts, are very much on side with this one element of the feminist movement's agenda. For women who came of age before the second wave, however, opinion is more divided: fewer than half believe that abortion is a matter of personal choice, and more women in this cohort than in any other believe that abortion should never be permitted. Attitudes on this issue reveal a decidedly linear pattern across the cohorts: subsequent

Table 11.3

Attitudes by Feminist Cohort (Percentages, with *N* in Parentheses)[a]

	Third Wave II	Third Wave I	Second Wave	Pre–Second Wave
Feminist movement				
Tries to get equal treatment for women	68.1	71.3	62.9	70.1
	(144)	(181)	(251)	(184)
Encourages women to be independent	78.3	79.8	80.9	81.3
	(152)	(203)	(277)	(198)
Abortion (Π^2)[b]				
Should never be permitted*	7.4	7.1	7.2	15.6
Should be permitted only after need established by a doctor*	23.8	26.7	32.1	37.3
Should be a matter of the woman's personal choice*	68.7	66.2	60.7	47.1
N (all responses)	(323)	(382)	(499)	(359)
Women and the workplace				
Lay off women whose husbands have jobs first*	7.4	4.6	9.0	28.1
	(177)	(221)	(300)	(221)
Discrimination makes it hard for women to get jobs*	58.7	68.9	63.7	71.9
	(172)	(209)	(300)	(213)
Use quotas in job hiring*	18.4	10.5	9.4	8.7
	(163)	(209)	(286)	(218)
Gender differences				
Gender equality can exist even with different responsibilities	76.9	79.0	75.7	78.1
	(169)	(214)	(301)	(219)
Men by nature are less caring and giving towards babies and children*	21.9	37.4	38.5	49.0
	(173)	(217)	(304)	(212)
Better off if women stayed home with children*	26.4	43.3	46.8	67.8
	(394)	480)	(620)	(456)
Feminist thought				
Gone too far pushing equal rights*	31.7	36.4	48.5	60.8
	(164)	(198)	(284)	(209)
Need greater tolerance for others**	70.7	69.0	67.6	63.5
	(171)	(213)	(293)	(211)
Newer lifestyles contributing to society's breakdown*	42.1	41.7	59.2	68.9
	(166)	(187)	(282)	(196)
Fewer problems if more emphasis on family values*	63.4	66.8	77.1	84.9
	(164)	(208)	(297)	(218)
Only married couples should have children*	22.9	25.6	37.1	56.9
	(397)	(477)	(620)	(444)
Homosexual couples should be allowed to marry*	74.4	52.0	44.1	22.5
	(164)	(196)	(288)	(196)

[a] Percentages of respondents selecting or agreeing with a particular statement. See Appendix, p. 175, for question wording; [b] Π^2= 50.04, *p*<.01
*p<.01; **p<.10

generations of women are more likely to believe that women should be provided access to abortion services whenever desired. The majority of second- and third-wave women are 'feminist' given their opinion on abortion.

Table 11.3 also breaks down results from the 1997 CES, tapping attitudes toward gender and the workplace. There appears to be a significant association between cohort and these attitudes—although not always in the anticipated direction. The vast majority of women in each of the cohorts disagreed with the statement that women whose husbands have jobs should be laid off first. Nevertheless, some differences in attitudes do exist: the three youngest cohorts were far less in agreement with the statement than women in the Pre–Second Wave Cohort.

On the second question, dealing with discrimination, the pattern is reversed. Although a majority of women in each cohort agreed that 'discrimination makes it extremely difficult for women to get jobs equal to their abilities', this share was highest among the three oldest cohorts. This pattern may reflect the fact that the youngest cohort has yet to experience such discrimination at first hand and as such is less willing to acknowledge its existence.

On the last question, addressing the use of job quotas to increase the number of women in good jobs, the cohort least accepting of the existence of discrimination appears to be the most willing to adopt quotas for job hiring. Equally puzzling is the unwillingness of the Pre–Second Wave cohort to adopt quotas in spite of their overall agreement that there is discrimination in job hiring. Correlation analysis of these two questions reveals that for only the two middle cohorts is a connection, although modest, made between the questions at the individual level.[14]

Table 11.3 next presents the cohort breakdown for a set of questions dealing with core differences between the sexes. The results suggest that Canadian women in the youngest cohort are the least accepting of essentialist arguments. On the first question, dealing with gender equality in spite of different responsibilities, women across the cohorts appear to be in agreement. On the next two questions, however, differences in attitude are more apparent. When read the statement 'When it comes to caring for babies and small children, men by nature are less patient and giving than women', younger women are much less likely than older women to agree. The same pattern appears in responses to the following statement: 'Society would be better off if women stayed home with their children'. Younger women, it appears, are far less willing to accept gender-defined roles, especially those directed at caring for children and those suggesting that a successful society requires women to remain at home to care for their children.

Finally, Table 11.3 reports cohort attitudes on several questions included in the 1997 CES that are related to feminist thought but not directly concerned with women or gender equality. Breaking opinion down by cohort reinforces the distance separating younger and older women in their attitudes on various issues. The first statement, 'We have gone too far in pushing equal rights in this country', reveals a significant degree of attitudinal difference between the cohorts: almost 30 percentage points separates Third Wave II women from Pre–Second Wave women, with the latter group far more likely to agree that an equal rights agenda has been too forcefully promoted. The question does not specifically mention equal rights for women but nevertheless taps into opinion on the extension of equality to all Canadians.

The second question reveals far less distance between the cohorts but nevertheless reinforces the conclusion that younger women are more tolerant of diversity. Agreement with the statement 'We should be more tolerant of people who choose to live according to their own standards, even if they are very different from our own' decreased with each cohort from 71 per cent of Third Wave II women to 64 per cent of Pre–Second Wave women. The difference was greater on the related statement, 'Newer lifestyles are contributing to the breakdown of our society'. Young women are far less willing to attribute societal problems to the appearance of 'newer lifestyles' than are older women.

The final three questions in Table 11.3 (p. 185) relate to 'family values' and the belief that the moral fibre of Canadian society is dependent in part of the maintenance of the traditional family structure: mother, father, and children. There is very little agreement across cohorts on the need for protecting this traditional institution. A majority of respondents in each cohort does believe that fewer problems might exist if there was a greater emphasis on 'traditional family values'. This majority is at its weakest, however, among the Third Wave cohorts and increases steadily with the Second Wave and Pre–Second Wave cohorts. Thus, while tolerance for diversity might be highest among the youngest cohort of Canadian women, this in no way means that they have completely dismissed a role for the traditional family unit.

When the question shifts to restricting access to legally accessible marriage or to who ought to care for and raise children, the distance separating the cohorts increases dramatically. When presented with the statement 'Only people who are married should be having children', only roughly one in four women in the Third Wave cohorts agrees, compared with more than half of the women in the Pre–Second Wave cohort. And when the question is one of extending legally recognized marriage to homosexual couples, the difference becomes larger still: from almost three out four in the Third Wave II cohort to less than one out of four in the Pre–Second Wave cohort. Thus, while the youngest cohort agrees in the importance of 'family values', these women's definition of a family appears to differ significantly from that of previous cohorts.

On many questions, then, Canadian women who came of age at the time of the third wave possess opinions and values very much in line with those of the most recent period of feminist thought and activism. These young women are more likely to support access to abortion and the use of quotas for job hiring. They are also more inclined to believe that different gender responsibilities need not translate into inequality and to dismiss arguments that women are better at caring for children and that children are better off if women stay home to care for them. Yet they are also more likely to believe that some things are much better than they were in the past, including workplace equity.

More broadly, young Canadian women are more tolerant, more supportive of past efforts at securing equal rights, and more supportive of newer lifestyles. Yet, interestingly, a majority of younger Canadian women also believes that 'family values' deserve greater emphasis, although this share is lower than in each of the remaining cohorts. In many respects, feminism has found a home among the values and attitudes of the youngest of Canadian women if not in their affect toward feminists themselves.

DISCUSSION AND CONCLUSION

Canadian women do not appear on the surface to be particularly open to feminists and the feminist movement. They respond that they 'like' feminists less than they do many other groups, and they believe that feminists deserve less influence than they currently possess. Feminists, and the feminist movement, appear on the surface to have not been particularly successful at winning women over.

There is a hint, however, that this rejection may reflect the effects of a backlash against the movement as much as a rejection of feminists and their objectives. The first clue is the significant degree of uncertainty among women of all ages as to the objectives of the movement. This uncertainty may stem from the many mixed messages that women receive about feminists and the feminist movement in the popular press and in popular culture.

The second hint is that many women, particularly young women, have nevertheless wholeheartedly endorsed many feminist beliefs and policy prescriptions. This unwillingness to 'identify' with feminists belies, then, a significant degree of feminist thinking among many Canadian women: the vast majority of third-wave women would be labelled 'feminist' given the set of beliefs that they hold about women's roles and gender equality. Despite such thinking, however, the cohort is no more likely to 'like' feminists than are women who came of age earlier in the twentieth century. The 'but I'm not a feminist' phenomenon appears to be alive and well among the youngest cohort of Canadian women.

In other ways, however, the differences that appear in the waves of feminist thought are reflected in the corresponding generations of Canadian women. In particular, the third wave of Canadian women, those born after 1957, is distinctive for its adoption of feminist beliefs and values and also for its greater acceptance of diversity, one of the defining characteristics of the youngest wave of feminist thought. This greater acceptance of diversity is striking and undoubtedly reflects in some measure the Charter of Rights and Freedom's impact on ideals of equality and tolerance. But the Charter is broader than the feminist movement, and the shift in attitudes may also reflect larger changes in the beliefs and opinions of Canadian women. Women of succeeding generations differ on many counts, including their weaker religious commitment, their higher educational attainment, and the fewer number of children they bear (O'Neill 2002). The changes have been many, and our ability to disentangle the causes of attitude shifts based on one cross-sectional survey is limited.

Furthermore, the electoral consequences of this particularly liberal set of attitudes among younger Canadian women may not be as large as one might immediately suppose. Feminist values and attitudes generally fall on the liberal end of the ideological spectrum: for example, advocating a governmental role in promoting and protecting equal rights for women in the private and public spheres, and promoting a more tolerant attitude toward gays and lesbians and supporting efforts to ensure equality for them. One could suggest that the adoption of these more liberal attitudes by young Canadian women might translate into the election of more liberal governments in the future.

A number of conditions would have to be met, however, before the election of an overtly feminist-friendly government were to occur. First, these young women would have to get out and vote in significant numbers. Not all women are particularly liberal in their opinions; women of previous generations are more conservative on a number of the attitudes measured here. Unfortunately, research suggests that today's young Canadians are unlikely to vote in numbers similar to previous generations (O'Neill 2001a). Second, the adoption of a particular set of attitudes need not translate directly into support for a political party whose platform includes a related set of policy prescriptions. Voting decisions are tremendously complex and reflect more than support for or opposition to particular party platforms. Although young women voters may support a particularly liberal party platform, the party leader, its performance during the campaign, and the salience of feminist and other policies could all translate into a vote against a feminist-friendly party. Additionally, an examination of women's attitudes and values in the end provides only half of the picture: men make up almost half of the voting population. The ability to elect feminist-friendly governments requires more than the votes of young Canadian women—it also requires the votes of young Canadian men. Finally, the ability to cue these particular attitudes and values at the ballot box requires that political parties include such policy recommendations in their campaign platforms. Past practice among Canadian political parties, their brokerage style, and the recent shift of the party system to the ideological right suggest that this is unlikely to occur any time soon (Young 2000). In the end it may take the reform of the electoral system to allow for the election of a feminist party: until vote shares are more closely reflected in seat shares, there seems to be little chance of overcoming the dominance of centrist political parties in Canada.

APPENDIX: QUESTION WORDING, TABLE 11.3

Attitudes to the Feminist Movement
- The feminist movement just tries to get equal treatment for women OR puts men down.
- The feminist movement encourages women to be independent and speak up for themselves OR to be selfish and think only of themselves.

Attitudes Related to Abortion
Of the following three positions, which is closest to your own opinion:
1. Abortion should never be permitted.
2. Abortion should be permitted only after need has been established by a doctor.
3. Abortion should be a matter of the woman's personal choice.

Attitudes to Women and the Workplace

- If a company has to lay off some of its employees, the first workers to be laid off should be women whose husbands have jobs.
- Discrimination makes it extremely difficult for women to get jobs equal to their abilities.
- When it comes to job hiring, quotas should be used to increase the number of women in good jobs OR hiring should be based strictly on merit.

Attitudes to Gender Difference

- Which comes closest to your own view: Men and women can only be equal when they have the same responsibilities in government, business, and the family OR Equality can exist even when men and women have very different responsibilities.
- When it comes to caring for babies and small children, men by nature are less patient and giving than women.
- Society would be better off if women stayed home with their children.

Attitudes Related to Feminism

- We have gone too far in pushing equal rights in this country.
- We should be more tolerant of people who choose to live according to their own standards, even if they are very different from our own.
- Newer lifestyles are contributing to the breakdown of our society.
- This country would have many fewer problems if there were more emphasis on traditional family values.
- Only people who are married should be having children.
- Homosexual couples should be allowed to be legally married.

NOTES

1. The author wishes to thank Tyler Jivan for his research assistance.
2. Much of the literature identifying this phenomenon comes from the United States. See, for example, Baumgardner and Richards (2000).
3. As Arneil points out, the second wave of feminism is identified in part by its many hybrids: liberal feminism, socialist feminism, psychoanalytic feminism, and radical feminism among others. Despite the diversity of thinking across the approaches, Arneil nevertheless provides an account of the commonality among them (Arneil 1999).
4. As one young feminist declared in explaining her decision to launch a Web site (GirlCrush) for girls between the ages of 13 and 18,

   > GirlCrush is feminist, yet girly (we have fashion and makeup sections) . . . because 'feminist' and 'girly' are NOT opposites. I want girls to know that you don't have to be one or the other; that there are stereotypes they don't need to conform to, and that there are definitely more than one or two or a hundred ways to be a feminist and to be a girl. (Anna Humphrey, Par-L discussion list, 22 December 2000)

5. The first such Web site, <www.cybergrrl.com>, launched in 1995 by Aliza Sherman, has since mushroomed into a globally linked network of chapters, with some, such as the Toronto chapter, providing technical training and advice, community work, social events,

and job and housing help to members (Cameron 2001). For Canadian examples, see <www.goodgirl.ca>, <www.girlcrushzine.com>, and <www.marigoldzine.com>.

6. Data from the 1997 CES were provided by the Institute for Social Research, York University. The survey was funded by the Social Sciences and Humanities Research Council of Canada, grant number 412-96-0007, and was completed for the 1997 CES Team of André Blais (Université de Montréal), Elisabeth Gidengil (McGill University), Richard Nadeau (Université de Montréal), and Neil Nevitte (University of Toronto). Neither the Institute for Social Research, SSHRC, nor the CES Team are responsible for the analyses and interpretations presented here.

7. The data have been weighted to accurately reflect a Canadian national sample. See 1997 CES, *Technical Documentation*, at the CES Web site: <http://www.fas.umontreal.ca/pol/ces-eec/ces.html>.

8. This breakdown roughly approximates that adopted by Everitt in her study of the relevance of the feminist movement to public opinion in Canada. The dates in her study are selected to correspond to the changes taking place in feminist activism and thought. Where Everitt adopts a single post-1958 cohort to identify those who came of age 'after the initial mobilization of the second-wave women's movement' (1998b: 750), however, this paper breaks this cohort into two distinct groups to allow for a more detailed examination of differences across the youngest Canadian women given the more recent data set employed.

9. Sample sizes for each group varied from these numbers depending on which of the three waves of the survey the question appeared in (campaign period, post-election period, and mail-back). The reported samples are from the campaign-period group. Group sample size is reported in all tables.

10. The strength of association is assessed with a Chi-square measure of association. Although the age groups and many of the dependent variables examined are ordinal measures that would allow for the use of stronger statistical tests, such tests very often do not allow for the existence of non-linear relationships in the data, and there is little theoretical justification for assuming linearity in the relationship between age and feminism.

11. Others have employed similarly worded survey questions in their research on feminist opinion (Conover 1988; Cook 1989; Gurin 1985). Additionally, Rhodebeck has shown that the feeling thermometer for the women's liberation movement (using slightly different wording than that employed here) 'serves as a more reliable indicator of feminist identity than does the index of closeness to women' (1996: 391–93).

12. The groups that scored above average on the level of influence the groups should possess are, in descending order, consumers, small business, farmers, environmentalists, seniors, and big business.

13. The order in which the three responses were given to respondents was altered in order to evaluate whether order mattered for responses.

14. For the Third Wave I cohort, $r=.19$; for the Second Wave Cohort, $r=.29$. Both were significant at the $p<.01$ level.

Part IV

Political Women and the Media

Chapter 12

Tough Talk:
How Television News Covers Male and Female Leaders of
Canadian Political Parties[1]

Joanna Everitt and Elisabeth Gidengil

Introduction

Canada is among a small group of Western industrialized nations that have had
women as the leaders of major political parties. While the representation of women
in national legislative assemblies is slowly creeping upwards, few women have suc-
cessfully made the leap to the most elite office in party politics. Since 1993,
however, federal Canadian elections have included at least one established party led
by a women. Going into the 1993 federal election, Kim Campbell was leader of the
Progressive Conservative party and the incumbent prime minister, and Audrey
McLaughlin was leader of the NDP. In 1997 and 2000, the NDP was again led by a
woman, Alexa McDonough, the former leader of the party in Nova Scotia. The
presence of these women in these elections provides an all too rare opportunity to
examine gender differences in media coverage of candidates for top political office.

Female politicians often cite gender-differentiated media coverage as an imped-
iment to their political careers (Ross and Sreberny 2000; Tremblay 1999). This is
true even for women running as leaders of national parties. During the 1993 election Campbell laid part of the blame for her electoral misfortunes on the media:
'new politics, old media . . . when you're not a traditional politician, they don't know
what to make of you' ('Campbell Not Making Many Personal Plans After Oct. 25
Election', *The Gazette* 12 October 1993: A8).

Past studies of media coverage of female politicians have tended to focus on
explicit examples of bias, such as women's lack of visibility and the presentation of
female candidates as having stereotypically feminine traits and issue competencies
and as being less viable than their male counterparts (Carroll and Schreiber 1997;
Kahn 1994; Kahn and Goldenberg 1991; Robinson and Saint-Jean 1995;
Robinson, Saint-Jean, and Rioux 1991; Ross 1995). There is evidence, however,
that such overtly gender-differentiated coverage may be diminishing (Norris 1997d;
Smith 1997). This chapter focuses on a more subtle form of gender-differentiated
treatment. Drawing on the notion of gendered mediation (Sreberny-Mohammadi
and Ross 1996), we investigate the possible biases that arise when conventional
news frames are applied to female politicians.

MEDIA BIAS

The growing literature on women and politics has long been concerned with the lack of neutral reporting on female politicians. Paralleling US studies (Kahn 1994; Kahn and Goldenberg 1991; Norris 1997d), past studies in Canada have high-lighted the lack of coverage received by female politicians. François-Pierre Gingras's examination of Ottawa-area newspapers (1995) revealed that in 1991 fewer than one-fifth of stories about politics referred to women. This underrepresentation of female politicians is emphasized by the fact that this coverage was notably below the proportion of women holding office in the federal government and in those provincial and municipal governments representing the readership of these papers. Furthermore, Gingras found that a significant proportion (on average 38 per cent) of the political coverage awarded to women was negative, in that it criticized the women or presented them in an unfavourable light. Finally, Gingras's studies revealed that the women who were presented in political stories were often those with little political power, such as the wives of the prime minister and other male politicians.

Gertrude Robinson and Armande Saint-Jean's research on the media's portrayal of female politicians across time (1995; with Rioux 1991) suggests that not only have journalists underrepresented female politicians, they have also relied on a series of gender-based stereotypes in their depictions, ranging from spinster and *femme facile* to superwoman and 'one of the boys'. While these stereotypes have changed over time, they nonetheless serve to emphasize the distinctiveness of those women engaging in political activity. Robinson and Saint-Jean also found that when women were covered, their coverage focused on personal characteristics such as clothing or hair rather than on the substance of their speeches, gave little recognition of women's political experience, made female politicians responsible for representing all women as a group, used 'feminism' to connote a negative personal attribute, held women up to higher standards of excellence than men, judged women only by extremes (good and bad), and imposed a moral code of sexual abstinence on female politicians that was not imposed on men (Robinson, Saint-Jean, and Rioux 1991).

More recent studies suggest that the tendency to apply feminine stereotypes may be declining (Carroll and Schreiber 1997; Norris 1997d; Smith 1997; Tremblay and Bélanger 1997), indicating that in some ways women are being treated more like their male counterparts. There remain, however, subtle forms of gender-differentiated coverage that result from the news values that govern political reporting; these continue to present a challenge to women in political life (Gidengil and Everitt 1999, 2000a, 2000b; Tremblay 1999; Tremblay and Bélanger 1997; see also chapter 13).

These differences are evident in Manon Tremblay and Nathalie Bélanger's 1997 examination of political cartoons found in major Canadian newspapers during the 1993 election. Tremblay and Bélanger wondered whether there was evidence of blatant stereotyping of Campbell or McLaughlin in traditional 'feminine' roles linked to the private sphere of the home and family. While they found that this was not the case, they found numerous other ways in which the female party leaders were presented differently than the men. For example, 67 per cent of the caricatures of the women portrayed them as dependent, fearful, and powerless, while over half the men in the cartoons were depicted as independent, brave, and assured. The women were also portrayed as being less in control of their environment and the action surrounding them (68.4 per cent)—and implicitly less capable of managing the country—than the men (32.8 per cent). Finally, in over half of the cartoons in which Campbell and McLaughlin appeared, they were presented in stereotypical terms as witches or Cinderellas, or even as victims of violence (Tremblay and Bélanger 1997: 53, 57, 61). In other words, the female leaders were shown in various roles typically assigned to women but not to men. The male leaders had fewer gender-typed images applied to them, but those that were used depicted them as supermen, businessmen, or elite athletes, such as race-car drivers. Even when the women were shown in non-traditional activities, such as sliding into home plate in a baseball game, they were still drawn wearing skirts and high heels.

These examples of gender-differentiated coverage present significant roadblocks in and of themselves to women seeking political office in Canada. The under-reporting or negative coverage given to women in political life and their presentation in stereotypical or powerless roles provide clear messages to voters that politics is a male game and that women just do not belong. However, even if journalists make conscious attempts to cover female politicians in the same manner as they cover male politicians, the news values governing political reporting can still undermine women's opportunities in the political arena.

STUDIES OF GENDERED MEDIATION

Our own work has explored these more subtle biases that arise from the stereotypically masculine conception of politics that guides political reporting. We build on Annabelle Sreberny-Mohammadi and Karen Ross's concept of gendered mediation, which argues that 'the way in which politics is reported is significantly determined by an orientation which privileges the practice of politics as an essentially male pursuit' (1996: 112). As a result of this gendered mediation, 'masculine' behaviours are treated as the norm and women who engage in political activities appear out of place, breaking with traditional gender-role expectations as they try to compete in an environment that is presented as being implicitly unnatural to them. At the same time, those women who do not adopt a 'masculine' or confrontational approach will tend to be discounted as unnewsworthy and will be ignored by the media. The 'masculine narrative' (Rakow and Kranich 1991: 8) is reinforced by the metaphorical language that journalists use in their coverage of political events, invoking images of wars or boxing matches (Blankenship 1976; Blankenship and Kang 1991; Gingras 1997; Gidengil and Everitt 1999; Patterson 1980), by the visuals used to accompany stories (Gidengil and Everitt 2000a), and by the choice of verbs used to report politicians' statements (Geis 1987; Gidengil and Everitt 2000b; see also chapter 13).

Masculine norms are also embodied in the news values governing political reporting. An abundance of information, combined with the limitations on the time and space available in nightly newscasts, means that media personnel have to choose which information to convey to viewers about politicians and events. This is the essence of the media's role as gatekeepers (Woodward 1997). As a result, 'we normally get only what journalists feel is newsworthy and what we get will normally be highly edited' (Geis 1987: 8). The decisions that media personnel make about what to report and how to report it are affected by the prevailing news values. As Allan Bell notes, 'the values of news drive the way in which news is presented. . . . They approximate to the—often unconscious—criteria by which newsworkers make their professional judgements as they process stories' (1991: 155). Of the many values that affect news reporting, the most frequently cited are the values of 'conflict' and 'unexpectedness' or 'novelty' (Bell 1991; Patterson 1980). Stories that contain these elements are considered to be more interesting and exciting. This makes for a ready audience, and so those stories are judged more newsworthy by those with the job of selling the news. Confrontations between politicians become the lead-off stories, and novel or unexpected behaviours get more attention than those that fit with general expectations.

It is important to recognize that news values 'are not neutral, but reflect ideologies and priorities held in society' (Bell 1991: 156). Indeed, the media often defend themselves from criticisms of bias by claiming to act as a mirror of society, reflecting back the social values and understandings common to the public they serve (Taras 1990). News reporting is shaped by 'preconceptions about the social groups . . . from which the news actors come' (Bell 1991: 156). However, as Robinson, Saint-Jean, and Rioux have argued, the role of the media often goes beyond being a passive mirror. Instead, the media act 'like active prisms through which our public understandings are fashioned' (1991: 147).

The idea that the media filter and shape our understanding of what is politically relevant is at the core of the gendered-mediation argument. Politics has traditionally been and is still dominated by men. The number of female MPs has increased over the past few decades, but with only 21 per cent of the seats in Parliament (as of 2002), women are still dramatically underrepresented. Likewise, women still remain underrepresented among media personnel. As a result, the dominant 'masculine' news frames continue to subtly highlight the 'unnatural' position of women in politics. Battles, boxing matches, and street brawls are activities that we conventionally associate with men. Suggestions that a woman might 'land a blow' or deliver 'a knockout punch' challenge traditional social expectations of appropriate gender-role behaviours. If women adopt traditional masculine behaviours and behave combatively, those behaviours are likely to be overemphasized in the coverage they receive. Combative behaviour is newsworthy, but combative behaviour on the part of a woman is doubly newsworthy. We have argued elsewhere (Gidengil and Everitt 1999, 2000a) that the resulting schema incompatibilities may disadvantage women competing for electoral office by reflecting negatively upon them. Actions that run counter to stereotypes are often viewed as more extreme, making a women's assertive behaviour appear downrightly aggressive. On the other hand, if women do not behave in an assertive or combative manner during an election campaign, they will often receive less than their fair share of media coverage.[2]

This is indeed the pattern that we observed in a series of studies focusing on the

1993 Canadian federal election. This election provided an excellent opportunity to explore the concept of gendered mediation: for the first time, two of the major parties were led by women. Our studies of that election have found distinct differences between the coverage received by Kim Campbell and Audrey McLaughlin and that of their male counterparts (Gidengil and Everitt 1999, 2000a, 2000b). In one study, in which we compared the metaphorical reconstructions of the leaders' debates in the nightly news with the participants' actual behaviour, we found that masculine metaphors invoking images of warfare, violence, or sports dominated the political commentary and that this imagery was evoked in strikingly gender-differentiated fashion (Gidengil and Everitt 1999). Both women were portrayed as warriors on the attack much more frequently than the male leaders, a portrayal that was at odds with their actual performances in the debates.

The idea that television news coverage of women leaders will focus disproportionately on behaviour that is counter to feminine stereotypes received further support in a second study examining sound bites (Gidengil and Everitt 2000a). The women were shown interrupting and using other aggressive behaviours such as shaking their fist or pointing their finger far more often than their behaviour in the debates warranted, confirming that media coverage tends to marginalize women when they fail to conform to traditional masculine norms of combative political conduct and yet overemphasizes the counter-stereotypical behaviour when they do behave assertively.

In a third study, examining verbs of reported speech, we found that statements made by the female leaders were less likely than those made by the male leaders to be left to speak for themselves (Gidengil and Everitt 2000b). Rather than relying on the neutral verbs *say* and *tell* to report what the women said, news personnel apparently felt the need to interpret their speech by using more expressive and unconventional verbs. These non-neutral verbs, such as *accuse* and *attack*, were more affect-laden than those used to report on the men. As with other aspects of political reporting, they played up the women's combativeness and emphasized their status as novelties on the electoral scene.

Finally, we have shown that the women's behaviour in the 1993 debates was more heavily mediated in news reports in the sense that it was not simply described but interpreted to a much greater extent than the men's behaviour (Gidengil and Everitt 2000a). Because women party leaders have traditionally been considered less viable electorally than men, the media tend to devote more attention to the horse-race aspects when reporting on women (Kahn 1996) and feel more need to explain their strategy and evaluate its success.

These studies beg the question of whether gender-differentiated media treatment continues to hinder women's participation in political life or whether it diminishes when the novelty of female party leaders begins to wear off. By 2000, McDonough was no longer a novelty, and so we would expect her behaviour to have been less subject to analysis and interpretation. However, other forms of gendered mediation are likely to persist. Politics remains an overwhelmingly male activity, and the news values of conflict and unexpectedness continue to govern the manner in which news is reported. If a female party leader fails to behave combatively, her low-key behaviour will fail both tests of newsworthiness and her visibility in the news will suffer. This chapter assesses these arguments by examining the degree to which change occurred (or did not occur) between 1993 and 2000 in the type and amount of coverage accorded to female party leaders.

METHODOLOGY

Our earlier work on the 1993 leaders' debates enabled us to confirm a number of the empirical implications of the gendered-mediation thesis (Gidengil and Everitt 1999, 2000a). In this study, we extended our previous analysis to include coverage of the 1997 and 2000 leaders' debates. This enables us to examine whether the process of gendered mediation was affected by the fact that female leaders were less of a novelty in the 1997 and 2000 election campaigns. Because the NDP was led by women in all three elections, we can, in effect, control for party in making these cross-time comparisons.[3] Extending the time frame also enables us to provide additional tests of our conclusions regarding the coverage of Campbell in 1993. Three possibilities need to be considered: that Campbell's coverage reflected not her gender but the party she was leading; that her incumbency as prime minister affected her coverage; and that she suffered from the type of negative coverage afforded candidates who have received favourable coverage early in their tenure only to pay for it later (Zaller and Hunt 1994, 1995).

We analyze the coverage of both the English and French debates on Canada's two major English-language television networks, CBC and CTV.[4] The newscasts under study for the 1993 election include those broadcast from the evening of October 3, immediately following the French-language debate, through October 5, the evening after the English-language debate. No stories mentioning either debate were run after this date. In 1997, the French-language debate took an unexpected turn when Claire Lamarche, the moderator, collapsed 30 minutes before the scheduled end of the debate. As a result, the concluding segment of the debate was postponed until almost a week later. This extended the period of time during which the debate was reviewed by reporters. Hence, our analysis of the 1997 election includes any mention of the leaders' performances in the debates from May 12 through May 18. For the 2000 election, we limited our study to the newscasts for November 8, the evening the French-language debate was held, through November 10, the evening after the English-language debate, when debate coverage ended.

Our focus on debate coverage is driven by the recognition that debates receive a high degree of public attention during election campaigns. Few campaign events are covered in as much detail by the media or are watched by as many voters; an even greater number of people watch the post-debate analysis. Past research has shown that the impact of debates is greatest for new leaders and that the influence of debates is strongest when it comes to forming impressions of the leaders and their personalities (Lanoue 1991; LeDuc 1997). Research on American televised debates suggests that this post-debate coverage has as much potential as the debates themselves, if not more, to influence voter perceptions of the party leaders (Lang and Lang 1979; Lemert et al. 1991; Patterson 1980). For many viewers of the debates, the post-debate television analysis helps to focus their attention on the successes, failures, strengths, and weaknesses of the participants. Meanwhile, for those who do not watch the debates (and for many of those who do), the post-debate coverage provides a critical source of information on the leaders' performances. Thus, any gender biases that appear in the post-debate commentary have the potential to significantly affect voters' assessments of women seeking the highest political office.

More important, leaders' debates provide an excellent opportunity to compare the leaders' own behaviour with the mediated version of their behaviour as presented in the nightly newscasts. The gendered-mediation argument that forms the basis of our research suggests that post-debate coverage will focus on elements of conflict and confrontation, leaving leaders who do not assume an aggressive stance in the debates with little coverage. At the same time, because assertive behaviour on the part of women challenges deeply embedded social expectations of appropriate gender-role behaviour, the news value of unexpectedness will lead the media to focus disproportionately on female debaters who behave in this manner. We also argue that women's novelty on the electoral scene will mean that their debate performances are subject to more analysis and evaluation than their male counterparts'. Anchors and reporters are increasingly assuming a self-appointed role as interpreters of political events, and the extensive post-debate coverage presents an important avenue for mediation because 'it is in "explaining" and "making sense out of" events that elements of bias can enter into news reports' (Geis 1987: 108). Given the greater media attention to novelties and unexpected actions, this blurring of the line between objective reporting and commentary is likely to be greatest in the coverage given to women in their first election as party leader.

In order to test these propositions, we first needed to establish an objective way of measuring just how combatively each leader behaved. To do this we identified five indicators of aggressive debating behaviour.[5] These indicators measure how often a leader addressed another leader as 'you' or by name, pointed a finger, clenched a fist, or was shown interrupting another leader. The coding of the English-language debates in each election was performed by a graduate student in Communication Studies at McGill University.[6]

Second, we looked at the amount of coverage received by each leader and compared it to the amount of time he or she each participated in the debate. The gendered-mediation thesis suggests that women who fail to conform to the dominant confrontational norms will tend to receive less attention from the media. Comparing the leaders' behaviour in the debates to the amount of coverage that they received enables us to assess the degree to which the media focused on women who behaved combatively and ignored those who did not.

Finally, an analysis of the proportion of descriptive, analytical, and evaluative coverage received by the different leaders helped us to assess the extent to which female leaders were perceived as novelties whose actions needed to be interpreted and evaluated for the public. Comparing coverage across the three elections enabled us to address a crucial question in this regard: Does the degree of gendered mediation found in election news coverage decline as women leaders become more common?

Female party leaders were a novelty in the 1993 election, but by the time of the 1997 and 2000 elections, this novelty may have worn off. If so, we expected to find that McDonough's performance was subjected to less analysis and evaluation than Campbell's and McLaughlin's had been in 1993.

DEBATE BEHAVIOURS

Figure 12.1 reveals that while Campbell was clearly the more combative of the two women who participated in the 1993 English-language debate, she was not obviously more aggressive than the men in the debate. Admittedly, she used the most aggressive type of debating behaviour, gesturing with her fist clenched, as often (12 times) as Chrétien (11 times). However, she ranked behind the men when it came to the other aggressive behaviours. McLaughlin's debating style in 1993 was much more low-key than any of the other leaders. To the extent that she behaved combatively, that combativeness was in the form of the least aggressive type of behaviour, referring to other leaders as 'you'.

An examination of the behaviour of the male leaders in the 1997 and 2000 debates provides little evidence that Campbell's behaviour was out of line with typical debate performances. Both Jean Charest in 1997 and Joe Clark demonstrated debate behaviours in 2000 that were every bit as aggressive as, if not more aggressive than, Campbell's. And on every dimension other than finger pointing, Chrétien was more combative in 1997 and 2000 than Campbell had been when she was the incumbent prime minister. Finally, Stockwell Day was more prone than Campbell to interrupt and to address the other leaders directly.

McLaughlin's successor, Alexa McDonough, adopted a more combative stance in the 1997 debate. She was more likely than McLaughlin to interrupt other speakers (29 times) and to use a clenched fist (7 times), and just as prone as her predecessor to addressing other leaders as 'you' (55 times) and to use their names (24 times). However, when her behaviour is compared to that of the men in the debate, there is not a single indicator of confrontational behaviour on which McDonough ranked first or even second. In the 2000 debate, McDonough reverted to a more low-key style of debating.

The key point is that McLaughlin and McDonough alike generally engaged in less confrontational behaviour than their male counterparts in all three debates, while Campbell clearly opted for a more combative style of debating. That said, it would be difficult to argue that Campbell was the most aggressive of the leaders in the 1993 debate or that she was more confrontational than any of the male party leaders in the 1997 and 2000 debates. This makes a comparison of the amount of coverage received by the different leaders all the more revealing.

COVERAGE OF THE LEADERS

Canadian debates are structured events, and participating party leaders are provided with equal time for opening and closing remarks. They are also given time to respond to the questions posed by journalists before other party leaders can jump

Figure 12.1

Aggresive Debating Behaviour by Leader (Number of Instances)

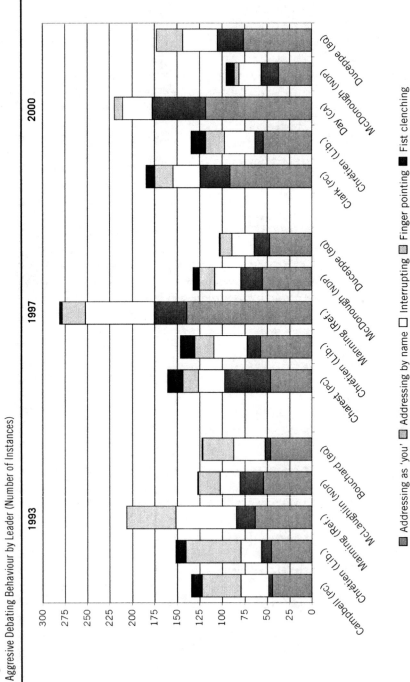

in and challenge them. This establishes an element of balance in the opportunities that the various leaders have to participate in the debates. Table 12.1 shows the amount of time each leader spoke in the English-language debates. While some leaders did end up participating more than others, it is clear that no leader was effectively sidelined. Instead, the pattern is for the incumbent prime minister and the leader of the opposition to speak slightly more than the other party leaders.[7]

In 1993 Campbell and Chrétien participated equally, but more than McLaughlin, who participated as often as Preston Manning and Lucien Bouchard. In 1997 McDonough spoke longer than McLaughlin had, but less than the other, male leaders. In 2000 she again spoke for about the same time, this time slightly more than Duceppe and Clark but less than Day or Chrétien.

It is in the mediated version of the debates, in the post-debate news coverage, that balance is lost. Given the limited time available in television newscasts, journalists focus on those aspects of the debate that they deem to be particularly newsworthy. This is where gendered mediation occurs. When female politicians engage in confrontational behaviour, they are violating deeply held notions of how women should behave. The gendered-mediation thesis suggests that the unexpectedness of this behaviour will make it especially newsworthy. If this argument is correct, we should expect to see extensive news coverage of Campbell's performance in the debate. On the other hand, we should expect much more perfunctory coverage of both McLaughlin and McDonough. When women conform to expectations and adopt a more low-key approach than their male counterparts, as McLaughlin and McDonough did, the gendered-mediation thesis predicts that they will attract little

Table 12.1
Speaking Time of and Statements Referring to Each Leader

	Speaking Time (Minutes)	Referrals (Number)
1993		
Campbell (PC)	22	107
Chrétien (Lib.)	22	74
Manning (Ref.)	15	22
McLaughlin (NDP)	15	20
Bouchard (BQ)	14	54
1997		
Charest (PC)	32.67	77
Chrétien (Lib.)	33.51	63
Manning (Ref.)	22.63	39
McDonough (NDP)	18.42	17
Duceppe (BQ)	16.23	39
2000		
Clark (PC)	17.67	30
Chrétien (Lib.)	25.81	60
Day (CA)	21.05	37
McDonough (NDP)	19.33	12
Duceppe (BQ)	17.13	18

media attention. Lacking as it does the critical ingredients of either conflict or unexpectedness, such behaviour is just not particularly newsworthy.

To test these propositions, we identified every statement made in the post-debate coverage that referred to the leaders by name or by the relevant personal pronoun (see Table 12.1). In 1993, 278 statements referring to the five party leaders were made by anchors, reporters and correspondents.[8] In 1997, this number had dropped slightly. In 2000 there was even less post-debate coverage as the Canadian leaders' debates occurred within days of the American election and the post-debate analysis was in competition with news stories about the still unknown Florida election results.

As expected, in the aftermath of the 1993 debates, reporters devoted more attention to Campbell's performance than to Chrétien's. McLaughlin received much less coverage, approximately the same number of references as did Manning, even though Manning participated only in the English-language debate and McLaughlin had participated in the French-language debate as well. As the first female prime minister, and as a woman who behaved combatively, Campbell's behaviour in the debates clearly received more attention from the media than that of the other party leaders. In fact, Campbell received the most coverage of all the leaders in the three elections under study. McLaughlin, on the other hand, was apparently deemed less newsworthy despite being a woman and was therefore largely ignored. The pattern is even more striking in subsequent elections. In 1997 her successor, McDonough, was the subject of a mere 17 statements in coverage of the debates, less than half the coverage of Duceppe or Manning, and much less than Chrétien or Charest. In the 2000 election, McDonough received even less coverage.

While we cannot rule out the possibility that McLaughlin's and McDonough's lack of coverage reflected their party's standing, it bears emphasis that the two women's behaviour in the debates did not conform as closely to the dominant confrontational norms as that of most of their male counterparts. It is also notable that in 1997 Charest was leading a party with a mere two seats in the House of Commons and that his party ended up winning one seat less than McDonough's party. Similarly, in 2000, the NDP came out one seat ahead of Clark's Conservatives. If 'hopeless cases' do 'get hopeless coverage', McDonough's party was not the only potential qualifier.

DESCRIPTION AND ANALYSIS

A comparison between the degree to which the women's coverage was analyzed or evaluated in 1993 and that in more recent elections enables us to assess the impact of the novelty factor. Following the example of Michael Robinson and Margaret Shehan (1983), each of the statements referring to a party leader was coded as being either descriptive, analytical, or evaluative. *Descriptive sentences* 'present the who, what, where, when of the day's news, without any meaningful qualifications or elaboration' (Robinson and Shehan 1983: 49). As such, they are the most objective form of coverage. Examples of such statements would be 'Chrétien shot back that the previous Tory governments left Canada bankrupt' (Jim Munson, *CTV National News*, 8 Nov. 2000) and 'Preston Manning led off in English, saying that particular piece of history will be irrelevant in the next century' (Neil MacDonald, CBC *National News*, 13 May 1997). *Analytical statements* go beyond simply reporting events and 'tell us why something occurs or predicts as to whether it might. Analytical sentences either draw inference or reach a conclusion based on facts not observed' (Robinson and Shehan 1983: 49–50). In other words, they reflect a reporter's interpretation of a leader's comments, motivations, or behaviours. Reporter Saša Petricic's statement that 'McDonough's goal was to differentiate herself from those other three, to present her party as the only alternative on the left' (CBC *National News*, 12 May 1997) is an obvious analytical statement. *Evaluative statements* represent the most heavily mediated form of coverage as they go beyond the *why* to provide an assessment of *how well*. These are statements of judgment containing 'explicit criticism, complaint, or praise' (Robinson and Shehan 1983: 43) that, even if true, reflect the journalists' own opinions rather than the assessments of other legitimate sources. Both 'Jean Charest was very successful at getting into the debate as often as he wanted by often cutting people off and just jumping into the debate' (Jason Moscovitz, CBC *National News*, 13 May 1997) and 'All in all, Day did very well by not hurting himself at all' (Craig Oliver, CTV *National News*, 8 Nov. 2000) are evaluative statements. Statements were considered evaluative if they contained any explicit evaluation on the part of the media personnel, and analytical if they contained any analysis of the leaders or their performances.[9]

What interested us were gender differences in the amount of analytical and evaluative coverage and whether those differences diminished between 1993 and 2000. In 1993, coverage of the two women leaders was clearly more heavily mediated than was coverage of the men (see Figure 12.2). Campbell's performance was more likely than that of any of her male counterparts to be analyzed and evaluated rather than simply described. Similarly, a higher proportion of McLaughlin's coverage was analytical or evaluative than was the case for either Manning or Bouchard. And while Chrétien rivalled the female leaders in terms of the relative amount of evaluative coverage he received, his evaluations were more likely than theirs to be positive. Indeed, Campbell received more negative than positive evaluations.

In 1997, the news environment had changed; reporters were more likely to incorporate their own views and assessments into their political commentary. Almost one-third of the statements made about the leaders in the post-debate coverage in 1997 contained an element of evaluation, as compared to only 13 per cent of the statements in the 1993 election. This shift came at the expense of analytical statements because reporters moved beyond an attempt to make sense of the leaders' actions to assess how well they had performed. These assessments carried with them both positive and negative elements.

Of the five leaders, Chrétien received the most 'objective' post-debate coverage; almost two-thirds of the 63 statements referring to him were descriptive in nature. Manning came second in descriptive coverage with 23 of the 39 references to him (59 per cent) being descriptive. While Charest received the most coverage of any leader in the debate (77 statements), he was also the most analyzed of the five leaders, with over one-third of the references to him attempting to explain his motivations. Duceppe received the most negative assessments from the anchors and

Figure 12.2
Mediated Coverage for Each Leader (Percentage)

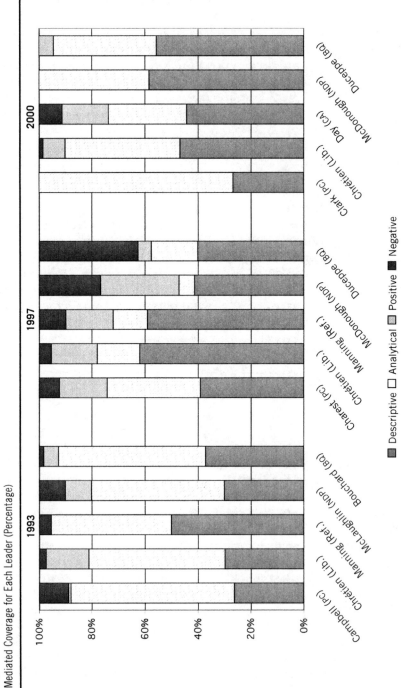

journalists with 15 of his 39 references (38 per cent) including elements of criticism. This was partly due to his party's position on the Canadian unity issue. It also reflected the fact that the collapse of the moderator impeded his ability to raise this topic in the French-language debate.

It was McDonough, though, who stood out as being the leader whose coverage was the most evaluative. Women leaders may have become less of a novelty by 1997, but the media still apparently felt a greater need to assess a woman's behaviour, to the extent that they reported it at all. McDonough received the least coverage of all of the leaders, with only 17 references to her debate performances in the week between the first English-language debate and the final segment of the French-language debate. However, over half (53 per cent) of those references involved an assessment of how well she had done. While 5 of these 9 references could be considered positive in nature, none was particularly glowing, and they were often tied to a more negative comment. A good example is CBC reporter Jason Moscovitz's near-afterthought in discussing the French-language debate: 'And Alexa McDonough was a participant as well, but she had a terrible time in French. Although she made a valiant effort, she did have great difficulty communicating' (*CBC National News*, 13 May 1997).[10] Another is CTV's Craig Oliver's comments, 'Ms McDonough, you sure know she was there. At times she went over the top, I think a lot of us thought, but nevertheless she did what she had to do here, which was to increase her profile substantially' (*CTV National News*, 12 May 1997). It is interesting that McDonough was by no means the most aggressive debater, and yet she was still perceived to have gone 'over the top'.

Even given the more limited coverage of the 2000 debates, the commentary on the leaders and their performances in the debates was generally more mediated than descriptive in nature. Chrétien, Day, and Clark—the leaders who were discussed the most in the post-debate coverage—received more analytical and evaluative coverage than descriptive, although the amount of evaluative coverage was much less than in 1997. Duceppe and McDonough were virtually absent from the post-debate newscasts. While Duceppe gave a stronger performance in the 2000 debate than he had in 1997, his party did not pose the same threat to national unity that it had in earlier elections and he was therefore less newsworthy. Nonetheless, he still received more coverage than McDonough. This is consistent with the gendered-mediation argument. Now that she was no longer a novelty on the electoral scene, McDonough's low-key debating style was reflected in the sparse coverage that she received.

A cross-time comparison of the three debates allows us to compare Campbell's coverage in 1993 to the coverage given to the men who followed her as leader of the Conservative party. While reports on Charest's performances in the debates were the most mediated of all of the leaders in 1997 and Clark received the lowest proportion of descriptive coverage in 2000, their experiences still did not compare to Campbell's. Charest's coverage was clearly more descriptive than Campbell's, and Clark's was clearly less evaluative. Likewise, Chrétien's treatment by the media in 1997 and 2000 was both less mediated and much more positive than Campbell's. This makes it difficult to argue that the high degree of analysis and evaluation in Campbell's coverage was due to her position as incumbent prime minister. Finally, while Day experienced the same rise-and-fall phenomenon in 2000 that Campbell had experienced seven years earlier, his post-debate coverage was significantly less mediated than hers had been. True, a higher proportion of his coverage was evaluative, but most of that was positive, suggesting that Campbell's coverage can not be attributed to the media's attempt to 'correct for their earlier favourable coverage . . . by growing tougher on candidates they perceive themselves as having helped' (Robinson and Shehan 1983: 128). There is little doubt that of all leaders in the three elections, it was Campbell whose debate performances were the most mediated in the subsequent news coverage. This gives credence to the argument that the novelty of a women in the position of party leader, let alone in the position of prime minister, leads media personnel to subject their performances to greater scrutiny.

DISCUSSION

Despite the fact that women have led national political parties in the last three Canadian elections as of the time of writing, it is clear that gendered mediation still represents a challenge to women's equal participation in political life. The news values of conflict and unexpectedness continue to govern what gets reported in the evening news. Women who participate in key election events such as leaders' debates are confronted by the need to adopt combative behaviours if they want to draw the media's attention. However, in doing so they risk appearing to violate traditional gender-role expectations and having those behaviours overemphasized. In asserting herself in the debates, Campbell faced just this dilemma. On the other hand, when McLaughlin and McDonough displayed less combative behaviours, they received little attention from the media.

The decline in the amount of analytical and evaluative coverage for McDonough in 2000 suggests that female leaders (or at least female leaders who are no longer new to the scene) were no longer perceived as being unusual enough within the political realm to warrant greater assessment than their male counterparts. As a result, the media's need to analyze and evaluate McDonough's behaviour was less than it had been in previous elections. While this is a positive finding, it remains to be seen whether it would still be the case if a woman were to lead a more competitive party or if that woman were to behave more combatively. And it is counterbalanced by the finding that McDonough received so little coverage in the aftermath of the 2000 debates. When the novelty wears off, it seems, a woman who fails to conform to the dominant conflictual norms is likely to suffer benign neglect.[11]

What is clear from this study is that despite attempts by the media to be fair in the coverage they provide to different party leaders, gender bias embedded in dominant news values and in traditional gender-role expectations still creeps into election news coverage. The increase in the number of women competing for elite elected office has done little to change the norms of political journalism, and these norms continue to reinforce the image that politics is a man's game. Given that the masculine narrative guiding political news coverage is unlikely to change in the foreseeable future, the media will continue to present a serious obstacle to women seeking elite elected office. Female party leaders such as Kim Campbell who try to fit in by adopting combative debating styles will find that their aggressive behaviours are overemphasized. As a result they will appear 'too aggressive' and will elicit criticism of their non-stereotypical behaviour. Paradoxically, those women who do not conform to the traditional masculine approach to politics will continue to be sidelined, receiving far less coverage than a similar low-key performance by a male leader.

Notes

1. We would like to thank Robin Sutherland (University of New Brunswick), Albert Bannerjee (McGill University), and Valisa Smith (McGill University) for their research assistance. This research was supported by a grant from the Social Science and Humanities Research Council of Canada and by the Fonds FCAR.

2. 'Fair share of media coverage' can be defined as the amount of coverage received by a competitor leading a party of comparable strength.

3. In an ideal world, though, we would want to be able to include a male NDP leader in the comparison to ensure that the patterns observed reflected the leaders' gender and not their party's standing.

4. We are grateful to the Fraser Institute for making transcripts of the coverage of the debates for 1993 and 1997 on both networks available to us. The Fraser Institute does not bear any responsibility for the analyses and interpretations presented here. The CBC coverage for the 2000 debates came from the CBC Web site. The CTV coverage for the 2000 debates came from Newscan.com. We did not study the French-language coverage of these debates on Radio-Canada or TVA.

5. In adopting this approach, we have followed the procedures used by Monière (1994; cf. Tiemens et al. 1985) in his analysis of the 1993 French-language debate. For more details about the coding of these behaviours, see Gidengil and Everitt (1999).

6. Our analysis of aggressive behaviours focuses solely on the English-language debates. It is possible that the leaders may have changed their debate strategy between the English- and the French-language debates in 1997 and 2000. However, a comparison of our results with Monière's analysis of the 1993 French-language debate (1994) suggests that while the leaders were more combative in English, their relative standings in terms of combativeness did not change significantly.

7. This was not true in 1997 when Duceppe was leader of the Opposition, as he was debating in English, his second language.

8. We did not code the remarks made by commentators such as pollsters or party officials as we felt that they would be heavily evaluative and biased. We did, however, code remarks made by journalists from media organizations other than the CBC or CTV as we felt that they have a professional obligation to be neutral and one could argue that because they were journalists they provided a credible source of objective reporting. We also omitted the CBC's 'Reality Check' segments on the grounds that this coverage was explicitly evaluative.

9. The coding for this study was conducted slightly differently than the coding presented in our earlier work (Gidengil and Everitt 2000a). Here, the unit of analysis was the statement, whereas previously we had coded by sentence. Given that reporters seldom spoke in complete sentences and that some sentences had more than one idea in them, we felt that there were valid reasons for basing our current analysis on statements rather than sentences. The coding of the 1993, 1997, and 2000 coverage was performed independently by one of us and a research assistant. The level of intercoder reliability was 98 per cent for the 1993 data, 89 per cent for the 1997 data, and 98 per cent for the 2000 data. Any discrepancies in the coding were resolved by discussion; where ambiguity

remained, the statement in question was coded into the category representing the lower level of mediation. In all of the analyses, there was complete intercoder agreement on the direction of evaluative statements as either positive or negative.

10. This quotation was considered to contain two statements, one negative and the other positive.

11. It may also be the case that the decline in interpretive coverage in 2000 is directly related to the reduced attention paid to the Canadian debates by the television networks in the wake of the Florida election results in the United States. It is possible that if the networks had devoted the normal amount of news space to the debates, the proportion of evaluative coverage would have been higher.

Chapter 13

'Wham, Bam, No Thank You Ma'am': Gender and the Game Frame in National Newspaper Coverage of Election 2000[1]

SHANNON SAMPERT AND LINDA TRIMBLE

INTRODUCTION

On 16 September 2000, anticipating an early election call by the governing Liberals, the *Globe and Mail* ran a tongue-in-cheek profile of Canada's five federal party leaders (McCarthy 2000). With a picture entitled 'Ready to Rumble', the piece cast the leaders as pugilists, eagerly anticipating their turn in the electoral ring. Like boxer's scorecards, the profiles listed each leader's alias, age, 'experience in the ring', 'brag line', and 'most effective punch', and even provided a pithy assessment of ('the skinny on') the leaders' capacity to land a 'knockout punch'. The lone female party chief, the NDP's Alexa McDonough, was ostensibly treated like one of the guys in the article. McDonough ('a.k.a. Lefty'), was recognized for her 'left jab' and for her 'plodding but dogged style'. But 'the skinny' on McDonough was 'float like a butterfly, sting like a, er, mosquito'. The article presented McDonough as an electoral lightweight and political weakling. The message underlying this leadership-as-boxing-match news frame, commonly referred to as the game frame, is that women don't have the right stuff for the competitive political arena.

This chapter analyzes coverage of the 2000 federal election campaign by scrutinizing election-related headlines that appeared in English Canada's national newspapers, the *Globe and Mail* and the *National Post*, over the course of the 36-day campaign.[2] We distinguished between a *game frame* for campaign coverage (headlines that focused on the leaders, the horse race, campaign gaffes and strategies, and poll results) and an *issue frame* (headlines highlighting policy issues, party policy stances, ideological differences between parties, and the party or government record). Since the game frame is imbued with the masculine language of the battlefield, the sports arena, and the boxing ring and laden with gender-differentiated assumptions, we hypothesized that its application by the print media would differentiate between the male leaders and the lone female party leader, Alexa McDonough. In other words, we anticipated that Canada's two national newspapers would, through their use of priming and framing devices, suggest that McDonough was a lesser player in the electoral game.

While it is true that McDonough and the NDP were not major contenders in the

2000 federal election, neither were Joe Clark and his Progressive Conservative party. Therefore, greater attention by the two newspapers to Clark and assessments of Clark as the more significant and commanding political actor were construed as evidence of a gendered game frame, an approach to election coverage that poses a clear disadvantage to female party leaders.

HORSE RACES, BOUTS, AND BATTLEFIELDS: MEDIA FRAMING OF ELECTIONS

To understand how the media shape public opinion about prominent news stories, it is important to define agenda setting, priming, and framing. *Agenda setting* refers to the ability of the news media to select and filter news stories and thereby determine the significant issues of the day (Iyengar and Simon 1993). The media focus attention on a particular news story by, for instance, placing it on the front page and giving it a catchy headline or dramatic photograph. *Priming* refers to the effects of agenda setting's emphasis on certain events or issues. By giving primacy to certain actors, issues, or ideas, the media influence readers' evaluations and shape the criteria by which political events are judged (Terkildsen and Schnell 1997).

The concept of *media framing* is particularly important to our study. *News frames* are mechanisms for selecting, interpreting, and presenting information (Gitlin 1980). Framing allows reporters to 'process and "package" large amounts of diverse and often contradictory information, quickly and routinely' (O'Sullivan et al. 1994: 122). For instance, an event like a natural disaster can be framed as a human interest story, featuring the stories of individuals coping with the consequences. Alternatively, it can be framed as a 'government to the rescue' tale, complete with information about disaster relief and prominent politicians' visits to the disaster site. Frames provide the reader or viewer with cues identifying the meaning and importance of the story. As Pippa Norris explains, 'news frames give "stories" a conventional "peg" to arrange the narrative, to make sense of the facts, to focus the headline, and to define events as newsworthy' (1997c: 2). Thus the language and metaphors used to describe an issue or event are very important and shape its interpretation. By fitting complex and even novel events into familiar categories, and by choosing and organizing stories according to dominant discourses and assumptions, the media offer the audience interpretive shorthand for making sense of the news.

Many media commentators in Canada and the United States have identified a prevalent frame for political reporting, called the *game*, or *strategic, frame*. This approach emphasizes the contest between competing forces by focusing on strategy and outcomes (Lawrence 2000). News reports adopting the game frame tell the tale of who's winning, who's losing, and why. This type of story is easily signalled with sports or battlefield language. As with sports or war stories, the electoral game frame includes tales of strategic advantage and disadvantage. Observers of media and politics note that the game frame now dominates mainstream news reporting of politics, especially elections (Frizzell and Westell 1989; Mendelsohn 1993; Soderlund et al. 1984; Wilson 1980–81). Electoral reporting tends to focus on the 'horse race' while neglecting analysis of party platforms and ideological differences.

David Taras (1990), Matthew Mendelsohn (1993), and Regina Lawrence (2000) are among those media analysts who argue that the organizational needs of television account, at least in part, for the increasing prevalence of leader-focused horse-race journalism. As Mendelsohn says, 'the language and culture of television encourages campaigns to be portrayed as a war, as a game, as drama, but rarely as a competition between alternate visions' (1993: 150). The game frame fits television's definition of newsworthiness: it offers elite conflict, winners and losers, personalities, drama, and immediacy. Moreover, the game frame packages events into easily understood stories, complete with accessible terminology, assumptions, and stereotypes. As Lawrence writes,

> Reporters often treat elections as if they fit into a 'master narrative' much like the 'Road to the National Championship' coverage so common in the sports pages. According to this narrative, election day is the goal line and everything that happens during the campaign is significant only as it pertains to a politician's (or a party's) chance of getting across the goal line. (2000: 96)

Feminist accounts of media framing reveal the gendered nature of the game frame. Political reporting in general, and election coverage in particular, employs a masculine narrative dominated by the images and language of the conflictual public sphere: the sports arena, the battlefield, and the boxing ring. The game frame, while using gender-neutral terminology, nevertheless assumes the male to be normative and is therefore profoundly gendered. Recall the boxing-match image in the *Globe and Mail* story cited in the introduction to this chapter, and try to imagine a woman stepping into the ring with the heavyweight champion of the world. Because men continue to dominate the realms of sports and armed conflict, and because patriarchal thinking classifies women as nurturing, caring, and non-combative, women are rendered to the margins or placed outside of the game frame.

When the media 'subscribe to a masculine conception of politics as a struggle between warring armies or competing teams', women politicians are put at a distinct disadvantage (Gidengil and Everitt 2000b: 109). Female leaders who behave assertively fall within the game frame but are seen to violate assumptions about how women should behave and are only considered newsworthy because of their 'unexpectedly' aggressive behaviour (see chapter 12). Female leaders confront a dilemma. If they conform to the media script, their assertiveness may be exaggerated and criticized by the press. On the other hand, female politicians who fail to play the game fall outside of the strategic news frame and may not receive much media attention. This is a key issue for women politicians, as several studies have shown that female candidates receive less coverage than do male candidates (Kahn and Goldenberg 1991; Serini, Powers, and Johnson 1998).

Shirley Serini, Angela Powers, and Susan Johnson argue that under some circumstances, a woman leader might capture media attention by 'playing the game like a man'. Their examination of press reporting of the 1994 Illinois Democratic gubernatorial primary in two Chicago newspapers found that the white female candidate received more game-frame coverage than her white male opponent, attention that may have helped her win the election (1998: 202). The female candidate's innovative advertising strategy captivated the print media, and her ability to 'emulate a man, speak a man's language and to position herself as a man' helped engineer a 'long-shot victory' (Serini, Powers, and Johnson 1998: 202). This approach was not available to NDP leader Alexa McDonough, however. In the 2000 Canadian federal election, the lone woman party leader was in no position to stage a come-from-behind victory: the NDP entered the election with a handful of seats in the House of Commons and an unpromising standing in opinion polls. As the *Globe and Mail* article referred to in the introduction illustrates, McDonough was written out of the game before it even began.

THE POLITICAL AND MEDIA CONTEXT OF ELECTION 2000

Prime Minister Jean Chrétien called a federal election on 22 October 2000, a mere three and a half years into his five-year term. At the time the writ was dropped, the Liberals held 161 seats and the Canadian Alliance, as the official opposition, had 58. The Bloc Québécois held 44 seats, the NDP 19, and the Conservatives 15. There were 4 independent MPs. This was Chrétien's third election as leader of the Liberals; he had won majority governments in the two previous elections and presided over a five-party Parliament. The prime minister's early election call was in response to polls showing the Liberals had a 19- to 33-point lead over their nearest contenders, the newly formed Canadian Alliance party (Fife 2000: A1).

The Alliance, formed out of the unsuccessful 'unite the right' initiative of Reform leader Preston Manning, featured a newly elected leader, Stockwell Day. Day barely had time to set up an Ottawa team before the election call. Still, when the writ was issued, the Alliance was enjoying its highest-ever level of popularity, with support near 25 per cent in national polls (Alberts 2000: A4).

Chrétien also faced another relatively new leader: Joe Clark. Clark had won entry to the Commons in a Nova Scotia by-election just six weeks before the writ was dropped, but he was no newcomer to politics. As prime minister, Clark had had the dubious distinction of holding power for a mere nine months before Pierre Trudeau's Liberals toppled his minority government in 1980. For Clark, the campaign began at a time when political pundits were anticipating that the Conservatives could lose official party status.

Similarly, the NDP began the election with just 10 per cent support in the polls and with McDonough deflecting some serious criticisms of her stewardship of the party. McDonough had lost one MP to the Liberal ranks early in 2000, when Rick Laliberte crossed the floor. Another MP, Angela Vautour, had joined the Tories the year before. Even the NDP's traditional union support appeared to be fading, with union representatives suggesting the party was heading for annihilation (Hunter 2000). McDonough went into the election facing an uphill battle to retain the party's 19 seats.

BQ leader Gilles Duceppe vowed that the 2000 election would not be a repeat of the 1997 campaign, which had featured media attention on a series of logistical problems in the new leader's tour. Indeed, the 1997 images of Duceppe wearing a hair net while visiting a cheese factory surfaced several times during the 2000 campaign as well, illustrating the media focus on leader gaffes and strategic errors.

In short, the polls indicated another Liberal victory, and too much predictability for a press corps seeking a real horse race. The only question about the front runner was whether the Liberal party would be returned to office with a minority or a majority government. As a result, the media had to settle for middle-level game framing, focusing on the strength of the Alliance outside the West, the ability of the Liberals to regain seats in the Atlantic provinces while hanging on to Western support, and the issue of whether or not the NDP and Conservatives would lose official party status.

Another factor shaping media framing of elections, and of politics generally, is the underrepresentation of women as journalists, editors, and managers in Canada's leading newspapers. Mainstream media are dominated by male voices, and Canada's national English-language newspapers are no exception. The *Globe and Mail* has 10 news editors listed on its Web site; only 2 are women (<www.globeandmail.com/services/site/help.html#sections>, accessed 15 May 2001). Moreover, the 2000 *Globe and Mail* election team featured 15 men and only 2 women (*Globe and Mail* 26 October 2000: A4). The *National Post*'s editorial board is also predominantly male. Of the 12 news editors listed on its Web site, 2 are women (<www.nationalpost.com>, accessed 15 May 2001). Male reporters and columnists also dominated the new paper's first national election team; the *Post* had only one woman riding the election buses, Justine Hunter, covering the NDP. Additionally, its 9 regular commentators on the election were all men.

METHODOLOGY

We conducted a content and discourse analysis of all election headlines appearing in the *Globe and Mail* and the *National Post* over the course of the campaign. Our analysis of the election headlines began the day after the writ was dropped (23 October 2000) and continued until the day after the election (28 November 2000). The two national newspapers were chosen because of their nationwide distribution and large audiences. In 2000, the *Globe* had a weekly readership of over 2 million, and the *Post* reached 1.7 million readers (Canadian Newspaper Association, <www.can-acj.ca/newspapers/facts>, accessed 15 May 2000). Stories that appear in the national newspapers are often put on the national news wire, to be picked up by other newspapers as well as television and radio stations. Moreover, journalists working for national newspapers are considered pre-eminent in their field and as a result, some of their columnists and reporters may act as political pundits for television and radio and comment on the election campaign as it evolves. The *National Post* and the *Globe and Mail* helped set the tone for media coverage throughout Canada. As well, the 2000 election was the first federal election reported by the upstart, controversial *National Post*, and we were curious about how the new newspaper would cover the parties and leaders in this campaign.[3]

We decided to focus on headlines because their prominence in the news story positions them as key framing devices, expressing the main topic of the news event, illustrating the social or political opinions of the newspaper, and influencing the interpretation of the story by readers (van Dijk 1991). Headlines are also often the only component of the story readers look at or the only information about the story they will later recall. As Teun van Dijk puts it, headlines define stories so power-fully that readers 'would have to make an extra effort to derive an alternative main topic from the text' (1991: 50). Because we were concerned with editorial decisions about election news framing, we examined headlines appearing in the front sec-tions, editorials, and special election sections, and did not code headlines from the business section of either paper. Nor did we analyze headlines from the letters to the editor. Although the letters to the editor appear in the front section of both newspapers, the associated headlines reflect the views of readers, not editors. We did include the special election sections in the *Globe and Mail* as these were clearly indicative of editorial decision making about the issues, events, and personalities central to Election 2000. In total, we coded headlines for 1,141 election news stories, 615 from the *Post* and 526 from the *Globe*.

Headlines were analyzed according to where they appeared in the paper (front page, editorial page, front section, special section), the type of story (hard news, per-sonality profile, opinion column, editorial), and the main and secondary topics con-veyed by the headline.[4] We categorized each headline according to its overall frame, distinguishing between a game frame and an issue frame. News stories are shaped as inverted pyramids, with the most important idea or source placed at the begin-ning of the story and the less important dimensions of the story placed near the end. Because this is also the case with headlines, we determined which party or party leader was mentioned first, second, and third in the headlines.

In addition to assessing the priming of the actors and topics emphasized by the headlines, we used discourse analysis to evaluate the context in which the words were used and the position of the actors in relation to one another. We determined which political actor was given agency by being mentioned first, and which actor was relegated to a passive role by being placed in a second (or even third) position. For example, in the following headline from the *Globe and Mail*, Clark is the first named, and dominant, actor, with the Liberals and Alliance described as the recip-ients of Clark's action: 'Clark Hurls One-Two Punch: Tory Leader Attacks Liberals, Alliance in Bid to Become Opposition Choice' (24 Nov. 2000: A9). This headline also illustrates the use of game metaphors, with Clark's attack on oppo-nents framed as a boxer's blow. This was very important to our analysis of gendered news frames, therefore we carefully examined the language used to describe the party leaders, paying particular attention to the use of masculine game-frame ter-minology. We sought to determine whether the language of sport (skates, runs, race, pitch), of boxing (punch, jab, bash, hammer), or of battle (warriors, weapons, ammunition, troops) was more strongly associated with the male party leaders than with NDP leader, Alexa McDonough.

Based on Canadian and American studies of election coverage, we hypothesized that the headlines would employ an unreflective and unabashed use of the game frame, complete with sports metaphors, boxing terminology, and the language of the battlefield (Cappella and Jamieson 1997; Fletcher and Everett 1991; Gilsdorf and Bernier 1991; Lawrence 2000; Mendelsohn 1993; Patterson 1994). Given the political and media context of the election, we expected the dominant print narrative to focus most of its attention on the ruling Liberal party and its leader, Jean Chrétien. We did not think either paper would give McDonough and the NDP much coverage, as the dominant discourse about the left is that it is passé, thus uninteresting and unappealing to voters. Additionally, we anticipated that the headlines would slot the male leaders into the prevalent game frame while associating McDonough and the NDP with issues, thereby implying that the female leader wasn't up to the (masculinist) demands of the electoral game. Finally, from a critical discourse perspective, we expected that McDonough would be placed in a passive second-actor position, portrayed as reacting to the male-dominant first-actor position. This hypothesis reflects Manon Tremblay and Nathalie Bélanger's (1997) finding that political cartoons in major Canadian papers during the 1993 federal election depicted the female leaders, Kim Campbell and Audrey McLaughlin, as less powerful, independent, and assertive than male leaders. Finally, we anticipated that the language of the aggressor would be applied less often to McDonough than to the male party chiefs.

FRAMING THE ELECTION AS A GAME

As we predicted, the majority of the headlines adopted a game frame. Indeed, 81 per cent (400) of the *Globe*'s headlines foregrounded the game . In contrast, the *Post* emphasized this strategic frame in 66 per cent (406) of its stories. This suggests that although both papers looked at issues in their election coverage, the issues were interpreted in the context of the horse race or of leader evaluations. An example of a headline that framed issues as secondary to the electoral game is provided by the *Globe*: 'Day Can't Shake Hot-Button Issues: Former Alliance Pollster Says Party Needs 4 More Years to Convince Voters It Does Not Have a Hot-Button Agenda' (20 Nov. 2000: A6). In this headline, the emphasis was not on the issues themselves, but on the ability of the Alliance to capture votes in an effort to win the next election. An example of an issue couched in game-frame terms by the *Post* is 'Day Not Fit to Lead Country, Clark Says: "A Secret Agenda" on Health' (16 Nov. 2000: A6). In this case, the issue of health care was relegated to a secondary headline, apparently considered less important than Day's leadership abilities.

A majority of the headlines in the *National Post*, 311 (50.6 per cent), and a plurality of those in the *Globe and Mail*, 239 (45.4 per cent), employed masculinist game-frame words, such as *fires*, *attacks*, *battle*, *race*, *blitz*, *tackle*, *skate*, and *hammer*, and metaphors, such as 'takes aim', 'sure-footed', 'gang up', 'shifts target', 'fractious troops', and 'one-two punch'. In summary, we established that most of the election headlines in the *National Post* and the *Globe and Mail* adopted the game frame, and many employed a gendered narrative of masculine combat and competition.

WHO'S IN THE GAME? PRIMING LEADERS AND PARTIES

Table 13.1 shows the distribution of overall party and leader mentions in the headlines by paper compared with the percentage of seats the party held at dissolution. Here we see that the Liberals got the most attention but received disproportionately fewer overall mentions given their percentage of seats. The Alliance received more mentions than party standings would suggest, especially from the *Globe*. The other parties were relegated to the sidelines, especially the Bloc, which was mentioned the least often in both papers despite the party's standing (and prior status as official opposition, 1993–97). It is interesting that Clark and the Conservatives got more mentions than did McDonough and the NDP. The Conservatives held fewer seats at dissolution than did the NDP, both the NDP and Conservatives were low in the polls going into the election campaign, and commentators suggested both parties would lose seats. So the slightly higher level of attention to Clark and the Conservatives is interesting and suggests that evaluations of Clark and McDonough were shaped by gender-based assumptions about the best 'players' in the electoral game.

The first political actor mentioned in a headline grabs centre stage and dominates the action of the headline, so first mentions are a sign of the actor's perceived importance in the news event. Table 13.2 shows a couple of key differences between the newspapers on this measure. First, the *Globe* focused more attention on Day and the Alliance than did the *Post*; indeed, Day captured almost as many

Table 13.1

Total Leader and Party Mentions by Newspaper

| | Newspaper | | Seats at Dissolution |
	National Post	*Globe and Mail*	
Liberal	311 (41.7%)	290 (40.3%)	53.5%
Alliance	204 (27.4%)	233 (32.3%)	19.3%
Bloc	50 (6.7%)	46 (6.4%)	14.6%
NDP	74 (9.9%)	63 (8.8%)	6.3%
PC	106 (14.2%)	88 (12.2%)	5.0%
Total	745 (100%)	720 (100%)	98.7%[a]

[a] Does not add up to 100% because there were also 4 independent MPs at dissolution (1.3%).

Table 13.2

First Actor Mentioned, by Newspaper

	National Post	*Globe and Mail*
Chrétien	101 (23.8%)	73 (19.7%)
Liberal party	85 (20.0%)	73 (19.7%)
Day	58 (13.6%)	68 (18.4%)
Alliance party	52 (12.2%)	59 (15.9%)
Duceppe	20 (4.7%)	3 (.8%)
Bloc Québécois	11 (2.6%)	22 (5.9%)
McDonough	22 (5.2%)	7 (1.9%)
NDP	23 (5.4%)	22 (5.9%)
Clark	26 (6.1%)	16 (4.3%)
Conservative party	17 (4.0%)	23 (6.2%)

first mentions in the *Globe* as did Chrétien. Second, McDonough captured very few first mentions in the *Globe*. The *Post* gave McDonough more attention. Clark's name, on the other hand, appeared first in slightly more of the *Post*'s election headlines, but in twice as many headlines in the *Globe*.

Not only was McDonough given a passive role in the coverage of the election campaign in the *Globe* and the *Post*, she was further marginalized by editorial decisions on story placement (see Table 13.3). Of the 67 headlines that ran on the front page of the *National Post*, McDonough and the NDP never rated a single mention, indicating that neither the party nor the leader were considered important enough to be on the front page. By comparison, Clark, whose party was also facing annihilation at the beginning of the election campaign, was the first actor mentioned on the front page in the *National Post* almost 7 per cent of the time. McDonough and the NDP fared slightly better in the *Globe*, but still not as well as Clark and the Conservatives. That Clark and the Conservatives got better front-page attention than McDonough and the NDP indicates that although both parties faced a similar electoral fate, they were treated differently by the press. This may reflect the ideological orientation of both newspapers, which is more congruent with the fiscal conservatism of the PCs. Or it could have resulted from the view that Clark outperformed McDonough on the campaign trail. However, it is also

Table 13.3

First Actor Mentioned by Location in Paper, by Newspaper

	National Post			*Globe and Mail*		
	Front Page	Front Section	Op/Ed Section	Front Page	Front Section	Op/Ed Section
Chrétien	27	66	8	22	39	8
	(49%)	(19%)	(28%)	(36%)	(14%)	(20%)
Liberal party	10	65	10	13	50	6
	(18%)	(19%)	(35%)	(21%)	(20%)	(15%)
Day	8	48	2	15	41	10
	(14%)	(14%)	(7%)	(24%)	(16%)	(24%)
Alliance party	3	42	7	6	42	10
	(6%)	(12%)	(24%)	(8%)	(16%)	(24%)
Duceppe	1	19	0	0	3	0
	(2%)	(6%)	(0%)	(0%)	(1%)	(0%)
Bloc Québécois	0	11	0	1	19	22
	(0%)	(3%)	(0%)	(2%)	(7%)	(5%)
McDonough	0	22	0	0	7	0
	(0%)	(6%)	(0%)	(0%)	(3%)	(0%)
NDP	0	23	0	1	20	1
	(0%)	(7%)	(0%)	(2%)	(8%)	(2%)
Clark	4	20	2	1	14	1
	(7%)	(6%)	(7%)	(2%)	(6%)	(2%)
Conservative party	2	15	0	3	19	1
	(4%)	(4%)	(0%)	(5%)	(7%)	(2%)

possible that McDonough and the NDP received less front-page coverage than Clark and the PCs because McDonough is not easily characterized by the stereotypically male game frame favoured by headline writers.

Another indication of gendered priming is illustrated by the relegation of the NDP and McDonough by the *Post* to standing head stories. *Standing head stories* are regular features with common headlines signalling a particular type of campaign coverage. The *Globe and Mail* featured a brief daily analysis of election trends, written by pundits, always headlined 'Colour Commentary'. Standing heads were used frequently, often daily, by both newspapers throughout the campaign. Those appearing in the *Globe* were quite bland in tone (for instance, 'Election Notebook' and 'In Brief'), did not name leaders or parties, and were tucked into the middle of the election coverage. In contrast, the *National Post* used these features to give colour to the campaign by enticing readers with provocative and even silly headlines placed at the top of pages dedicated to election coverage. For instance, the *Post* ran a standing feature, 'We Wanna Know', that asked party leaders such questions as 'What's your favourite perfume?' 'Do you have a tattoo?' and 'What was the name of your first pet?'

These headlines are examples of soft journalism, designed to entertain rather than inform. They reflect a lifestyle or personality approach, and evoke stereotypically private, feminine concerns. So it is not surprising that McDonough was the leader mentioned first most often in the *Post*'s standing headlines (see Table 13.4). McDonough was mentioned first in only 5 per cent of the *Post* headlines overall and 2 per cent of the *Globe* headlines. But when she was mentioned first in the *Post*, invariably it was in the frivolous, superficial standing head stories.

When it came to hard news (defined as regular, balanced news coverage, not opinion pieces, columns, personality profiles, or editorials), McDonough was ignored. While all the leaders except Chrétien and Day received few first mentions in the hard news stories, overall McDonough had proportionally less coverage in the *Post*'s hard new stories than any male leader, and less than all leaders but Duceppe in the *Globe*. Both the *Post* and the *Globe* also viewed McDonough and the NDP as largely unworthy of editorial comment. None of the *Post*'s columnists discussed the NDP or McDonough in their headlines, and the *Globe* mentioned the party as a second actor in only one of its column headlines.

The electoral game frame places leaders in the foreground, as they are seen as personifying the party. As Taras writes, television's 'need to focus on individuals and to personify complex issues, and the need of the parties in the face of this to provide a single spokesperson and a neat, tightly wrapped message, have elevated party leaders to be the supreme contestants of elections' (1990: 166). Mendelsohn showed, in his analysis of the 1988 campaign (1993), that news coverage primed leadership, and Gidengil and colleagues confirmed this result for the 1993 and 1997 campaigns (2000b). Thus we expected all the leaders to be mentioned more often than their parties.

Table 13.5 explores the relationship between party and leader mentions; it shows that, with a few exceptions—the *Globe* put Clark and Duceppe behind their parties in first mentions—the male leaders were indeed cited more frequently than their

Table 13.4

First Actor Mentioned by Type of News Story, by Newspaper

	National Post				Globe and Mail[a]		
	Hard News	Editorial	Column	Standing Head	Hard News	Editorial	Column
Chrétien	74	4	15	5	58	1	13
	(24%)	(44%)	(28%)	(10%)	(21%)	(10%)	(17%)
Liberal party	62	3	12	7	49	2	20
	(20%)	(33%)	(23%)	(15%)	(18%)	(20%)	(26%)
Day	44	0	8	5	49	1	18
	(14%)	(0%)	(15%)	(10%)	(18%)	(10%)	(24%)
Alliance party	32	0	11	8	41	2	16
	(10%)	(0%)	(21%)	(17%)	(15%)	(20%)	(21%)
Duceppe	18	0	0	2	2	0	1
	(6%)	(0%)	(0%)	(4%)	(1%)	(0%)	(1%)
Bloc Québécois	9	0	1	1	20	1	1
	(3%)	(0%)	(2%)	(2%)	(7%)	10%	(1%)
McDonough	12	1	0	8	7	0	0
	(4%)	(11%)	(0%)	(17%)	(3%)	(0%)	(0%)
NDP	18	0	0	5	20	1	1
	(6%)	(0%)	(0%)	(10%)	(7%)	(10%)	(1%)
Clark	18	1	4	2	13	0	2
	(6%)	(11%)	(8%)	(4%)	(5%)	(0%)	(3%)
Conservative party	12	0	2	3	18	1	3
	(4%)	(0%)	(4%)	(6%)	(7%)	(10%)	(4%)

[a] A breakdown of standing head stories is therefore not provided for the *Globe* because these stories made up a much smaller proportion of *Globe* election coverage and the headlines for this type of story in the *Globe* were generic, not mentioning party leaders.

Table 13.5

Leader Mentions as a Proportion of Total Leader and Party Mentions, by Paper

	1st Mention		2nd Mention		3rd Mention	
	Post	Globe	Post	Globe	Post	Globe
Chrétien	101/186	73/146	41/95	48/94	15/32	25/50
	(54%)	(50%)	(43%)	(51%)	(47%)	(50%)
Day	58/110	68/127	33/55	43/70	6/29	22/36
	(53%)	(54%)	(51%)	(51%)	(21%)	(61%)
Duceppe	20/31	4/25	5/15	6/10	2/5	5/11
	(65%)	(12%)	(33%)	(60%)	(40%)	(55%)
McDonough	22/55	7/29	8/19	12/25	2/10	3/9
	(45%)	(24%)	(42%)	(48%)	(20%)	(33%)
Clark	26/43	16/39	23/42	22/30	9/21	13/19
	(61%)	(41%)	(55%)	(73%)	(43%)	(68%)

parties. Yet the lone female leader, Alexa McDonough, was *always* mentioned less frequently than her party, above all for first mentions in the *Globe*. The assumption that leaders are more important than their parties applied to the male leaders in newspaper headlines, but not to McDonough.

GAME FRAMING AS GENDERED MEDIATION

As we have seen, both newspapers framed the election coverage as a game and neither paper engaged in much issue framing. The game frame was particularly dominant in *Globe and Mail* headlines. We hypothesized that McDonough and the NDP would be more strongly associated with the issue frame than with the game frame for two reasons: first, because McDonough is female, she does not 'fit' within the masculinist assumptions and discourses of the game frame; second, the NDP was judged to be a minor player in the electoral game. In this sense, McDonough and the NDP provide an interesting contrast to Clark and the Conservatives, as the PCs were also seen to be out of the race and, like the NDP, were struggling to survive the election with official party status intact. However, Clark, as a male leader who had played the game (and won) before, was more likely to be perceived as fitting within the strategic frame.

Table 13.6 illustrates the framing of the all-important first mentions, that is, the first party or leader mentioned in the headlines. While a game frame predominated in all coverage, an issue frame was used more often in relation to McDonough and the NDP when they were mentioned first than for any other party, particularly in the *National Post*. The *Post*'s negative evaluations of the Liberal party record and campaign promises placed coverage of Chrétien and the Liberals in the issue camp quite often, but not as often as McDonough and the NDP. Similarly, the *Globe* associated the Alliance more strongly with the issue frame than any party other than the NDP. This reflects the *Globe*'s (critical) attentiveness to Alliance policy slip-ups, or 'idea gaffes', such as support for two-tier health care, the 3 per cent referendum quota, and Day's belief in creationism.

The pattern of applying the issue frame more often to McDonough and the NDP became even more evident in the *National Post* when we collated first, second, and third mentions and distinguished between the framing applied to leaders and that applied to their political parties (see Table 13.7). Adding first, second, and third mentions shows a slightly different trend for the *Globe*, which was more likely than

Table 13.6
First Actor Mentioned (Percentages) by Frame and by Newspaper

	Game Frame		Issue Frame	
	Post	*Globe*	*Post*	*Globe*
Liberal	69	88	31	12
Alliance	78	72	22	28
Bloc	80	92	29	8
NDP	62	65	38	35
PC	72	92	28	8

the *Post* to associate McDonough with the game frame, though she was framed this way less often than were other party leaders. It is likely that the dominance of the game frame, coupled with the very few mentions of McDonough within *Globe* headlines, washed out the gender effect.

Indeed, when we look at the link between leader mentions and game language in the headlines, the differential treatment of male and female leaders becomes clear (see Table 13.7). Game language and metaphors were used in just over half of the *Post*'s election headlines and almost half of the *Globe*'s headlines, but they were not applied evenly to male and female leaders. As predicted, aggressive game language and imagery were applied most often to the male party leaders and less often to McDonough. In both newspapers, game metaphors were employed less frequently in the headlines when McDonough was the dominant actor (that is, the first actor mentioned). That her party was slightly more likely than the Liberal party and significantly more likely than the Alliance to be associated with game metaphors when mentioned first by the *Globe* indicates that it was McDonough, not her party, who was regarded as not in the game.

Similarly, in the *National Post*, the NDP was almost as likely as other parties, and more likely than the Bloc, to be linked with the aggressive aspects of the electoral game. Yet less than half of the *National Post* headlines where McDonough was mentioned first used game language to describe the situation. Clearly editorial writers—in both the *Post* and the *Globe*—found it easier to characterize the NDP as a player or fighter than to frame the party's female leader with these masculine metaphors.

DISCOURSE ANALYSIS

The content analysis does not show how the language and priming of the headlines work to firmly place male leaders within the strategic frame by situating them as the dominant actor, in charge of the action and capable of aggressively playing the

Table 13.7

Game Framing and Use of Game Metaphor (Percentages)

	Game Framing of Parties and Leaders (All Mentions)		Use of Game Metaphor by First Actor Mentioned	
	Post	*Globe*	*Post*	*Globe*
Chrétien	70	87	53	59
Liberal party	79	84	62	49
Day	74	80	62	52
Alliance	85	64	60	39
Duceppe	82	100	45	67
Bloc	82	94	46	55
McDonough	59	77	41	43
NDP	57	63	52	50
Clark	76	92	6	56
PC	70	89	71	57

game. For this reason, we felt it was necessary to provide a discourse analysis of the headlines used during the election campaign.

We found that in both newspapers the headlines used the language of sports or of aggression to define the campaign events. Because these headlines were so imbued with masculine themes, they tended to sideline McDonough. For instance, McDonough was never characterized with the sports metaphors applied to male leaders, such as in this headline in the *National Post*: 'Chrétien Keeps Puck in Unfriendly Territory: Wife's Silent Urging like Talia Shire's in *Rocky*' (20 Nov. 2000: A5). In this headline, Chrétien has the role of the goalkeeper and his wife is forced into the stereotypical role of the supportive 'little woman'—the good wife who does not speak. Another hockey metaphor was used in this *Globe* headline: 'Chrétien Skates On Despite Slips' (24 Oct. 2000: A5). Sports metaphors were not exclusively used for Chrétien; Clark and Day were also included. One headline in the *Globe* opined, 'Day Showing Strain of Losing Race' (23 Nov. 2000: A7). A *Post* headline suggested, 'Tories Need to "Get in the Game": Clark' (4 Nov. 2000: A4). That McDonough was not considered 'in the game' is implied by the fact that neither paper featured McDonough in a headline that used a sports metaphor.

Boxing or fighting terms were also used in the headlines to describe action. For instance, in the *Globe*, Day 'Bashed' the Liberal Red Book (3 Nov. 2000: A9), and in the *Post*, a fired up Day 'Came Out Swinging' (4 Nov. 2000: A8). With the use of the boxing or fighting metaphor, the politician is given a position of power and is cast as acting offensively in the campaign. In this *Globe* headline—'Clark Hurls One-Two Punch' (24 Nov. 2000: A4)—Clark was effectively given agency over the campaign and his opponents.

Closely related to the boxing or fighting metaphor is the war motif, which was also quite prominent in the election coverage. One *Globe* headline read, 'Clark Fires Broadside at Chrétien's Ethics' (24 Oct. 2000: A9), while another suggested, 'Young Warriors Seek Weapons for Clark' (9 Nov. 2000: A4). The *Post*, meanwhile, suggested in one headline that an election is war and in another wrote that the 'Liberal Master Plan Is to "Carpet Bomb" Day' (9 Nov. 2000: A1). Again, this type of masculinist framing gives power to the male politician and leaves little room for a female voice. As such, it inhibited editors from describing McDonough as a participant in the headlines.

The male leaders were regularly portrayed as in charge of the aggressive strategic activity; for instance, 'PM Fights Tory Tide from East' (*Globe and Mail* 23 Nov. 2000: A1). In contrast, there were few examples of McDonough being put a position of agency with a headline that portrayed her in aggressive terms. In the *Post*, there were only two headlines that had McDonough as the first actor and used a battlefield or fighter metaphor. The first read, 'McDonough Breaks with Attacks on Liberals to Take a Swipe at Alliance: NDP's War in the West' (28 Oct. 2000: A9). The second declared that 'McDonough Takes Aim at Bay Street' (24 Oct. 2000: A9). The *Globe* never put McDonough in this position of power without qualification. One of only two times the *Globe* described McDonough as on the attack was in the following headline: 'McDonough, Broadbent Gang Up Against Rivals' (6 Nov. 2000: A9). Here McDonough needed the help of a former (male) NDP leader to help her attack other parties. The relegation of McDonough to the position of 'other' was continued in a second headline in the *Globe*: 'McDonough Takes Swipe at Macho Politics: Testosterone Can Dull the Mind, She Jokes Before Launching an Appeal to Women to Vote for Her Party' (7 Nov. 2000: A8). For the *Globe*, McDonough was assertive only with a male by her side or when making appeals, as a woman leader, to female voters.

For the most part, McDonough was not portrayed as an active, dominant, and competitive politician in the headlines. Instead, she was relegated to a passive position; for example, 'Grits Ignore Toxic Pond: McDonough' (*Globe* 25 Oct. 2000: A6) or 'Alliance Abortion Vote "Cowardly": McDonough' (*Post* 4 Nov. 2000: A11). With few exceptions, she was framed as reactive and passive and with more neutral language than her male counterparts. Indeed, when McDonough did go on the attack, she was condemned for it. When McDonough criticized the Alliance party, the headline in the *Post* read, 'McDonough Likens Day to Cockroach: Closing Days Find NDP Leader on the Defensive' (23 Nov. 2000). The *Globe* was similarly critical with this headline: 'McDonough Veering off the High Road: NDP Leader's Recent Verbal Venom Contrasts Her Stated Vow to Run Clean Campaign' (23 Nov. 2000: A10). By contrast, Day was urged to become aggressive. One headline in the *Globe* suggested that 'Day Faces Pressure to Go on the Attack' (26 Oct. 2000: A11), and the paper later reported, 'Day Turns Aggressive with Attack on Chrétien' (27 Oct. 2000: A1). In the *Post*, Day was castigated for being too nice: 'No More, Please, Mr. Nice Guy' (4 Nov. 2000: A17). Still another *Post* headline read, 'As Gentle as Day Is Long: The Camera Loves St. Day: Telegenic, Kinetic, Charismatic, So Why Has the Image-Savvy Alliance Leader Been So Reluctant to Engage Fully in the Campaign Battle?' (4 Nov. 2000: A9). Clearly there is a double standard at work in these leader evaluations: male leaders are expected and even urged to treat the election as a war or aggressive contest; female leaders, on the other hand, cannot 'go on the attack' without risking censure.

CONCLUSIONS

We hypothesized that coverage of the 2000 federal election in *Globe* and *Post* headlines would give McDonough and the NDP relatively little attention and would more strongly associate the lone female leader and her party with the underreported issue frame than with the central game frame. We were particularly attentive to comparisons between McDonough and the NDP, on the one hand, and Clark and the Conservatives, on the other.

First, as we predicted, Clark and the Conservatives were mentioned more often in the headlines than were McDonough and the NDP, and Clark was mentioned first more often than McDonough. McDonough was far less visible than Clark in all but frivolous standing head stories. Moreover, while the male leaders were mentioned more often than their parties, indicating the pre-eminent position of party leaders within the game frame, McDonough was considered by headline writers to be less important than her party.

Second, was we expected, McDonough and the NDP were more strongly associated with the issue frame than any other leader or party, particularly in the *National Post*. The reluctance of headline writers in both papers to describe McDonough in aggressive strategic terms was illustrated by the fact that headlines mentioning McDonough first were significantly less likely to use aggressive game metaphors than headlines mentioning male leaders first.

Finally, the language of the headlines firmly placed male leaders within the game frame by situating them as dominant, active, and pugilistic actors. In contrast, McDonough was portrayed as passive and as reacting to the action, not initiating it (for a similar finding regarding the 1993 election, see Tremblay and Bélanger 1997). More important, she was rarely described with aggressive action words. And when McDonough used harsh words to criticize the leaders of the Liberal and Alliance parties, headlines in both papers criticized her for going on the attack. In short, we found that by applying the strategic frame's aggressive language and gender-differentiated assumptions to election coverage, the *National Post* and the *Globe and Mail* marginalized the lone female party leader, placing her on the side-lines of the electoral 'game'.

A 1996 headline in the *Ottawa Citizen* asked, 'Why Don't Female Leaders Last in Canadian Politics?' (29 Nov.: A1). Arguably, one of the reasons they don't last is that the mass media judge them unfit to play the electoral game. Our findings support Annabell Sreberny-Mohammadi and Karen Ross's argument that 'far from being neutral, . . . the imagery and language of mediated politics is heavily gen-dered, supporting male as norm and regarding women politicians as novelties' (1996: 112). The competence of women leaders continues to be assessed, at least by Canada's English-language national newspapers, according to a gender-based double standard. Achieving the goal of gender parity requires acceptance by parties, media, and voters of women politicians as capable political actors. Unless electoral politics are mediated in a truly gender-neutral fashion, press representations of female leaders will continue to act as barriers to the fair and effective representation of women.

NOTES

1. The authors gratefully acknowledge the research assistance of Mark Blythe (University of Alberta), who performed the intercoder reliability test for this study.

2. Alberta editions of both newspapers were used for the analysis.

3. Although Conrad Black sold his Hollinger group of newspapers and his 50 per cent ownership in the *National Post* to CanWest Global in the summer preceding the 2000 election, his editorial team remained in place during the election.

4. All headlines were coded by the authors. However, to ensure accuracy in coding results, we trained an independent researcher to randomly select and code 20 per cent of the headlines in each newspaper. The formula used to determine intercoder reliability was the number of questions in agreement divided by the total number of questions. Intercoder reliability was determined to be 89.4 per cent for the *Globe and Mail* and 84.4 per cent for the *National Post*, with a cumulative agreement of 86.6 per cent. This result is above the desired agreement percentage of 80.0 per cent.

References

Abu-Laban, Yasmeen (1998). 'Keeping 'em Out: Gender, Race, and Class Biases in Canadian Immigration Policy'. In Veronica Strong-Boag, Sherrill E. Grace, Avigail Eisenberg, and Joan Anderson, eds, *Painting the Maple: Essays on Race, Gender, and the Construction of Canada*, 69–82. Vancouver: UBC Press.

—— (2002). 'Challenging the Gendered Vertical Mosaic: Immigrants, Ethnic Minorities, Gender, and Political Participation'. In Everitt and O'Neill, eds (2002), 268–82.

Adamson, Nancy, Linda Briskin, and Margaret McPhail (1988). *Feminist Organizing for Change: The Contemporary Women's Movement in Canada*. Toronto: Oxford University Press.

Agnew, Vijay (1996). *Resisting Discrimination: Women from Asia, Africa, and the Caribbean and the Women's Movement in Canada*. Toronto: University of Toronto Press.

Alberts, Sheldon (2000). 'Day Urges Voters to Deny PM "Three-Peat"'. *National Post* 23 October: A4.

Allen, Judith (1990). 'Does Feminism Need a Theory of the State?' In Sophie Watson, ed., *Playing the State: Australian Feminist Interventions*, 21–38. London: Verso.

Andrew, Caroline (1984). 'Women and the Welfare State'. *Canadian Journal of Political Science* 17: 667–83.

—— (1991). 'Le pouvoir local: Stratégie de pouvoir ou nouvelle impasse pour les femmes'. In Conseil du Statut de la Femme, *L'Égalité, les moyens pour y arriver: Actes du colloque 'L'Égalité, les moyens pour y arriver', tenu à Sherbrooke le 22 mai 1991*, 63–75. Quebec City: Les Publications du Québec.

Appleton, Andrew, and Amy G. Mazur (1992). 'Party Organizations and Positive Action Strategies in France'. Paper presented at the annual meeting of the American Political Science Association, Chicago, September.

—— (1993). 'Transformation or Modernization: The Rhetoric and Reality of Gender and Party Politics in France'. In Lovenduski and Norris (1993), 86–112.

Archer, Keith, and Alan Whitehorn (1997). *Political Activists: The NDP in Convention*. Toronto: Oxford University Press.

Archibald, Linda, Leona Christian, Karen Deterding, and Dianne Hendrick (1980). 'Sex Biases in Newspaper Reporting: Press Treatment of Municipal Candidates'. *Atlantis* 5: 177–84.

Arend, Sylvie, and Celia Chandler (1996). 'Which Distinctiveness? Major Cleavages and the Career Paths of Canadian Female and Male Politicians'. *Women & Politics* 16: 1–29.

Arneil, Barbara (1999). *Politics and Feminism*. Malden, MA: Blackwell.

Arscott, Jane (1997). 'Between the Rock and a Hard Place: Women Legislators in Newfoundland and Nova Scotia'. In Arscott and Trimble, eds (1997), 308–37.

Arscott, Jane, and Manon Tremblay (1999). '"Il reste encore des travaux à faire": Feminism and Political Science in Canada and Québec'. *Canadian Journal of Political Science* 32: 125–51.

Arscott, Jane, and Linda Trimble (forthcoming). 'The Electoral Glass Ceiling for Women'. In Keith Brownsey, ed., *Reinventing Political Parties*. Peterborough, ON: Broadview.

Arscott, Jane, and Linda Trimble, eds (1997). *In the Presence of Women: Representation in Canadian Governments*. Toronto: Harcourt Brace.

Arseneau, Thérèse (1999). 'Electing Representative Legislatures: Lessons from New Zealand'. In Milner, ed. (1999), 133–44.

Bacchi, Carol Lee (1983). *Liberation Deferred? The Ideas of the English-Canadian Suffragists, 1877–1918*. Toronto: University of Toronto Press.

Banducci, Susan A., and Jeffrey A. Karp (2000). 'Gender, Leadership, and Choice in Multiparty Systems'. *Political Research Quarterly* 53: 815–48.

Bashevkin, Sylvia (1982). 'Women's Participation in the Ontario Political Parties, 1971–1981'. *Journal of Canadian Studies* 17.2: 44–54.

——— (1983a). 'Social Background and Political Experience: Gender Differences Among Ontario Provincial Party Elites, 1982'. *Atlantis* 9: 1–12.

——— (1983b). 'Social Change and Political Partisanship. The Development of Women's Attitudes in Quebec, 1965–1979'. *Comparative Political Studies* 16: 147–72.

——— (1991). 'Women's Participation in Political Parties'. In Megyery, ed. (1991b), 61–79.

——— (1993). *Toeing the Lines: Women and Party Politics in English Canada*, 2nd ed. Toronto: Oxford University Press.

——— (1998). *Women on the Defensive: Living Through Conservative Times*. Toronto: University of Toronto Press.

Bashevkin, Sylvia B., and Marianne R. Holder (1985). 'The Politics of Female Participation'. In Donald C. MacDonald, ed., *Government and Politics of Ontario*, 3rd ed., 275–88. Scarborough, ON: Nelson.

Baumgardner, Jennifer, and Amy Richards (2000). *Manifesta: Young Women, Feminism, and the Future*. New York: Farrar, Straus and Giroux.

Beckwith, Karen (1986). *American Women and Political Participation: The Impacts of Work, Generation, and Feminism*. New York: McGraw-Hill.

——— (1992). 'Comparative Research and Electoral Systems: Lessons from France and Italy'. *Women & Politics* 12: 1–33.

Beaud, Jean-Pierre (1982). 'Hiérarchie partisane et sélection sociale: L'exemple du Parti Québécois (1968–1978).' In Vincent Lemieux, ed., *Personnel et partis politiques au Québec*, 227–52. Montreal: Boréal Express.

Beaulieu, Carole (1985). 'Pauline Marois s'engage à promouvoir l'accès des femmes à l'égalité en politique'. *Le Devoir* 31 August: 3.

Beaulieu, Carole, and Renée Rowan (1985). 'Pour les femmes, Marois et Johnson sont les plus concrets et innovateurs'. *Le Devoir* 16 September: 2.

Bell, Allan (1991). *The Language of News Media*. Oxford: Blackwell.

Biersack, Robert, and Paul S. Herrnson (1994). 'Political Parties and the Year of the Woman'. In Elizabeth Adell Cook, Sue Thomas, and Clyde Wilcox, eds, *The Year of the Woman: Myths and Realities*, 161–80. Boulder, CO: Westview.

Binder, Sarah (1998). 'Candidate Highlights Focus on Women'. *Toronto Star* 27 November: A7.

Black, Jerome H. (1997). 'Minority Women in the 35th Parliament: A New Dimension of Social Diversity'. *Canadian Parliamentary Review* 20: 17–22.

———. (2000a). 'Entering the Political Elite: The Case of Minority Women as Parliamentary Candidates and MPs'. *Canadian Review of Sociology and Anthropology* 37: 143–66.

———— (2000b). 'Ethnoracial Minorities in the Canadian House of Commons: The Case of the 36th Parliament'. *Canadian Ethnic Studies* 32: 105–14.

———— (2001a). 'Immigrants and Enthnoracial Minorities in Canada: A Review of Their Participation in Federal Electoral Politics'. *Electoral Insight* 3.1: 8–13.

———— (2001b). *Quebec and the Representation of Minority Diversity at the Federal Level: Minorities as Quebec MPs, 1993–2000.* Unpublished study for Conseil des Relations Interculturelles, Quebec.

———— (2002a). 'Representation in the Parliament of Canada: The Case of Ethnoracial Minorities'. In Everitt and O'Neill, eds (2002), 355–72.

———— (2002b). 'Ethnoracial Minorities in the Canadian House of Commons: An Update on the 37th Parliament'. *Canadian Parliamentary Review* 25: 24–28.

Black, Jerome H., and Lynda Erickson (2000). 'Similarity, Compensation or Difference? A Comparison of Female and Male Office-Seekers'. *Women & Politics* 21.4: 1–38.

Black, Jerome H., and Aleem S. Lakhani (1997). 'Ethnoracial Diversity in the House of Commons: An Analysis of Numerical Representation in the 35th Parliament'. *Canadian Ethnic Studies* 29: 1–21.

Black, Jerome H., and Nancy E. McGlen (1979). 'Male–Female Political Involvement Differentials in Canada, 1965–1974'. *Canadian Journal of Political Science* 12: 471–97.

Black, Naomi (1993a). 'The Canadian Women's Movement: The Second Wave'. In Sandra Burt, Lorraine Code, and Lindsay Dorney, eds, *Changing Patterns: Women in Canada*, 2nd ed., 151–76. Toronto: McClelland & Stewart.

———— (1993b). 'Les Yvettes: Qui sont-elles?' In Anita Caron and Lorraine Archambault, eds, *Thérèse Casgrain: Une femme tenace et engagée*, 165–70. Montreal: Presses de l'Université du Québec.

Blais, André, and Elisabeth Gidengil (1991). *Making Representative Democracy Work: The Views of Canadians.* Toronto: Dundurn.

Blais, André, and Louis Massicotte (1997). 'Electoral Systems'. In Lawrence LeDuc, Richard G. Niemi, and Pippa Norris, eds, *Comparing Democracies: Elections and Voting in Global Perspectives*, 49–82. Thousand Oaks, CA: Sage.

Blais, André, Neil Nevitte, Elisabeth Gidengil, and Richard Nadeau (2000). 'Do People Have Feelings Towards Leader About Whom They Say They Know Nothing?' *Public Opinion Quarterly* 64: 452–63

Blankenship, Jane (1976). 'The Search for the 1972 Democratic Nomination: A Metaphorical Perspective'. In Jane Blankenship and Hermann G. Stelzner, eds, *Rhetoric and Communication: Studies in the University of Illinois Tradition*, 236–60. Urbana: University of Illinois Press.

Blankenship, Jane, and Jong Guen Kang (1991). 'The 1984 Presidential and Vice-Presidential Debates: The Printed Press and "Construction by Metaphor"'. *Presidential Studies Quarterly* 21: 307–18.

Brock, Kathy (1997). 'Women and the Manitoba Legislature'. In Arscott and Trimble, eds (1997), 180–200.

Brodie, Janine (1977). 'The Recruitment of Canadian Provincial Women Legislators, 1950–1975'. *Atlantis* 2: 6–17.

———— (1985). *Women and Politics in Canada.* Toronto: McGraw-Hill Ryerson.

———— (1987). 'The Gender Factor and National Leadership Conventions in Canada'. In George Perlin, ed., *Party Democracy in Canada: The Politics of National Party Conventions*, 172–87. Scarborough, ON: Prentice-Hall.

———— (1988). 'The Gender Factor and National Leadership Conventions in Canada'. In George Perlin, ed., *Party Democracy in Canada: The Politics of National Party Conventions*, 172–87. Scarborough, ON: Prentice-Hall.

———— (1994). 'Women and Political Leadership. A Case for Affirmative Action'. In Maureen Mancuso, Richard G. Price, and Ronald Wagenberg, eds, *Leaders and Leadership in Canada*, 75–96. Toronto: Oxford University Press.

———— (1996). *Women and Canadian Public Policy.* Toronto: Harcourt Brace.

———— (1998). 'Restructuring and the Politics of Marginalization'. In Tremblay and Andrew, eds (1998), 19–37.

Brodie, Janine, with Celia Chandler (1991). 'Women and the Electoral Process in Canada'. In Megyery, ed. (1991b), 3–50.

Brodie, Janine, and Jill Vickers (1981). 'The More Things Change . . .: Women in the 1979 Federal Campaign'. In Howard R. Penniman, ed., *Canada at the Polls, 1979 and 1980: A Study of the General Elections*, 322–36. Washington, DC: American Enterprise Institute for Public Policy Research.

———— (1982). *Canadian Women in Politics: An Overview.* (CRIAW Papers 2). Ottawa: Canadian Research Institute for the Advancement of Women.

Brown, Robert, and Ramsay Cook (1974). *Canada 1896–1921: A Nation Transformed.* Toronto: McClelland and Stewart.

Brown, Rosemary (1989). *Being Brown: A Very Public Life.* Toronto: Random House.

Burt, Sandra, and Elizabeth Lorenzin (1997). 'Taking the Women's Movement to Queen's Park: Women's Interests and the New Democratic Government of Ontario'. In Arscott and Trimble, eds (1997), 202–27.

Butler, Judith (1990). *Gender Trouble.* New York: Routledge.

Bystydzienski, Jill (1992). 'Influence of Women's Culture on Public Policies in Norway'. In Jill Bystydzienski, ed., *Women Transforming Politics: Worldwide Strategies for Empowerment*, 11–23. Bloomington and Indianapolis: Indiana University Press.

———— (1995). *Women in Electoral Politics: Lessons from Norway.* Westport, CT: Praeger.

Cameron, Stevie (2001). 'The Boy Trouble at Web Grrls'. *Herizons* 14 (Winter): 9–10.

Canadian Alliance (2002). *Declaration of Policy*, May. Available at: <http://www.canadianalliance.ca/english/policy/index.asp>, accessed 10 Oct. 2002.

Cappella, J., and Katherine Hall Jamieson (1997). *Spiral of Cynicism: The Press and the Public Good.* New York: Oxford University Press.

Carbert, Louise (1997). 'Governing on "the Correct, the Compassionate, the Saskatchewan Side of the Border"'. In Arscott and Trimble, eds (1997), 154–79.

Carroll, Susan J. (1987). *Women as Candidates in American Politics.* Bloomington: Indiana University Press.

———— (1988). 'Women's Autonomy and the Gender Gap: 1980 and 1982'. In Mueller, ed. (1988), 237–57.

———— (1992). 'Women State Legislators, Women's Organizations and the Representation of Women's Culture in the United States'. In Jill M. Bystydzienski, ed., *Women Transforming Politics: Worldwide Strategies for Empowerment*. Bloomington: Indiana University Press.

———— (1994). *Women as Candates in American Politics*, 2nd ed. Bloomington: Indiana University Press.

Carroll, Susan J., and Ronnee Schreiber (1997). 'Media Coverage of Women in the 103rd Congress'. In Pippa Norris, ed., *Women, Media and Politics*, 131–48. Oxford: Oxford University Press.

Carty, R. Kenneth (1991). *Canadian Political Parties in the Constituencies.* Toronto: Dundurn.

Carty, R. Kenneth, William Cross, and Lisa Young (2000). *Rebuilding Canadian Party Politics.* Vancouver: University of British Columbia Press.

Carty, R. Kenneth, and Lynda Erickson (1991). 'Candidate Nomination in Canada's National Political Parties'. In Herman Bakvis, ed., *Canadian Political Parties: Leaders,*

Candidates and Organization, 97–189. Toronto: Dundurn.

Caul, Miki (1998). 'Political Parties and Candidate Gender Quotas: A Cross-National Study of the Influences on Adoption'. Paper presented at the annual meeting of the Midwest Political Science Association, Chicago, 23–25 April.

——— (1999). 'Women's Representation in Parliament: The Role of Political Parties'. *Party Politics* 5.1: 79–98.

Clark, Campbell (1998). 'Women Take a Bigger Role in New Bouchard Cabinet'. *National Post* 16 December: A7.

Clark, Lorenne M.G., and Lynda Lange (1979). *The Sexism of Social and Political Theory*. Toronto: University of Toronto Press.

Clarke, Harold, Jane Jenson, Lawrence LeDuc, and Jon Pammet (1980). 'Voting Behaviour and the Outcome of the 1979 Federal Election: The Impact of Leaders and Issues'. *Canadian Journal of Political Science* 15: 517–52.

——— (1991). *Absent Mandate: The Politics of Discontent in Canada*, 3rd ed. Toronto: Gage.

Clarke, Harold D., and Allan Kornberg (1979). 'Moving up the Political Escalator: Women Party Officials in the United States and Canada'. *Journal of Politics* 41: 442–77.

Clarke, Harold D., Allan Kornberg, Faron Ellis, and Jon Rapkin (2000). 'Not for Fame or Fortune: A Note on Membership and Activity in the Canadian Reform Party'. *Party Politics* 6: 75–93.

Cleverdon, Catherine (1974). *The Woman Suffrage Movement in Canada*, 2nd ed. Toronto: University of Toronto Press.

Cohen, Yolande (1997). 'Suffrage féminin et démocratie au Canada'. In Christine Fauré, ed., *Encyclopédie politique et historique des femmes*, 535–50. Paris: Presses Universitaires de France.

Comité d'Action Politique des Femmes (CAPF) (1980a). 'Lettre aux présidents de région et aux permanents régionaux', 11 August.

——— (1980b). 'Lettre aux responsables des comités de condition féminine de comté', 11 August.

——— (1982a). 'Lettre aux permanents et permanentes', 26 April.

——— (1982b). 'Lettre aux présidentes et aux présidents de région', 24 March.

——— (1986a). 'Appel du CAPF aux membres du Conseil national', January.

——— (1986b). 'Journée d'études', 24 May.

——— (1986c). 'Plan d'action et budget', Summer.

——— (1986d). 'Rapport au Conseil national de novembre (1986)', November.

——— (1986e). 'Rapport d'activités au Conseil national', June.

——— (1986f). 'Rapport du Comité d'action politique des femmes', February.

——— (1986g). 'Rapport du Comité d'action politique des femmes', circa 1986.

——— (1986h). 'Rapport du Comité d'action politique des femmes au Conseil national', 27–28 September.

——— (1987). 'Rapport au Conseil national', 31 January.

——— (1988a). 'Lettre aux présidentes et présidents de comté et de région', c. December.

——— (1988b). 'Rapport au Conseil national', 10–11 September.

Comité National d'Action Politique des Femmes (CNAPF) (1993). 'Présentation du CNAPF', July.

——— (1993–94). 'Bilan des réalisations pour le mandat: Avril 1991 à décembre 1993', Winter.

——— (1994). 'Rapport du Comité national d'action politique des femmes au Conseil national du Parti québécois', May.

Comité National de la Condition Féminine (CNCF) (1977). 'Lettre aux présidents de comté et de région', 17 October.

——— (1978). 'Document d'aide à la mise sur pied de comités de condition féminine', February.

Conover, Pamela (1988). 'Feminists and the Gender Gap'. *Journal of Politics* 50: 985–1010.

Conseil du Statut de la Femme (CSF). 1978. *Pour les Québécoises: Égalité et indépendance.* Quebec City: Service des Publications.

Cook, Elizabeth (1989). 'Measuring Feminist Consciousness'. *Women & Politics* 9.3: 71–88.

Copps, Sheila (1986). *Nobody's Baby: A Survival Guide to Politics.* Toronto: Deneau.

Crête, Jean, and André Blais (2000). 'Le système électoral et les comportements électoraux'. In Manon Tremblay, Réjean Pelletier, and Marcel R. Pelletier, eds, *Le parlementarisme canadien*, 89–119. Sainte-Foy, QC: Presses de l'Université Laval.

Crossley, John (1997). 'Picture This: Women Politicians Hold Key Posts in Prince Edward Island'. In Arscott and Trimble, eds (1997), 278–307.

Czudnowski, Moshe M. (1975). 'Political Recruitment'. In Fred I. Greenstein and Nelson W. Polsby, eds, *Handbook of Political Science: Micropolitical Theory*, vol. 2, 155–242. Reading, MA: Addison Wesley.

Dahl, Jens, Jack Hicks, and Peter Jull, eds (2000). *Nunavut: Inuit Regain Control of Their Lands and Their Lives.* Copenhagen: International Work Group for Indigenous Affairs.

Dahlerup, Drude (1988). 'From a Small to a Large Minority: Women in Scandinavian Politics'. *Scandinavian Political Studies* 11: 275–99.

D'Amours, Martine (1995). 'Entre les élues et les groupes de femmes, le courant passera-t-il?' *La Gazette des femmes* 16 (January/February): 16.

Dandurand, Renée, and Évelyne Tardy (1981). 'Le phénomène des Yvettes à travers quelques quotidiens'. In Yvonne Cohen, ed., *Femmes et politique*, 21–44. Montreal: Le Jour.

Darcy, R., Susan Welch, and Janet Clark (1994). *Women, Elections, and Representation.* Lincoln: University of Nebraska Press.

D'Augerot-Arend, Sylvie (1991). 'Why So Late? Cultural and Institutional Factors in the Granting of Quebec and French Women's Political Rights'. *Journal of Canadian Studies* 26: 138–65.

Deitch, Cynthia (1988). 'Sex Differences in Support for Government Spending'. In Mueller, ed. (1988), 192–216.

De Sève, Micheline (1985). *Pour un féminisme identitaire.* Montreal: Boréal Express.

Desrochers, Lucie (1993). *Femmes et pouvoir: La révolution tranquille.* Quebec City: Publications du Québec.

——— (1994). *Femmes et démocratie de représentation: Quelques réflexions.* Quebec City: Bibliothèque de l'Assemblée nationale.

Desserud, Don (1997). 'Women in New Brunswick Politics: Waiting for the Third Wave'. In Arscott and Trimble, eds (1997), 254–77.

De Vaus, David, and Ian McAllister (1989). 'The Changing Politics of Women: Gender and Political Alignment in 11 Nations'. *European Journal of Political Research* 17: 241–62.

Dobrowolsky, Alexandra (2000). *The Politics of Pragmatism: Women, Representation, and Constitutionalism in Canada.* Toronto: Oxford University Press.

Dobrowolsky, Alexandra, and Jane Jenson (1993). 'Reforming the Parties: Prescriptions for Democracy'. In Susan D. Phillips, ed., *How Ottawa Spends, 1993–1994: A More Democratic Canada . . .?* Ottawa: Carleton University Press.

Drouilly, Pierre, and Jocelyne Dorion (1988). *Candidates, députées et ministres: Les femmes et les élections.* Quebec City: Bibliothèque de l'Assemblée Nationale.

Duverger, Maurice (1964). *Political Parties: Their Organization and Activity in the Modern*

State, 2nd ed. London: Methuen.

Dyck, Rand (2000). *Canadian Politics: Critical Approaches*, 3rd ed. Scarborough, ON: Nelson.

Eady, Mary (1970). 'Text for Women's Leaflet'. Presented to Federal NDP Council, Ottawa, 19 September 1970. National Archives of Canada: MG 28 IV 1 Vol. 458, File: Literature, 1962–1980.

Eagly, Alice H., and Mona G. Makhijani (1994). 'Are People Prejudiced Against Women? Some Answers from Research of Attitudes, Gender Stereotypes and Judgments of Competence'. *European Review of Social Psychology* 5: 1–35.

Eagly, Alice H., Mona G. Makhijani, and Bruce C. Klonsky (1992). 'Gender and the Evaluation of Leaders: A Meta-analysis'. *Psychological Bulletin* 111: 3–22.

Eichler, Margrit (1979). 'Sex Equality and Political Participation of Women in Canada: Some Survey Results'. *International Review of Sociology* 15.7: 49–75.

Elections Canada. (1988). *Official Voting Results of the 1988 General Election*. Ottawa: Minister of Supply and Services Canada. Available at: <http://www.parl.gc.ca>, April 2001.

Elshtain, Jean Bethke (1984). 'Reclaiming the Socialist-Feminist Citizen'. *Socialist Review* 74.14: 23–30.

Erickson, Lynda (1991a). 'Les candidatures de femmes à la Chambre des communes'. In Kathy Megyery, ed., *Les femmes et la politique canadienne: Pour une représentation équitable*, 111–37. (Études de la Commission Royale sur la Réforme Électorale et le Financement des Parties 6). Montreal: Wilson & Lafleur.

———— (1991b). 'Women and Candidacies for the House of Commons'. In Megyery, ed. (1991b), 101–25.

———— (1993). 'Making Her Way In: Women, Parties and Candidacies in Canada'. In Lovenduski and Norris, eds (1993), 60–85.

———— (1997a). 'Canada'. In Norris, ed. (1997), 33–55.

———— (1997b). 'Might More Women Make a Difference? Gender, Party and Ideology Among Canada's Parliamentary Candidates'. *Canadian Journal of Political Science* 30: 663–88.

———— (1997c). 'Parties, Ideology, and Feminist Action: Women and Political Representation in British Columbia Politics'. In Arscott and Trimble, eds (1997), 106–27.

———— (1998). 'Entry to the Commons: Parties, Recruitment, and the Election of Women in 1993'. In Tremblay and Andrew, eds (1998), 219–55.

Erickson, Lynda, and R. Kenneth Carty (1991). 'Parties and Candidate Selection in the 1988 Canadian General Election'. *Canadian Journal of Political Science* 24: 331–49.

Erickson, Lynda, and Brenda O'Neill (forthcoming). 'The Gender Gap and the Changing Woman Voter in Canada'. *International Journal of Political Science*.

Erie, Steven P., and Martin Rein (1988). 'Women and the Welfare State'. In Mueller, ed. (1988), 173–91.

Everitt, Joanna (1998a). 'The Gender Gap in Canada: Now You See It, Now You Don't'. *Canadian Review of Sociology and Anthropology* 35: 191–219.

———— (1998b). 'Public Opinion and Social Movements: The Women's Movement and the Gender Gap in Canada'. *Canadian Journal of Political Science* 31: 743–65.

———— (2002). 'Gender Gaps on Social Welfare Issues: Why Do Women Care?' In Everitt and O'Neill, eds (2002), 110–25.

Everitt, Joanna, and Brenda O'Neill, eds (2002). *Citizen Politics: Research and Theory in Canada Political Behaviour*. Toronto: Oxford University Press.

Faludi, Susan (1991). *Backlash: The Undeclared War Against American Women*. Toronto: Doubleday.

Farrell, David M. (1997). *Comparing Electoral Systems*. Hemel Hempstead, UK: Prentice

Hall/Harvester Wheatsheaf.

Fife, Robert (2000). 'PM Attacked for Fall Election "Vanity"'. *National Post* 23 October: A1.

Flanagan, Tom (1995). *Waiting for the Wave: The Reform Party and Preston Manning.* Toronto: Stoddart.

Fletcher, Fred, and Robert Everett (1991). 'Mass Media and Elections in Canada'. In Frederick J. Fletcher, ed., *Media, Elections and Democracy*, 179–222. (Research Studies for the Royal Commission on Electoral Reform and Party Financing 19). Toronto: Dundurn.

Forbes, E.R. (1978). 'In Search of Post-Confederation Maritime Historiography, 1900–1967'. *Acadiensis* 8: 3–21.

Fraisse, Geneviève (1994). 'Quand gouverner n'est pas représenter'. *Esprit* 3/4: 103–14.

Fraser, Graham (1984). *René Lévesque and the Parti Québécois in Power.* Toronto: Macmillan.

Frizzell, Allen, and Anthony Westell (1989). 'The Media and the Campaign'. In Alan Frizzell, Jon Pammett, and Anthony Westell, eds, *The Canadian General Election of 1988*, 75–90. Ottawa: Carleton University Press.

Gaudet, Jeanne d'Arc, and Ginette Lafleur (1988–89). 'La non-accessibilité des femmes au pouvoir'. *Égalité* 24: 15–30.

Geis, Michael L. (1987). *The Language of Politics.* New York: Springer-Verlag.

Gidengil, Elisabeth (1995). 'Economic Man—Social Woman? The Case of the Gender Gap in Support of the Canada–U.S. Free Trade Agreement'. *Comparative Political Studies* 28: 384–408.

——— (1996). 'Gender and Attitudes Toward Quotas for Women Candidates in Canada'. *Women & Politics* 16.4: 21–44.

Gidengil, Elisabeth, André Blais, Richard Nadeau, and Neil Nevitte (2000a). 'Are Party Leaders Becoming More Important to Vote Choice in Canada?' Paper presented to the American Political Science Association, Washington, DC, September.

——— (2000b). 'Do Election Campaigns Prime Leadership? Evidence from Recent Canadian Elections'. Paper presented at the ECPR 28th Joint Session Workshops, Copenhagen, 14–19 April. Available at: <www.fas.umontreal.ca/pol/ces-eec/ces.html>

——— (2000c). 'Women to the Left, Men to the Right? Gender and Voting in the 1997 Canadian Election'. Paper presented at the 2000 Congress of the International Political Science Association, Quebec City, 1–5 August.

Gidengil, Elisabeth, and Joanna Everitt (1999). 'Metaphors and Misrepresentation: Gender Mediation in News Coverage of the 1993 Canadian Leaders' Debates'. *Press/Politics* 4.1: 48–65.

——— (2000a). 'Filtering the Female: Gender Mediation in Television Coverage of the 1993 Canadian Leaders' Debates'. *Women & Politics* 21.4: 105–31.

——— (2000b). 'Talking Tough: Gender and Reported Speech in Campaign News Coverage'. July. Available at: <http://www.ksg.harvard.edu/presspol/publications/gidengil.htm>

Gilens, Martin (1988). 'Gender and Support for Reagan'. *American Journal of Political Science* 32: 19–49.

Gilligan, Carol (1982). *In a Different Voice: Psychological Theory and Women's Development.* Cambridge, MA: Harvard University Press.

Gilsdorf, William O., and Robert Bernier (1991). 'Journalistic Practice in Covering Federal Election Campaigns in Canada'. In Frederick J. Fletcher, ed., *Reporting the Campaign: Election Coverage in Canada*, 3–78. (Research Studies for the Royal Commission on Electoral Reform and Party Financing 22). Toronto: Dundurn.

Gingras, Anne-Marie (1997). 'Les métaphores dans le langue politique'. *Politique et Sociétés* 30: 159–71.

Gingras, Anne-Marie, Chantal Maillé, and Évelyne Tardy (1989). *Sexes et militantisme.* Montreal: CIDIHCA.

Gingras, François-Pierre (1995). 'Daily Male Delivery: Women and Politics in the Daily Newspapers'. In Gingras, ed. (1995), 191–207.

Gingras, François-Pierre, ed. (1995). *Gender and Politics in Contemporary Canada.* Toronto: Oxford University Press.

Gitlin, Todd (1980). *The Whole World Is Watching: Mass Media in the Making and Unmaking of the New Left.* Berkeley: University of California Press.

Gotell, Lise, and Janine Brodie (1991). 'Women and Parties: More Than an Issue of Numbers'. In Hugh G. Thorburn, ed., *Party Politics in Canada*, 6th ed., 53–67. Scarborough, ON: Prentice-Hall.

Gottlieb, Amy (1993). 'What About Us? Organizing Inclusively in the National Action Committee on the Status of Women'. In Linda Carty, ed., *And Still We Rise: Feminist Political Mobilizing in Contemporary Canada*, 368–85. Toronto: Women's Press.

Greenberg, Anna (2000). 'Why Men Leave: Gender and Party Politics in the 1990s'. Paper presented at the Annual Meeting of the American Political Science Association, Washington, DC, September.

Guadagnini, Marila (1993). 'A "Partiocrazia" Without Women: The Case of the Italian Party System'. In Lovenduski and Norris, eds (1993), 168–204.

Guénette, Françoise (1981). 'Quand les femmes du Oui disent Non'. *La Vie en rose* (March–May): 28–29.

Gurin, Patricia (1985). 'Women's Gender Consciousness'. *Public Opinion Quarterly* 49: 143–63.

Hamilton, Roberta (1993). 'Les Yvettes douze ans après.' In Anita Caron and Lorraine Archambault, eds, *Thérèse Casgrain: Une femme tenace et engagée*, 171–78. Montreal: Presses de l'Université du Québec.

Harrison Smith, H.S. (1964). Report of the National President. National Archives of Canada, MG 28 IV 2, Vol. 477, File: Annual Meeting 1964.

Hayes, Bernadette C., and Ian McAllister (1997). 'Gender, Party Leaders, and Election Outcomes in Australia, Britain and the United States'. *Comparative Political Studies* 30: 3–26.

Hébert, Chantal (1998). 'No Place for a Woman'. *National Post* 14 November: B9.

Holt, Alene (1973). Letter to May Lambert, 10 July. National Archives of Canada, MG 28 IV 2 Vol. 645, File: Women's Association (1) 1972–1973.

Hopkin, Jonathan (2001). 'Bringing the Members Back In? Democratizing Candidate Selection in Britain and Spain'. *Party Politics* 7: 343–61.

Hosek, Chaviva (1983). 'Women and the Constitutional Process'. In Keith Banting and Richard Simeon, eds, *And No One Cheered: Federalism, Democracy and the Constitution Act*, 280–300. Toronto: Methuen.

Howe, Paul, and David Northrup (2000). 'Strengthening Canadian Democracy: The Views of Canadians'. *Policy Matters* 1.5: 1–102.

Howell, Susan E., and Christine L. Day (2000). 'Complexities of the Gender Gap'. *The Journal of Politics* 62: 858–74.

Huang, Agnes, and Fatima Jaffer (1993). 'Interview with Judy Rebick'. *Kinesis* 3: 10–11.

Hunter, Alfred A., and Margaret A. Denton (1984). 'Do Female Candidates "Lose Votes"? The Experience of Female Candidates in the 1979 and 1980 Canadian General Elections'. *Canadian Review of Sociology and Anthropology* 21: 395–406.

Hunter, Justine (2000). 'Campaign Targets Tax Cuts'. *National Post* 23 October: A4.

Hyde, Janet Sybley (1991). *Half the Human Experience: The Psychology of Women.* Lexington, MA: D.C. Heath.

Ignazi, Piero (1992). 'The Silent Counter-revolution: Hypotheses on the Emergence of Extreme Right-Wing Parties in Europe'. *European Journal of Political Research* 22.1: 3–34.

Inglehart, Ronald (1990). *Culture Shift in Advanced Industrial Society*. Princeton, NJ: Princeton University Press.

Inglehart, Ronald, and Pippa Norris (2000). 'The Developmental Theory of the Gender Gap: Women and Men's Voting Behavior in Global Perspective'. *International Political Science Review* 21: 441–63.

Inter-Parliamentary Union (2002). 'Women in National Parliaments'. May. Available at: <www.ipu.org/wmn-e/classif.htm>.

Iyengar, Shanto, and Adam Simon (1993). 'News Coverage of the Gulf Crisis and Public Opinion: A Study of Agenda-Setting, Priming, and Framing'. *Communication Research* 20: 365–83.

Jennings, M. Kent (1988). 'Preface'. In Mueller, ed. (1988), 1–13.

Jennings, M. Kent, and Barbara G. Farah (1981). 'Social Roles and Political Resources: An Over-Time Study of Men and Women in Party Elites'. *American Journal of Political Science* 25: 462–82.

Jenson, Jane, and Mariette Sineau (1995). *Mitterrand et les Françaises: Un rendez-vous manqué*. Paris: Presses de la sciences.

Joly, Karine (2001). 'Cabinet Landry, le nouveau gouvernement québécois'. Available at: <http://canadactualite...alite/library/weekly/aa030901a.htm>, 15 May 2001.

Kahn, Kim Fridkin (1994). 'The Distorted Mirror: Press Coverage of Women Candidates for Statewide Office'. *Journal of Politics* 56: 154–73.

——— (1996). *The Political Consequences of Being a Woman: How Stereotypes Influence the Conduct and Consequences of Political Campaigns*. New York: Columbia University Press.

Kahn, Kim Fridkin, and Edie N. Goldenberg (1991). 'Women Candidates in the News: An Examination of Gender Differences in US Senate Campaign Coverage'. *Public Opinion Quarterly* 55.2: 180–99.

Kanter, Rosabeth Moss (1977). 'Some Effects of Proportions on Group Life: Skewed Sex Ratios and Responses to Token Women'. *American Journal of Sociology* 82: 965–90.

Katz, Richard S. (1999). 'Electoral Reform Is Not as Simple as It Looks'. In Milner, ed. (1999), 101–8.

——— (2001). 'The Problem of Candidate Selection and Models of Party Democracy'. *Party Politics* 7: 277–96.

Kay, Barry J., Ronald D. Lambert, Steven D. Brown, and James E. Curtis (1987). 'Gender and Political Activity in Canada, 1965–1984'. *Canadian Journal of Political Science* 20: 851–63.

——— (1988). 'Feminist Consciousness and the Canadian Electorate: A Review of National Election Studies, 1965–1984'. *Women & Politics* 8.2: 1–21.

Kenny, James (1999). 'Political Culture in Fin-de-Siècle Atlantic Canada'. *Acadiensis* 29: 122–37.

Kite, Mary E. (2001). 'Changing Times and Changing Gender Roles'. In Rhoda K. Unger, ed., *Psychology of Women and Gender*, 215–27. New York: Wiley.

Kitschelt, Herbert (1995). *The Radical Right in Western Europe: A Comparative Analysis*. Ann Arbor: University of Michigan Press.

Klein, Ethel (1984). *Gender Politics: From Consciousness to Mass Politics*. Cambridge, MA: Harvard University Press.

Kohn, Walter S.G. (1984). 'Women in the Canadian House of Commons'. *American Review of Canadian Studies* 14: 298–311.

Kolinsky, Eva (1991). 'Political Participation and Parliamentary Careers: Women's Quotas in West Germany'. *West European Politics* 14: 56–72.

Kopinak, Kathryn (1987). 'Gender Differences in Political Ideology in Canada'. *Canadian Review of Sociology and Anthropology* 24: 23–38.

Krashinsky, Michael, and William J. Milne (1985). 'Additional Evidence on the Effect of Incumbency in Canadian Elections'. *Canadian Journal of Political Science* 18: 155–65.

———— (1986). 'The Effect of Incumbency in the 1984 Federal and 1985 Ontario Elections'. *Canadian Journal of Political Science* 19: 337–43.

Kymlicka, Will (1998). *Finding Our Way: Rethinking Ethnocultural Relations in Canada.* Toronto: Oxford University Press.

LaMarsh, Judy (1968). *Memoirs of a Bird in a Gilded Cage.* Toronto: McClelland and Stewart.

Lamoureux, Diane (1986). *Fragments et collages: Essai sur le féminisme québécois des années 70.* Montreal: Remue-ménage.

———— (1989). *Citoyennes? Femmes, droit de vote et démocratie.* Montreal: Remue-ménage.

Lamoureux, Diane, and Micheline De Sève (1989). 'Faut-il laisser notre sexe au vestiaire?' *Politique* 15: 5–22.

Lamoureux, Diane, and Jacinthe Michaud (1988). 'Les parlementaires canadiens et le suffrage féminin: Un aperçu des débats'. *Revue canadienne de science politique* 21: 319–29.

Lane, Jan-Erik, and Svante O. Ersson (1991). *Politics and Society in Western Europe.* London: Sage.

Lang, Gladys E., and Kurt Lang (1979). 'Immediate and Mediate Responses: First Debate'. In Sidney Kraus, ed., *The Great Debates: Carter vs. Ford, 1976,* 298–313. Bloomington: Indiana University Press.

Langevin, Liane (1977). *Missing Persons: Women in Canadian Federal Politics.* Ottawa: Advisory Council on the Status of Women.

Lanoue, David J. (1991). 'Debates That Mattered: Voters' Reaction to the 1984 Canadian Leadership Debates'. *Canadian Journal of Political Science* 24: 51–65.

Lawrence, Regina G. (2000). 'Game-Framing the Issues: Tracking the Strategy Frame in Public Policy News'. *Political Communication* 17.2: 93–114.

Laxer, Krista Maeots (1970). 'The Burdens of Discrimination'. Presented to Federal NDP Council, Ottawa, 19 September 1970. National Archives of Canada, MG 28 IV 1 Vol. 458, File: Literature 1962–1970.

LeDuc, Lawrence (1997). 'The Leaders' Debates: (. . . And the Winner Is . . .)'. In Alan Frizzell and Jon H. Pammett, eds, *The Canadian General Election of 1997,* 207–224. Toronto: Dundurn.

Legault, Ginette, Guy Desrosiers, and Évelyne Tardy (1988). *Militer dans un parti provincial: Les différences entre les femmes et les hommes au P.L.Q. et au P.Q.* Montreal: Centre de Recherche Féministe.

Léger, Huguette, and Judy Rebick (1993). *The NAC Voters' Guide.* Hull, QC: Voyageur.

Léger, Marcel (1986). *Le Parti québécois: Ce n'était qu'un début.* Montreal: Québec/Amérique.

Lemert, James B., William R. Elliott, James M. Bernstein, William L. Rosenberg, and Karl J. Nestvold (1991). *News Verdicts, the Debates, and Presidential Campaigns.* New York: Praeger.

Lessard, Denis (1989). 'Mme Marois: "Je m'explique mal ce qui retient les femmes"'. *La Presse* 4 March: B1.

Lévesque, Michel (1993). 'Vingt ans d'action politique féminine: La Fédération des femmes libérales du Québec'. In Anita Caron and Lorraine Archambault, eds, *Thérèse Casgrain: Une femme tenace et engagée,* 335–53. Montreal: Presses de l'Université du Québec.

Lijphart, Arend (1994). *Electoral Systems and Party Systems: A Study of Twenty-Seven Democracies, 1945–1990.* Oxford: Oxford University Press.

Lips, Hilary M. (1993). *Sex and Gender: An Introduction*. Mountain View, CA: Mayfield.

Lovenduski, Joni (1986). *Women and European Politics: Contemporary Feminism and Public Policy*. Amherst: University of Massachusetts Press.

Lovenduski, Joni, and Pippa Norris. (1993). 'Gender and Party Politics in Britain'. In Lovenduski and Norris, eds (1993), 35–59.

Lovenduski, Joni, and Pippa Norris, eds (1993). *Gender and Party Politics*. London: Sage.

MacInnis, Grace (1972). 'Women and Politics'. *The Parliamentarian* 53.1: 8–12.

MacIvor, Heather (1996). *Women and Politics in Canada: An Introductory Text*. Peterborough, ON: Broadview.

—— (1999a). 'A Brief Introduction to Electoral Systems'. In Milner, ed. (1999), 19–34.

—— (1999b). 'Proportional and Semi-Proportional Electoral Systems: Their Potential Effects on Canadian Politics'. Presentation to the Elections Canada Advisory Committee, Ottawa, May.

MacKinnon, Catherine (1989). *Toward a Feminist Theory of the State*. Cambridge, MA: Harvard University Press.

MacQueen, Ken (1996). 'Why Don't Female Leaders Last in Canadian Politics?' *Ottawa Citizen* 29 November: A1.

Maillé, Chantal (1990a). *Les Québécoises et la conquête du pouvoir politique*. Montreal: Saint-Martin.

—— (1990b). *Vers un nouveau pouvoir: Les femmes en politique au Canada*. Ottawa: Conseil Consultatif Canadien sur la Situation de la Femme.

—— (1994). 'Women and Political Representation'. In James P. Bickerton and Alain-G. Gagnon, eds, *Canadian Politics*, 2nd ed., 156–72. Peterborough, ON: Broadview.

Mallen, Chantal (1985). 'Le Comité d'action politique des femmes du Parti québécois et l'élection à la présidence.' *Le Devoir* 12 August: 6.

Manza, Jeff, and Clem Brooks (1998). 'The Gender Gap in U.S. Presidential Elections: When? Why? Implications?' *American Journal of Sociology* 103: 1235–66.

Marsden, Lorna, and Busby, Joan (1989). 'Feminist Influence Through the Senate: The Case of Divorce, 1967'. *Atlantis* 14.2: 72–79.

Marzolini, Michael (2001). 'The Politics of Values: Designing the 2001 Liberal Campaign'. In Jon H. Pammett and Christopher Dornan, eds, *The Canadian General Election of 2000*, 263–90. Toronto: Dundurn.

Massicotte, Louis, and Blais, André (1999). 'Mixed Electoral Systems: A Conceptual and Empirical Survey'. *Electoral Studies* 18: 341–66.

Matland, Richard E. (1993). 'Institutional Variables Affecting Female Representation in National Legislatures: The Case of Norway'. *Journal of Politics* 55: 737–55.

—— (1995). 'How the Election System Structure Has Helped Women Close the Representation Gap'. In Lauri Karvonen and Per Selle, eds, *Women in Nordic Politics: Closing the Gap*, 281–309. Dartmouth, UK: Aldershot.

—— (1998). 'Women's Representation in National Legislatures: Developed and Developing Countries'. *Legislative Studies Quarterly* 23.1: 109–25.

Matland, Richard E., and Donley T. Studlar (1996). 'The Contagion of Women Candidates in Single-Member District and Proportional Representation Electoral Systems: Canada and Norway'. *Journal of Politics* 58: 707–34.

—— (1998). 'Gender and the Electoral Opportunity Structure in the Canadian Provinces'. *Political Research Quarterly* 51.1: 117–40.

Matland, Richard E., and Michelle M. Taylor (1997). 'Electoral System Effects on Women's Representation: Theoretical Arguments and Evidence from Costa Rica'. *Comparative Political Studies* 30: 186–210.

Mayer, Lawrence C., and Roland E. Smith (1995). 'Feminism and Religiosity: Female Electoral Behaviour in Western Europe'. In Sylvia Bashevkin, ed., *Women and Politics in Western Europe*, 38–49. London: Frank Cass.

McCarthy, Shawn (2000). 'PM Pushes for Early Election'. *Globe and Mail* 16 September: A1, A4.

McLaughlin, Audrey, with Rick Archbold (1992). *A Woman's Place: My Life in Politics*. Toronto: Macfarlane Walter & Ross.

Megyery, Kathy, ed. (1991a). *Ethno-cultural Groups and Visible Minorities in Canadian Politics*. (Research Studies for the Royal Commission on Electoral Reform and Party Financing 7). Toronto: Dundurn.

—— (1991b). *Women in Canadian Politics: Toward Equity in Representation*. (Research Studies for the Royal Commission on Electoral Reform and Party Financing 6). Toronto: Dundurn.

Mendelsohn, Matthew (1993). 'Television's Frames in the 1988 Canadian Election'. *Canadian Journal of Communication* 18: 149–71.

—— (1996). 'The Media and Interpersonal Communications: The Priming of Issues, Leaders and Party Identification'. *Journal of Politics* 58: 112–25.

Mettler, Suzanne (1998). *Divided Citizens: Gender and Federalism in New Deal Public Policy*. Ithaca, NY: Cornell University Press.

Milner, Henry, ed. (1999). *Making Every Vote Count: Reassessing Canada's Electoral System*. Peterborough, ON: Broadview.

Moncrief, Gary F., and Donley T. Studlar (1996). 'Women Cabinet Ministers in Canadian Provinces 1976–1994'. *Canadian Parliamentary Review* (Autumn): 10–13.

Moncrief, Gary F., and Joel A. Thompson (1991). 'Urban and Rural Ridings and Women in Provincial Politics: A Research Note on Female MLAs'. *Canadian Journal of Political Science* 24: 831–37.

Monière, Denis (1994). 'Le contenu du débat des chefs en français'. In Denis Monière and Jean H. Guay, *La bataille du Québec: Premier épisode: Les élections fédérales de 1993*, 69–91. Saint-Laurent, QC: Fides.

Morton, Desmond (1986). *The New Democrats 1961–1986: The Politics of Change*. Toronto: Copp Clark Pitman.

Mueller, Carol M., ed. (1988). *The Politics of the Gender Gap: The Social Construction of Political Influence*. Beverly Hills, CA: Sage.

Myers, Patricia A. (1989). 'A Noble Effort: The National Federation of Liberal Women of Canada, 1928–1973'. In Linda Kealey and Joan Sangster, eds, *Beyond the Vote: Canadian Women in Politics*, 36–62. Toronto: University of Toronto Press.

Nadeau, Richard, André Blais, Neil Nevitte, and Elisabeth Gidengil (2000). 'It's Unemployment, Stupid! Why Perceptions About the Job Situation Hurt the Liberals in the 1997 Election'. *Canadian Public Policy* 26.1: 77–94.

National Women's Liberal Commission (NWLC) (1978). 'Election '78: Information on Issues of Particular Concern to Women'. National Archives of Canada, MG 28 IV 3 1377, File: 1.4.20, WLC National Executive Meeting, 1978.

—— (1981). 'Report to Members of National Executive'. March. National Archives of Canada, MG 29 IV 3 1407, File: Irma Melville, President, WLC, 1981.

—— (1982). 'Guidelines for Political Action'. National Archives of Canada, MG 28 IV 3 1377, File: 4.1.8: Guidelines for Political Action.

Nelson, Barbara J., and Najma Chowdhury (1994). *Women and Politics Worldwide*. New Haven, CT: Yale University Press.

Nevitte, Neil (1996). *The Decline of Deference: Canadian Value Change in Cross-national Perspective*. Peterborough, ON: Broadview.

Nevitte, Neil, André Blais, Elisabeth Gidengil, and Richard Nadeau (2000). *Unsteady State: The 1997 Canadian Federal Election.* Toronto: Oxford University Press.

New Brunswick New Democratic Party (NDP) (1998). *Guidelines for the Candidate Search Committees / Lignes directrice pour les comités de recherche de candidat/candidate.* Fredericton: NDP.

New Democratic Party (NDP) (1970a). 'The Canadian Women's Movement and the New Democratic Party'. National Archives of Canada, MG 28 IV 1 Vol. 458, File: Literature 1962–1970.

———— (1970b). 'NDP Women's Liberation Movement: Our Aims'. National Archives of Canada, MG 28 IV 1 Vol. 458, File: Literature 1962–1970.

New Democratic Party (NDP). BC Participation of Women (POW) Committee (1974). *BC Women's Manifesto.* National Archives of Canada, MG 28 IV 1 Vol. 458, File: Literature, 1962–80.

New Democratic Party (NDP). Participation of Women (POW) Committee (1975). 'Minutes of POW Committee Meeting'. 16 January. National Archives of Canada, MG 28 IV 1 Vol. 463, File: Participation of Women Committee, 1970–76.

Normand, Gilles (1989). 'Et pourquoi pas une femme Premier Ministre?' *La Presse* 26 August: B7.

Norris, Pippa (1987). *Politics and Sexual Equality: The Comparative Position of Women in Western Democracies.* Boulder, CO: Lynne Rienner.

———— (1993). 'Conclusion: Comparing Legislative Recruitment'. In Lovenduski and Norris, eds (1993), 309–30.

———— (1996). 'Legislative Recruitment'. In Larry LeDuc, Richard G. Niemi, and Pippa Norris, eds, *Comparing Democracies: Elections and Voting in Global Perspective*, 184–215. London: Sage.

———— (1997a). 'Choosing Electoral Systems: Proportional, Majoritarian and Mixed Systems'. *International Political Science Review* 18: 297–312.

———— (1997b). 'Conclusions: Comparing Passages to Power'. In Norris, ed. (1997), 209–31.

———— (1997c). 'Introduction: Women, Media and Politics'. In Pippa Norris, ed., *Women, Media, and Politics*, 1–18. Oxford: Oxford University Press.

———— (1997d). 'Women Leaders Worldwide: A Splash of Color in the Photo Op'. In Pippa Norris, ed., *Women, Media, and Politics*, 149–65. Oxford: Oxford University Press.

———— (1999). 'Gender: A Gender–Generation Gap?' In Geoffrey Evans and Pippa Norris, eds, *Critical Elections: British Parties and Voters in Long-term Perspective*, 148–63. Thousand Oaks, CA: Sage.

———— (forthcoming). 'The Gender Gap: Old Challenges, New Approaches'. In Susan Carroll, ed., *Women and American Politics: Agenda-Setting for the 21st Century.* New York: Oxford University Press.

Norris, Pippa, ed. (1995). 'The Politics of Electoral Reform'. *International Political Science Review* 16.1: special issue.

———— (1997). *Passages to Power: Legislative Recruitment in Advanced Democracies.* Cambridge, UK: Cambridge University Press.

Norris, Pippa, R.J. Carty, Lynda Erickson, Joni Lovenduski, and Marian Simms (1990). 'Party Selectorates in Australia, Britain and Canada: Prolegomena for Research in the 1990s'. *Journal of Commonwealth & Comparative Politics* 28: 219–45.

Norris, Pippa, and Joni Lovenduski (1989). 'Women Candidates for Parliament: Transforming the Agenda?' *British Journal of Political Science* 19: 106–15.

———— (1995). *Political Recruitment: Gender, Race and Class in British Parliament.* Cambridge, UK: Cambridge University Press.

Nunavut Implementation Commission (1997). 'Two-Member Constituencies and Gender

Equality: A "Made in Nunavut" Solution'. In Arscott and Trimble, eds (1997), 374–80.

Ollivier, Michèle, and Manon Tremblay (2000). *Questionnements féministes et méthodologie de la recherche*. Paris: L'Harmattan.

O'Neill, Brenda (1995). 'The Gender Gap: Re-evaluating Theory and Method'. In Sandra Burt and Lorraine Code, eds, *Changing Methods: Feminists Transforming Practice*, 327–56. Peterborough, ON: Broadview.

——— (1998). 'The Relevance of Leader Gender to Voting in the 1993 Canadian National Election'. *International Journal of Canadian Studies* 17: 105–30.

——— (2001). 'A Simple Difference of Opinion? Religious Beliefs and Gender Gaps in Public Opinion in Canada'. *Canadian Journal of Political Science* 34: 275–98.

——— (2002). 'Sugar and Spice? Political Culture and the Political Behaviour of Canadian Women'. In Everitt and O'Neill, eds (2002), 40–55.

O'Sullivan, Tim, John Hartley, Danny Saunders, Martin Montgomery, and John Fiske (1994). *Key Concepts in Communication and Cultural Studies*, 2nd ed. New York: Routledge.

Palamerek, Michael (1989). *Alberta Women in Politics: A History of Women and Politics in Alberta*. Report for Senator Martha P. Bielish.

Pammett, John H. (2001). 'Youth in the Electoral Process'. *Electoral Insight* 3: 14–17.

Parti Libéral du Québec (PLQ) (2000). 'La Constitution du Parti libéral du Québec'. Available at: <http://www.minfo.net/plq/constitution2001.pdf>, 15 May 2001.

Parti Québécois (PQ) (1994). *Des idées pour mon pays: Programme du Parti québécois*. Montreal: PQ.

——— (2001). *Régions et circonscriptions: Régions*. Available at: <http://partiquebecois.org/regions_regions.phtml>, accessed 15 May 2001.

Parti Québécois (PQ). Conseil National de Sherbrooke (1977). '33ème proposition', 24–25 September.

Patterson, Thomas E. (1980). *The Mass Media Election: How Americans Choose Their President*. New York: Praeger.

——— (1994). *Out of Order*. New York: Vintage.

Payette, Lise (1982). *Le pouvoir? Connais pas!* Montreal: Québec/Amérique.

Pelletier, Alain (1991). 'Politics and Ethnicity: Representation of Ethnic and Visible-Minority Groups in the House of Commons'. In Megyery, ed. (1991a), 101–59.

Pelletier, Réjean, and Manon Tremblay (1992). 'Les femmes sont-elles candidates dans des circonscriptions perdues d'avance? De l'examen d'une croyance'. *Revue canadienne de science politique* 25: 249–67.

Peterson, Robert A. (1994). 'A Meta-analysis of Cronbach's Coefficient Alpha'. *Journal of Consumer Research* 21: 381–91.

Phelan, Shane (1990). 'Feminism and Individualism'. *Women & Politics* 10.4: 1–18.

Phillips, Anne (1995). *The Politics of Presence*. New York: Oxford University Press.

Pinterics, Natasha (2001). 'Riding the Feminist Waves: In with the Third?' *Canadian Woman Studies* 20/21:15–21.

Pitkin, Hanna Fenichel (1967). *The Concept of Representation*. Berkeley: University of California Press.

Pitre, Sonia (1998). 'Les femmes et le pouvoir municipal au Nouveau-Brunswick'. *Égalité*, no. 43: 37–67.

——— (forthcoming). 'Attitudes of Local Riding Executives Toward Women in Politics: Are There Party Differences in New Brunswick?'

Piven, Francis Fox (1984). 'Women and the State: Ideology, Power and the Welfare State'. *Socialist Review* 74.14: 11–19.

Pratto, Felicia, Lisa M. Stallworth, and Jim Sidanius (1997). 'The Gender Gap: Differences in Political Attitudes and Social Dominance Orientation'. *British Journal of Social Psychology* 36.1: 49–68.

Praud, Jocelyne (1993). 'Quotas and Women's Political Representation in the Norwegian Labour Party and the Parti Socialiste Français.' Paper presented at the meeting of the Canadian Political Science Association, Ottawa, May–June.

——— (1995). 'The Beginnings of Affirmative Action for Women in the Ontario New Democratic Party'. In Jean-Pierre Beaud and Jean-Guy Prévost, eds, *La sociale-démocratie en cette fin de siècle/Late Twentieth-Century Social Democracy*, 201–22. Sainte-Foy, QC: Presses de l'Université du Québec.

——— (1997). 'Feminizing Party Organizations: The Cases of the Parti Socialiste Français, the Parti Québécois and the Ontario New Democratic Party'. Ph.D. dissertation, University of Toronto.

——— (1998a). 'Affirmative Action and Women's Representation in the Ontario New Democratic Party'. In Tremblay and Andrew, eds (1998), 171–93.

——— (1998b). 'La seconde vague féministe et la féminisation du Parti socialiste français et du Parti québécois'. *Politique et sociétés* 17.1–2: 71–90.

Prentice, Alison, Paula Bourne, Gaill Cuthbert Brandt, Beth Light, Wendy Mitchinson, and Naomi Black (1996). *Canadian Women: A History*, 2nd ed. Toronto: Harcourt Brace.

Progressive Conservative (PC) party (1972). 'Campaign Document—Women in Society'. National Archives of Canada, MG 28 IV 2 Vol. 713, File: Women—Research (1) 1971–1974.

——— (1980). 'The Progressive Conservative Response to the Advisory Council on the Status of Women Questionnaire'. National Archives of Canada, MG 28 IV 2 Vol. 660, File: Campaign 1980, Policy, Women's Issues.

Putnam, Robert D. (1976). *The Comparative Study of Political Elites.* Englewood Cliffs, NJ: Prentice-Hall.

Rae, Douglas (1971). *The Political Consequences of Electoral Laws.* New Haven, CT: Yale University Press.

Rahat, Gideon, and Reuven V. Hazan (2001). 'Candidate Selection Methods: An Analytical Framework'. *Party Politics* 7: 297–322.

Rakow, Lana F., and Kimberlie Kranich (1991). 'Women as Sign in Television News'. *Journal of Communication* 41.1: 8–23.

Raney, Tracey (1998). 'Redrawing the Map of Canada: Identity and Community Constructions in the Citizenship and Nationalist Discourses of the Reform Party of Canada'. Unpublished MA thesis, Carleton University, Ottawa.

Rankin, L. Pauline, and Jill Vickers (1998). 'Locating Women's Politics'. In Tremblay and Andrew, eds (1998), 341–67.

Rasmussen, Jorgens (1981). 'Female Political Career Patterns and Leadership Disabilities in Britain: The Crucial Role of Gatekeepers in Regulating Entry to the Political Elite'. *Polity* 13: 600–20.

——— (1983). 'Women's Role in Contemporary British Politics: Impediments to Parliamentary Candidature'. *Parliamentary Affairs* 36: 300–15.

REAL Women of Canada (1998). *REALity.* Nov./Dec. Available at: <http://www.realwomenca. com/html/newsletter>.

Région Montréal-Centre du Parti Québécois (1976). 'Compte rendu des ateliers du colloque sur la condition féminine "Solitaires ou solidaires"', March.

Reform Party of Canada (1989). *The Blue Book.* Calgary, AB.: Reform Party of Canada.

Rhodebeck, Laurie A. (1996). 'The Structure of Men's and Women's Feminist Orientations:

Feminist Identity and Feminist Opinion'. *Gender & Society* 10: 386–403.

Richer, Jocelyne (1991). 'Femmes de pouvoir: On revient de loin'. *La Gazette des femmes* 12: 17–20.

Robinson, Gertrude, and Armande Saint-Jean (1995). 'The Portrayal of Women Politicians in the Media: Political Implications'. In Gingras, ed. (1995), 176–90.

Robinson, Gertrude J., and Armande Saint-Jean, with Christine Rioux (1991). 'Women Politicians and Their Media Coverage: A Generational Analysis'. In Megyery, ed. (1991b), 127–69.

Robinson, Michael J., and Margaret A. Shehan (1983). *Over the Wire and on TV: CBS and UPI in Campaign '90*. New York: Russell Sage Foundation.

Ross, Karen (1995). 'Gender and Party Politics: How the Press Reported the Labour Leadership Campaign'. *Media, Culture & Society* 17: 499–509.

Ross, Karen, and Annabelle Sreberny (2000). 'Women in the House: Media Representation of British Politicians'. In Annabelle Sreberny and Liesbet van Zoonen, eds, *Gender, Politics and Communication*, 79–99. Cresskill, NJ: Hampton.

Rowan, Renée (1976a). 'Colloque du PQ sur la condition féminine: La femme devra se résoudre à être menaçante politiquement'. *Le Devoir* 29 March: 2.

——— (1976b). '"Solitaires ou solidaires": Colloque du PQ sur la condition féminine'. *Le Devoir* 24 March: 2.

——— (1979). 'Au Parti québécois, la politique devient l'affaire de toutes les femmes'. *Le Devoir* 17 October: 2.

Royal Commission on Electoral Reform and Party Financing (Lortie Commission) (1991). *Reforming Electoral Democracy: Final Report*, Vol. 1. Ottawa: Minister of Supply and Services Canada.

Royal Commission on the Status of Women (Bird Commission) (1970). *Royal Commission on the Status of Women in Canada: Report*. Ottawa: Minister of Supply and Services Canada.

Ruddick, Sara (1989). *Maternal Thinking: Toward a Politics of Peace*. Boston: Beacon.

Rule, Wilma (1987). 'Electoral Systems, Contextual Factors and Women's Opportunity for Election to Parliament in Twenty-Three Democracies'. *Western Political Quarterly* 40: 477–98.

——— (1994a). 'Parliaments of, by and for the People: Except for Women?' In Wilma Rule and Joseph F. Zimmerman, eds, *Electoral Systems in Comparative Perspective: Their Impact on Women and Minorities*, 15–30. Westport, CT: Greenwood.

——— (1994b). 'Women's Underrepresentation and Electoral Systems'. *PS: Political Science and Politics* 27: 689–92.

——— (2001). 'Political Rights, Electoral Systems, and the Legislative Representation of Women in 73 Democracies'. In Stuart S. Stuart and Amy Robb, eds, *Handbook of Global Social Policy*, 73–91. New York: Marcel Dekker.

Rule, Wilma, and Pippa Norris (1992). 'Anglo and Minority Women's Underrepresentation in Congress: Is the Electoral System the Culprit?' In Wilma Rule and Joseph F. Zimmerman, eds, *United States Electoral Systems: Their Impact on Women and Minorities*, 41–54. New York: Greenwood.

Sainsbury, Diane (1993). 'The Politics of Increased Women's Representation: The Swedish Case'. In Lovenduski and Norris, eds (1993), 263–90.

Sapiro, Virginia, with Pamela Johnston Conover (1997). 'The Variable Gender Basis of Electoral Politics: Gender and Context in the 1992 US Election'. *British Journal of Political Science* 27: 497–523.

Sayers, Anthony M. (1998). *Parties, Candidates, and Constituency Campaigns in Canadian Elections*. Vancouver: UBC Press.

Sears, David O., and Leonie Huddy (1990). 'On the Origins of Political Disunity Among Women'. In Louise Tilly and Patricia Gurin, eds, *Women, Politics and Social Change*, 249–77. New York: Russell Sage.

Séguin, Rhéal (1996). 'Bouchard Lays Out PQ Agenda, but Fiscal Details Are Lacking'. *Globe and Mail* 30 January 30: A7.

Seidle, F. Leslie (1996). 'The Canadian Electoral System and Proposals for Reform'. In A. Brian Tanguay and Alain-G. Gagnon, eds, *Canadian Parties in Transition*, 2nd ed., 292–300. Scarborough, ON: Nelson.

Seltzer, Richard, Jody Newman, and Melissa Leighton (1997). *Sex as a Political Variable: Women as Candidates and Voters in U.S. Elections*. Boulder, CO: Lynne Rienner.

Serini, Shirley A., Angela A. Powers, and Susan Johnson (1998). 'Of Horse Race and Policy Issues: A Study of Gender in Coverage of a Gubernatorial Election by Two Major Metropolitan Newspapers'. *Journalism & Mass Communication Quarterly* 75: 194–204.

Sharpe, Sydney (1994). *The Gilded Ghetto: Women and Political Power in Canada*. Toronto: HarperCollins.

Ship, Susan Judith (1998). 'Problematizing Ethnicity and "Race" in Feminist Scholarship on Women and Politics'. In Tremblay and Andrew, eds (1998), 311–40.

Short, Clare (1996). 'Women and the Labour Party'. *Parliamentary Affairs* 49.1: 17–25.

Siaroff, Alan (2000). 'Women's Representation in Legislatures and Cabinets in Industrial Democracies'. *International Political Science Review* 21: 197–215.

Sigurdson, Richard (1994). 'Preston Manning and the Politics of Post-modernism in Canada'. *Canadian Journal of Political Science* 27: 249–76.

Simard, Carolle (1999). *La représentation politique des élus issue de groupe ethniques minoritaires à Montréal*. Faculté de Science Politique et de Droit, Université du Québec à Montréal, Cahiers de Recherche no. 8.

Simard, Carolle, with Sylvie Bélanger, Nathalie Lavoie, Anne-Lise Polo, and Serge Turmel (1991). 'Visible Minorities and the Canadian Political System'. In Meygery, ed. (1991a), 161–261.

Sineau, Mariette (2001). *Profession femme politique: Sexe et pouvoir sous la Cinquième République*. Paris: Presses de Sciences.

Skjeie, Hege (1988). *The Feminization of Power: Norway's Political Experiment*. Oslo, Norway: Institute for Social Research.

——— (1991). 'The Rhetoric of Difference: On Women's Inclusion into Political Elites'. *Politics and Society* 19: 233–63.

Smith, Jennifer (1991). 'Representation and Constitutional Reform in Canada'. In David E. Smith, Peter MacKinnon, and John C. Courtney, eds, *After Meech Lake: Lessons for the Future*, 69–82. Saskatoon, SK: Fifth House.

Smith, Kevin B. (1997). 'When All's Fair: Signs of Parity in Media Coverage of Female Candidates'. *Political Communication* 14: 71–82.

Smith, Tom (1984). 'The Polls: Gender and Attitudes Towards Violence'. *Public Opinion Quarterly* 48: 384–96.

Soderlund Walter C., E. Donald Briggs, Walter I. Romanow, and Ronald H. Wagenberg (1984). *Media and Elections in Canada*. Toronto: Holt, Rinehart & Winston.

Spelman, Elizabeth (1988). *Inessential Woman: Problems of Exclusion in Feminist Thought*. Boston: Beacon.

Spencer, Samia (1985). 'The Female Cabinet Members of France and Quebec: Token Women?' *Contemporary French Civilization* 9: 166–91.

Spencer, Samia, and William Spencer (1992). 'Female Deputies and Cabinet Ministers in Québec: Past and Present'. *American Review of Canadian Studies* 22: 329–50.

Sreberny-Mohammadi, Annabelle, and Karen Ross (1996). 'Women MPs and the Media:

Representing the Body Politic'. *Parliamentary Affairs* 49: 103–15.

Stasiulis, Daiva K. (1999). 'Feminist Intersectional Theorizing'. In Peter S. Li, ed., *Race and Ethnic Relations in Canada*, 2nd ed., 347–97. Toronto: Oxford University Press.

Stasiulis, Daiva K., and Yasmeen Abu-Laban (1991). 'The House the Parties Built: (Re)constructing Ethnic Representation in Canadian Politics'. In Meygery, ed. (1991a), 3–99.

Statistics Canada (1995). *Interdepartmental Group on Employment Equity Data, Projections of Visible Minority Population Groups, Canada, Provinces and Regions, 1991–2016.* Cat. No. 01-541-XPE. Ottawa: Statistics Canada.

——— (2000). *Women in Canada, 2000: A Gender-Based Statistical Report.* Cat. No. 89-503-XPE. Ottawa: Statistics Canada.

Steed, Judy (1988). *Ed Broadbent: The Pursuit of Power.* Toronto: Viking.

Steenbergen, Candis (2001). 'Feminism and Young Women: Alive and Well and Still Kicking'. *Canadian Woman Studies* 4 (1): 6–14.

Studlar, Donley T., and Richard E. Matland (1994). 'The Growth of Women's Representation in the Canadian House of Commons and the Election of 1984: A Reappraisal'. *Canadian Journal of Political Science* 27: 53–79.

——— (1996). 'The Dynamics of Women's Representation in the Canadian Provinces: 1975–1994'. *Canadian Journal of Political Science* 29: 269–93.

Studlar, Donley T., and Gary F. Moncrief (1997). 'The Recruitment of Women Cabinet Ministers in the Canadian Provinces'. *Governance* 10: 67–81.

Tahon, Marie-Blanche (1998). 'La revendication de la démocratie paritaire'. *Politique et Sociétés* 17.1–2: 13–48.

Taras, David (1990). *The Newsmakers: The Media's Influence on Canadian Politics.* Scarborough, ON: Nelson.

Tardy, Évelyne (1980). 'Les femmes et la campagne référendaire'. In Robert Boily, ed., *Québec: Un pays incertain: Réflexions sur le Québec post-référendaire*, 183–203. Montreal: Québec/Amérique.

——— (1993). 'Le caratère paradoxal de l'engagement des Québécoises au tournant des années quatre-vingt'. In Anita Caron and Lorraine Archambault, eds, *Thérèse Casgrain: Une femme tenace et engagée*, 179–86. Montreal: Presses de l'Université du Québec.

Tardy, Évelyne, Anne-Marie Gingras, Ginette Legault, and Lyne Marcoux (1982). *La politique: Un monde d'hommes?* Montreal: Hurtubise HMH.

Tardy, Évelyne, and Ginette Legault (1996). *Qui sont les mairesses et les maires du Québec?* Montreal: Institut de Recherches et d'Études Féministes, Université de Québec à Montréal.

Tardy, Évelyne, Manon Tremblay, and Ginette Legault (1997). *Maires et mairesses: Les femmes et la politique municipale.* Montreal: Liber.

Terkildsen, Nayda, and Frauke Schnell (1997). 'How Media Frames Move Public Opinion: An Analysis of the Women's Movement'. *Political Research Quarterly* 50: 879–901.

Terry, John (1984). 'The Gender Gap: Women's Political Power'. *Current Issue Review* 84-17E. Ottawa: Library of Parliament.

Thomas, Sue (1994). *How Women Legislate.* New York: Oxford University Press.

Thorburn, Hugh (1961). *Politics in New Brunswick.* Toronto: University of Toronto Press.

Tiemens, Robert K., Susan Hellweg, Philip Kipper, and Steven L. Phillips (1985). 'An Integrative Verbal and Visual Analysis of the Carter–Reagan Debate'. *Communication Quarterly* 33: 34–42.

Togeby, Lise (1994). 'The Political Implications of Increasing Numbers of Women in the Work Force'. *Comparative Political Studies* 27: 211–40.

Tremblay, Manon (1992). 'Quand les femmes se distinguent: Féminisme et représentation politique au Québec'. *Revue canadienne de science politique* 25: 55–68.

—— (1994). 'Les opinions des nouvelles et des nouveaux politologues francophones concernant les rôles des femmes et des hommes en politique'. *Revue québécoise de science politique* 26: 103–59.

—— (1995a). 'Les femmes, des candidates moins performantes que les hommes? Une analyse des votes obtenus par les candidates et candidats du Québec à une élection fédérale canadienne, 1945–1993'. *Revue internationale d'études canadiennes* 11: 59–81.

—— (1995b). 'Gender and Support for Feminism'. In Gingras, ed. (1995), 31–55.

—— (1997). 'Quebec Women in Politics: An Examination of the Research'. In Arscott and Trimble, eds (1997), 228–51.

—— (1998a). 'Do Female MPs Substantively Represent Women? A Study of Legislative Behaviour in Canada's 35th Parliament'. *Canadian Journal of Political Science* 31: 435–65.

—— (1998b). 'Femmes et représentation à la Chambre des communes du Canada: Un modèle des orientations du rôle de représentation des femmes'. *Revue internationale d'études canadiennes* 17: 67–92.

—— (1999). *Des femmes au Parliament: Un stratégie feministe?* Montreal: Remue-ménage.

—— (2000–1). 'La parité femmes/hommes en politique: Un élément de réforme des institutions politiques canadiennes'. *Journal d'études canadiennes* 35.4: 40–59.

—— (2002a). 'L'élection fédérale de 2000: Qu'est-il donc arrivé aux candidates?'. *Politique et Sociétés* 21.1: 89–109.

—— (2002b). 'Québec Women in Politics: An Examination of the Research: A Reappraisal'. In Veronica Strong-Boag, Mona Gleason, and Adele Perry, eds, *Rethinking Canada: The Promise of Women's History*, 375–93. Toronto: Oxford University Press.

—— (2003). 'Femmes, représentation et parité: Pour un élargissement des débats sur le nationalisme québécois'. In Claude Couture, ed., *Points de vue sur le fédéralisme canadien*. Centre d'études canadiennes, University of Alberta, Saint-Jean.

Tremblay, Manon, and Caroline Andrew, eds (1998). *Women and Political Representation in Canada*. Ottawa: Ottawa University Press.

Tremblay, Manon, and Nathalie Bélanger (1997). 'Femmes chefs de partis politiques et caricatures éditoriales: L'élection fédérale canadienne de 1993'. *Recherches féministes* 10.1: 35–75.

Tremblay, Manon, and Réjean Pelletier (1993). 'Les femmes et la représentation politique vues par des députées et députés du Québec'. *Recherches féministes* 6.2: 89–114.

—— (1995). *Que font-elles en politique?* Sainte-Foy, QC: Les Presses de l'Université Laval.

—— (2000). 'More Women or More Feminists? Descriptive and Substantive Representations of Women in the 1997 Canadian Federal Election'. *International Political Science Review* 21: 381–405.

—— (2001). 'More Women Constituency Party Presidents: A Strategy for Increasing the Number of Women Candidates in Canada?' *Party Politics* 7: 157–90.

Tremblay, Manon, and Réjean Pelletier, with Sonia Pitre (forthcoming). *Mary Wollstonecraft's Dilemma: Women and the 1997 Canadian Federal Election*. Vancouver: UBC Press.

Trimble, Linda (1993). 'A Few Good Women: Female Legislators in Alberta, 1972–1991'. In Catherine A. Cavanaugh and Randi R. Warne, eds, *Standing on New Ground: Women in Alberta*, 87–118. Calgary: University of Alberta Press.

—— (1997). 'Feminist Politics in the Alberta Legislature, 1972–1994'. In Arscott and Trimble, eds (1997), 128–53.

—— (1998). 'Who's Represented? Gender and Diversity in the Alberta Legislature'. In Tremblay and Andrew, eds (1998), 257–89.

—— (1999). 'The Politics of Gender'. In Janine Brodie, ed., *Critical Concepts: An*

Introduction to Politics, 303–19. Scarborough, ON: Prentice-Hall.

Trimble, Linda, and Jane Arscott (forthcoming). *Still Counting: Women in Politics Across Canada*. Peterborough, ON: Broadview.

United Nations. Centre for Social Development and Humanitarian Affairs (1992). *Women in Politics and Decision-Making in the Late Twentieth Century: A United Nations Study*. Dordrecht, Netherlands: Nijhoff.

Vallance, Elizabeth (1984). 'Women Candidates in the 1983 General Election'. *Parliamentary Affairs* 37: 301–9.

van Assendelft, Laura, and Karen O'Connor (1994). 'Backgrounds, Motivations and Interests: A Comparison of Male and Female Local Party Activists'. *Women and Politics* 14: 245–62.

van Dijk, Teun (1991). *Racism and the Press*. New York: Routledge.

Vickers, Jill (1997). 'Toward a Feminist Understanding of Representation'. In Arscott and Trimble, eds (1997), 20–46.

———— (1978). 'Where Are the Women in Canadian Politics?' *Atlantis* 3.2: 40–51.

Vickers, Jill, and M. Janine Brodie (1981). 'Canada'. In Joni Lovenduski and Jill Hills, eds, *The Politics of the Second Electorate: Women and Public Participation*, 52–82. London: Routledge & Kegan Paul.

Vickers, Jill, Pauline Rankin, and Christine Appelle (1993). *Politics as If Women Mattered: A Political Analysis of the National Action Committee on the Status of Women*. Toronto: University of Toronto Press.

Vowles, Jack (2000). 'Evaluating Electoral System Change: The Case of New Zealand'. Paper presented to the 2000 meeting of the International Political Science Association, Quebec City, 1–5 August.

Vowles, Jack, Peter Aimer, Susan Banducci, and Jeffrey Karp, eds (1998). *Voters' Victory? New Zealand's First Election Under Proportional Representation*. Auckland, NZ: Auckland University Press.

Vowles, Jack, Peter Aimer, Jeffrey Karp, Susan Banducci, Raymond Miller, and Ann Sullivan (2002). *Proportional Representation on Trial: The 1999 New Zealand General Election and the Fate of MMP*. Auckland, NZ: Auckland University Press.

Wearing, Peter, and Joseph Wearing (1991). 'Does Gender Make a Difference in Voting Behaviour?' In Joseph Wearing, ed., *The Ballot and Its Message: Voting in Canada*, 341–50. Toronto: Copp Clark Pitman.

Welch, Susan (1985). 'Are Women More Liberal than Men in the US Congress?' *Legislative Studies Quarterly* 10: 125–34.

Whitehorn, Alan, and Keith Archer (1995). 'The Gender Gap Amongst Party Activists: A Case Study of Women and the New Democratic Party'. In Gingras, ed. (1995), 2–30.

Wilcox, Clyde (1997). 'Racial and Gender Consciousness Among African-American Women: Sources and Consequences'. *Women & Politics* 17: 73–94.

Wilson, R. Jeremy (1980–81). 'Media Coverage of Canadian Election Campaigns: Horserace Journalism and the Meta-campaign'. *Journal of Canadian Studies* 15: 56–68.

Wilson, V. Seymour (1993). 'The Tapestry Vision of Canadian Multiculturalism'. *Canadian Journal of Political Science* 26: 645–59.

Woodward, Gary (1997). *Perspectives on American Political Media*. Boston: Allyn and Bacon.

Young, Iris Marion (1990). *Throwing like a Girl and Other Essays in Feminist Philosophy and Social Theory*. Bloomington and Indianapolis: Indiana University Press.

Young, Lisa (1991). 'Legislative Turnover and the Election of Women to the Canadian House of Commons'. In Megyery, ed. (1991b), 81–99.

———— (1994). *Electoral Systems and Representative Legislatures: Consideration of Alternative Electoral Systems*. Ottawa: Canadian Advisory Council on the Status of Women.

—— (1997). 'Fulfilling the Mandate of Difference: Women in the Canadian House of Commons'. In Arscott and Trimble, eds (1997), 82–103.

—— (1998). 'The Canadian Women's Movement and Political Parties, 1970–1993'. In Tremblay and Andrew, eds (1998), 195–217.

—— (2000). *Feminists and Party Politics.* Vancouver: UBC Press.

—— (2002a). 'Going Mainstream? The Women's Movement and Political Parties in Canada and the US'. In Everitt and O'Neill, eds (2002), 413–25.

—— (2002b). 'Women's Electoral Participation'. Paper presented at a Metropolis sponsored seminar, Bringing the Worlds Together: The Study of the Political Participation of Women in Canada and Lessons for Research on Newcomers' Minority Political Participation, Ottawa, 22–24 March.

Zaborszky, Dorothy (1988). 'Feminist Politics: The Feminist Party of Canada'. In Peta Tancred-Sheriff, ed., *Feminist Research: Prospect and Retrospect*, 205–62. Montreal: CRIAW/McGill-Queen's University Press.

Zaller, John, and Mark Hunt (1994). 'The Rise and Fall of Candidate Perot: Unmediated Versus Mediated Politics—Part I'. *Political Communication* 11: 357–80.

—— (1995). 'The Rise and Fall of Candidate Perot: Unmediated Versus Mediated Politics—Part II'. *Political Communication* 12: 97–123.

Index

divorce, 83

Dobrowolsy, Alexandra, 2, 33

double-value hypothesis, and minority women, 69–71

Duceppe, Gilles, 164–72, 203–7, 214–26

Dyck, Rand, 43, 55

Eagly, Alice H., 81, 161, 166, 169

education: and female politicians, 41, 53–4; and minority MPs, 67–9

Eichler, Margrit, 17

election, as game, 217

election(s), federal: (1972) 81; (1979) 83; (1980) 7, 83; (1983) 88; (1984) 79, 89; (1988), 62, 143; (1993) 12, 15, 16–17, 18, 30, 47–8, 62–3, 67–71, 92, 140, 162, 194; (1997) 5–6, 7, 16–17, 26, 62–3, 66,140, 162–76, 198; (2000) 6, 7, 14, 16–17, 62–3, 66, 88, 92, 109, 111, 140, 144, 146, 154, 211–26

election(s), provincial: New Brunswick (1999), 109, 112–22; Ontario (1990), 111; Quebec (1985), 129; (1989), 17, 130; (1998), 134

election, US, 161–2

electoral system(s), 13, 22–35; characteristics of, 28–9; formula, 24; and incentive structures, 29–32; measuring effect of, 27–8; types of, 24–7

eligibility, of candidates, 114

elites, political, 12–19

employment: background, 41, 42, 54–5, 141–2, 147, 186; equity, 82, 83

entry, vertical and horizontal, 8–9

equal rights, attitudes towards, 186–7

Erickson, Lynda, 6, 11, 12, 13, 15, 16, 18, 30, 31, 39, 40, 41–2, 46, 49, 76, 91, 99, 109

Erie, Steven P., 141

Ersson, Svante, 113

ethnicity, 16; and female politicians, 38, 40, 47–9; *see also* country of birth; ancestry; minority

Everett, Robert, 216

Everitt, Joanna, 5, 6–7, 16, 17, 140, 153, 160, 180, 213

Faludi, Susan, 177

family: attitudes towards, 187; law reform, 83; and Reform party, 86–7

Farah, Barbara G., 76

Fédération des Femmes du Québec, 1

female/male party members, 9–12, 93–4

feminism, 3, 4, 7, 12, 17–19; attitudes towards, 181–4; and diversity, 40; and gender, 149–51; and leader assessment, 172; liberal, 76–7, 78–9; and party politics, 76–89, 91, 102–3, 125; radical, 77, 78, 79; as radicalizing, 142, 148; waves of, 177, 178–80

Feminist Party of Canada, 78

feminization, in Quebec, 125–36

Femmes Regroupées pour l'Accès au Pouvoir Politique et Économique (FRAPPE), 130, 135

fighting position, in list-PR, 28, 32

Flanagan, Tom, 86

Fletcher, Fred, 216

Forbes, E.R., 120

formula, electoral, 24

frame(s), and media, 211–26

France, electoral system in, 27, 33

free enterprise, and gender gap, 144–9

Friedan, Betty, 178

Frizzell, Allen, 212

Front de Libération des Femmes, 78

Gagnon, Luc, 128

game frame, 211, 212–13, 216–21, 223–6; as gendered mediation, 221–3

gays and lesbians: attitudes towards, 182–4; and marriage, 151

Geis, Michael L., 196, 197

gender: equality, 79; gap, 5–8, 32; parity, 5, 33, 84; and political beliefs, 140–57; quotas, 30, 33, 84; roles, 149

gender-generation gap, 148–9, 151, 153, 177–91

Gidengil, Elisabeth, 6, 7, 16, 17, 22, 160, 161, 162–3, 164, 178, 213, 220

Gilens, Martin, 164

Gilligan, Carol, 142–3, 152, 168

Gilsdorf, Wiliam O., 216

Gingras, Anne-Marie, 9–10, 11, 16, 126

Gingras, François-Pierre, 195